Copyright © 2001 by Sheridan Morley

First published in Great Britain in 2001 by Hodder and Stoughton
A division of Hodder Headline

10 9 8 7 6 5 4 3 2 1

A CIP catalogue record for this title is available
from the British Library

ISBN 0 340 36803 9

Typeset by Palimpsest Book Production Limited,
Polmont, Stirlingshire
Printed and bound in Great Britain by
Mackays of Chatham plc, Chatham, Kent

Hodder and Stoughton
A division of Hodder Headline
338 Euston Road
London NW1 3BH

JOHN G

The Authorised Biography of John Gielgud

Sheridan Morley

Hodder & Stoughton

JOHN G

The Authorised Biography of John Gielgud

For my darling Ruth Leon; who has been living with John nearly as long as I have; for my mother, Joan Morley, who once shared a stage with Ellen Terry; and for my lifelong friend Ion Trewin, who commissioned this book at Hodder and then had to wait a decade to read it.

CONTENTS

LIST OF ILLUSTRATIONS

Section One

1. Family album, 1912: Kate Gielgud with her four children, Lewis, Val, John and Eleanor
2. John feeding the chickens (1907)
   With his sister Eleanor in family charades (1912)
   The four Gielgud children with their father Frank
3. John in his first major prep-school role as Mark Antony
   John at 16 in an amateur *As You Like It*
   His great-aunt Ellen Terry, circa 1890
4. Trofimov in the 1925 Oxford Playhouse *The Cherry Orchard*
5. Konstantin in *The Seagull*, Little Theatre 1925
   Replacing Noël Coward in *The Constant Nymph* in 1926
6. 'Baylis was a fearful old bat but it was at her Old Vic that I really made my Shakespearian debut as Romeo, Hamlet and Richard II'
7. The Matinee idol of the 1920s and 1930s
8. John Worthing, first played at the Lyric Hammersmith in 1930

Section Two

9. West End stardom in March 1933: Vintage Bordeaux at £100 a week
10. His first Prospero at the Old Vic
    Back in the West End for the play (and then the film) of Priestley's *The Good Companions*
    John's first King Lear at the Old Vic
11. *Richard of Bordeaux*
12. The production that led John to the creation of the first classical repertory company in the West End: with Jessica Tandy as Ophelia
13. John directing Laurence Olivier, Peggy Ashcroft and Edith Evans in the 1935 *Romeo and Juliet*
    As Mercutio
    As Romeo
14. John at the christening of Emlyn Williams' son Alan, with Noël Coward holding the baby
    Gibraltar, Christmas 1942

Picture Acknowledgements

BFI Stills, Posters and Designs: 15 below. Ronald Grant Archive: 21 below, 24. Hulton Archive: 3 below, 7 above right, 10 above, 11, 14 above, 17, 18 above left and below, 19 below right, 20, 22 below, 23 above. Mander and Mitchenson Theatre Collection: 5, 6, 7 above left and below, 8, 9, 10 below, 12, 13, 15 above (photo Angus McBean), 16, 18 above right, 19 above, below left (photo Angus McBean), 21 above, 23 below (photo Anthony Crickmay). PA Photos: 22 above. Private Collections: 1, 2, 3, 4, 14 below.

ACKNOWLEDGEMENTS

A word or two of explanation about how this book came to be written. Almost twelve years ago, back in 1989, John Gielgud rang me one morning. We were not perhaps close friends, but in a way I had known him almost all my life: he had directed my grandmother Gladys Cooper in *The Chalk Garden*, and Robert my father in *Halfway Up the Tree*, and my mother Joan had been an early friend of his own first great love, John Perry; another of his great friends and colleagues across almost fifty years was the actor Robert Hardy who married my Aunt Sally, she too becoming a close friend. John had also been wonderfully helpful to me in many of my earlier biographies, writing several prefaces to them and filling in, as only he could, a wealth of theatrical detail and gossip for such lives as those I had written of Noël Coward and David Niven and Sybil Thorndike and Robert and Gladys themselves. I had also very frequently interviewed him for radio and television, newspapers and magazines, and had spent some happy hours with him at Wotton Underwood as well as in California when he was out there filming *The Loved One* with my father for Tony Richardson in the early 1960s. I had even once been assigned to greet him at Honolulu Airport when I was teaching there and he en route to play his solo *Ages of Man* in Australia; he had the grace to look only mildly surprised as I covered him in a flowered kind of necklace, a local tradition which I think we somehow failed to explain to him.

By the time we began our telephonic life, in I suppose the early 1980s, he had already acquired the habit of starting his phone calls with no kind of pre-emptive greeting or introduction, as if aware that his voice alone would be enough. 'My biographer,' this particular 1989 conversation began, partly wistful and partly almost accusatory, as though it were somehow my fault, 'seems to have died.'

The biographer in question was Richard Findlater, a distinguished and long-serving arts editor of the *Observer*, who had indeed been engaged for several years on the project for Ion Trewin, then an editor at Hodder & Stoughton and an old friend of mine from the years we spent together as journalists on *The Times*. Richard's death, although at an eminently respectable age, left John and Ion in something of a quandary. Ion wanted the authorised biography, and John wanted at least an answer with which to fend off the many other writers who were now beginning to approach him asking for permission to write his life.

They decided that I might prove a suitable candidate, and it took me all of about ten seconds to agree. Thanks to Richard's widow, I was able to buy all his research notes with my original advance, and discovered that although he had not yet started to write John's life, he had interviewed several crucial witnesses, from Olivier to Redgrave, Vivien Leigh to Sybil Thorndike, whose subsequent deaths made them unavailable to me. He had also painstakingly annotated John's own volumes of theatrical memoirs, and what was already a small bookcase full of other books about him and his remarkable career.

There were two immediate issues to be resolved: would it be possible to write an authorised biography that would add sufficiently to what already existed in print (and on tape, since John had given both radio and television interviewers remarkably long and detailed accounts of his working life); and could we agree on precisely when the book should appear? For John's ninetieth, which was already close, or his ninety-fifth, or at the time of his death which was somewhat harder to predict, since almost throughout John's last decade he gave every indication of planning to live forever?

I soon realised that the issues were inextricably linked: the only way of writing fully about John's life, as opposed to his work, which had already been handsomely chronicled elsewhere, was to confront the issue of his arrest for homosexual soliciting in 1953, and that was precisely what John wished me to avoid. His argument was eminently understandable: he knew that the arrest was on the files, and public knowledge at least to those who were around at the time. But such was the devotion in which he was held towards the end of his long life that there had grown up an unspoken, and in my experience unprecedented, agreement among those of us who wrote about him that we would simply not mention it. What John feared was not a straightforward account of the facts, such as I have tried to write in what is I believe unique detail after years of research in police and other files, but the interest this would arouse in an old case. He feared, not my book so much, but the phone calls and the prurient enquiries that it would doubtless elicit from gossip columnists eager to get a paragraph or two out of his apparently scandalous past.

This then became the major problem; I realised very early on that my book could not appear in his own lifetime, but he also realised what I was up to, and became increasingly eager to see, if not to censor, the text. He would ring on a regular basis: 'How old am I now, dear boy?' he would ask, and for several years I was able to pretend that he was still in his twenties. Along the way I also wrote some other books, always taking care to explain that they were secondary to his, but I think we both knew that I was playing for time.

'I suppose you want me dead?' was the start of another phone call, and I had to explain that although it might technically make my book easier to write and publish, the thought of living without his voice, unquestionably the greatest of the twentieth century, either begging or imparting some new and splendid gossip about the actors we both knew and sometimes loved, would be far too high a price to pay. For the first and (I hope) only time in my life, I had backed myself into a biographer's cul-de-sac; although I spent these last ten years doing literally hundreds of interviews about John at home and abroad, watching again and again his every film and television appearance, listening to every radio broadcast and even (thanks to John Miller and John Powell) the unbroadcast offcuts of the hours of autobiography they recorded with him, I couldn't actually bring myself to start writing the book, because that would have been in my own mind some kind of acknowledgement that John was on the way out, given that we had already come to the reluctant conclusion that it couldn't be published in his lifetime without hurting the actor whom above all others outside my immediate family I had come most to love, but with a love that encompassed the knowledge that the truth about him had eventually to be told.

Other books about him began to appear with increasing frequency and sometimes even his cautious blessing, but none was able to deal in any detail with his private life, not least because by now John had given me all his own letters and private papers, boxes and boxes of them neatly stored by his mother. But again, we never could bring ourselves to discuss precisely what use I was to make of these; John must have known what was in them, and that by showing them to me he was offering a considerable time-bomb which would destroy the secrecy in which he had managed to shroud his past. On reflection, I think I know now what he knew: that in his lifetime I would never publish anything that he might in his late nineties consider damaging to his reputation. This meant, logically, that I must be working on a book designed to appear after his death, but even that was not entirely satisfactory, since he clearly wished to read it.

One issue on which we did agree was that of the Bricks. John had, from a very early age, been famous for saying the wrong thing as almost a reflex action, covering a curious, unworldly shyness which years of fame never quite erased. But just as all the best one-liners eventually end up being ascribed to Oscar Wilde or Dorothy Parker or Noël Coward (and having written two of these biographies I have some evidence of this), rightly or wrongly, so John was eventually lumbered with all the clangers ever made backstage, and we agreed that I would only include in the book those that could be accurately documented. The only one of these that I have failed to find room for is the morning he rang me in some horror: 'You'll never believe this; in America they are actually about to name a theatre after a drama critic. Oh my God, you are one. Goodbye.'

So that, more or less, was the state of play when he died on 21 May 2000, soon after his ninety-sixth birthday; and that Sunday night, when I was first told of his death, I began for the first time to write the opening of chapter one, as if somehow I could at last see how to do it and even perhaps keep him with me for a few more months. I wrote this book every day and many nights from May to December, drawing on almost two decades of my own and Richard Findlater's research, and papers of John's going back to the early 1920s. I owe many tremendous debts to John himself and his immediate and extended family; to my own darling Ruth Leon, who has lived with me in a house that effectively became the Gielgud Archives for several years; to Mrs Richard Findlater, for allowing me to acquire her late husband's meticulous and pioneering work; to Ion Trewin, who first gave me the assignment and, from his subsequent desk as managing editor at Weidenfeld, has kept a watchful eye over it ever since, wondering like me if we would ever manage to get it together, or simply sink under a mountain of memories; to Roland Philipps at Hodder who never once (in all the ten years during which I signally failed even to hand over an outline) pointed out that I was somewhat late in delivery; to Michael Korda, who picked up the American rights with commendable speed once I had a book to show him; to Paul Webb, who did much of the research and for the last year and more has kept the book in some kind of computerised shape, living patiently from day to day with my increasing technophobia; to my agent Michael Shaw, whose patience has also been far above and beyond what I had any right to expect; and to all of the following, living and sometimes alas now dead, who have helped me in some way to complete the Gielgud jigsaw. Many of them gave me their time and their memories; others simply let me read what they had written about John, or hear what they had said about him on the air, and as a comprehensive bibliography would consist of virtually every theatre book written in the twentieth century, I have simply listed the authors here who were most immediately helpful, including those who directly or indirectly answered questions about John from Richard Findlater, many of whom therefore now appear in somewhat ghostly form.

I also wish here to record my deep gratitude to Barbra Paskin (herself now a distinguished biographer) for indexing all of John's letters, Angela Herlihy at Hodder, Michael Levett for the index, Juliet Brightmore for her wonderful work on the photographs, and to the librarians and archivists at many research centres here and in the USA, principal among them Sandra Archer at the Library of the Academy of Motion Picture Arts and Sciences in Los Angeles, Alan Pally at the New York Public Library for the Performing Arts at Lincoln Center, Cathy Haill at the British Theatre Museum, Richard Mangan at the Mander-Mitchenson Collection, and the keepers of the archives of the British Film Institute, the Royal Shakespeare Company, the National

ACKNOWLEDGEMENTS

Theatre, the Garrick Club, the Players Club (New York), the BBC, Colindale, the British Museum and the British Library. My thanks also go to Peter Coller, Sally-Anne Pinnington and Mark Gold for holding off the rest of the world for long enough to let me get this eventually to press.

Biography is, I have always believed, a form of Pentimento: just as, in days when artists could seldom afford new canvas, they would paint over already existing pictures which would eventually break through to the surface in shadow, so you start a biography with one picture and end up with quite another. Let me thank here all the people, listed or not, who helped me to find the Gielgud beneath the surface of his remarkable and historic career; after a decade in all their various and very varied company, I am going to miss them almost as much as I already miss John himself.

In Los Angeles: John Houseman, Roddy McDowall, Dudley Moore. In Mexico: Brian Bedford, Peter Glenville. In Switzerland: Adrianne Allen, Noel Coward, Graham Payn. In Sydney: John McCallum, Greta Scaachi, Googie Withers. All other interviews were conducted in London or New York in the last twenty years, either by Richard Findlater or Paul Webb or the author; the following list includes many now sadly no longer with us, and several who supplied written or recorded material over the same period.

Edward Albee, Mark Amory, Peggy Ashcroft, Frith Banbury, Keith Baxter, Simon Russell Beale, Richard Bebb, Alan Bennett, Michael Billington, Kitty Black, Claire Bloom, Dirk Bogarde, Gyles Brandreth, Peter Brook, Michael Bryant, Peter Bull, Barry Burnett, Richard Burton, Sally Burton, Simon Callow, Judy Campbell, Humphrey Carpenter, John Casson, Michael Coveney, Hume Cronyn, Rosalie Crutchley, Constance Cummings, Molly Daubeny, Judi Dench, Michael Denison, Edith Evans, Laurie and Mary Evans, Ralph Fiennes, Richard Findlater, Bryan Forbes, Meriel Forbes, Clive Francis, David Frost, Christopher Fry, Patrick Garland, Eleanor Gielgud, Maina Gielgud, Marius Goring, Martin Gottfried, Morton Gottlieb, Derek Granger, Dulcie Gray, Hubert Gregg, George Grizzard, Valerie Grove, Alec Guinness, Piers Haggard, Peter Hall, Edward Hardwicke, Robert Hardy, Sally Hardy,

Margaret Harris, Ronald Harwood, Frank Hauser, Ronald Hayman, David Hemmings, Jocelyn Herbert, John Higgins, Wendy Hiller, Clive Hirschhorn, Michael Hordern, Sue Hyman, Barry Ingham, Julie Kavanagh, Rachel Kempson, Gavin Lambert, Anna Massey, Geraldine McEwan, Ian McKellen, Sarah Miles, John Miller, John Mills, Liza Minnelli, Julian Mitchell, Adriana Mnuchin, Tanya Moiseiwitch, Joan Morley, Robert Morley, Cathleen Nesbitt, John Neville, Benedict Nightingale, Garry O'Connor, Laurence Olivier, Tarquin Olivier, Tony Palmer, Michael Pennington, John Perry, Margot Peters, Eric Phillips, Robin Phillips, Harold Pinter, Joan Plowright, John Powell, Anthony Quayle, Corin Redgrave, Michael Redgrave, Vanessa Redgrave, Ralph Richardson, James Roose-Evans, Daniel Rosenthal, Millie Rowland, Peter Sallis, John Schlesinger, Paul Scofield, Marian Seldes, Michael Shaw, Ned Sherrin, Donald Sinden, Lord Snowdon, John Standing, Marguerite Steen, Robert Tanitch, Elizabeth Taylor, Sybil Thorndike, Wendy Toye, Ion Trewin, J.C. Trewin, Wendy Trewin, Dorothy Tutin, Kathleen Tynan, Peter Ustinov, Hugo Vickers, Alexander Walker, Mavis Walker, Eli Wallach and Anne Jackson, Susannah Walton, Geoffrey Wansell, Irving Wardle, John Warner, Elizabeth Welch, Brook Williams, Hugh Whitemore, Audrey Williamson, Irene Worth, Michael York.

Chapter One

AN EDWARDIAN YOUTH
(1904–1921)

If your great-aunt happens to be Ellen Terry, your great-uncle
Fred Terry, your cousins Gordon Craig and Phyllis Neilson-Terry,
and your grandmother the greatest Shakespearean actress in all
Lithuania, you are hardly likely to drift into the fish trade.

Whatever other achievements may yet be claimed for the twentieth century, one is already beyond all doubt or dispute: it produced in Britain the greatest generation of classical actors that the world has ever known. It took almost eighty years to get from David Garrick to Edmund Kean, and then at least another fifty to get to Henry Irving, and they were essentially on their own, loners unchallenged by any immediate rivals. Yet in the middle of this past century it was possible to see, in the same city and sometimes even the same stage or screen productions or acting companies, Laurence Olivier, Ralph Richardson, Michael Redgrave, Paul Scofield, Alec Guinness, Peggy Ashcroft, Edith Evans and Sybil Thorndike. And, of course, the greatest survivor of them all, John Gielgud, who had no place in the history of twentieth-century British theatre, for the simple reason that he was that history.

The coming together in roughly the same lifetime of this classical galaxy has never been adequately explained, and is unlikely ever to be repeated; those of us lucky enough to have witnessed it will just have to be content to describe it to anyone who will listen, illustrated only by often inadequate film or television records, and above all aware that, like any of the magic kingdoms from Prospero's to Peter

Pan's, it was just there for a while and then, suddenly and equally mysteriously, it wasn't. Like the boy Thomas Malory, who is sent by King Arthur behind the lines at the end of *Camelot* to spread the word of what once was, we just have to be aware that, for one brief shining moment, from approximately 1925 to 1975, the British classical theatre was at its all-time zenith.

Kenneth Tynan, the greatest theatre critic of this mid-century period, and the one lucky enough to be writing about this amazing generation in its prime, once suggested the following analogy: 'You have to imagine the English stage as a vast chasm, with two great cliffs either side towering above a raging torrent. Olivier gets from side to side in one great animal leap; Gielgud goes over on a tightrope, parasol elegantly held aloft, while down there in the rapids you can just discern Redgrave, swimming frantically against the tide.'

This, then, is the story of the man on the tightrope: although written with his approval and active co-operation in the last decade of his long life, it is intended as a critical biography of an actor who indeed spent much of that life working on the high wire without a net. And although in retrospect it now seems also to have been a charmed life, that of a man from an already theatrical family who simply carried on their tradition all the way to solo supremacy, we need to recall at the outset that we are also attempting to record the life of the only leading actor of the twentieth century to have come to the very edge of a prison sentence for homosexual soliciting, a man who then, albeit briefly, considered suicide, a man who had no real financial security until he was well into his sixties, a man who had constantly to cope with the frantic jealousy of his only acknowledged rival, Laurence Olivier, a man who only really learned to live happily in his own skin once he realised that, against all early odds and forecasts, he had outlasted and outperformed all the competition.

But this was also the man who, with his beloved brother Val, was in at the beginning of radio drama, and remained both on stage and radio his century's longest-running Hamlet, a role he played for almost thirty years at home and abroad. Long before the coming of the Royal Shakespeare Company or the National Theatre in the early 1960s, Gielgud alone in the West End effectively invented what we think of now as the classical repertory company. He was the actor and director who dragged Shakespeare out of the Victorian era of his own starry ancestors, and towards something vastly more psychologically complex. His early partnerships with his cousin Edward Gordon Craig, the director Komisarjevsky, and the Harris sisters who, with Elizabeth Montgomery, made up the radical costume and set-design team of the Motleys, meant that he was at the cutting edge of all the revolutionary 1930s changes in how Shakespeare was staged. With Ralph Richardson, in a late-life partnership dubbed by Richardson himself 'the broker's men', Gielgud was also the first classical stage actor to excel in Harold Pinter and Alan Bennett and David Storey, and the first player king ever to hold the Order of Merit as well as the title Companion of Honour.

Knighted far later than he deserved, overlooked for the theatrical peerages that have thus far gone only to Olivier and (amazingly) Bernard Miles, John G yet managed to end the century having not just outlived but also overtaken all his competition. There is a lot to be said for sheer survival. Gielgud spent his ninety-sixth birthday in April 2000 working with Harold Pinter and David Mamet on a play by Samuel Beckett. He died peacefully on a Sunday afternoon, at home, barely a month later, and only then was the sound of what Alec Guinness once called 'the silver trumpet muffled in silk' silenced for the first and last time, just three months before Sir Alec himself died at eighty-six, thereby ending the generation of stage and screen giants of which Gielgud was the first and Guinness the last.

Unlike Guinness, who managed to go to his grave (and even beyond it) without ever having been 'outed' as a late-life alcoholic and a man who had once been picked up for soliciting in Liverpool just after the war, Gielgud had to live with public knowledge of his 1953 arrest. But it says a great deal for the affection in which he was generally held that the journalists of all papers obeyed, almost until his death, a rule of silence despite the fact that the press cuttings of the 1953 case were always available in libraries.

In many ways, John G's death was as perfectly timed and placed as his life; his lover Martin Hensler, with whom John had lived for the last forty years of his life, had died of cancer in considerable agony almost sixteen months earlier, and John was appalled by the prospect of a hospital end. With Martin's death, just before Christmas 1998 while John himself was in the same local Aylesbury hospital with a sprained ankle, something in Gielgud also started to die; until then, he had been happily going out to film small but richly paid and showy roles in critical hits such as *Shine* and *Elizabeth*, as well as several more obscure parts in minor tele-movies. He would only accept two or three days' work at a time, knowing now his own fragility, but he loved the gossipy life of a film set, catching up with the lives of those actors whose names he could still recall, and escaping (albeit briefly) Martin's dominant, craggy, reclusive demands at home. Theirs was not, as we shall see, a marriage made in heaven, and Martin was towards the end by no means an easy, or even perhaps a very suitable, partner for the older John; but there is no doubt that Hensler's death was the moment when John himself started to die.

He also became convinced that, although he still wanted to take every role that came his way (and indeed in the last few months of his life hired a new young agent, Paul Lyon Maris, on the retirement of his old friend Laurie Evans), he must avoid even the possibility of sudden death on the set. John became hilariously obsessed with the idea that, if he were to die in mid-scene, they would send for Michael Denison to replace him, and that was not precisely how Gielgud wished to have his seventy-year career come to a close. Sadly, Denison died a few months before him, but ironically enough it was his widow, Dulcie Gray, who alone took to visiting John almost daily when Martin was no longer around.

John left strict instructions that there was to be no memorial service, according to a pact he had once made with an old friend and colleague, Emlyn Williams, and that even his funeral was to be held as privately as possible. His estate was eventually valued for probate in November 2000 at rather more than £1 million, of which a large proportion would be accounted for by the sale of South Pavilion in Wotton Underwood, where John and Martin had lived for almost thirty years, having bought the magnificently theatrical property from the historian Arthur Bryant.

A few days after his death, John's niece and principal heiress, the dancer and choreographer Maina Gielgud, talked about his last few months:

I had grown up with John and Martin, and although I know that many found Martin dour and difficult, I got on with him very well, and I knew how much John loved him, even though of course they often irritated each other tremendously. They were like an old married couple, mutually dependent, but also sometimes aching for their individual freedom. Martin was very eccentric, kept all kinds of exotic animals like iguanas in cages in the bathroom, and was obsessed by growing bonsai trees which Uncle John kept tearing out of the soil in the belief that they were weeds.

But when Martin died, a terrible change came over Uncle John; he always thought he'd be the first to go, not surprisingly as he was twenty years older than Martin, and he began to complain about his ankle injury and a back or hip problem. He could barely walk without a stick, and his wonderful voice had faded to a kind of whisper. Sometimes he would rally and there would be an adventure, like going to see *The Lion King*, but he was still desperate to work and even his last role, in the Beckett play with Pinter, sadly was silent. 'They won't let me have any lines,' was the last thing he said to me, oblivious to the fact that the role had been written silent by Beckett.

Arthur John Gielgud was born on 14 April 1904 at 7 Gledhow Gardens in South Kensington. 'We had only been living in Gledhow Gardens,' recalled John's mother some years later, 'for five weeks, when our third son was born, and we named him Arthur John. I wanted Arthur James, but John was a traditional Gielgud name. It was inevitable that, as everyone insisted on calling him Jack, I failed to persuade him to answer to Arthur, though if asked his name, he would as a baby always say, very distinctly, "I am Arthur John."'

He was the third of four children of a father, Frank Gielgud, who served almost fifty years on the London Stock Exchange, working for the family firm of Leonard Messel, who was himself the great-grandfather of the designer Oliver Messel. John's mother, Kate Terry Lewis, came from what was then the royal family of the British theatre. Her father Arthur Lewis was a wealthy haberdasher who founded the Arts Club, and in Kate's childhood their circle included Oscar Wilde, the painters Watts and Millais, Lewis Carroll, and the artists John

Tenniel and George du Maurier. Two dozen of her close relatives had all worked on or backstage, and she herself had only given up a promising theatrical career to marry Frank; it was always believed by her family that, had she stayed in the business, she would have become the most impressive actress of her Terry generation.

Their courtship had been surprisingly brief. Frank, a young widower, and Kate had met at one of the tennis parties which were then fashionable, and within a few weeks he had proposed to her at a charity ball. They married on 18 July 1892. Kate was six years younger than Frank, but far from being put off by his air of melancholy she rose to the challenge, determined to make him happy again. In due course he responded to her subtle but effective campaign to woo him away from his rather self-indulgent gloom, and the marriage went ahead, with the honeymoon being spent at a Thames-side inn at Streatley, and then in Scotland.

Kate's decision to opt for her own family life, rather than the theatre in her blood, was heartily endorsed by a husband who, despite the fact that his great-grandparents had both been eminent Polish actors, now viewed stage life with considerable misgivings, especially as his many in-laws were later inclined to erupt into his Kensington home, bringing with them noisy histrionics when quiet evenings at the piano were what he usually craved after a tough day in the City.

Also resident at Gledhow Gardens when John was born were his two older brothers, Lewis, who was ten, and Val, who was four. At the time of his birth, his mother was thirty-five and his father forty-one; after the birth of the two elder boys, both were hoping for a daughter. They were disappointed on this occasion, but three years later, in 1907, their final attempt to produce a girl succeeded, when Eleanor was born.

The most reliable witness to John in these very early family years was his elder brother Val, later to become a distinguished BBC Radio director and producer. Val always believed that their mother had regretted her decision to relinquish the theatre in favour of housewifery, and his own recollections of life in those early Gledhow Gardens days tended to be on the darker side. His mother, he said, always hotly denied any kind of sacrifice, but somehow the family had a strong awareness of her emotional displacement. There was, as one critic was later to say of the Lloyd Webber household, rather more linoleum than carpet on the floors of their house, and hot water was at a premium, but in the fashion of the times there was still enough money to employ several maids and a cook.

One of the very few of Gielgud's contemporaries to live as long as the century, his beloved Gwen Ffrangcon-Davies, once noted that the relationship between John's parents was coloured by his father's occasional 'unkindness' towards his mother, as he fell sometimes out of sympathy with her histrionic nature. John himself was to recall his father as 'very alarming when he was angry, and very charming at other times', while for Val he was 'withdrawn, and consequently formidable'. Their younger sister Eleanor, who later became John's secretary and a tower of strength in his time of trouble, added, 'We had a happy childhood, but it was very strict . . . we were all very frightened of Father; he never used force, but he could be very sarcastic. If you did something wrong, you always knew it.'

The year of John's birth was also the year in which Bernard Shaw's *Candida* first opened, the year that the foundations of the Royal Academy of Dramatic Art (of which John was later to become president and then their first Fellow) were established, the year Sybil Thorndike made her stage debut, and the year that the Court Theatre in Sloane Square was taken over by Harley Granville-Barker, who was to play a major role in John's later life.

1904 also saw the birth of J.M. Barrie's *Peter Pan*, and it is tempting to see the real-life Gielguds as a counterpart to the Darling family – Bohemian, eccentric, sometimes short of ready cash, but always individually and collectively fascinating, precisely because they were an extraordinary family in an apparently very ordinary London street, with John as the perennially youthful, starry Peter and his father as the recalcitrant Mr Darling.

Although the real-life Terrys were thoroughly rooted in what was then becoming, for the very first time, an almost respectable theatrical profession (Henry Irving had after all been knighted by Queen Victoria nine years before John was born), the Gielguds came of an altogether different background. Frank was Polish on both his paternal and maternal sides, but a generation or two further back the Gielguds had emerged from a village in Lithuania that to this day still bears the family name, Gielgaudskis. For three hundred years the family had lived in what is now a ruined castle beside the River Niemen. They were not, however, renowned for their brilliance; one forebear, General Anthony Gielgud, managed to get himself killed by one of his own soldiers during a Polish rising against Russia in 1831, while another was killed by Napoleon's troops.

Poland, constantly fought over, divided and reunited in ever more contentious ways, ceased to be a safe place to live and, finally, Gielgud's great-grandfather (also called John) decided that enough was enough. He fled to England and settled in Chelsea, where his son, Adam, was to find work first as a schoolmaster and then as a clerk in the War Office. Adam's eldest son, Frank, was born in 1860.

As far as his own family were concerned, John was later to recall early life in South Kensington: 'I was always supposed to be the delicate one of the family, because I enjoyed and exaggerated quite minor illnesses like measles, since they guaranteed me special food and added attention. I was the baby of the family until my sister was born, and Mother always spoiled me, particularly as I was inclined to be overly sensitive, and as a result I became as strong as a horse.'

'John was always the fragile one of the boys,' wrote his mother Kate plaintively, 'and in the first years of his life he absorbed most of my time . . . I had to supervise his food continuously and, with several unlucky changes of nurses, he slept so badly that I often had to take charge of him at night lest he disturb Val too frequently . . . His first summer was an exceptionally fine one but the heat could be trying, and thunderstorms were frequent. In the course of one of these, with the thermometer up to 93 degrees, John terrified me by going into a dead faint as I lifted him into his cot for his morning rest. The doctor found that heat-stroke had affected his heart. He was on his back for several days in a dark room, wan and limp, and we had to carry him about for months afterwards.'

In her memoirs, published in 1953, sixteen years after John had written *Early Stages*, Kate refers surprisingly seldom to her youngest son, noting somewhat irritably that the reader should read the actor's own early memoirs, and concluding: 'In my early days I was presented to strangers as Kate Terry's daughter; now other people meet "the mother of John Gielgud".'

All other evidence points to Lewis being their mother's favourite son, which left John and Val always striving for her attention; unsurprisingly, they were both in later life to be the great achievers of their respective professions, theatre and broadcasting, as if somehow they were always looking for the approval that Kate, hovering in their wings, was never quite able to give them.

Val remembered that John was, from a very early age, determined to ally himself with his maternal Terry relatives rather than with the paternal Gielguds:

The Terrys lay all about us in our infancy . . . a toy playhouse, pillared and elaborately gilded, was the pride and joy of our nursery . . . but John was to owe his career to nothing but his own persistence. Our parents looked distinctly sideways at the stage as a means of livelihood, and when John showed some talent for drawing, our father spoke crisply of the advantages of an architect's office. One of our more managing aunts even extolled the navy, saying that John would look very nice in the white tabs of the youthful cadet.

What John possessed from the very beginning was singleness of heart and mind, together with a remarkable capacity for hard work. When he was not acting in the theatre, going to the theatre or talking about the theatre, he was to all intents and purposes not living. All through his life, he was only to experience genuine happiness either on stage or in a dressing-room.

On the other hand, 'If I had been a pure Terry,' John said later, 'my acting talents might have developed in a much more conventional way, especially as at first I never thought that my father's ancestry had any influence on my work. But now I realise that I've always had a tremendous feeling for Russian plays and ballets and music, and it may well be that my Eastern European background gave me a real understanding of Chekhov.'

The year of John's birth was the year of the first productions of not only *Peter Pan* but (in Moscow) *The Cherry Orchard*, and it could be argued that these two plays neatly represented the twin poles of what came to be Gielgud's theatre: on the one hand a kind of magic sentimentality, and on the other a Russian regret for another type of Neverland alienation. That year, 1904, also saw the births of Graham Greene, Christopher Isherwood, George Balanchine and Cecil Beaton, all of whose lives were at some point to cross John's, however tangentially. It was, by any standards, a vintage and important year, effectively the opening of twentieth-century British theatre.

John and Val shared a bedroom and a bed at the top of the house, and with all the authority of his four-year seniority, Val used to insist that John should get into the bed first, thereby making it nice and warm for him. Relations were not improved between the brothers when Val took to writing acid reviews of John's earliest childhood theatrical endeavours, centred on their toy theatre, of which John took instant control. His early directorial efforts were usually dramatic epics starring Val's toy soldiers, despite his early-developed and strong distaste for all things military.

In Gledhow Gardens, where number seven is in fact on the corner of the Old Brompton Road, the young Gielguds led, as Marguerite Steen has noted:

> a rarefied life, initially controlled by a German governess, a staff of servants, an elder brother at public school, and strict parental conventions . . . John was a nervous and neurotic little boy, brought up (at least to start with) in privileged conditions . . . Naturally he was also to become a conceited little boy, yet he never appeared to be spoiled – he was far too serious for that . . . His grandmother Kate, his parents and aunts, knew everybody; so he grew up, not in the limited world of the theatre, but against a broad and impressive background of Important People. His parents were deeply and intellectually interested in the arts – his father in music, his mother in theatre and literature. The Gielguds moved in a wide social circle of cultured friends, whose means kept pace with their tastes. There always seemed to be enough money, but above all there was always security . . . John was indubitably an artist, from the time he played with his first toy theatre – which to him was not a toy at all, but an intrinsic part of his childish life, and the foundation of his career. Later, he would often retire into a private world of books and music.

Christmas provided the annual opportunity for yet more family drama. Every year, on the feast day itself, Ellen Terry and her sister Marion would arrive for a family lunch and then encourage charades around the fireside, as John was later to recall:

> Ellen was of course the great star of our family, and I fell madly in love with her the first time she ever came to our house. But she had led, to say the least, a somewhat irregular social and sexual life, and Mother always found her rather restless and fidgety. When I first saw her act, I realised that restlessness was part of her glory because although she was then an old lady, deaf and rather blind and very vague in mind, when she came onstage you really believed that she was either walking on the flagstones of Venice or in the fields of Windsor. I remember her so well, moving with extraordinary swiftness and grace, though of course Shaw said that she also had a genius for standing still. She was a pre-Raphaelite actress, and she had known all the great men of her time, from Browning and Ruskin to Rossetti and Wilde. And although she had learned so much from them, she also had a marvellous humility – she was ready to learn from us children, and she had a wonderful sense of humour, which the rest of my family rather lacked. I think Marion and Fred and Kate all considered Ellen to be the scapegrace – she was the one who had been received into all the great houses in England and America, despite having two illegitimate but enormously talented children [Edith and Edward Gordon Craig]. I have always believed that in my childhood I saw only three great actresses: Sarah Bernhardt, Eleanora Duse and my own Aunt Ellen. They were all old and infirm, but they could still stop the traffic and form queues right down Shaftesbury Avenue.

The Ellen Terry that John remembered had been born in 1847, herself also the child of a theatrical family. After a brief and unhappy marriage to the artist George Frederick Watts – 'He wanted a model, not a wife' – she had joined Henry Irving's company at the Queen's in 1867, and within a year went to live with the married architect E.W. Godwin. This alliance led to her two remarkable children, Gordon and Edy, and to a deeper relationship with them than any Ellen was to achieve in her three marriages.

At the Lyceum, from 1878 to 1900, she was Irving's Ophelia,

Portia, Desdemona, Juliet, Beatrice, Viola, Cordelia, Imogen and Lady Macbeth. When their partnership eventually broke up, Ellen Terry went into management by herself, and was the first to stage Ibsen's *The Vikings* (1903) in a vastly expensive and disastrous production, with scenery by her son Gordon Craig.

But Ellen was always a survivor; soon after Irving's death she was working with Beerbohm Tree, and in 1906 Bernard Shaw wrote for her the role of Lady Cicely in his *Captain Brassbound's Conversion*. In the years that John knew her, she was making a series of five silent films (among them, in 1922, *The Bohemian Girl*, in which she co-starred with Ivor Novello and another actress whose beauty was often to get in the way of her acting, Gladys Cooper), and also giving solo lectures on the heroines of Shakespeare, as well as returning intermittently to the stage. Because of her somewhat scandalous extramarital affairs, she had to wait until 1925 to be made a dame, only the second actress to receive such an honour after Genevieve Ward. Ironically, Irving had overcome the scandal of his marital breakdown to get the first theatrical knighthood; but this was still a time when women were expected to follow a higher moral code – at least in public – and although Ellen Terry was, before Peggy Ashcroft and after Mrs Siddons, the dominant actress of her age, this elderly and much loved public figure remained, so far as her family were concerned, something of a black sheep. John's connection to Ellen was romantic and emotional, but it had one practical outcome, which was that all through his early career he made a point of playing special one-off matinées at Smallhythe, the barn in Kent which had been Ellen's home and remains to this day her miniature theatre.

If, in John's early years, Ellen was the shining (albeit still somewhat distant) star of the family, there was no shortage of lesser players closer to home. Both John's parents had come from unorthodox backgrounds with strong European connections, and although on his father's side the relatives included a number of professional soldiers and a former Chief Justice of Lithuania, his mother could deliver at least five working Terrys, as well of course as Gordon and Edith Craig. Life in Gledhow Gardens was therefore never less than theatrical: one year, the boys' audience for their Christmas show even included G.K. Chesterton. A handwritten programme survives for just one of the Gielguds' home-made entertainments, a play written by John himself, entitled *The Nightingale* and subtitled 'A Set of China in Five Pieces from the famous fairy tale of Hans Andersen'. The many scenes and settings included: The Lake, The Palace, A Corridor, The Fisherman's Hut and (most intriguingly) The Emperor's Bed. The cast list for *The Nightingale* included: Death, A Spiteful Geisha, The Voice of the Nightingale, and The Mother of the Fisherman.

Surprisingly, given all the theatricality around the house, it wasn't until he was seven that Gielgud was taken to his first theatre. As for most London children of his generation, it was *Peter Pan*, with Pauline Chase in the title role, the part she played for ten of the production's first twelve years, and Holman Clark as Captain Hook. It could well be argued that for a stage-struck child to get his first glimpse of real theatre in a play about a strange, sexless boy forever trying to coerce his friends into joining him on a magical never-never island was not at all a bad start for John's life in the theatre.

As John himself was later to recall:

I was thrilled by the first entrance of the Pirates, drawn on a kind of trolley with Hook enthroned at the centre of the group, and the sinister song that heralded them as they approached from behind the scenes. I loved Nana taking the socks in her mouth from the nursery fender. Was she a real St Bernard, I wondered, or a man dressed up and walking on all fours? But I resented the wires on the children's backs which I could see glittering in the blue limelight, and guessed that their nightgowns had bunched-up material on the shoulders to hide the harnesses they had to wear underneath. And I wished the wallpaper at the top of the scenery didn't have to split open, as well as the tall windows, when the time came for them to fly away. The doors immediately fascinated me – the one in *Peter Pan*, through which the little house rose slowly at the end of the play, with Peter and Wendy waving to the audience from its windows, and the one in *Where the Rainbow Ends* which suddenly whisked the wicked Aunt and Uncle to the nether regions. And of course I loved the fights in both plays: Peter and Hook, St George and the Dragon King, and the double scene above and below ground in *Peter Pan*, and the hollow tree with stairs inside it, with Hook in a green limelight, leaning over the low door at the bottom, leering at the children as they lay asleep.

For the young Gielgud, the most important place to be was already the second star on the right, and to find that you had to keep straight on till morning. But already a curious contradiction lay at the heart of John's childhood. Whereas most of his great-aunts and uncles on the Terry side were deeply involved in theatre, his own parents were really only enthusiastic in the abstract:

My mother talked about it a good deal, but my father was never keen on the gossipy side of theatre; he was a much more serious and intellectual character than my mother. He liked music very much, and would take us to concerts on the very hard seats behind the organ at the Albert Hall, which gave me my appetite for music. He also took us to museums and galleries, which bored me rigid. I think you could say that my two brothers and young sister and I were intelligently brought up, but we were not encouraged ever to play games, because my parents had no interest in that – neither did they swim, or ride, or shoot, or fish, so if we ever went away, it was always just to the seaside.

We had three or four servants, a nurse and a governess, although my father never made more than £2,000 a year, but in those pre-war days of course that was all quite possible. I do remember, very clearly, the London of my early youth: the straw thrown down outside houses to muffle the noise of horses when people were ill, and the muffin man with the green baize apron, and the coal-man who carried great sacks on his head, like Dolittle in *Pygmalion*, and would throw the coal down the manhole in front of your house with a terrible crash. In those days, the horses made far more noise than the cars which came later, and everything was for me a kind of excitement and an exhibition.

As soon as I was able to, I started exploring London on foot and fell totally in love with the West End, the marquees, the queues at the stage doors and the photographs in front of theatres, all very discreet, with none of the blaring advertisements and quotes from newspapers that you see today. How elegant and dignified it all was.

There followed other theatre treats, mostly involving members of the Terry family, and among John's earliest memories was his cousin Phyllis Neilson-Terry as Queen Elizabeth in *Drake* with real white horses on stage, and his uncle, Fred Terry, swashbuckling his way through *Henry of Navarre*. John was already completely obsessed by the theatre and, from this time forward (despite a brief flirtation with architecture and stage design), considered no career alternative. Especially not poetry, despite this early effort, written when he was nearly seven:

> *Life in Mamma's Balloon*
> I went right to the moon
> Far in the sky, ever so high
> I went, and had tea with the moon.

The poem is signed 'Arthur John Gielgud, six years and ten months' and is his first known writing.

But now, everything was about to change abruptly. In the autumn of 1912, when he was just eight, he was sent away by his parents to Hillside, a preparatory school near Godalming in Surrey where both his elder brothers had been head boy. Aldous Huxley had also been a pupil, as, in John's time, was the future playwright Ronald Mackenzie in whose work Gielgud was later to appear onstage.

The fraternal tradition was not at first one that John seemed likely to sustain. As he noted later: 'It was an altogether ghastly place; a great deal of bullying went on, the headmaster was far too old, and between lunch and the next morning's breakfast, all we ever got were three chunks of bread, thinly buttered, with a scraping of jam.'

If John's early years had come straight out of *The Forsyte Saga* (which, when he read it a few years later, seemed to him to be an amazingly accurate account of his own family life), he now appeared to be moving rapidly into *Tom Brown's Schooldays*. But here, as so often in John's recollection, one has to allow for a certain theatrical exaggeration.

Most important of all, it was at Hillside that he first decided he really might like to be an actor, after giving a duly tearful Mock Turtle in *Alice In Wonderland* ('I sang "Soup of the Evening" with increasing volume and shrillness in each verse'), followed by an equally successful *Humpty Dumpty*. But nothing was yet certain. At the same time that the acting first became important, he also discovered a strong talent for sketching. Every week the boys of Hillside had to write compulsory letters home, and either because John did not want to betray his loneliness and unhappiness to a doting mother, or because he simply had very little to report, he took to filling the pages of his letters with ink and crayon drawings of the staff and fellow pupils. Three-quarters of a century later, several of his early theatrical sketches of pantomime figures were triumphantly published as charity Christmas cards.

John stayed at Hillside until almost the end of the First World War. In these five years he found that Divinity and English were the subjects he liked best, and he especially enjoyed singing in the choir at Sunday services, already working out how to make his voice louder and more identifiable. Gradually, life at Hillside ceased to seem so terrible. As his height and stage experience increased, he was entrusted with Shylock in *The Merchant of Venice* which he also stage-managed, allowing him, for the first time, to incorporate some design ideas of his own. He was also able to send his mother an ink sketch of himself as Shylock, although there was at this time the very real feeling that art rather than drama would be his eventual career.

John's final year at Hillside, 1917, was surprisingly successful for the boy who had so hated being there. Although by his own admission, 'always a funk at games', he had managed to score in football, rugby and cricket; but the real joy of these last few terms came when he followed his brothers as head boy. This meant that at cricket matches he could appoint himself scorer, thus giving himself time to prepare for his last Hillside dramatic role as Mark Antony in *Julius Caesar*.

In this summer of 1917, Zeppelin raids were apt to interrupt the school curriculum with increasing regularity, though at first John was inclined to find them fascinating rather than frightening. When nearby Guildford was bombed, resulting in a lot of flying glass, he felt inspired to write a poem which here makes its first appearance in print:

THE ZEPPELIN RAID ON GUILDFORD by A.J. Gielgud
One fine evening (so 'twas said)
While we boys were all in bed
Zeppelins passed overhead
Out to show us 'kultur'
Back to Germany went they
(They don't like the light of day)
Leaving bombs about this way
'Specially at Guildford
We, excited, rushing round
All believing every sound
'Martha's Chapel's on the ground'
said our music master.
This was not quite true, I fear
We the real truth did not hear
'Til the riders with a jeer,
Said; 'It's standing happy'
On the Sunday there we went,
Tried to get some bomb, all bent,
But the Guildford men had sent
All *their* boys to get it.
Back to Hillside went we sad
Not a bit of bomb *we* had
But we saw some houses had
Had some bombs inside 'em.

Back at Gledhow Gardens, as at so many other addresses, the long summer of the pre-war world had been abruptly ended by telegrams bearing news of young men killed at the front. For the Gielgud family the bad news was of Lewis, who had been seriously wounded at the Battle of Loos. After several weeks in hospital in Boulogne, it was suggested by the Red Cross that Kate herself should go out to nurse her son, and it was here that, like so many other women of the time, she really came into her own. While Frank stayed nervously at his desk in London, Kate became the life and soul of the Red Cross hospital where Lewis was forced to stay for several months. As soon as she could, Kate brought him home to England and Lewis was transferred to a small clinic for convalescent officers, which had just been opened in a wing of Kensington Palace. There, Kate noted proudly, his first visitors included two of his pre-war Oxford contemporaries, the writer Aldous Huxley and the scientist J.B.S. Haldane.

A few months later still, Lewis was allowed to return home, classified 'Permanently Disabled', although by the end of 1918 he was sufficiently recovered to be back in France as a cypher clerk at the signing of the Armistice. Lewis's war ended in a blaze of glory, as he was variously attached to the staffs of Clemenceau, Maréchal Foch and Field Marshal Sir Douglas Haig.

The atmosphere back home at Gledhow Gardens was however rather less victorious: Frank was no longer having much success on the Stock Exchange, there were still school fees to be paid for the younger children, domestic staff had to be let go, and the house now seemed, like so many others, to be in mourning for its pre-war life.

John, with all the single-minded selfishness of the adolescent, was meanwhile discovering a whole new world for himself, blithely ignorant of the fact that his parents' social universe was in some ways coming to an end. Whenever possible, on half-holidays or weekends, he would hang around Shaftesbury Avenue, greedily gobbling up every production for which he could afford a stool in the gallery queue. In these wartime years he saw every kind of performance from *Chu Chin Chow* (no fewer than five times), to *Peg o' My Heart*. A year earlier he had also seen the Drury Lane gala celebration of the Shakespeare Tercentenary, which brought together every star in the West End firmament, from Henry Ainley and Gerald du Maurier to Genevieve Ward and, from his own family, Ellen, Fred and Marion Terry.

During the interval King George V had summoned Frank Benson to the royal box and knighted him, a ceremony only slightly spoiled (in John's recollection) by the fact that His Majesty had no sword, and had to send round the corner to a local theatrical costumier's for a false one.

The Edwardian theatre of my boyhood was dominated by the great actor-managers like George Alexander, Beerbohm Tree and Gerald du Maurier. At the time, I accepted their style of acting completely, and I suppose I longed to be like them. I thought that was the way to act. I much preferred the panache of Fred Terry or Robert Lorraine in

Cyrano to the naturalistic but brilliant acting of Du Maurier or Charles Hawtrey . . . but I had no conception of the various methods necessary to achieve such fine results. Du Maurier often put on rubbish, just as Fred did – they both catered to the public taste for sentimental dramatists like J.M. Barrie. Ibsen and Chekhov had only just arrived in translation, but they certainly weren't what most theatre-goers then wanted. Actors in those days read very little, did not like to be taken too seriously, and had little faith in foreign writing. People were also still curiously snobbish about the theatre. My Aunt Mabel was very close to Gerald du Maurier's brother Guy, who was killed in the First War, and I once asked her if she had been in love with him. 'In love? With an actor?'

As the First World War came to its close, the Gielguds' life in South Kensington was slipping into a kind of genteel poverty. Essentially, theirs had been an Edwardian household and, like so many of its kind, it had undergone an almost imperceptible downgrading during the war. The pre-war seaside holidays and large family Christmas parties had of course come to an abrupt end in 1914, and as the four children began to move away, to war or public school, the house took on the faintly ghostly air of a theatre just after the audience has gone home. Where before there had been servants and warmth and hospitality, now there was a general air of decay, ameliorated by Kate Gielgud's theatrical determination not to let any family problems show 'from the front'.

With the family now in considerable economic difficulty, it was imperative for John to gain a scholarship to his senior school; having failed both Eton (to which Lewis had won a scholarship) and Rugby (where Val had enjoyed a similar triumph), the nearby Westminster School, though very much a third choice, proved willing to accept the young John on a fee-paying basis, and only then after some tough coaching.

No sooner had he arrived, at the age of thirteen, for the September term of 1917, than John knew it was the place to be, not least because one of the vergers in the neighbouring Abbey gave him a black-edged card which had once been attached to an Irving wreath. On it was simply written 'Rosemary for Remembrance' but the initials were unmistakably those of his great-aunt – 'E.T.'.

More importantly still, had he in fact gone to either Eton or Rugby, he would effectively have become a prisoner within school grounds; Westminster by contrast, less than a mile away from his home or Shaftesbury Avenue, meant that the whole of central London could become his playground.

Even so, John only survived a couple of terms as a weekly boarder at Grant's House before he was writing home in desperation to his mother: 'Please, dearest Mama, let me become a day boy. All I feel inclined to do is either cry or shriek, and it is so awful trying to fight such unhappiness and homesickness. I feel vilely rotten. Woke up this morning with a deadly fear of getting up, the day, the house, the work, the play, the meals and then going to bed again. I shiver and shake and think and worry. It is all too beastly. One can't enjoy a moment.'

Even allowing for schoolboy exaggeration and John's already highly developed sense of drama, this sounded ominously like a premature nervous breakdown, and John soon got his way, through an appeal not to his mother's rather non-sentimental nature, but to her sense of the practical. Soon after her son's arrival at Westminster, the now almost nightly air-raids would force the whole school to run through the cloisters into one of the oldest Abbey vaults. There too, as Gielgud later recalled, 'all the canons and the dean would gather with their wives, families and servants . . . One night the buttresses of the Abbey were covered with snow. They sparkled in the brilliant moonlight, while the bursting shells overhead and the searchlights swinging to and fro made an extraordinary picture in the sky.'

By using these air-raids and the consequent loss of sleep as an alibi, he now persuaded his parents to re-cast him as a day boy; this also represented a considerable economic saving, which came in useful as his father was by now a Special Constable patrolling Chelsea and, specifically, guarding the Lot's Road power station while awaiting the all-clear. John also joined a Westminster cadet group and, hating it deeply, was at least reassured to find that he looked and felt better in uniform than in the top hat and stiff collar that Westminster pupils were still required to wear.

I was still a boy, but lucky enough to have been born just in time to touch the fringe of the great nineteenth century of theatre. I saw

Sarah Bernhardt die in battle, I saw Adeline Genée dance, I heard Albert Chevalier sing 'My Old Dutch', and I saw Vesta Tilley and Marie Lloyd in their last days. I also stood in the gallery, ridiculous and mocked in my Westminster school uniform, to see Duse make her farewell appearance in *Ghosts* . . . what impressed me most was the tremendous reception the audience gave her, their breathless silence during her performance, and the air of majestic weariness with which Duse seemed to accept it all. There was something poignant and ascetic about her when she was old and ill, quite different from the indomitable gallantry of the crippled Bernhardt, and the ageless beauty and fun that Ellen Terry still brought with her upon a stage.

What most appealed to John about Westminster was not the education, which he could take or leave, and usually left, but the sheer sense of drama; as a young teenager, he began to experience his lifelong fascination with tombs and statues and weddings and funerals and memorial services, all of which had a theatricality utterly central to his character.

Like Noël Coward, whom he was to understudy and replace in his first West End engagement less than ten years later, John was now finding in religion a kind of musical theatricality which much appealed to the showman already in his childhood nature. But where Coward had to content himself with appearances as a boy soprano in the suburban churches of Teddington and Battersea, John's stage was Westminster Abbey itself, where the school choir was often to be found in twice-daily performance, albeit without the applause that Coward (born five years before Gielgud) and John already craved.

It was by no means clear at this stage that John was cut out to be any kind of an actor. His extramural interests at Westminster were still art and architecture; at home, he set up an easel in what was now his own bedroom and soon paintings displaced the model theatre: 'I have always had such a love of the pictorial side of theatre that the very first things in a production that really strike me are always the scenery and costumes. If they delight me, I am already halfway towards enjoying myself.' Although he was not to meet him for several more years, there is no doubt that by the time John was fifteen the relative who most intrigued him was no longer Ellen Terry but her illegitimate son,

Edward Gordon Craig, already perceived as a great and revolutionary stage designer.

Temporarily religious, like many adolescents, John was unsure whether his Church of England background gave him enough emotional support. One possibility would have been High Church or even Roman Catholicism, and he often went to smell the incense at Brompton Oratory, just round the corner from Gledhow Gardens. He was searching for a sense of ceremony and ritual, and one of the few things that made up for his hatred of the Westminster cadet training was being allowed to play a very small part, as an usher's attendant, at the 1919 Burial of the Unknown Soldier in the Abbey itself.

At Westminster many of his friends were Jewish, and he became aware of their segregation at prayers and mealtimes. Mostly, he admired and felt comfortable with their almost theatrical openness and their unashamed love for the arts, an interest often either dormant or suppressed in more conventional English schoolboys. One of his best friends, Arnold Haskell, was already a fervent ballet addict, and he took John to such classic events as the Bakst *Sleeping Beauty* and the dancing of great prima ballerinas such as Karsavina, Lopokova and Tchernicheva, all of whom were working in London during the war. This was also the heyday of the Ballets Russes at the Alhambra, and John was soon able to make the connection with his own partly Russian background: 'Haskell, who of course became a leading ballet critic, and I used to save all our pocket money and, after school on wet Saturday afternoons we would stand for hours together in queues – that first production of *Boutique Fantasque*, the exquisite blue backcloth for *Carnaval*, the enchanted tower in *Thamar* and the glory of Bakst's rococo palaces in *The Sleeping Princess* were all early ecstasies, although my youthful admiration also extended quite indiscriminately to *The Beggar's Opera* and *The Bing Boys Are Here Again*.'

Many years later Gielgud was to write of the first time he saw the Ballets Russes: 'the entrancing mixture of music, mime and spectacle enraptured me immediately . . . For *Boutique*, the scenery was extremely avant-garde . . . I was able to appreciate the acting as well as the dancing, which seemed to merge together with incredibly skilful ease and grace . . . The elegance of *Carnaval*, the high spirits of

Boutique . . . the savage dances in *Prince Igor*, as the music crashed out and the curtain fell to tumultuous applause.'

For John G this experience was not just an artistic revelation, but the rite of passage of another sort: 'I left the theatre in a dream. Soon I was to become an aficionado of all the Diaghilev seasons that were to follow . . . Standing in the Promenade beside my father, and walking about with him in the intervals among the cigar smoke and clinking glasses in the bar, I felt I had really grown up at last.'

The influence of the Ballets Russes was not just restricted to this stage-struck public schoolboy. Their explosive combination of the best of modern design, dance and music had an enormous impact on the English cultural scene, inspiring a generation of ballet dancers, choreographers and patrons, and appealing to a wider audience of artists and actors, among them the poet Rupert Brooke. The Edwardian age is now looked back on as a golden Eden, removed from the modern world; but culturally at least it was, in large measure thanks to Diaghilev's extraordinary ability to conjure up new talent (particularly in the work of Vaslav Nijinsky, his lover and protégé and the most famous male ballet dancer of all time), an age of enormous excitement and change, led not from Paris but from what was then still St Petersburg. The Russian Empire provided not only an ancestral home for the Gielguds, but, in the form of Chekhov, it was to offer their most famous son some of his best roles and greatest professional satisfaction.

From now on, as a would-be artist and even as a theatre-goer, he was to be constantly torn between the ornate grandeur of Diaghilev and the avant-garde minimalism of Gordon Craig. John was still by no means certain precisely what he was going to do with the rest of his life, but at this late teenage moment if you had asked him, the answer would certainly have been designing scenery rather than appearing in front of it:

I think at this time I was tempted by the idea of being a designer, at least partly because I was terrified of the thing I most wanted, which was to be an actor. At home and in school plays, I really hadn't got much further than wandering around with a rug draped over my shoulder, thinking I was a king or something. Years later, when my friends got bored of all my theatrical chat, they used to say, 'Oh, for God's sake, put a crown on his head and send him on,' which always mortified me.

I was always very vain, and very fond of my voice and my looks, so it took me years to break free and learn to be a real actor; at first, what frightened me was that I moved very badly. I have always hated sport, I played no games, I couldn't swim, I couldn't really do anything. Later, when I learned to drive a car, I even had to give that up because I was so clumsy. I've always dropped things, and it was only on stage that I eventually found my confidence; but I was still very conceited and rather effeminate, and much too fond of the sound of my own voice. It took me an amazingly long time to stop showing off, and start acting.

His lack of interest in sport was in strong contrast to his love of walking around London:

I was a great walker, finding my way all over London – Lincoln's Inn, Chelsea, Chiswick, Kew Gardens and Hampton Court . . . but my Mecca was the West End, and the triangle of streets radiating from Piccadilly Circus, where so many theatres stood . . . I walked up Shaftesbury Avenue, skirting on my left the narrow streets of Soho . . . but ignoring, to the right-hand side, the temptations of Gerrard Street and Lisle Street, where the tarts lingered provocatively all day long, as well as at night . . . These walks around theatreland allowed me to examine minutely all the photographs and bills outside the theatres, while I tried to decide which of them seemed most likely to encourage me to invest my pocket money, and to savour the never-ending delight of standing in a queue for several hours waiting for the Pit doors to open.

John's last year at Westminster was 1921, and clearly decisions had to be made. Lewis, after his wartime service and rehabilitation, had returned to win a scholarship to Magdalen College, Oxford, and Val had just got into Trinity. Visiting them there, John fell in love with both the city and the university, but he was still woefully unacademic. The problem, as usual, was his utter inability to cope with maths and, despite some expensive private coaching, he humiliatingly failed his college entrance no fewer than three times.

Putting the bravest possible face on his failure, his mother Kate recalled: 'John declined the university course we had planned for him. He declared that it would be a waste of his time and his father's money, as he wished to spend those three years studying for the stage . . . I think he always realised that he had my wholehearted backing. I was always certain that there was too much of the artist in him to let him settle down on an office stool, and though an architect's office was offered as a halfway concession, his very poor records at school in maths and geometry did not hold out much promise in that direction.'

Ironically, this left him in a rather stronger bargaining position with his reluctant parents, and they rapidly came to an understanding: John would apply to Lady Benson, who ran a private drama school close to his grandmother's house in the Cromwell Road. If accepted, he would be allowed to train with her for the theatre on the strict understanding that if, by the age of twenty-five, he had not become self-supporting, he would turn to a career in art or architecture.

Meanwhile, at Gledhow Gardens, the toy theatre was put away in the attic for the very last time, and John was about to find a real one just around the corner.

Chapter Two

❧❦❧

WATERLOO ROAD TO GOWER STREET
(1921–1923)

*Lady Benson was a very bad actress but a splendid teacher. She
ran her school in a ramshackle little drill hall, and on my very
first day told me that I walked like a cat with rickets.*

John was now seventeen. His early years, according to his
own memoirs and other evidence, were a curious mixture of
privilege and fading gentility. The Terry family had reached the
apex of their stardom with Ellen and Fred, but there was as yet no
indication that any of the next generation would enjoy the same
success. John did not, unlike his near-contemporary Noël Coward,
have to fight his way out of south London boarding-houses, but nor
did he have the great advantage of Sybil Thorndike and Laurence
Olivier, both born into the Church and therefore accustomed to
hearing their fathers declaiming from the pulpit every Sunday. By
contrast, John's father was still a shy, retiring figure, and it was
therefore left to his numerous aunts and distant cousins to start his
theatrical education.

Life at Gledhow Gardens had certainly been distinguished by the
number of famous theatrical guests who visited regularly, but money
was now always tight, and John from an early age knew his only assets
were a famous family and a passionate desire to be in the theatre. He
would always have to make his own living and, while he never starved,
he was never to make 'real' money until well into his sixties.

By the time he arrived at Lady Benson's, where he was one of only four boys in a class of thirty, he had already progressed from the early family plays in the attic to a couple of amateur appearances, thanks to his older brothers at Oxford. The first of these was a production of a First World War drama at a theatre in the King's Road, Chelsea. The cast included not only John as a young Greek officer, but, playing a British prisoner of war, the scientist Julian Huxley who, like his brother Aldous, had by now become a friend of all the Gielgud brothers.

John had also played a couple of very minor roles for Rosina Filippi's drama school in Chelsea, and made his Shakespearean debut, somewhat disastrously, in an amateur production of *As You Like It*, played in the open air at Battle Abbey. Aged sixteen, and cast as Orlando, he proudly went to the local barber shop demanding to have his hair waved – for a play, he added, cautiously. 'Certainly, sir,' said the barber. 'I assume sir is with the Pierrots on the Pier this week?' He might as well have been. As a duly coiffed Orlando, he strode on to the lawn, drew his sword, declaimed his opening line, 'Forbear and fight no more,' and promptly fell over a large log. Thus it was that the greatest Shakespearean actor in the history of the world made his stage debut flat on his face.

But even during his time at Lady Benson's, John still half thought he might prefer to be a designer rather than an actor. He had a deep dislike of the fencing, dancing and gesture classes that were central to the acting course. He was interested in text, but terrified of the physical side of acting: 'As a young man, I was vain and foppish; I pranced around, looking very self-conscious. Then I became too graceful and posed; later I had to control my physical mannerisms by having them checked by others but, at this age, I was still far too shy to ask anyone about them.'

Though his parents still had grave doubts about allowing their youngest boy to go into the family business, Kate Lewis Terry, his grandmother, was overjoyed: 'Dear old Jack,' she wrote him in 1921, 'I am delighted to hear of your intended real start in a profession you love, and wish you every success. You must not anticipate a bed of roses, for on the stage, as in every other profession, there are "rubs and arrows" to contend with. "Be kind and affable to all your co-mates, but if possible be intimate with none of them." This is a quotation of my parents' advice to me, and I pass it on, as I have proved it to be very sound. Theatrical intimacy breeds jealousy of a petty kind which is very disturbing. I hope you may have many chances with your various studies and prove yourself worthy.'

By John's own admission, he was a talented but conceited pupil at Lady Benson's; yet he now began to develop serious doubts about whether he could ever really make it as an actor: 'I became acutely self-conscious, knowing that my laziness and my dislike of games had prevented me from learning, when I was a boy, to move freely and naturally. I walked from the knees instead of from the hips, and bent my legs when I was standing still, instead of holding them straight. I am sure that if I had been forced to run and swim when I was a child, I should not have developed these mannerisms so badly, but it was too late to think of that now. Such a discovery in my first term at Lady Benson's was extremely depressing; however, it dealt a severe blow to my conceit, which was a good thing.'

As a result of all these insecurities, John now decided that the only way he might get by as an actor was in wheelchair roles, or those that required him to lie in bed, but he soon worked out that this would mean a necessarily limited career. He did however appear during term-time in a couple of charity matinées, one of Noël Coward's first play *I'll Leave It To You*, and the other of the play that was later to become almost his own personal property, Wilde's *The Importance of Being Earnest*.

While at Lady Benson's, he made the happy discovery that the Old Vic in the Waterloo Road, then as always strapped for cash, was in the habit of using drama students as free extras. Thus it was that, still only seventeen, on 7 November 1921 Gielgud made his first professional, albeit unpaid, appearance onstage as the Herald in *Henry V*, directed by Robert Atkins who kept shouting to 'that boy in the brown suit, for God's sake, take your hand out of your pocket when holding a spear'.

For John, susceptible, romantic, uneasy, but convinced by his Terry heritage of the absolute magic of the theatre, the Old Vic came as a rude awakening. The rehearsal room was filthy, extras had to change in a box above the stalls with only a curtain to hide them from the audience, and John had said his one line, 'Here is the number of the slaughtered French,' so badly that for the rest of the season he was not given another word to speak. So unpromising did he seem to the 'real' actors in the company that many of them, including Ernest Milton and Sybil Thorndike's brother, Russell, took the trouble to come over and tell him that despite his theatrical heritage he would be well advised to give up any thought of the professional stage. Curiously, it was this opposition that finally tipped the balance and made him now, for the first time, determined to be an actor.

Daunted but not defeated, John returned for two more terms to Lady Benson, and got his first review playing a vicar in an end-of-term farce called *Lady Huntsworth's Experiment*. True, he wasn't mentioned by name, but the critic of the *Stage* noted: 'The worthy parson, unctuously played by quite a beginner, drew much laughter from a critical audience.'

By the end of the year's course, John was not really much further forward. Lady Benson's was not regarded as a fully fledged drama school, and as for his family, although they had shown polite and loyal interest in his teenage endeavours as both actor and artist, they were not now exactly falling over themselves to find him work. On the other hand, he did already have a few credits, a little humility and a now unshakeable determination to make his future in the theatre.

When help did come, it was inevitably from one of the Terrys, albeit one he hadn't seen since early childhood. Phyllis Neilson-Terry was the daughter of Fred, and therefore a cousin of John's. She had been on the road in America for several years but on her return, hearing of his interest in the theatre, she wrote offering him £4 a week for a long tour of fifteen weeks around the provinces to understudy and speak a few words at the end of *The Wheel*. He would also, for the money, be required to work as an assistant stage manager, and after a very few rehearsals (because most of the cast had already done the play in London), they opened at the Theatre Royal in Bradford on 4 September 1922.

The idea of Bradford was to John the height of romantic theatricality – it was, after all, the city where Irving had died, a few hours after giving his last performance as Becket in 1905. Seventeen years later, when John got there, he found, to his surprise, an infinitely depressing vista of smoke-stacks and the universal greyness of northern factory life. He stayed in a small back room in digs largely occupied by the singers and dancers working at the local music hall and felt, this young boy from a classical royal family, rather out of his element amid the rough and tumble of popular entertainers. Even in the theatre, he found he still had a lot to learn, especially about greasepaint; most nights he would arrive on stage as a British naval officer, but bizarrely resembling a Cherokee Indian, because he kept forgetting to powder his make-up before going under the lights.

The tour proceeded to Sheffield, Hanley, Preston and Leeds, where John was not best pleased to find in his digs a sign reading, 'Lav in pub opposite'. Things could only improve, and they did so at Aberdeen, where one of the principals fell ill and John had to go on in his place. Phyllis was so pleased with her cousin's achievement that a couple of weeks later, when the tour reached Oxford, she asked the now-recovered leading man to stand down for one night so that John's parents might be invited to come and see him. Something about their presence destroyed his performance, however, and Frank and Kate returned sadly to London, convinced that their boy had made an unwise choice of career. Salvation came in the form of another young actor on the tour, Alexander Sarner, who gently suggested to John that a year with Lady Benson was not exactly the ultimate in theatrical training, and perhaps he would now be wise to apply to RADA (the Royal Academy of Dramatic Art) for a more advanced theatrical education.

By now much more experienced than any of the other applicants, John easily achieved the scholarship that had eluded him everywhere else. His contemporaries during the year, 1922–23, that John spent in Gower Street at RADA included its star pupil, Robert Harris, and such other future classical players as Beatrix Lehmann, Veronica Turleigh, George Howe and Mervyn Johns, all of whom were to work in John's companies in later years. Their principal teachers were Elsie Chester, a formidable and disabled old bat who used to hurl her crutch at students who displeased her, and Claude Rains, who went on to an extremely starry Hollywood career in such classics as *Casablanca* and Hitchcock's *Notorious*.

Forty years later the actor and raconteur Peter Ustinov was to find himself in St Louis, Missouri, where John was playing his solo Shakespeare recital *The Ages of Man* at a local theatre. To publicise it, he had agreed to give a television interview to a local college professor, and it was this that Ustinov caught.

'One final question,' said the interviewer. 'Sir . . . Sir Gielgud . . . did you . . . oh, you must have had . . . we all did . . . at the start of your very wonderful . . . very wonderful and very meaningful . . . let me put it this way . . . did you have someone . . . a man . . . or even a woman . . . at whom you could point a finger and say Yes! This person helped me when I . . .' By now John seemed to have grasped the question. 'Yes,' he replied thoughtfully, 'there was somebody who taught me a very great deal at drama school, and I am certainly grateful to him for his kindness and consideration. His name was Claude Rains.' And then, as an afterthought, John added, 'I don't know what happened to him. I think he failed, and had to go to America.'

Certainly, at RADA, Rains was more to Gielgud than a failed actor: he was a significant teacher and it was through his encouragement that John at last began to lose some of his acute self-consciousness. At the end of the first term, Gielgud played the title role in the Academy's production of *The Admirable Crichton*, J.M. Barrie's classic comedy about the butler and the aristocrats stranded on a desert island, and he was seen by Nigel Playfair, one of the most revered and adventurous producers and directors of his day. So keen was Playfair to have John join his company that a deal was reached whereby, while continuing at the Academy, he would also play the Poet Butterfly in Karel Kapek's *The Insect Play*, a revolutionary piece which flopped badly, because the sexual content which had made it such a success on the continent had been removed by the puritanical Lord Chamberlain (a member of the royal household who had been appointed to censor plays in the eighteenth century and was, amazingly, to go on doing so until 1968), in order to save the blushes of an English audience. 'Looking back, I am amazed that the audience refrained from throwing things at me . . . I wore white flannels, a silk shirt, a green laurel wreath and a golden shuttlecock . . . The production was a disaster, and I certainly didn't help it.'

At this early stage it would have been a brave critic who forecast that John really had any future at all as a leading player; still very frail and sensitive, sheltered even now by a dominant mother, and always having been allowed to escape any kind of physical activity at school, he was deeply uneasy in his own skin – awkward, ungainly, physically inhibited and already aware that he had to be careful about appearing in any way homosexual, since this was then reckoned anathema to most audiences, and of course still against the law, even for consenting adults in the privacy of their own homes.

At this time John G was about as unlikely an actor as could have been found. Here was no Olivier, eager to appear before an audience; instead, John's magically lyrical voice and artistic inclinations suggested a poet or a painter rather than a public performer. He seemed more likely to be found at the top of an ivory tower than pinned under a spotlight.

Even so, Gielgud already had his supporters, a group not limited to his relatives. Nigel Playfair, for instance, retained such faith in the young RADA student, still only nineteen, that he kept him on at the Regent Theatre for the next and very different production, a staging of *Robert E. Lee* by the poet John Drinkwater, who had just scored a huge success with *Abraham Lincoln*. But his second stab at American Civil War history was by no means as popular as the first, and John's only role was that of an orderly, following Felix Aylmer around the stage and trying not to count the empty seats through his field glasses. He did, however, get to understudy Claude Rains and went on for him in a couple of performances in the title role where, again, he found he was very good on the first night and very bad on the second: 'I seemed at this time always to lose confidence after I had played a part once, but people were agreeably surprised at my ability in the emotional scenes. The feeling of them came to me without much difficulty, and the sincerity of that feeling got over to the audience, despite my lack of technical accomplishment, whereas in the other part, as the orderly, my clumsiness and slovenly movement were conspicuous, and there were no moments of emotion or drama in which I could atone.'

Back at RADA, Rains was still giving the young Gielgud what amounted to a series of master-classes, putting him through everything from Tolstoy to Shakespeare and even a scene from *L'Aiglon* which he played in French. But, with money still very tight, and a constant awareness that under the deal he had made with his father he had only until the age of twenty-five to establish himself in the acting profession, John decided at the end of his first RADA year that the Academy had taught him enough and it was time to head out into the real theatrical world. At this point, the only advice on which teachers and pupils at RADA were agreed was that John would certainly have to change his surname, since no one seemed able to pronounce or spell it with any degree of accuracy, and he was usually to be found on theatre posters and programmes as 'Mr Guilguid', suggesting a Scots background rather than an East European one.

John G had however already attracted the attention of one important admirer: 'I was,' recalled Sybil Thorndike some years later, 'doing a little teaching at RADA and I was horrified by the students – they all acted like governesses, with no power, and I said, "You are all terrible, no fire, no guts, you've none of you got anything in you except that boy over there, the tall one, what's your name?" And he said, "It's John Gielgud," and I said, "Well, you're the only one with possibilities." None of the rest of them had any voices or style of their own, they were all trying to be Gerald du Maurier, and that's no way to approach Greek tragedy.'

John was soon to discover that a mere year at RADA was not in fact nearly enough, but he did now have the experience of a range of Academy and semi-professional roles which, although none too successful, had at least given him the feeling of what it was like to go out in front of an audience in a series of vastly different and rapidly learned and rehearsed plays. He had also begun to keep a critical first-night diary which suggests that he could have had an entirely other career as a sharp, not to say waspish, Fleet Street reviewer; among his earliest notices, neatly inscribed on the covers of programmes he was to keep for more than three-quarters of a century, are reflections on *The Beggar's Opera*, *Ghosts*, John Barrymore's *Hamlet* and O'Neill's *The Emperor Jones*, as well as such more lightweight productions as *White Cargo* and *Advertising April*. Gielgud notes that at *Mary Rose* he 'wept buckets'; *Heartbreak House* he found 'dull and ill-constructed', *The Second Mrs Tanqueray* 'far more dramatic and less dated than I had thought from reading it', *Anna Christie* 'a very fine play, sordid but intensely dramatic'. Duse in *Ghosts* 'seemed to be somewhat selfish in her playing', and Coward in *London Calling* 'definitely not good, lacked charm and personality'. As for *The Sleeping Prince* at the Alhambra in November 1921, with a score by Tchaikovsky and a production by Leon Bakst, 'far too long and under-rehearsed; disappointing scenery, marvellous clothes, some good dancing but some very dull, wants pulling together, very enjoyable apart from that'.

Chapter Three

❧❦❧

A DISUSED MUSEUM IN THE WOODSTOCK ROAD
(1923–1925)

'Your name and college, sir?'
'I fear I am not a member of this university.'

Leaving RADA behind, John now went on the inevitable rounds of agents' and managers' outer offices in search of a job. Unlike most aspiring actors of his time, something in his background, whether the Terry connection or the enthusiasm of such influential figures as Rains and Playfair, meant that he was almost immediately able to find work, and indeed hardly ever to be out of it again for almost exactly three-quarters of a century.

To this day, it is still debatable whether a famous family background (and Gielgud was of course not nominally a Terry) is generally an advantage. The widespread view seems to be that it can help you to get the work, but not necessarily to keep it and, in John's case, there was the added problem of his extreme social and sexual nervousness. He was, in every sense but the most immediately theatrical, a late developer. Coupled with an innate shyness went the feeling that he was somehow not like other hopeful young actors of his time.

His background was therefore at once an asset and a hindrance; he did not mix easily, and on the rare occasions when he found a real friend, he was somehow embarrassed to admit the grandeur of his connections – a grandeur that had nothing at all to do with money or even class, but everything to do with talent. His family were always outsiders, not only because they had first chosen to act at a time when this was still widely considered socially scandalous, but also because a name like Gielgud scarcely suggested reliable British stock. Once again, the timing was against him; actors might have begun to become respectable while he was still in his teens, but only by desperately trying to acquire the manners and even the clothing of the squirearchy. Something about John was irredeemably foreign and artistic, at a time around the First World War when to be one or the other was suspect, and to be both little short of intolerable.

Nevertheless, his first job after drama school came easily and quickly enough, even if it wasn't quite the beginning that might have been hoped for a leading classical actor of the future. The role he was offered was a Christmas season in *Charley's Aunt* at the Comedy Theatre. The play had already become an annual fixture in London and on the road since 1892 and neither the author, Brandon Thomas, nor his daughter Amy, who was now the director, would allow any changes. John's dreams, therefore, of playing Charley in a rather more 'modern' manner were rapidly defused in rehearsal, and he was told simply to act it as it always had been acted, move by move, and intonation by intonation. It was not a happy engagement but it only lasted six weeks, and what came next was something altogether more satisfactory.

J.B. Fagan was the Irish author, producer and director who had already done some very distinguished work at the Royal Court, including *Othello* with Godfrey Tearle, and he had now founded the first Oxford Playhouse Company in a disused big-game museum on the Woodstock Road, affectionately known as the Red Barn. This soon became one of the most respected regional repertory companies in the country, and by the time John joined it during that first season, early in 1924, Fagan had already gathered an amazing team of young players including Raymond Massey, Flora Robson, Tyrone Guthrie, Reginald Denham, Richard Goolden and Glen Byam Shaw; while among their audiences were the young historians A.J.P. Taylor and A.L. Rowse.

Over the next eighteen months, John was to appear in a total of eighteen different productions for Fagan, frequently just walking on; but he seems to have made so little impression on the company that neither Raymond Massey nor Tyrone Guthrie in their memoirs indicate any recollection of having met him until years later.

But for John himself this was to be a magical time. Guthrie remembered 'a building on the fork of two arterial roads which, because it had once been a museum, seemed to me haunted by the ghosts of a moose, an elk and a lion, whose stuffed and mouldering corpses had been the melancholy sole exhibits. The building also trembled and reverberated like thunder every time a truck or bus went past, roughly every six seconds.'

John's brother Val agreed. 'The Playhouse,' he wrote later, 'was a building devoid of cheer, foyer or bar, which had surely the most uncomfortable seats of any theatre in the world. John, undaunted by any of this, loved every minute.'

For Gielgud himself: 'It was very pleasant to be living in Oxford, having meals in college and drinks with the OUDS [Oxford University Dramatic Society], everything I had of course missed by not being a student there. The Playhouse was indeed terribly cramped, there was no foyer, and the stalls groaned and squeaked when anyone got up or sat down or even moved their legs. On the other hand, we did a very interesting season of plays by Congreve, Sheridan, Wilde, Pinero, Shaw, Ibsen, Chekhov and Pirandello.'

Years later, Tyrone Guthrie, fired at the end of his first season at the Red Barn for general belligerence, was still taking no prisoners: 'At the first cast meeting, Fagan announced that because ours was a presentational stage, we should be giving Presentational Productions. None of us had the faintest idea what this meant, not even Fagan himself who insisted that everything should be white. A white curtain set in a white proscenium, white curtains forming the scenery for all our plays, and a few white tables and chairs around which to act. This, it soon became clear, was not a very good idea and audiences soon became extremely tired of all that white.'

The first production of the new season was Shaw's *Captain Brassbound's Conversion*, and although John was only one of the pirate crew, with barely half a dozen lines, *The Times* reported that: 'He showed both imagination and restraint in the small part of Johnson.' He also displayed considerable ingenuity when, one night, all the lights failed and the last act had to be played in the beams of two car lamps, held proudly aloft by Gielgud like follow-spots.

He got his reward in the second production: 'Our big success in my first season was Congreve's *Love For Love*.' John was cast as Valentine with Guthrie as his servant, Jeremy. For the actor who had so recently been told that he walked like 'a cat with rickets' and that his voice sounded consumptive, here surely was the chance to establish some real credentials.

In the audience one night was an undergraduate who was later to become very important to John.

'I saw, in his first leading role, in *Love For Love*,' recalled Emlyn Williams, 'a youth whose name in the programme caused a woman behind me to say, "Poor boy! How does he pronounce it? John Jeelgud?" . . . When he got going, all nose and passion and dragging calves, and unbridled oboe of a voice . . . the tall, haughty creature held the stage all right.'

John was now living in a tiny flat in the High, and earning all of £8 a week – a reasonable salary for the time. He was also getting more and more involved with the undergraduates who ran an active drama society under Gyles Isham, and fervently began to make up for what he now realised had been his first great lost opportunity, that of becoming an Oxford student when that university was at its most theatrical in the high-camp early 1920s. In later years he was to befriend and work with George 'Dadie' Rylands, the English don at Cambridge who (like Nevill Coghill at Oxford) was, across a long twentieth-century life, to establish very firm connections between Oxbridge and the classical theatre, connections both homosexual and professional, which were in turn to lead to an unusual number of undergraduates of the 1950s and 1960s starting their theatrical careers even before they had graduated. Its ultimate outcome could indeed be considered the establishment in the early 1990s of the Cameron Mackintosh Chair of Theatre at Oxford, even though drama itself has still not been accepted as a degree course by the university.

But for John, in these early 1920s, when he was not needed in rehearsal at the Red Barn, it was suddenly possible to lead the life he had only ever managed to play in *Charley's Aunt*, that of a languid student in chambers. Thanks to his new friend Gyles Isham, who was then living in college, John almost persuaded himself that he too was a student, at least until he was one night stopped by proctors, the university police, for singing bawdy songs in the High after hours.

'Name and college, sir?' 'Alas,' replied John with considerable regret, 'I am not a member of this university.'

On another occasion, Gyles invited John to lunch in his rooms at Magdalen, rooms that had once been occupied by Oscar Wilde, to tell him that he had an ambitious plan to play Romeo in London during the next vacation. On his way home that night, John's neck began to swell and it became clear that he had mumps. He was immediately expelled from the Playhouse Company for the duration. Guthrie was deputed to fumigate his dressing-room and take over his roles, 'while Mother took me home in a hired car with large pillows on which to rest my face, which now looked so like Humpty Dumpty's that I had to laugh every time I caught sight of myself in the window'.

But even this story has a happy ending of sorts. When John returned, as soon as he was able, to the Oxford Playhouse Company, he discovered that Isham had caught his mumps and, through gritted teeth, had now to ask John to take over not only the rehearsals but also the leading role in his *Romeo and Juliet*. To John's fury, Isham recovered in time for the first night, but Gielgud was asked to stay on in the role of Paris, after which (as the first Playhouse season was now at an end), he returned to London where, in April 1924, he received a letter from the agent Akerman May: 'Dear Mr Gielgud,' it read. 'If you would like to play the finest lead among all the plays by the late William Shakespeare, will you please call upon Mr Ayliff at the Regent Theatre on Friday at 2.30 p.m. Here is an opportunity to become a London Star in a night.'

What had happened was that Gwen Ffrangcon-Davies was in desperate need of a Romeo for her Juliet, and although John was still only nineteen, and she had been less than impressed by his performance as the Poet Butterfly in *The Insect Play*, she decided, after three long auditions, that, on this occasion, he would have to do.

Rehearsals went reasonably well because both were word-perfect at the outset, John having learned the role for Gyles Isham and Gwen Ffrangcon-Davies having just played it in Birmingham. 'She was wonderfully helpful, extraordinarily keen and unself-conscious. From the very first rehearsal she threw herself wholeheartedly into every moment of her part, running the whole gamut of emotions and telling me not to be frightened of our "clinches". So when the moment came to embrace her passionately, I was amazed to find how naturally she slipped into my arms, sweeping her draperies in the most natural and yet artful way so that they should not lose their line or impede her movement, and arranging her head and arms in a position in which we could both speak and breathe in comfort.'

It began to look as though John was at last losing some of his physical inhibitions, but shortly before the first night he also lost his nerve: 'I was given white tights with soles attached to them underneath and no shoes. My feet looked enormous, and it was most uncomfortable to fight or run around. My wig was coal black and parted in the middle. Wearing an orange make-up and a very low-necked doublet, my Romeo looked like a mixture of Rameses of Egypt and a tetchy Victorian matron.'

Not surprisingly, the reviews were very mixed. Gwen Ffrangcon-Davies's child-Juliet was warmly acclaimed, but Ivor Brown considered that 'Mr Gielgud is niminy-piminy and from the waist downwards he looks absolutely nothing. He has the most meaningless legs imaginable, a sort of hysterical laugh and generally lacks experience . . . he is also scant of virility.'

As was the custom of the time, John and Ffrangcon-Davies were also engaged to play special nights at the London Coliseum, doing the balcony scene on a music-hall bill: 'They gave us a terrible set, with a sort of cardboard balcony, which made it look as if Juliet was standing in a picnic box. The audience never knew what to make of it, but one of the stage hands was kind enough to say to me, during the last performance, "You are doing it a bit better now."'

They were preceded on the bill by Teddy Brown on his xylophone, and followed by the Houston Sisters, one of whom, Renée, was a character actress who spent much of the rest of her life at backstage parties doing a lethal parody of the young Gielgud.

The worst was still to come. Two weeks into an unhappy run, in which the over-sensitive young actor knew he was not being remotely good enough, John developed pneumonia and neither of his understudies, Ion Swinley and Ernest Milton, managed to fill in without carrying the book. The run therefore came to an ignominious end after six weeks, and it was with some relief that John returned for a second season to the Oxford Playhouse.

He had regained some measure of confidence by dint of simply being invited back to rejoin Fagan, since both Flora Robson and Tony Guthrie had been unceremoniously dumped after the previous season. This second Oxford stay, in 1924–5, proved considerably more successful than the first. The reason was a major production of *The Cherry Orchard* in which John made his first real success as Trofimov: 'It was the first time I ever went out on stage feeling that perhaps, after all, I could really be an actor.' All the same, this was not an altogether easy time for him: 'We had only a week to rehearse, and I did not understand the play at all, but there was no time for the director to explain it, so it was all rather clumsy and tentative.'

It is important, seventy years later, to recall that at this time Chekhov was virtually unknown in Britain and his plays, when performed, invariably divided both audiences and critics. Of the new Oxford production, James Agate wrote in the *Sunday Times*: 'I suggest that *The Cherry Orchard* is one of the great plays of the world, and young Gielgud as Trofimov is perfection itself.'

Audiences were still far from certain, but the *succès de scandale* inspired a new management, that of Nigel Playfair, to transfer *The Cherry Orchard* to his Lyric, Hammersmith. Here John again played Trofimov; the first performance was well received and there were even cries of 'author', but the reviews were hostile and audiences were poor, at least until the critic James Agate made a very early radio broadcast urging listeners to go to the Lyric, Hammersmith. Playfair also printed a poster quoting radically different reviews of the play including 'This imperishable masterpiece' (Agate) and 'This fatuous drivel' (MacDonald Hastings).

Yet it was precisely because of this controversy that John G now became one of the most talked-about actors in town. The BBC, barely five years old, offered him Malcolm in a live wireless production of *Macbeth*, and unlike Tony Guthrie who 'can't *bear* broadcasting, although I can see it has a future', John was thrilled to be in at the beginning of a new medium which he was to make his own for the next seventy years, while his brother Val became the founding father of BBC Radio drama.

A few weeks later, John got in at the start of another new medium, though one in which he was always to be much less at home. He was unexpectedly offered a leading role in a silent film, called *Who Is The Man?*, a script which had been played on the Paris stage by his idol, Sarah Bernhardt. He had even seen her do it. Her godson, Louis Verneuil, had written it for her soon after her leg was amputated, so that she could play on a divan covered in rugs. This clearly was not going to do for the film, in which John was required to play an opium-addicted sculptor undergoing a series of frantic emotional tantrums. The studio hired a violinist and piano player to get him into the right mood, but the results were so deeply embarrassing that nowhere in his memoirs does John ever refer to it. The film does exist, at least in the British Film Catalogue, but all other traces would seem to have vanished, a fate to which all too many silent films have been consigned, some more happily than others.

It was now clear that, with John's natural affinity for Chekhov and his tentative success in *The Cherry Orchard*, he was ready at last to leave Oxford for the brighter lights of the big city with some confidence. Fagan let him go, having neatly arranged that his brother, Val, would take on some of his roles at the Playhouse, and John was to leave, looking back at some of the happiest days of his professional career. It had been a good time to be around Oxford: undergraduates of the period included Oliver Messel, Evelyn Waugh, Graham Greene, Claud Cockburn and John Betjeman, all of whom were later to write or talk about the first time they had seen John act, howsoever tentatively, in the Red Barn.

But the ambitious plan (by the impresario Philip Ridgeway) to run a complete Chekhov season in London fell rapidly apart. After *The Cherry Orchard*, a nervous hit, they moved on to *The Three Sisters*, at the tiny Q Theatre in Barnes, whose budget was appropriately small – John was to be paid only £1 a week. He recalled this as:

> a beautiful production, very simply done, and with a lot of very good actors. Komis's [Komisarjevsky, the director] main idea for me was that I should play Tusenbach as a very handsome young man, although in the text Chekhov calls him ugly. Komis believed that English audiences were now badly in need of a romantic hero, and he was an enormous influence in teaching me not to act from outside, not to seize on obvious, showy effects and histrionics, not so much to exhibit myself,

as to be within myself trying to impersonate a character who is not aware of the audience, to try to absorb the atmosphere of the play and the background of the character, to build it outwards so that it came to life naturally. This was something I had never thought of, and it seemed to me a great relaxing exercise . . . relaxation which is the secret of good acting. I remember our first rehearsals in someone's Bloomsbury flat, with the floor marked out in bewildering lines of coloured chalk – the groupings, entrances and exits were all most accurately planned, though at first we could none of us imagine why we were being shuffled about in such intricate patterns of movement.

During the brief run of *The Three Sisters*, Gielgud also played for Komisarjevsky a Sunday-night performance of another, now much less familiar, Russian drama, Andreyev's *Katarina*, in which he appeared as a jealous husband of fifty, whose wife dances almost naked in front of him during a party, to the despair of both him and his host.

The Three Sisters was not a success, but it had at least brought Gielgud together, for the first time, with the legendary Russian director and Stanislavsky disciple Komisarjevsky, who was later to marry Peggy Ashcroft, and was already widely known in rehearsal as 'Come and Seduce Me' on account of his passion for young actresses.

In more recent theatrical times, perhaps only Lee Strasberg at the Actors' Studio in New York had the same revolutionary impact on actors as that of Komisarjevsky in the London theatre of the early 1920s. Komis was, at least in John's experience, one of the very first directors to exist, and certainly the first ever to free his cast from the simple instruction to learn their lines and not crash into the furniture. In that sense, Komis was also the first psychiatrist of the British theatre and John, who had always been fascinated by Russian theatre, was among the first to pick up on what had until then been a very foreign concept: 'For the first time, working for Komisarjevsky, I realised that I need no longer worry whether I was moving gracefully or looking handsome. I had not to declaim or die or express violent emotions in fine language. Instead, I must try to create a character utterly different from myself, and then behave as I imagined the creature would behave, whose odd appearance I suddenly saw in my looking glass.'

It was during the break between leaving Fagan early in 1925 and joining the Ridgeway season at Barnes that John took what many have seen as one of the most curious career decisions of his early life. Sensing perhaps that the future for an Oxford actor specialising in Chekhov was bound to be limited, John was actuely aware that he had as yet played no part in the commercial theatre, which was at this time all-important. Accordingly, he took up an offer to understudy Noël Coward in *The Vortex*, Coward's first major playwriting hit, with the understanding that when Coward took it to America a few months later, John would inherit the role of Nicky Lancaster, the drug-addicted son, in the West End transfer from Hampstead. It was, after all, the nearest he could then get to a modern-dress *Hamlet*, complete with a bedchamber scene and at least the suggestion of incest. Intriguingly, the mother-obsessed Nicky is also probably homosexual, although this, for 1924, had to remain unspoken in front of an audience who seem to have had no trouble with drug-taking, but were not yet up for homosexuality in their drawing-room dramas.

John had first met Noël Coward a few months earlier at a party given near his home in South Kensington by their mutual friend, Betty Chester. Both Coward and John were also now taken up by the wealthy Lord Lathom, a stage-struck homosexual aristocrat who was to spend most of his inheritance putting money into Coward's plays and giving country-house parties of extraordinary extravagance, at which footmen would welcome the West End guests by pouring perfume into heated spoons to fill the entrance hall with a thick scent. Gielgud later described him as 'a delightful friend who gave me the first expensive gift I ever received – a silver clock from Asprey'. For him as for Coward, this was an introduction to a world of unimaginable opulence which only came to an end in the 1930s, by which time Lathom had run through his considerable fortune; not the least of his extravagances was building a Greek swimming pool and a bowling alley inside the house, where he also created his own personal perfumery. On one occasion he sent a footman down to London on the night train to return in time for luncheon the next day with a special brand of chocolate almonds. In his short reign as the Playboy of the West End World, Lathom was more than generous to both John and Coward, and these weekends at his country house were undoubtedly homosexually arranged.

John's initial impression of Noël Coward, before their weekends with Lathom became a regular feature, had been of someone 'dreadfully precocious and rather too keen to show off at the piano'; but when, a few weeks later, John went with his parents to see *The Vortex* at the little Everyman Theatre in Hampstead, in the October of 1924, he abruptly changed his mind: 'In that tiny auditorium the atmosphere was extraordinarily tense, and the curtain of the second act, with Noël sitting in profile to the audience, his white face lifted, chin jutting forward, head thrown back, playing that infuriating little tune over and over, louder and louder, until the curtain fell, was one of the most effective things I had ever seen in the theatre . . . after the performance, clattering back in the half-empty tube on the long journey home to South Kensington, my parents and I all sat silent in that state of flushed exhaustion that only a really exciting evening in the theatre can produce.'

When, a few months later, *The Vortex* transferred to the West End, it was essential for Coward to have an understudy who could play the piano, and John was therefore asked to audition. He was still not quite twenty-one.

Understudying Coward proved, however, to be both an irritating and a thankless task; Coward, who (unlike John) was already leading an extremely active social life as not only a writer but also a party entertainer to the upper classes, was in the habit of arriving at the stage door only moments before his first entrance. This is turn meant that John had, almost every night, to get into full costume and make-up, only to see Coward rush onstage with seconds to spare. Although John's recollection was that Coward was always charming to him and offered any help he could, it wasn't until almost six months into the London run, when Coward wanted to go to Manchester to see the opening night of his new revue, *On With the Dance*, that John was therefore able to take over the role, however briefly.

'There are few occasions more nerve-racking than playing a leading part in the absence of a principal. Before I went on that evening, some kind person knocked at my door to tell me that several people had asked for their money back because they had seen the notice, posted at the box-office, announcing that Noël was not appearing. But audiences are extraordinarily fair and well-disposed towards young understudies, especially if the play is an interesting one, and by the end of the evening the applause was just as warm as it had been on other nights.'

Although Noël Coward was already far better established in the West End than John (not only as an actor but also, already, as director, playwright and songwriter), the two men had a great deal in common and were indeed to go on working together across the next half-century, in such plays as Coward's own *Nude With Violin*, and Mike Todd's all-star travelogue, *Around the World in Eighty Days*. But, at this point, their relationship was not particularly close, despite the fact that they were working in the same theatre, and both coming to realise that their innate homosexuality was going to create considerable personal and professional problems, unless carefully guarded from all but their most reliable friends.

At twenty-five Coward was already far more socially and sexually confident, and even world-weary, than John. For Gielgud, just turning twenty-one, sex was still largely an undiscovered country, but it did not take long for both the actor himself and his closest friends to realise that women were seldom if ever going to be a part of his offstage life. At this point, both Coward and John were already obsessed by their work, and inclined to regard any sexual encounter as at best an interruption, and at worst a threat, to their budding careers. For neither of them was sex much more than a diversion. And if, in later life, either actor did allow himself to fall in love, it was usually an experience of short, sharp shock from which they fled to the arms of a much lower-maintenance male lover, so that most of their energies could still be reserved for what happened across the footlights.

But sitting in the understudy dressing-room night after night, even after the brief glory of giving two almost flawless performances while Coward was otherwise engaged in Manchester, proved a depressing time for John, especially in the weeks around his twenty-first birthday in April. It did however allow him a considerable pause for thought, as well as the chance to look closely at the state of the commercial theatre on and around Shaftesbury Avenue.

At this time, far more evidently than later, there were essentially two British theatres: that of the commercial London and all-important touring circuit; and that of the small club theatres and Sunday societies and university venues like Fagan's, or summer festivals like Stratford's, where either classic Shakespeare or revolutionary Chekhov and Ibsen could be experimentally staged on minimal budgets. Essentially, John's heart was with the former, and his intellect with the latter; though always unworldly with money, he rapidly came to realise that Coward's was the most desirable of lives. To be the 'shock boy' of the West End, already making two if not three salaries as star, director and writer, was also to be the latest wonder of theatrical London society, and John immediately began to envy Coward his facility both on and off the boards, his ability to play leading roles in restaurants and at parties as well as in his own plays.

John still came from the unfashionable theatre; it was around this time that the greatest of West End stars, Sir Gerald du Maurier, had to explain to an eager fan that he would not be playing Richard III because 'my audience would find my appearance in such a play embarrassing', and certainly the gentlemen actors of Du Maurier's time were not expected to inflict anything intellectual, in either translation or verse, on their loyal followers.

Reflecting on all this backstage at *The Vortex*, John realised that if he was to achieve the first and principal dream of his working life, to make classical and even foreign drama acceptable to mainstream, chauvinist and still very conservative audiences, then he would have first of all to make his own name, one that many people were still having considerable trouble in either spelling or pronouncing correctly. At this time, the only hope for an 'intellectual theatre' was the rapidly proliferating Sunday-night play societies, where new or difficult or even dangerous work would be given an often fully fledged performance, though for one night only, frequently by actors and actresses such as Edith Evans and Esmé Percy who were already tiring of their mindless Monday-to-Saturday runs on Shaftesbury Avenue, and aching to do more serious and demanding work.

Thus it was that, even while he was understudying Coward, John gave his next performance for the Phoenix Society in May 1925, a few weeks after his coming of age, in Thomas Otway's *The Orphan* for one Sunday only, a performance caught by the critic Desmond MacCarthy who noted prophetically that 'Mr Gielgud, with his charming voice and pleasing vivacity, is sure to make his mark quickly.' John was now whenever possible making himself available for one-night stands, whether for play-reading societies or school productions (he was at Charterhouse for *French Leave* in December 1924), or anywhere else that he could get the experience of another role.

At Oxford, he had already briefly appeared in Shaw, Congreve, A.A. Milne and Oliver Goldsmith, not to mention Synge, Ibsen and Maugham during the 1924–5 season, and his long stay backstage at *The Vortex* only served to make him hungrier for the classical roles which he already knew were his home territory, even if they were not likely to make him as instantly rich or famous as Coward.

Chapter Four

❧❧❧

NOËL AND THE NYMPH

(1925–1929)

Although by now I was beginning to get some quite promising
reviews, I also received a good deal of personal criticism from my
family and a few discriminating friends, who told me that my
mannerisms were becoming extremely pronounced, my walk as
bad as ever, and my diction slovenly and affected.

By the time John finally replaced Coward in *The Vortex*, he
had in less than four years on the stage already played thirty-
four roles, admittedly many of them in college, semi-
professional or Sunday-only productions. No other actor of his time
had done so much so fast, but as John's more discriminating friends
were beginning to warn him, facility and theatricality alone were by
no means enough. He had begun to play the shadows, but not the
substance, and yet he was already too old and too experienced to
complete the three-year training which he had abandoned at RADA.

Even his regional repertory apprenticeship at Oxford had stopped
abruptly before he was twenty-one, and there was now a strong
feeling (among those few who really cared about his future) that
he was running dangerously fast before he could really walk with
any confidence on stage. But at least his next engagement took him
back to Chekhov; it was in fact a transfer of the *Cherry Orchard* that
he had first played in the previous year at Oxford.

The producer, Nigel Playfair, had been so impressed by the production that he now took it into his Lyric, Hammersmith, with

Gielgud still playing Trofimov in a play which he admitted he found 'absolutely bewildering', although he had managed to hide himself behind rimless spectacles and a make-up closely based on his brother Val.

But London audiences were still not yet ready for Chekhov, and when John came on at the first night to utter the line, 'All these clever people are so stupid,' a woman in the stalls shouted back, 'How very true!' Unlike the Oxford producer, J.B. Fagan, who was inclined to take refuge in the academic theatre, Nigel Playfair was a showman, and he realised at once that he had a controversial production to sell when, on the first Sunday of the Hammersmith run, James Agate, for the *Sunday Times*, declared it 'the best production in London' while MacDonald Hastings for the *Observer* thought it 'the worst'. Even John was inclined to agree:

'Before *The Cherry Orchard* I just felt I could exhibit myself, and I rather enjoyed the business of going to the theatre and walking about onstage . . . I suppose I always used it as an escape. To go through a stage door, shut myself up in a dressing-room, and come out as some-body else, gave me tremendous pleasure. I was always living in some sort of fantasy world, and I was still very englamoured by the older members of my own family. The great thing about Playfair and Fagan was that they were wonderful talent-spotters. I know I must have been very clumsy and conceited as a young actor, silly and vain, but those two men never made me feel hopeless or wretched as a beginner.'

John's Trofimov ('Perfection itself' according to Agate) led him back to Fagan's Oxford company for two last appearances in the late summer of 1925, first as the Stranger in Ibsen's *Lady from the Sea*, and then as the title character in Pirandello's *The Man With the Flower in his Mouth*. But by the autumn of that year, John was back in London, and in Chekhov. Cast as Konstantin in *The Seagull* at the Little Theatre, he confirmed his reputation as what *The Times* called 'an unequalled interpreter' of Russian drama.

Writing to Gabrielle Enthoven, the theatre-goer and long-time Gielgud fan whose unrivalled collection of programmes was to form the basis of the Theatre Museum collection, John said how glad he was that she had noticed the way that 'I am getting rid of a few of the bad tricks. It's a difficult part, and the producer wasn't much use as a helper, so I have had to go tentatively about my own improvements and developments since the first night. I hope it's getting better by degrees, but it's so irritating to realise suddenly, after one has been playing for some time, some perfectly obvious thing that one has been missing all along.'

It was now that John began to take an increasing interest in the idea of directing as well as acting; although it was Valerie Taylor whose performance as Nina made her a star overnight, it was not long before John was back with Komisarjevsky, planning yet another season of Chekhov at Barnes.

But Gielgud was still picking up other work whenever and wherever he could: during the run of *The Seagull* he also turned up for special matinées as the Good Angel in *Doctor Faustus*, Harrington in Gwen John's *Gloriana* pageant, the hero of *L'Ecole des Cocottes*, opposite Gladys Cooper, and even Ferdinand in Shakespeare's *The Tempest*, though none of these made any special impression on audiences or passing critics. What they did was to keep John in permanent rehearsal, unable or unwilling to form any lasting relationships in his private life, but ready and eager to join whatever production or company was up and running for a few days or weeks.

In one sense London was ready for a new classical star, but just how unprepared Gielgud was for that role had become all too clear in 1925 when John Barrymore first brought his swashbuckling *Hamlet* to England from its Broadway triumph. At this time Barrymore was the marker for any stage *Hamlet*, and John missed that mark by a mile. Everything that Barrymore did, and perhaps above all his easy, relaxed relationship with the audience, was something that Gielgud could only wonder at from a seat in the gallery.

But even John, by now, was able to feel part of the community of London theatre players; on Sunday nights and Monday afternoons he would turn up in a range of non-Chekhovian roles, everything from Valentine in *Two Gentlemen of Verona* to Rosencrantz in an uneasy modern-dress *Hamlet*, though the most notable of these performances was as the young lover Armand in the first London staging of Dumas's *La Dame Aux Camélias*. This in turn led him to another long run, although here once again he was to be overshadowed by Noël Coward.

Early in 1926 there was no doubt around the West End that the big hit of the season was likely to be Basil Dean's staging of *The Constant Nymph*, Margaret Kennedy's bestseller about the Bohemian Sanger family, leading lives of elegant artistic degradation in the Tyrol. The obvious casting for the role of the romantic, pipe-smoking Lewis Dodd, a musical genius who spends most of the play strumming the piano and uttering witty one-liners, was either Coward or the other great matinée idol of the time, Ivor Novello. Basil Dean eventually opted for Coward, on the grounds that he was currently hotter than Novello after the London and Broadway success of *The Vortex*. At first, Coward seemed unenthusiastic about the role however and Dean, always a man to cover his options, quietly offered it to Gielgud, who was therefore less than thrilled to overhear Coward a few days later, at the then as now theatrically fashionable Ivy restaurant, announce that he would after all be opening as Lewis Dodd, despite the fact that the author had already come out in favour of John.

As is often the way, all three actors eventually had their turn as Lewis Dodd: Coward opened it, John succeeded him for the bulk of the first run, and two years later Novello made the silent movie. But Coward had been right to approach *The Constant Nymph* with misgivings; the role of Lewis required him to grow his hair long, smoke a pipe and generally behave on stage as he never had in any of his own work. Dean was determined in rehearsal to get him away from familiar 'Noël Coward mannerisms', and Coward spent a fair amount of his time setting fire to his hair, since he had never before worn it long or smoked a pipe. Asked why he had agreed to take on the role, since it was the first in five years not also written by himself, Coward replied, 'To see if I am any good in other people's work,' and the short answer was that he wasn't, or at least not yet. At the end of a long and tough rehearsal period, during which Coward threatened to resign roughly twice a week (and Dean therefore kept Gielgud on a kind of semi-permanent standby), Mrs Patrick Campbell rang him to beg for dress-rehearsal tickets on the grounds that she was a poor, lonely, unwanted old woman who couldn't afford to buy any. She duly arrived at the final run-through half an hour late, bearing a yapping dog, but in ample time to tell Coward afterwards that although she thought Edna Best quite good in her role, he was deeply miscast, lacked the necessary glamour for the character, and should anyway be wearing a beard.

His first-night reviews were not a lot better, and barely three weeks into the run an already overtired and stressed Noël Coward suffered the first of his three major nervous breakdowns, played one entire performance in floods of tears, and was promptly told by his doctor to retire immediately from the role.

John, who had been half-prepared for the takeover for several weeks now, duly stepped in at the following matinée, and played the part of Lewis Dodd in London and then on the road for the whole of the following year. He too, though, was initially very unhappy: Dean refused to rehearse him for his first three months at the New Theatre and, which was very much more hurtful, insisted on leaving Noël Coward's name on the posters and his face on the front-of-house publicity photographs, as if to imply that he was somehow planning to return to the production at some future date.

Of course he wasn't, but in these uneasy working conditions John took a long time to find his feet:

My performance was far too closely modelled on Noël's, especially as I had been understudying him in *The Vortex* only a few months earlier, and although I felt at last that I was getting established in the West End and learning how to play a major contemporary role, I got no particular credit for it. The cast were very kind to me, and seemed to understand I had been badly treated by Dean, but of course the critics never came back, and when Basil Dean did finally come to see me, all he said was, 'Not bad for an understudy, but I need something rather better than that.' The next day he called a full rehearsal, at which he told me to use my mind on stage instead of just my emotions, which I did find rather good advice later on; but it still took me a long time to get over my nerves at following Noël in two plays, and I rather think that delayed me in finding a style of my own as an actor. When you start out as an actor, though, you do need a model and Noël was certainly mine; he knew how to hold the stage, and I was somehow aware even then that he was going to be a great star.

Once John had settled into the long run at the New, he too began to enjoy some of the perks of being a West End leading man; he was now twenty-two, and the weekly salary from *The Constant Nymph* allowed him for the first time to move out of the parental home in South Kensington and into a flat of his own in Upper St Martin's Lane, near Seven Dials, one that had been occupied by the actor Frank Vosper, who was soon to drown mysteriously at sea. 'There was,' John recalled, 'no proper kitchen, and the bathroom had a rather erratic geyser down a flight of stairs that was very draughty in winter. But otherwise the place was charming; Vosper had covered the sitting-room walls with brown hessian, and there was a Braque-like ceiling in one of the bedrooms, with a lot of large nudes sprawling about, which I thought very modern and original indeed.'

And there were soon to be one or two more nudes sprawled on the bed below; freed rather later than most from any parental supervision, and flush for the first time with a regular weekly income, John quickly began to lead a discreetly homosexual life around the Shaftesbury Avenue that was now on his doorstep. It was also during the run of *The Constant Nymph* he took into the flat his first real partner, a young Irishman called John Perry who was to remain a lifelong friend and colleague.

The truth about Gielgud's homosexuality is that although it conditioned his life, led to a court conviction, and undoubtedly caused him considerable uneasiness in an era when it was still a penal offence even among consenting adults, he (like Noël Coward) was always determined to find low-maintenance partners who would not get in the way of his true obsessions and ambitions, all of which were of course totally theatrical.

John Perry, an amiable and very good-looking if none too successful young actor, then working as a florist, fitted this bill admirably. His true love was really hunting in Ireland where, in these late 1920s, he made a considerable social reputation as a charming, witty if somewhat vain young man. He discovered very early on that he had no real talent as an actor; but he was more than happy to share John's flat, his bed and his life as an elegant companion with a constant interest in all things theatrical.

Perry died in the mid-1990s, leaving precious little behind him; but his writing partner Molly Keane (who signed her plays M.J. Farrell) made a remarkable return to the bestseller charts in very late life with a 1981 novel called *Good Behaviour*. In this there is a remarkable likeness of John Perry in the character of a young homosexual who fakes a relationship with a young girl rather than face his parents with the truth of a long Cambridge affair with another young man, one whose sudden death gives the novel its tragic quality. The background of Irish country life, prolonged house parties and a kind of decaying aristocracy is precisely the one from which John Perry came, and where he first met Molly.

In London and later a country house they shared for weekends, at Harpsden, in the hills above Henley-on-Thames, Perry and Gielgud now became inseparable. To some extent they were an odd couple, and they formed a male partnership not unlike that in later years of Noël Coward and Graham Payn. Where Gielgud was hard-working and theatrically obsessive, Perry was boyish, and always ready for a game of tennis or poker. Their circle was soon to include such elegant Oxford undergraduates of the period as Terence Rattigan and Giles Playfair.

Behind closed doors, theirs was an unashamedly homosexual world; but there was a very real danger which they all recognised in their increasingly public lives. This was the time when E.M. Forster could not publish his homosexual stories, when the Lord Chamberlain was still refusing to license any even cautiously homosexual plays and, even worse, when the rise of fascism all over Europe was leading to sustained bouts of homophobic incidents. In Britain every year more than three hundred people were being convicted and often imprisoned for 'acts of gross indecency', even those taking place in the privacy of their own homes.

So although the theatre was far more tolerant than the rest of society, it was still necessary for its workers to form a kind of secret network, behaving rather like spies. Although Oscar Wilde had been dead for thirty years, the gulf between homosexual and straight actors was as wide as ever, and this was to condition the lives of Gielgud and all his friends. In a famous phrase of the period, you could around 1930 either join the Comintern or the Homintern and, like Guy Burgess, sometimes even both.

At the very end of his life, I asked John Perry to think back to his earliest impressions of John G. Even at a distance of half a century Perry, still remarkably good-looking – tall, willowy, fair-haired and with theatrical charm – maintained the discretion about his private life that was partly a matter of his upbringing and partly an ingrained self-defence in a country that had criminalised his sexual behaviour for most of his adult life, but he did remember his fascination with John's 'sheer theatricality. There was something very sexy about his passion for the theatre, but it made him difficult to live with; John never really understood relaxation, and I think that although we enjoyed a few foreign holidays together, he was only really ever happy in rehearsal or performance. Like Coward, he regarded private life as something of an interruption to the rehearsing day, and he could never understand how I seemed happy doing nothing very much – except of course making sure that John had somewhere to come home to, and a place for the weekends.'

It was the run of *The Constant Nymph*, though John soon found it unrewarding theatrically, that allowed him to take his place at the heart of the West End acting community, and on equal terms with its other young stars. He soon became friendly with Gladys Cooper, then managing the Playhouse, as well as with Leslie Faber and other players who always proved eager to involve him in their Sunday and charity shows.

During the run came the excitement of the General Strike in May 1926, chiefly recalled by John Perry for the sight of Gielgud, 'immaculate in a large grey trilby and pearl-grey flannel trousers so wide you could hardly see the patent leather shoes beneath', putting in an appearance at a rally near Hyde Park Corner. Bleakly uninterested always in politics, John was yet eager to be a part of the London life all around him, and it was during the run of *The Constant Nymph* that he truly began to find his feet as a homosexual actor and a social figure, able for the first time to find his way around the nightclubs and late-night restaurants of London in the mid-twenties, even though his grasp of politics was to say the least unworldly. 'I can never remember,' he once told an astonished dinner guest, 'which are the Whigs and which the Conservatives nowadays.'

But if it was as Lewis Dodd that Gielgud effectively came of age, his value to the production remained minimal. When Dean decided that the play should go out on the road after nearly a year in the West End, he began to offer the leading role around to several other players before – all of them having declined the long tour – grudgingly agreeing that John could continue in the part, with a derisory salary increase to just £35 a week, for the next four months.

All in all, John was to spend fourteen months in *The Constant Nymph*, in London and on tour, an engagement which gave him the regular income with which to buy his first car, a snub-nosed Morris in which he and John Perry explored the countryside around each of the tour dates. The two Johns, John and Johnnie as they were always known, could now even afford a cook and they began to give a series of lunch parties, to which they always invited Val, now playing the small part of a policeman in Edgar Wallace's *The Ringer*, which was just across St Martin's Court at Wyndham's, while John was still at the New. Val in turn once brought the star of his show, Leslie Faber, with whom John had played a couple of Sunday-night 'specials', and Faber now became his greatest fan.

No sooner had the tour of *The Constant Nymph* come to an end than Faber suggested that John should take over, at the last minute, the role of the Tsarevitch in a play called *The Patriot*, which was about to open on Broadway. With only forty-eight hours to pack, John set off to join the rest of the company who were already rehearsing in New York; with a good salary, and a six-week guarantee, he set sail on New Year's Eve 1926 on a small German boat which had only two other English-speaking passengers – just as well, as he had to learn the role while at sea.

He arrived barely in time for the dress-rehearsal. At the theatre, he found a superb costume (a blue cloak with an ermine cape, silver and red facings, white breeches and boots) but no great enthusiasm for his acting. Indeed the producer, Gilbert Miller, and the legendary designer Norman Bel Geddes, spent much of their limited time shouting at John about his voice, movement and pace on stage.

After all that haste and anxiety, the play (though later a big success for Emil Jannings on film, and on stage in London under the title *Such Men Are Dangerous*) did not exactly take New York by storm. It closed after only eleven performances to a loss of $40,000, which for 1927 was a considerable shock. But, like Noël Coward a couple of years earlier, John did not allow an initial Broadway flop to colour his fascination with the city itself: 'We were there in icy weather but Fagan, my old Oxford producer, was playing at a theatre next door and I went to lots of backstage parties and even to "speakeasies", descending steep flights of slippery area steps to little doors, where there would be passwords and faces peering through the gratings before we could be admitted.'

John also found now, as had Noël Coward, an American patron in the columnist and critic Alexander Woollcott, who noted 'a young newcomer from the English stage named John Gielgud gave a good account of himself', an opinion not, alas, shared by Brooks Atkinson, who wrote in the *New York Times* of 'an appallingly earnest young Prince'. Gielgud quickly decided that, despite one or two quite promising offers in New York, including one from Constance Collier, who thought she might be able to put him into a revival of Maugham's *Our Betters*, he could not afford to stay too long away from home.

By March 1928 John had come back to the flat in St Martin's Lane, to John Perry, and to the life of a West End actor: 'Over the next eighteen months, I was to appear in ten different plays in London. Not one was a notable success, and they were all in fact pretty terrible, but I took everything that was offered to me. I was the leading man, which was a new experience for me; I was getting good billing and usually a good salary, and I had decided that acting was really a matter of staying in work, doing whatever came along.'

And of course, at twenty-four, he was already sure that he wouldn't have to honour the promise that he had made his father about going back to architecture if all else failed.

It was therefore with a real sense of pride and excitement that, a few months later, he opened his dressing-room door to find his uncle Fred Terry, 'the Golden Terry' as he was always called, coming towards him exclaiming, 'My dear boy, you are one of the family now!'

Back from Broadway, John's first engagement was a double-bill of Spanish plays (*Fortunato* and *The Lady from Alfaqueque*) which had been translated by Harley Granville-Barker and were to be directed by James Whale – later to make his name in Hollywood with *Journey's*

End and *Frankenstein*, before becoming, long after his death, the central figure in the movie *Gods and Monsters*.

But Whale, like John a homosexual and radical theatrical actor and director, was in fact fired in rehearsal, and the Court season came to a close just in time for John to be free for a series of special matinées of *Ghosts* to celebrate the centenary of Ibsen's birth. This was to be his first meeting with one of the legendary *grandes dames* of the British theatre, Mrs Patrick Campbell, and it was to stay in John's memory for ever. Although both Marion and Ellen Terry had been her rivals, she took an instant liking to John, who was mesmerised by her stage technique. In the one scene where Pastor Manders threatens to take the lead, Mrs Pat would focus attention on herself by first unpacking, and then hanging, a complete set of drawing-room curtains.

Her advice to John, playing Oswald, was simply 'to keep still, gaze at me, empty your voice of meaning, and speak as if you are going to be sick'. But the audiences were not good, and to add to their difficulties there were pneumatic drills laying tarmac in the Charing Cross Road just outside the theatre, with deafening results. 'I see,' whispered Mrs Pat to John as she came on to play yet another bad matinée, 'that the Marquis and Marchioness of Empty are in front again.'

Reviews here were good for John ('His Oswald will be as memorable as the play itself,' thought *The Times*) but James Agate, although finding John 'extremely fine', wrote famously of Mrs Campbell that she was 'like the Lord Mayor's coach, only with nothing inside it'.

John's next two engagements, while about as far from Ibsen as he could get, were no more successful: *Holding out the Apple* was a comedy entirely financed by its author, and *The Skull* was an American thriller in which, some thirty years before *The Mousetrap*, John played a detective who was also the murderer.

Gielgud's last appearance in 1928 was again for an American author, this time Don Marquis. In *Out of the Sea*, he was cast as a young American poet who played Wagner at the piano, while the heroine and villain were reincarnations of Isolde and King Mark. Most critics found it pretentious beyond belief, and the public did not find it at all: 'In the last act,' recalled John, 'the heroine threw herself off a cliff while I sat glooming in a raincoat on a neighbouring rock. We lasted less than a week.'

As if to set the seal on a bad season, this was also the year when Ellen Terry died, in her early eighties, and John was one of the hundreds who flocked to her funeral in St Paul's, Covent Garden:

The floor of the church was strewn with sweet-smelling herbs, and in the middle of the aisle was a catafalque covered by a golden pall, with candles burning around it, but there was no coffin, and nobody was allowed to wear mourning. By the time I knew her, she was finding it very hard to sustain the success she had always enjoyed with Irving at the Lyceum, but her memory, as with all us Terrys, was treacherously uncertain, and her concentration easily disturbed, though she had continued, to the end of her life, to enchant the public whenever they were lucky enough to see her on or off the stage. She had, like all of her family, a healthy appetite, enormous courage, and longevity, poor eyesight and intermittently indifferent health. She drew her characters with instinctive genius in broad strokes and generously flowing lines, but she was too restless to be confined within the walls of modern drawing-room comedy, and her loyalty to Irving meant that she listened too late to Shaw's entreaties and stayed too long at the Lyceum, with its fading fortunes. In her old age, I heard her at lecture readings, speaking Shakespeare as if she had only just left him in the next room.

Still unable to get back into the kind of classical or repertory company that Gielgud now knew was his only real way forward, John opened 1929 safely enough by reviving his Konstantin in *The Seagull*, in the production he had first played four years earlier at the Little Theatre. Valerie Taylor was again his Nina, but the repetition bored John and he was happy to move on to his next role, in the short-lived *Red Rust* where Ion Swinley usefully taught him how to break chairs over actors' heads without causing any real damage. The interest here was that it was the first post-revolutionary play to have reached London from Moscow, albeit not for very long.

There followed a takeover in a play about Florence Nightingale, *The Lady With the Lamp*, which, although not entirely distinguished, brought him together with two actresses later central to his career, Edith Evans and Gwen Ffrangcon-Davies. As was now his habit during any long West End run, John spent most of his Sundays in one-night performances of everything from J.M. Barrie (*Shall We Join the Ladies?*) to *The Return of the Soldier Ulysses*. Additionally, his ceaseless workload also meant that he would spend his occasional non-matinée days filming at local London studios. After his debut in *Who Is The Man?* (1924) he also played the title role in Komisarjevsky's Jules Verne silent, *Michael Strogoff* (1926), and the lead in an early Edgar Wallace thriller, *The Clue of the New Pin* (1929), in all of which John found himself embarrassingly inept.

He also returned to Komisarjevsky to play Trotsky in *Red Sunday*. Again, he made himself up to look remarkably like his brother Val, and took some delight in having to play a club theatre because the Lord Chamberlain considered that it was thoroughly impertinent to show Trotsky, Lenin and Rasputin on the same stage as the Tsar of all the Russias, barely a decade after his unfortunate demise.

It was during this run, in the June of 1929, that John happened to be lunching in the restaurant of the Arts Theatre off the Charing Cross Road when he received the unexpected offer of a return to the classical theatre repertory on which he had always set his heart.

Chapter Five

❧❧

TO THE VIC

(1929–1930)

Was it for this that I had forsaken a good salary in the West End,
a comfortable dressing-room for myself, good billing, new suits,
late rising, and suppers at the Savoy?

I f, at the end of almost a century, John Gielgud is to be
remembered for any single achievement, it would surely have to
be the way in which he redefined and recreated the resident
classical repertory company. Without his interest and involvement
in every aspect of this, from casting to costumes, from production
to publicity, it is doubtful whether either the National Theatre or
the Royal Shakespeare Company would have come into post-war
existence quite so heavily influenced by his pre-war work.

But this is not to suggest that John was immediately happy at the
Old Vic of 1930. The man who had invited him to join, at that brief
and unplanned Arts Theatre lunch-time encounter, was Harcourt
Williams, then a forty-nine-year-old actor who had himself just been
invited, by the redoubtable Lilian Baylis, to become the director of
productions in the Waterloo Road.

Baylis had inherited the Vic from her aunt Emma Cons in 1914,
and she had turned it from a Victorian temperance music hall into
a classical theatre so rapidly that by 1923 her first director, Robert
Atkins, had already staged all thirty-seven Shakespeare plays in the
canon, working on a minimal budget with very little scenery, but
attracting such talents as those of Sybil Thorndike, her brother Russell

and Edith Evans. By 1929, however, Baylis had decided that the time had come for a change and, in Harcourt Williams, she had found an excellent touring actor who was also a sandal-wearing vegetarian living in a country cottage with an outside lavatory, where he also kept a large store of cheese.

Williams had not initially been at all impressed by Gielgud's early work, but seeing him in *Ghosts* he drastically revised his opinion and offered John an open-ended contract to play at least three major Shakespearean roles in the 1929–30 season. Williams wanted to revolutionise Shakespeare at the Vic: to have it played faster, with more realistic settings, and to bid a belated farewell to the red-plush Victorian fustian that had hallmarked the Vic under Atkins.

For John, whose only other offer had been to replace Leslie Howard in *Berkeley Square*, this was not a hard decision to make, although at first he began to wonder what on earth he had got himself into.

There was a faint smell of size from the paint dock, and of steak and tomatoes from the office where Lilian Baylis's lunch was being cooked. I was ushered in through the glass door, and found her sitting behind her big roll-top desk, surrounded by vases of flowers, photographs, two dogs and numerous unwashed cups of tea. I had on my best suit, and tried to look rather arrogant, as I always do when money has to be discussed. 'How nice to see you, dear,' said Lilian. 'Of course we would love to have you at the Vic. I knew your dear aunt, you know, but we can never afford stars.' By the end of the interview, I was begging her to let me join the company, and we both evaded any question of payment for as long as possible. In the end it came down to £10 a week for leading roles, and £5 for all others.

His first three parts were to be Romeo, Antonio in *The Merchant of Venice* and Richard II, to which would be added both Oberon and Cléante in Molière's *Le Malade Imaginaire* before Christmas. In the rehearsal room, John found two other refugees from the West End, Martita Hunt (whom he had insisted should also be invited to join the company) and Adele Dixon, as well as more experienced Shakespeareans such as Donald Wolfit, Leslie French and Russell Thorndike.

From the first day of rehearsal in August, we were kept constantly busy; both Gordon Craig and Granville-Barker sent us messages of good luck, and among what you might call the more intellectual theatre community there was the very real sense that we were a new company starting on something very exciting. Baylis was her usual motherly self, never knew her arse from her elbow when it came to Shakespeare, but our great strength and rallying point was Harcourt Williams, whom I knew Ellen Terry had recognised as one of the best actors and directors of his generation. His main ambition was to preserve the continuity of the plays by natural and speedy delivery of the verse and very light settings which would allow quick changes of scene. He always ruled by trust, and any sign of selfishness or disloyalty to the Vic or Shakespeare would throw him into a mood of amazed disbelief. He would take dress-rehearsals with a stop-watch and if the text called for 'two hours traffic of our stage', that was precisely what Williams tried to deliver.

But despite such good and radical intentions, Harcourt Williams's first residency at the Vic got off to a very poor start. Critics, accustomed as they were to the more declamatory style of the Robert Atkins school, were less than happy with the new regime, and as the total budget for any one production was still only £20, the feeling of the church hall was never easily overcome. The actress and later director Margaret Webster, a lifelong friend of John's, recalled once being given an entire roll of cloth by the wardrobe mistress and told to wrap it around her, but not to cut it in any way, as it would be needed for other productions.

John was to play Romeo on three subsequent occasions, and often called it his milestone, but this first attempt was deeply unhappy; as Harcourt Williams himself was later to write: 'this was the least interesting performance of John's two years at the Vic. He never touched the last scenes. He failed to bring off the distracted boy, jolted by disaster into full manhood. The ecstasy, too, of Romeo's last moments transcending death, totally escaped him.'

The Times noted acidly that 'England won another world speed record last Saturday night, when at the Old Vic, Shakespearean blank verse was spoken faster than ever before'; while Donald Wolfit, playing Tybalt, was also convinced that speed was the problem. 'We were all blamed for taking the play at such a lick that the verse and poetry were entirely lost; as Tybalt I scraped past the post, but this was a deeply unpopular opening night, and traditional Vic audiences felt that we had somehow betrayed them with our new style.'

The critic of *Punch* concurred: 'Gielgud is not, I think, quite the ardent, love-sick stripling of our imagination. He is adequate in elocution, occasionally a little noisy, and spirited in movement; but there is no quality of rapture in his wooing while the rash Tybalt (Mr Donald Wolfit) is more plausibly Italianate than the rest, spitting the venom of vendetta through passionately compressed lips.'

John's second role in this 1929 season at the Vic was Antonio, the title figure in *The Merchant of Venice*, but this, as Harcourt Williams recalled, met with an equally hostile press:

> How well I remember the cast hiding from me the newspapers containing the worst notices. They must have been terrible, because I was so overwhelmed by an inferiority complex that I virtually tendered my resignation to Lilian Baylis . . . Gielgud played Antonio with real sympathy and distinction, he was far less solemn than most Antonios, and never dreary; one felt, for once, that this Merchant had the right to carry the title of the play. However, our only real fan seemed to be Harley Granville-Barker, who sent both John and me pages of very useful criticism. His main advice was to let the verse seem to be carrying the actors along, instead of them carrying it, and above all not to be so damned explanatory.

All through this first season it was widely known among the company that the role John already coveted was that of Hamlet, and Lilian Baylis, far more politically astute than was the impression she gave, would periodically dangle it in front of him, before adding, 'But of course, dear Gyles Isham is also very keen, and he has been in the company a little longer than you.'

Although the top salary at the Vic was now £10 a week, most of the company were still on £6. Moreover, each production only played an average of thirteen performances, because the Vic was still also being used for opera and ballet in alternate weeks.

John's third role was Cléante in Molière's *Le Malade Imaginaire*, a production that required him to sing with Adele Dixon, an experience only made bearable because by day John was now rehearsing his first Richard II. Although it is arguable that the role of John's career was Hamlet, there are those who still believe that it was in fact in the role of Richard that he was able to establish his greatest claim to Shakespearean immortality. As with his subsequent Hamlet, he was to go on playing Richard for the best part of the next thirty years, not only in the original text but also in what would be his greatest West End triumph, *Richard of Bordeaux*.

All the same, this first attempt was less than triumphant, despite the fact that, as its director Harcourt Williams was to recall: 'In my time I have seen some half a dozen Richards, some shining in other ways than John's brilliance in the part, but none have touched his poetic imagery and emotional power. His playing of the abdication scene will live in my mind as one of the greatest things I have ever seen in the theatre.'

Critics remained deeply unimpressed but one junior member of the company, Eric Phillips, had a vivid recollection of John 'sniffing at an orange stuck with cloves, or striding petulantly about the stage with a riding whip . . . the turn of his head, the curve of his body, the movement of his hands, each told a story of their own, and were beautiful to watch . . . at the end of the deposition scene Gielgud tottered down the steps and moved slowly towards the exit, dragging his feet behind him and tilting his chin upwards in a last exhibition of majesty.'

As for John himself, he was well aware that much was still wrong with this first, basic, under-rehearsed and poorly financed *Richard II*, even though it was here that for the very first time he felt he was finding his feet in Shakespeare:

I seemed to be immediately in sympathy with that strange mixture of weakness and beauty in the character. I had already seen both Leslie Faber and Ernest Milton play Richard, but although their pictorial qualities had impressed me greatly in the part of the King, I had taken in nothing of the intellectual or poetic beauties of the play. But as soon as I began to study the part myself, the subtlety of Shakespeare's characterisation began to fascinate and excite me. I felt sure I could do justice to some of the imagery and pathos of the character. Richard was such a shallow, spoiled young man, vain of his looks with lovely things to say. I found myself no end in the part, but even that seemed to help my acting of it. I could see from the company's attitude that at last they thought I was going to be good, and I felt a great sense of elation. We only ran three weeks and there were hardly any good reviews, but I began to feel that I had made a real personal success.

The main advantage of this 1929–30 season was the sheer range of work available to John: immediately after *Richard II* came a Jacobean *Midsummer Night's Dream* (Gielgud as Oberon, Adele Dixon as Titania, with Martita Hunt and Donald Wolfit among the young lovers), which was mainly notable for the night when a twelve-year-old Wendy Toye, playing one of the fairies and later to become one of England's greatest choreographers and pioneer female film-makers, managed to set John's flowing Oberon cape alight with her lantern. Within six weeks of that came his first *Macbeth* and a totally uncut *Hamlet*.

The *Macbeth* was less than triumphant, but years later John recalled James Agate wandering into his dressing-room after the murder of Duncan and saying, 'You were very good in that scene but I know you won't be able to manage the rest of the play, so I just thought I'd come round and tell you now.'

The general feeling among other critics was that John had made a brave stab at a part for which he was still vastly too young, but when, less than a month later, he played his first Hamlet – a role to which he would return more than half a dozen times in the next fifteen years, Agate was the first to cheer: 'At twenty-six, Gielgud is the youngest Hamlet in living memory, and I have no hesitation whatsoever in saying that it is the high-water mark of English Shakespearean acting in our time. This actor is young, thoughtful, clever, and sensitive. His performance is subtle, brilliant, vigorous, imaginative, tender and full of the right kind of ironic humour.'

This production included several performances of the complete text, known to the cast as the Eternity Version, and John was the first actor in a couple of centuries, since the prodigal child actor of the early nineteenth century, Master Betty, to play Hamlet so young. Indeed the production closed the 1929–30 season so triumphantly that it transferred to the Queen's Theatre, despite the fact that there were already two other Hamlets in the West End: Henry Ainley, the Edwardian matinée idol, was playing it at the Haymarket, and Alexander Moissi was playing it in German at the Globe.

Donald Wolfit, already at loggerheads with Gielgud, whom he wrongly accused of having the director Harcourt Williams cut Claudius down to the bone, did not improve their relationship by telling John how much better Moissi was in the role that John had already begun to regard as his alone. Because of his age, the youthful tantrums and despair of the opening scenes were more poignant than in John's later and more famous revivals, but he was also the first actor to bring out a dark and ugly streak in the Prince's nature.

Even so, divided by three, the West End audience proved very thin for John's version, especially in the stalls; as one critic sourly noted: 'Pit, Upper Circle and Gallery are crowded at every performance while the more expensive parts of the house decline to be filled. It is a horrible thing to have to say, but the rich have no taste in matters of the theatre, and those who have theatrical taste have no money. In other words the serious theatre in this country is entirely supported by people who can barely afford to support themselves.'

Of all the letters that John was now getting about his Hamlet, those that meant most to him came from his illustrious family. As his uncle Fred Terry wrote: 'I have in the past forty years seen many Hamlets, but none, I think, which Shakespeare himself would have liked as much as yours.' In a rare letter to his son, Frank Gielgud wrote: 'You must be thrilled with at least some of your notices, but what gave me the greatest pleasure last night was to see you in such command of the role. I do think you are speaking too fast still, and sometimes we lose some of the words, especially at the beginning of "The Readiness is All". Your quiet moments are very moving, and your mother was in tears by the end. Much love, and keep up the good work, from your critical old father.'

His mother added:

I have told you far too little of the delight I feel at your great success, and I can't tell you of the joy it gives me to have you give up your spare time and forsake your many new friends to come home to me, and let me share your interests, weigh the pros and cons of your future, show me your laurels and to be ever my dear and sympathetic and loving son as well as a brilliant actor. You can dominate the stage, but you never step out of the canvas to distort the picture. You do not demand the centre of the stage, but can hold your audience spellbound by a whisper, and their eyes with a gesture – not with mere tricks but with the breadth and truth of your imagination. Hamlet is many men in one and the wholeness, dignity, beauty, breadth, and simplicity of your delivery fills my heart with admiration and wonder.

Among the many non-family letters John received was one from one of the finest actresses of her generation, Sybil Thorndike, who wrote: 'Yours is the Hamlet of my dreams and I never hope to see it played better. I was swept off my feet into another world, and moved beyond words.' A young actress called Diana Wynyard, with whom John was to score some of his post-war Shakespearean triumphs, now wrote to him for the first time: 'I came to the matinée on Saturday, and want to thank you not only for the most completely satisfying and lovely acting I have ever seen, but also for the way you made me think about the play. Your performance seems to me to justify the decision we have made to go into the theatre, because you never drag acting down to the usual shoddy game of who's going to be next up the ladder.'

Another young actor, Alan Webb, later to be a lover of Noël Coward's, wrote: 'I came especially to London from the Liverpool Playhouse to see your Hamlet – it puts all others in the shade, and I am so glad that old theatrical bores now have something new to discuss. Most of them don't seem to have seen a *Hamlet* since Irving's.'

The West End transfer of *Hamlet* having proved to be more of a stagger than a run, John still had several summer months to fill in before he could go back to the Vic as its now unchallenged leading man.

❧❧❧

Chapter Six

THE IMPORTANCE OF
BEING RICHARD
(1930–1932)

*Between the two Old Vic seasons, I was asked to play John
Worthing in* The Importance of Being Earnest *with my aunt,
Mabel Terry-Lewis, as Lady Bracknell. The production was
entirely in black and white, in the manner of Beardsley drawings.
We had a great success in a very hot summer, except for one
matinée when I glanced at the audience and saw about six old
ladies in different parts of the theatre all hanging out of their
seats, fast asleep. I became quite hysterical, and was threatened
with the sack for giggling so disgracefully.*

John's first performance as John Worthing, in what was to
become (with Hamlet and Richard II) one of his three signature
roles, was, on this first occasion, directed by Nigel Playfair.
And after his recent disappointment with the transfer of *Hamlet*,
Gielgud could now enjoy the luxury of a commercial hit at the
Lyric, Hammersmith. He was also secure in the knowledge that he
had the Old Vic to go back to in the autumn, and the fact that Lilian
Baylis had unusually granted his request for a small rise in salary
suggested that, at long last, she had become aware of his value at the
box-office.

There was even, as John recalled, a useful link between John
Worthing and Hamlet: 'It was amusing to change the black weeds
of the Prince of Denmark for the top hat and black crepe band of

John Worthing, in mourning for his imaginary brother, and my recent association with the tragedy gave further point to Wilde's joke. I was very proud to be appearing for the first time with my Aunt Mabel, who shared with Marie Tempest and Irene Vanbrugh that rare distinction of style, deportment and carriage which was to vanish with them.'

The last time that Gielgud had worked with Nigel Playfair he had been way down the cast list; now he was appearing, albeit still in Hammersmith, as a leading man, and it was Playfair who for the very first time made John aware, a decade after he had come into the business, that he really might have the classical capacity to be a star.

The summer revival of *The Importance of Being Earnest* had to be cut short because of John's commitment to a second season at the Vic; but it is arguable that the Wilde connection first established Gielgud within the homosexual community as one of their own. Certainly by now, thirty years after his death, Oscar Wilde's reputation had escaped the stigma of his imprisonment, but it was to be another quarter of a century before John himself was to discover that, outside the theatre, Britain was still remarkably and even dangerously intolerant of homosexuality. If there is a subliminal, homosexual reading of *The Importance*, with the idea that John Worthing's secret other life (what he calls Bunburying) may be a metaphor for Oscar's own bisexuality, then John would have been the first to make this connection clear over the footlights.

As the critic Ronald Hayman has noted: 'John Gielgud, with his slim, straight back, his meticulous elegance and his air of nobility tilted into a lordly languor, had all the qualities for Wilde's mannered comedy . . . as in *Hamlet*, he conveyed the impression of being quite capable of inventing for himself the perfect lines which the author had given him.' But as so often in John's career, other critics were sharply divided: for the *Sunday Times*, James Agate thought that John was 'a tragic actor who should never attempt comedy', while the playwright and critic Charles Morgan, in *The Times*, wrote of Gielgud 'standing out as the model for the true interpretation of Wilde'.

John was now so well established as the leading man of the Old Vic, to which he returned in September of this year, that both the director Harcourt Williams and the manager Lilian Baylis consulted him over the constitution of the company. Undoubtedly the most interesting of the newcomers he chose was Ralph Richardson, with whom John was now to work for the first time at the start of a stage partnership that would last well into the 1970s.

Their first meeting, in the rehearsal room of the Vic, was not, however, exactly auspicious, as Richardson recalled: 'I sprang at the opportunity of going to the Vic not only because Johnny Gielgud was a kind of miracle, but also because I stood a really good chance of staying on there when he left at the end of the season. But when we first met, I found his clothes extravagant and his conversation flippant. He was the New Young Man of his time, and I didn't like him at all in rehearsal, although on stage you had to admire him because he was so brilliant, he shone, he was so handsome and his voice was so splendid.'

The two actors who were, with Olivier and Redgrave, to dominate the British theatre for most of the rest of the century had in fact fleetingly met a couple of years earlier, when they were both in a Sunday-night performance of *Prejudice*, but it wasn't until they got to the Vic that they really made any impression on each other, as John was later to recall: 'When we first acted together at the Old Vic in 1930, I little thought that we might ever become friends. At first we were inclined to circle round each other like suspicious dogs. In our opening production, I played Hotspur to his Prince Hal in *Henry IV Part 1*, and was relieved though somewhat surprised to discover that he was as reluctant as I was to engage in the swordplay demanded in the later, under-rehearsed scenes at Shrewsbury. On the first night I was amazed to hear him whispering, loudly enough surely for the audience to hear, "Now you hit me, cocky; now I hit you!"'

This was the attraction of opposites; Richardson was a year older than Gielgud, but he would have to wait until 1933 for his first taste of stardom. Gielgud, by contrast, had already played eight leading roles at the Vic and begun to make his name elsewhere, if not yet in the West End then certainly at Hammersmith. Richardson had also unwisely announced to his friends that 'Gielgud's acting often keeps me out of the theatre' but, precisely because they were so different, they achieved a remarkable kind of odd-couple success. Richardson was deeply embarrassed by any discussion of John's private life, and at first they only ever met in rehearsal. 'I was always,' said Ralph, 'rather amazed at him; he was a kind of brilliant butterfly, while I was always a gloomy sort of boy.'

For his part, Gielgud noted: 'Unlike me, Ralph was intensely interested in machinery and all the intimate details of science and engineering, but he despised the petty accessories of theatrical life, all the gossip and the theatre columns in the newspapers which always appealed so strongly to me.'

Their first Vic production, directed as usual by Harcourt Williams, got off to a bad start when Richardson brought a bottle of champagne which he then managed to explode all over the dressing-room, and it wasn't until they began working together on *The Tempest*, a few days later, that John found the courage to suggest to Richardson that they might like to take some time out for private rehearsals. Richardson immediately agreed, and thus began an initially wary friendship of fifty years.

In *The Tempest*, Richardson was Caliban to John's first Prospero; later in the season, Richardson was Sir Toby Belch to John's Malvolio and, in Shaw's *Arms and the Man*, Bluntschli to John's Sergius. John's first Prospero, half a century before he was finally to film it for Peter Greenaway, was a slender and shaky affair, and Gielgud's backstage mood was not helped by his first and very difficult meeting with his celebrated cousin, Edward Gordon Craig.

With Ellen Terry, his mother, Craig was the most famous member of the current Gielgud clan, but whereas Ellen was always encouraging and loving towards John, her son proved at first distinctly prickly. He sent a note backstage to John at the Vic, reading simply: 'Perhaps, as we are related, we ought to get to know each other, and you seem to be quite popular here in London.' Craig then announced that he had only stayed for the opening scene of *The Tempest*, despite the fact that Harcourt Williams, the director, was one of his oldest friends. Taking John out to dinner, Craig delivered a vitriolic dismissal of Williams, Lilian Baylis, and everything that the Old Vic stood for. Although a somewhat chastened and disappointed John was to remain considerably in awe of Gordon Craig's radical theatrical philosophy, the two cousins did not meet again until 1953, by which time Craig had become considerably more avuncular.

A far easier relationship was that which, through their working together, was now developing between Gielgud and Richardson, who always knew, said John once:

> that of every twelve suggestions I made to him, two would be of some use, and the rest could be thrown in the dustbin. We were neither of us wildly intellectual, but whereas I really adored the billing, the advertisements, the fan letters and the somewhat unbalanced adulation of certain people whose admiration was extravagant and often insincere, Ralph had enormous dignity and reserve where the public was concerned. I would think to myself, A jolly good house tonight, went marvellously and I made a lot of stunning effects, must remember to put them in again tomorrow night. That was not Ralph's way; he was a realistic actor, labouring to find the core of a character, and until he had time to study a role, he didn't want to be looked at, or even criticised. By contrast, I would conceitedly jump in and take a wild dash at a part from the first rehearsal. I find it difficult to work by myself at home; I develop a part in rehearsal with the company, make mad suggestions, then throw them out and try some more. I am feather-headed, where Ralph was always far more thorough.

During these two seasons at the Vic, John was often miscast, not least as Antony in *Antony and Cleopatra*. But the experience, now at £20 a week, of playing many different roles in front of an enthusiastic but broadly uneducated audience, gave him useful practice in sheer Shakespearean survival against the odds.

When it came to his *Macbeth*, towards the end of this second season, 'I had rather more success than when I came to study the part more thoroughly, twelve years later . . . I simply went for the broad lines of the character, without worrying about all the technical, intellectual and psychological difficulties. With only three weeks to rehearse, there was no time to do more than play it from scene to scene, but I do think one should dare to fly high when one is young. One may sometimes surprise oneself, and it is wonderful to give the imagination full play, hardly realising what an exciting danger is involved.'

Harold Nicolson, writing in his diary for 4 October 1930: 'Talk to Gielgud, who is a fine young man. He does not want to specialise in juvenile parts, since they imply rigidity. He takes a high view of his calling. I think he may well be the finest actor we have had since Irving. His voice and figure are excellent.'

It was also at the Vic in this season that Gielgud discovered another of the roles that were to be central to his later career. Benedick in *Much Ado About Nothing* was far more suited to his romantic, mercurial temperament than the soldier Antony, where John could only recall 'wearing a false beard and shouting and booming a lot'. When it came to Benedick, and later both *The Winter's Tale* and *Measure For Measure*, John found far more complex but closely fitting characters, and it was here that, for the first time, 'I began to trust the sweep of Shakespeare's verse, concentrating at last on the commas, full stops and semi-colons. I found that if I kept to them, and breathed with them, like an inexperienced swimmer, the verse seemed to hold me up, and even, at last, to disclose its meaning.'

But no sooner had he finally conquered Shakespeare, and begun to take an active part in both the direction and the design of the Vic's low-budget productions, than he began to yearn once again for some commercial success. Reluctantly, he therefore told Lilian Baylis and Harcourt Williams that he would be leaving the Vic for ever at the end of the current season. Williams offered him a choice of farewell role: he could either revive his now celebrated Hamlet or, at the age of just twenty-seven, he could tackle his first King Lear.

Unable to resist the challenge, John opted for Lear, and as usual he was his own best critic: 'I was wholly inadequate in the storm scenes, having neither the voice nor the physique for them. Lear has to *be* the storm, but I could do no more than shout against the thunder sheet. The only scene I thought I did at all well was the one with the Fool, when Lear leaves Goneril to go to Regan: "O let me not be mad, not mad, sweet heaven . . ."'

Critics generally agreed with John's verdict on himself and, for the *Spectator*, Peter Fleming also picked up on the scene with the Fool: 'I have never seen a better bit of acting than Mr Gielgud's "O fool, I shall go mad". He says the words in a voice become suddenly flat and toneless, quickened only with a chilling objective interest in their no longer contestable truth . . . but in general, the performance has the deliberate threat of distant gunfire, rather than the unpredictable menace of a volcano.'

John in fact opened his first Lear not only at the Old Vic but also Sadler's Wells, which Lilian Baylis had also now bravely started to run as a second stage. Richardson was his Duke of Kent, and Leslie French was the Fool; sometimes breaking with their usual tradition, the audience would applaud John's first entrance, and sometimes they would not: 'If I failed to get the round of applause as I mounted my throne, the expression of amused triumph on Ralph's face would be almost too much for me, and I used to have to turn away for a moment before I began "Attend the Lords of France and Burgundy".'

However patchy this first Lear, the idea of an actor of twenty-seven playing a king of eighty attracted considerable attention, even abroad. As the *New York Post* now wrote: 'There is a young actor in London, named John Gielgud, who has taken the town by storm the way John Barrymore first took New York, when he was known as Jack and was knocking the flappers out of their seats. Gielgud's pictures now sell like mad among the earnest young students who flock to his performances.' A rather more thoughtful appraisal of precisely where Gielgud now stood in the British theatrical hierarchy came from the director Harcourt Williams in his farewell speech to John at the Vic, handing over to him a glove which Henry Irving had once worn as Benedick. 'I know, from the foundations that stand beneath your power as an actor, that you will grow and expand until you shatter that theatre falsely termed "commercial" (all good theatres must function commercially) and create one of your own, either of brain or brick, that we shall all be proud of.'

Peggy Ashcroft and the publisher Rupert Hart-Davis, then at the start of the affair that was to lead to their marriage, were in the Old Vic audience one night, as Hart-Davis later wrote to John:

Peggy and I were so swept away by your magnificent Lear that we couldn't come backstage. Beforehand I could not believe that you would manage it, but my God I was wrong! It is far and away the best thing I have seen you do, vastly better than your Prospero or Malvolio. Your voice, your variety, and your physique are splendid. And although Regan looks like a cook in a sack-race, I thought Richardson was excellent. I'm afraid I thought Leslie French as the Fool wrong in every way – he should not be a maddeningly bright boy, but an ageless and weary man, desperately making jokes against Time. I doubt I shall ever see a better Lear, except of course when you play the part again in twenty years' time.

Leaving Richardson to lead the Vic through the next season, John now returned to the West End in Edward Knoblock's adaptation of J.B. Priestley's bestseller *The Good Companions*, which he was subsequently also to film, a year later, with Jessie Matthews. Knoblock, one of the most successful dramatists of his time, specialised in adaptations, and was years later to be on the receiving end of one of John's most celebrated conversational gaffes. The two men were lunching alone, when John described a friend as 'nearly as boring as Eddie Knoblock; no, no, not you of course, I mean the other Eddie Knoblock'.

The character that John played for nearly a year in the West End, Inigo Jollifant, is the young preparatory schoolmaster who, always theatre-struck, turns professional pianist and composer to join Priestley's band of wandering players. Several critics, while noting John's uneasiness at the piano, also took the view that after his Old Vic triumphs he should have been doing something rather more cerebral and serious than this unashamed crowd-pleaser. For John himself, the problem was rather different:

> This kind of play was quite a new departure for me, and demanded a considerable re-adjustment of my style of acting. The scenes were very short and sketchy, and there was hardly any development of character . . . Jollifant was a very ordinary juvenile, who had to carry off a few very slight love scenes and a couple of effective comedy situations with the aid of a pipe, undergraduate clothes, and his catchword 'Absolutely' . . . I had to attract the audience's interest with his first word and sweep my little scenes along to a climax in a few short minutes . . . I was playing with actors of several different schools, and I had to learn tricks of upstaging if I was to survive in a commercial environment.

The Good Companions was to change John's private life for ever; he could now afford late suppers at the Savoy, while a large number of scripts, some from very established authors, were finding their way to his dressing-room; two of these, Gordon Daviot's *Richard of Bordeaux* and Ronald Mackenzie's *Musical Chairs*, were soon to give him two more of his early West End successes.

John was also, albeit very hesitantly, starting on a film career which, unlike Olivier, Richardson and Redgrave, all of whom had established lucrative movie careers with Korda, Hitchcock or (in Olivier's case) Hollywood well before the war, he was not really to consolidate until long after it. But his earliest film appearance had in fact been in the 1924 silent, *Who Is The Man?* adapted from one of Sarah Bernhardt's last stage hits, one he only caught up with several months after the initial release:

> I was a sculptor in a beautiful smock, flinging clay at a half-finished nude lady. I had not then yet sat to Epstein, and therefore had no idea of how sculptors really worked, but I made great play with a sweeping thumb and a wire tool, and hoped for the best . . . there was a sofa draped with shawls, on which I flung myself at intervals, smoking a pipe of opium in close-up. I exhausted myself acting in a highly melodramatic manner, and we had to do some scenes over one weekend on location at Le Touquet. I suffered acute embarrassment marching around in yellow make-up and attempting to drive a car, which is not one of my accomplishments. When I finally saw the film there was just a strip of sand, which could have been photographed equally well at Margate. However, we all had a very jolly weekend.

John's next silent was an Edgar Wallace thriller, *The Clue of the New Pin*, which he shot in 1929: 'In this, I played the villain, fantastically disguised in a long black cloak, black wig, spectacles and false teeth, and always photographed from the back so that I could by no possible chance be recognised (even by the most adept villain-spotter in the audience) as the bright young juvenile whom I had to impersonate during the rest of the film.'

His first talking picture, *Insult*, made during the run of *The Good Companions*, was adapted from a long-running stage hit of which John's only recollection was that:

> The film was set in the Far East, and shot through clouds of smoke.

There was a donkey, a monkey, and several horses, one of which I rode gingerly in close-up down a narrow studio-village street, while my double stood close at hand to mount and dismount my fiery steed in long shot. I was fascinated and horrified by my acting in these three early pictures. Fascinated because seeing one's own back and profile is an interesting experience usually limited to one's visits to the tailor, and horrified at the vulturine grimaces on my face, and the violent and affected mannerisms of my walk and gestures. It was to be a very long time before I came to terms with the camera, and I think my embarrassment, at how bad I was, made me sound very snobbish and superior when I talked about not wanting to leave the stage for the screen. The truth is that unlike Larry and Ralph and Michael, it took me years to learn the difference between stage and screen acting.

As John began to enjoy his first real taste of West End stardom, there were also some subtle changes to his private life. He and John Perry were still effectively locked into a homosexual marriage, and still sharing the flat in St Martin's Lane, but for the first time their partnership now began to open up; John Perry had amiably abandoned his initial plans to be an actor, and was now spending a fair amount of his time in his native Ireland, where he was a keen rider and hunter.

Back in London, John G was by no means averse to the occasional sexual attentions of the many good-looking, and sometimes ambitious, young men who now began to cluster around his stage door. Moreover, just arrived in London from his native Cardiff was yet another gorgeous young man, Hugh 'Binkie' Beaumont, who, taken under the wing of the much older impresario Harry (H.M.) Tennent, would soon become not only the most successful West End theatre manager of the 1930s and 1940s, but also the man who was to break up the sexual (and for a short time even social) partnership of the two Johns.

During the run of *The Good Companions*, John became more and more determined not to lose the cultural and critical edge that he had achieved in his seasons at the Old Vic. He was therefore more than delighted, in the opening weeks of 1932, to receive an invitation from the then president of the OUDS (Oxford University Dramatic Society), George Devine, to direct *Romeo and Juliet* at New College, Oxford.

Devine's idea was, as his biographer Irving Wardle has noted, extremely astute. Although Gielgud had now had ten years of classical work behind him, and was emerging as the dominant London star, one who moreover had already appeared in three productions of *Romeo*, at the age of twenty-eight he had never actually directed anything, and in that sense Devine was offering him something very attractive. Not that John was initially that impressed: Devine struck him as 'rather ungainly and gross. Very greasy, spotty and unattractive. But he had great humour and charm, and was immediately very intelligent.'

In later years, Devine was to direct John in the controversial Noguchi *King Lear* and, as director of the Royal Court, to open up the English Stage Company which was to bring John into contact for the first time with post-Osborne playwriting and thereby rescue his post-war stage career when it had fallen to its lowest level.

The OUDS had been as all-male as the university itself until 1927; from then on, female undergraduates were theoretically allowed to take part in productions, but it was still the tradition to invite young professional actresses from London, as much for their talent as for the edification and entertainment of the young gentlemen. Peggy Ashcroft (now playing Juliet) had indeed first played with the OUDS a year earlier in Flecker's *Hassan*. John had not seen her in this, but he had been hugely impressed by her Desdemona to Paul Robeson's Othello at the Savoy Theatre in 1930. Playing the nurse was Edith Evans, with whom John had already worked in the short-lived *The Lady With the Lamp*.

The Romeo was to be Christopher Hassall (who later found his true vocation as the lyricist for most of Ivor Novello's enormously successful musicals), and also in that amazing student cast were George Devine himself, Hugh Hunt (for many years director of the Bristol Old Vic theatre school) and William Devlin, later a distinguished classical and modern actor who was frequently, as a professional, to work with Gielgud again. Indeed, only one student was really unhappy in this production, and he was an eighteen-year-old Terence Rattigan, who in the last act was so inept at announcing the death of Juliet, almost his only line, that the audience would regularly fall about with laughter on his 'Faith, we may put up our pipes and be gone.' Many years later, Rattigan's classic backstage comedy, *Harlequinade*, was to feature a small-part player with precisely the same problem.

Inevitably John had to focus most of his rehearsal time on the undergraduates, leaving Edith Evans and Peggy Ashcroft to their own devices. He had arrived in Oxford, as the OUDS historian Humphrey Carpenter relates, to find the student drama group torn apart by internecine warfare between the old guard and Devine's new men, all of whom were now determined to drag a somewhat Edwardian society into the twentieth century. Gielgud's first production of *Romeo and Juliet* was to be the barest outline for his subsequent triumph with Olivier in the West End three years later, but for now it would be naïve to pretend that John was commuting from *The Good Companions* to Oxford merely for the sake of his art. The OUDS at that time was a distinctly homosexual society with some very good-looking young men, among them Peter Glenville, Robert Flemyng and Rattigan himself, all of whom were keen to cluster around the visiting star. John G even started here a brief affair with James Lees-Milne, subsequently a distinguished architectural historian and diarist, and although this did not continue beyond Gielgud's weeks in Oxford, the two men were to remain distant friends for the rest of their lives. 'For six weeks,' recalled Lees-Milne, 'I was infatuated with him. Then it passed like a cloud; it was a very short-lived affair.'

The weekend cottage that the two Johns now shared at Harpsden was also a very homosexual retreat, though as always there was the vague threat of danger and exposure, one that was to come into sharp focus a year or two later when the young Beverly Nichols, incensed by a hostile review for one of his early plays by James Agate, seriously threatened to make Agate's homosexuality public. Nothing came of this, however, and for a few more years Gielgud and Perry were to sleep with each other in comparative safety.

But the most important connection that John made during his Oxford *Richard II* was with the three set and costume designers, Elizabeth Montgomery and the sisters Margaret and Sophia Harris, who were collectively known as the Motleys. The three of them had as yet no stage experience. As John was later to recall: 'When I was at the Vic they made some drawings of me as Richard II, Macbeth and Lear, which they shyly brought to my notice. In those days they were three silent and retiring young women, and it was some time before I could get them to speak about themselves in their gentle, hesitating voices . . . they later told me that my sudden unexpected arrivals in their tiny Kensington home would throw them all into paroxysms of shyness, as I hurled remarks at them, speaking so fast that they barely understood a word.'

Devine himself was not initially keen to bring in outside designers, but he was taken by John to visit 'the girls' at Kensington, and immediately offered them the job, as Elizabeth recalled: 'We rushed out and hired a couple of people to do the sewing for us. But we did almost everything else ourselves. That was really how we started – before that, we had only been making fancy dresses for the shops at Christmas.'

This meeting was in fact to be the start of two great partnerships: from now on, John was seldom to work without the Motleys, while Devine was later to marry Sophia Harris. Hardly surprisingly, Peggy and Edith and the Motleys took Oxford by storm at a time when the undergraduates seldom enjoyed the benefit of any female company at all, let alone that of five radical, intellectual Shakespeareans. John, commuting every night back to *The Good Companions*, also immediately found his feet as a director, bringing to the OUDS a touch of professionalism which that society was not to see again until long after the war. John was given one night off to run the first dress-rehearsal: 'The lights, the scenery and the orchestra were all being used together for the first time. I sat alone in the dress-circle, with my notebook and a torch. The house lights went down, the music began to play, and there was a faint glow from the footlights. A wonderful play was about to be performed, and it was for me alone. I felt like Ludwig of Bavaria.'

Nevertheless, by the end of the first night his nerves had got the better of him, and at the curtain call John G memorably referred to Edith Evans and Peggy Ashcroft as 'Two leading ladies, the like of whom I hope I shall never meet again'. Several years later, introducing the female members of one of his wartime touring companies, he announced to a somewhat amazed military audience: 'And now, the ladies I have brought to give you pleasure.'

This *Romeo* was of course still only a pro-am student production, playing for a few nights in New College, Oxford; it did not attract national attention although W.A. Darlington, in the *Daily Telegraph*, noted: 'although he is not present, it happens again and again in this production that one seems to hear Mr Gielgud's voice on the stage – which means not that the undergraduates are slavish imitators, but simply that they are indeed learning to speak the verse, and are sensitive enough to recognise a master when they hear him . . . Above all, Miss Ashcroft's Juliet is not rehearsing phrases, but passionately in love.'

Peggy Ashcroft herself later added: 'I see Romeo and Juliet as, in themselves, the most glorious, life-giving people . . . I discovered playing Juliet that the essential thing is youth, rather than being tragic. I think she's a victim of circumstance. The tragedy is simply something that happens to her.'

As the critic and biographer Michael Billington was to write: 'This OUDS *Romeo* was in every sense a momentous production: one that forged vital links between a group of people whose professional lives were to be interconnected over the next three decades. If there was a sense of family in the upper echelons of British theatre, it had its origins in this production.'

But it was John's original host at the OUDS, George Devine, who, in a personal letter to him, best captured what had been achieved here:

> I don't know how much other people realise it, but to my mind this whole success belongs to you. Some of the glory also goes to me, because I was the President who had the luck to invite you. But the ideas, the actresses, the costumes, the sets, the spirit and the acting are all your contribution. For your lessons in verse-speaking alone we should be more than grateful, and suffice it to say, you have made my OUDS Presidency everything I wanted it to be. I only hope you feel compensated for all the time and hard work which you have devoted to us. I have just managed to extract some money from the box-office, and I have bought you a cigarette lighter, as I don't think I ever saw you with one. It's a silly thing to buy, but I can't think of a book about the theatre that you would not already have.

With *Romeo* safely up and running in Oxford (Lord David Cecil thought it 'easily the best production of the play I have ever seen – straightforward in interpretation, but fresh with youthful, lyrical rapture'), John returned to *The Good Companions* and to his determination to find something rather more radical to play next.

A backstage letter from the playwright Ronald Mackenzie reminded John G that they had been together at the same prep school, Hillside. Since then, Mackenzie had not been so fortunate, and no fewer than six West End managements had turned down a play of his called *The Discontents*, a Chekhovian tragi-comedy set amid the oilfields of Galicia in Poland. John, however, always quick to respond to his own Polish ancestry, loved the script on first reading, and especially the central role of a cynical and consumptive pianist whose German fiancée had been killed during the First World War bombing of Düsseldorf, an air-raid in which the pianist had himself participated.

This was clearly the best contemporary role that John had ever been offered, above all because it neatly combined the two sides of his nature: the pianist was really a modern Hamlet, and yet the background was indisputably Russian. In its complexity and its challenge, *The Discontents* was a world away from the Shaftesbury Avenue safety of *The Good Companions*.

Immediately befriending Mackenzie, John made two suggestions. First that an off-putting title be changed to *Musical Chairs*, and second that the great Russian director Komisarjevsky be invited to direct. Ever since they had first met on *Three Sisters* in 1925 at Barnes, Gielgud had been desperately eager to work again with Komis, whom he felt alone could move the British classical theatre forward into the new century. The son of an operatic tenor and a Russian princess, Komisarjevsky had succeeded Meyerhold as artistic director of the major theatre in what was then still St Petersburg, after which he had gone on to run both the Imperial and the State Theatres in Moscow. In 1920, at the age of thirty-seven, he had fled the new communist regime to work first in Paris, then in New York before coming to London on a contract to produce operas for Sir Thomas Beecham.

Like Gielgud a man of many theatrical talents, he also designed his own sets and costumes, arranged the music and lit all his own productions with a revolutionary eye on what lighting could do for a play. He was also an architect, responsible for the Phoenix Theatre, which opened on the Charing Cross Road in 1930, and several suburban cinemas. As Ronald Hayman has noted: 'Komisarjevsky was a near-genius, phenomenally versatile, and violently moody, dynamic and charming, but liable to bouts of depression when he would sulk in silence for hours on end. He was a born rebel, and in each country where he worked he soon became resentful of the prevailing conditions. A man of great sensitivity, he was also capable of being extremely insensitive and even ruthless.'

Nevertheless, he was a perfect match for both the play and John G, whom he even allowed to take several rehearsals. John, however, found the emotional strain of this production nearly intolerable and, playing a consumptive, began to look all too realistic. As a friend of Ralph Richardson's said, 'I went to see Gielgud the other night – is he really as thin as all that?' Not everyone was thrilled with the play, or indeed the production. Noël Coward left at the end of the first act, later writing to John: 'I thought you were over-acting badly, and using voice tones and elaborate emotional effects – as I seriously think you are a grand actor, it upset me very much. I also thought that Frank Vosper [playing John's father] had a wig with such a bad join that it looked like a yachting cap.'

James Agate, for the *Sunday Times*, wrote one of his rare raves:

I am now ready to burn my boats. *Musical Chairs* is, in my view, the best first play written by any English playwright during the last forty years – better than *Widowers' Houses, Journey's End* or *Hindle Wakes*. My reasons for regarding this play as a small masterpiece are as follows: 1) it tells a credible and tragic story. 2) That story is enlivened by a magnificent sense of humour. 3) It is as taut and spare as a barrel, which means it is perfectly made and put together with maximum economy. 4) The characters are real, vivid, and do not overlap each other. 5) As parts they are magnificently laid out for actors. 6) This work of art has its own atmosphere, compounded of strangeness, melancholy and the wildest fun, and Mr Gielgud plays it with every nerve in his body and brain.

During this hot summer, the company was given two weeks off, and John, on holiday with John Perry in France, was horrified to pick up an English newspaper and read that Ronald Mackenzie, also on holiday in France, had been killed when a burst tyre overturned his car. This tragedy brought an end to *Musical Chairs*, not least because John now had another new play on offer, one that he was really keen to direct.

By chance this also came from a radical young dramatist, already intent on revolutionising the British theatre using techniques either learned or borrowed from Chekhov. Rodney Ackland's *Strange Orchestra* was a distant forerunner of Rattigan's *Separate Tables*, though on this occasion the paying guests were all sharing a rather run-down Bloomsbury flat. John's first idea for the leading role was the redoubtable Mrs Patrick Campbell, who from the very first rehearsal took an immediate dislike to the play: 'Who,' she demanded imperiously of John, 'are all these extraordinary characters? Where do they live? Would Gladys Cooper know them?'

It was soon abundantly clear that Mrs Pat was, neither for the first nor last time, unable to make it through to the first night, and her role was duly taken over by the more reliable if less charismatic Laura Cowie. This was to be Gielgud's first production of a modern play, and he found its characters infinitely engrossing: 'They are uncertain of their jobs, they quarrel, make love, indulge in scenes of hysteria, behave abominably to one another, and perform deeds of unselfish heroism, all the while dancing to a gramophone.'

Strange Orchestra received mixed reviews, and only survived a few short weeks, but James Agate reckoned that it was 'As much superior to the ordinary stuff of theatre as tattered silk is to unbleached calico'. And Gielgud himself pinpointed what made Ackland special: 'The moods and subtleties of his characters are woven together in a very distinctive pattern – his vision is apt to be limited to his own particular type of atmosphere, but at least he deals with real people.' One thing most critics were agreed on was that since the tragic death of Ronald Mackenzie, Ackland alone seemed interested in pursuing his dramatic line of what might be called 'English Chekhov', a line that was really only to reach a happy conclusion in the late 1940s work of N.C. Hunter, in which John was sometimes to star and often would direct.

This demand for reality, at a time when the West End was generally at its most artificial, characterised John's constant search for a new kind of theatre, one in which he and Komisarjevsky and the Motleys could break down the old Shaftesbury Avenue certainties with plays that would either disturb an audience or at the very least make them think. On the other hand, he was quick to recognise commercial necessities; having become a star and begun to enjoy the good life, John wasn't about to throw it all up for that of a penniless theatrical revolutionary, condemned always to work in attics and basements for very little money. As a result, he eagerly took up the offer of filming *The Good Companions* in which he was joined by Max Miller, Jessie Matthews and the young Jack Hawkins.

During the shooting John was embarrassingly required to do the usual round of fan-magazine interviews, in one of which he even had to pretend that he was in the market for a loving wife:

> My trouble is that as my work is my life, I have no real interests outside it. I therefore find it rather difficult to make friends with anyone who is not connected with the theatre. For me, age doesn't count at all. For example, Mrs Patrick Campbell, Edna Best, Gwen Ffrangcon-Davies, Lillian Braithwaite and Adele Dixon have all been the best of 'good companions' to me, and a supreme necessity of good companionship is understanding my need for solitude. I also think good temper and a sense of humour would be vital, more important than actual beauty. I would like a girl who was well-groomed and always appropriately dressed, a good reader and someone who could talk intelligently about pictures and music. I would also like her to be a good cook for, like all my Terry family, I have a thoroughly healthy appetite. I would also hope that she would be devoted to children and not give all her attention to pets, at least not when I am about.

Having thus dealt, as well as any homosexual man could, with the requirements of popular movie magazines, he returned to the film itself, which the critic C.A. Lejeune thought 'suggests a long screen career for John Gielgud'.

But he himself was still uneasy with his performance and the life on a film set:

> I hate the early rising, the long, endless days of spasmodic work, and I loathe to be patted and slapped and curled and painted, while I lie supine and helpless in the make-up equivalent of a dentist's chair . . . I detest the lack of continuity which insists I should idiotically walk

twenty times down a corridor with a suitcase in my hand, to enter
the door of a room in which I played some important scene three
weeks ago . . . I hate the meals in films, and the heat of the lights
which makes them still more disgusting. Above all, I get muddled by
all the details, and I hate the close-ups when the heroine is not called,
and you play the big moment of your emotional scene to nothing but
a camera, a yard away.

John might have been more enthusiastic about film at this time if he
had been able to find rather better scripts. Sadly, two projects for the
cinema which really did intrigue him both now fell through. One was
an Elisabeth Bergner *Saint Joan* in which he would have played the
Dauphin (thirty years later he was to be the Inquisitor to Jean Seberg)
and the other was Jerome K. Jerome's *Passing of the Third Floor Back*,
a role which he lost to Conrad Veidt, who was also to film *Jew Süss*,
another Gielgud favourite.

John's early days in the film studios led the drama critic of the
Evening News to reflect on the precise nature of his current standing
in the profession:

To the best of my knowledge, Mr Gielgud is the only real star of the
British theatre, under thirty. Many others are now in their forties and,
unlike Gielgud, were all on the stage either during or before the First
War. Mr Ivor Novello and Herr Richard Tauber are already in their
forties, and Mr Charles Laughton and Mr Noël Coward are thirty-five.
Stardom is a quality above and beyond sheer acting ability; it is a
personal, even an emotional quality, and it has undeniably a great
deal to do with sex appeal, which in turn has very little to do with good
looks. Mr Gielgud has this quality of stardom, not so much by virtue
of possessing wonderfully delicate features and colouring, as because
he has that most priceless of all theatrical gifts, the Terry voice at its
loveliest. His other great quality is his agelessness; he can be anything
from nineteen to ninety, from Romeo to Prospero, Constantin to King
Lear. I passionately hope that he will prove all this in one evening by
playing Peer Gynt.

This in fact was one of the few great classical roles that was always to elude John, but the *News* critic was surprisingly percipient: the other actors under thirty that he now tipped for triumph by 1950 included Ralph Richardson, Robert Donat, Maurice Evans and Jack Hawkins.

As so often, the filming of *The Good Companions* overran, which meant that John had to miss the early rehearsals of his first professional production of a Shakespeare play, *The Merchant of Venice*, due to open at the Old Vic in December 1932, with Peggy Ashcroft as Portia and Malcolm Keen as Shylock. Harcourt Williams stood in for him and Gielgud took no fee as director, because he wanted it to go instead to the Motleys for the first Old Vic production in which costumes were specifically designed. In fact, the total décor budget was less than £100, and Shylock's robe was made out of dishcloth at threepence a yard. Nevertheless Lilian Baylis was predictably appalled at this extravagance and less than thrilled with Gielgud's decision to use music from Peter Warlock to give the whole production an air of mystery and fantasy, instead of the usual penny-pinching Old Vic drabness.

Anthony Quayle, then a very junior member of the Vic company, recalled that with John, for the very first time, he felt he was involved in a production 'behind which there was a brain and a consistent point of view, whether it was one you liked or not; at least it was coherent. I remember being struck in rehearsal by the elegance of John's clothes – his suede shoes, his beautifully cut suits, his immaculate shirts, the long gold key chain that went around his waist before diving into his trouser pocket; I had never seen the like. I also remember how unfailingly courteous he always was to the older and more distinguished members of the company, although to me he himself already seemed God-like in his eminence.'

One of the most detailed reviews of this *Merchant* came not in the press, but in a private letter to John from Tyrone Guthrie:

> I was entranced, many thanks and congratulations – the casket scene is exquisitely pretty and amusing and the trial scene is perfect. Top marks to Motley, especially for the women's clothes, though some of the men's are rather feminine. Antonio seems nice and worthy but rather dull. And surely he, rather than Shylock, should dominate the trial scene until Portia arrives? Malcolm Keen is over-doing his exit

shamefully, and Peggy Ashcroft, just right in personality, like a school prefect, but barely adequate vocally. Why does the Duke of Venice look like a provincial lady mayoress planting a tree? Harcourt Williams was perfect as Aragon, and if you have read this far you will know that I for one found the whole thing stimulating and gay, and I do want to congratulate you.

As for Peggy Ashcroft, although her Portia attracted some wonderful reviews (*The Times* praised her for being the first actress ever to play the 'quality of mercy' speech quite naturally, with her hands behind her back, instead of as an oration), she herself had grave doubts about what Gielgud was trying to do. 'I think John at the time was very influenced by Komis and all his innovations, but I wasn't too sure about this production because I felt it was fancy dress, and John could never tell us what period we were supposed to be in.'

What John most loved about both Peggy Ashcroft and Edith Evans was that their faces had what he was to call 'enigmatic originality', meaning that they both almost cultivated their features into an impersonal canvas, on to which any character could be painted.

Unlike Edith Evans, who was to spend the later part of her life (when not living with Michael Redgrave) in mourning for a husband who had died much too young, Peggy Ashcroft's private life was a constant source of backstage gossip. What is known is that within less than a year of *The Merchant* she had married Komisarjevsky, only then rapidly to divorce him on discovering a series of his love letters to other actresses. In one of his superbly indiscreet and supposedly off-the-record comments, discussing the rival merits of Peggy Ashcroft and Celia Johnson, who were almost of an age, John once said, 'Look at Celia, totally happy, lots of money, nice husband, lovely daughters, beautiful house, big success, yet she looks like the back of a London bus. Whereas Peggy has been in and out of every bed in London, and not a line on her face. That must be what a really active sex life can do for a woman.'

What John now knew was that he wanted to bring *The Merchant* to an audience who were usually accustomed to an altogether lighter kind of theatre, as the young Tyrone Guthrie reported: 'Here, for the first time in my limited experience, was Shakespeare done with elegance and wit, light as a feather, and so gaily sophisticated that it makes Maugham and Coward seem like two non-conformist pastors from the Midlands.'

John made another of his famously uneasy curtain speeches on the first night, on this occasion thanking Harcourt Williams for 'doing all the donkey work', and thus ended a year in which he had played the nine-month run of *Musical Chairs*, appeared in two films, directed *Romeo and Juliet*, *The Merchant of Venice* and *Strange Orchestra*, and started to work on what was to be his next great West End success, *Richard of Bordeaux*.

Chapter Seven

VINTAGE BORDEAUX
(1933–1934)

Richard of Bordeaux was the success of the season. From the window of my flat, I could look down St Martin's Lane and see the queues coiled like serpents around the theatre. I was photographed, painted, caricatured, interviewed. I signed my autograph a dozen times a day, and received letters and presents by every post.

T he author of *Richard of Bordeaux* was in fact three people. Her real name was Elizabeth Mackintosh, but she had already written several successful historical novels as Josephine Tey, and was now to chose her third identity as Gordon Daviot for the play she sent to John because, as she was later to admit, she had been inspired by seeing Gielgud at the Old Vic in what might be called 'the original' *Richard II*. His playing of Richard made him the obvious casting for Daviot's urbane, romantic, and often witty retread of Shakespeare; to find another example of the rewriting of medieval history in light-hearted modern language, you would have to go forward thirty years to James Goldman's very similar treatment of Henry II and his quarrelsome family in *The Lion in Winter*.

The Richard of Daviot's play had a non-Shakespearean life of his own; although his homosexuality could only be suggested through the character of his friend Robert (a kind of amalgam of Shakespeare's Bushy, Bagot and Green), he was given a sort of weary cynicism in lines such as: 'The only people I can trust are my two thousand archers, paid regularly every Friday.'

From the moment, backstage at the Vic, that John first read *Richard of Bordeaux*, he realised that not only was it a wonderful vehicle for his talents but also, rather in the manner of Shaw's *Saint Joan*, that there was something very attractive in the still revolutionary idea of great kings and warriors from history now behaving and talking like modern human beings. He was able to insist on directing the play himself, and duly brought in his beloved Motleys to do the sets and costumes: 'This was a much more realistic play than the cloak-and-sword dramas of my uncle Fred Terry and Matheson Lang, but it still had plenty of melodrama and excitement as well as comedy.'

They tried it out for a couple of semi-staged Sunday nights at the Arts Theatre while John was still in his last season at the Vic, but as soon as they went into rehearsal for the West End he decided to go for such epic Edwardian stage effects as the burning down of Sheen Palace. It wasn't until a catastrophic dress-rehearsal, at which the fire nearly spread throughout the theatre, that John realised his mistake, and cut down the production at the last minute to very much more manageable proportions. His co-star was Gwen Ffrangcon-Davies as the unlucky Princess Anne, but also, in a strong cast, were such established character actors as Francis Lister, Richard Ainley (son of the matinée idol, Henry Ainley) and Donald Wolfit, who was to start here a lifelong enmity with John. Fifty years later, Gielgud found himself in Tuscany with John Mortimer (filming *Summer's Lease*), when their conversation turned to the missing Lord Lucan. Mortimer suggested that the vanished peer had been the victim of a contract killing for £3,000. 'Good Lord,' said John, 'is that all it costs to have a man killed? If Wolfit had known that, he would have taken out a contract on me, years ago. He really loathed me, you know, and the feeling was always entirely mutual.'

At the time of *Richard of Bordeaux* Wolfit was already unhappily married, with a small child and a career that seemed to be going nowhere very much. He still viewed Gielgud with violent jealousy, as a man who, unlike himself, had come from a privileged and charmed theatrical background and who apparently had never been out of work since leaving drama school. Wolfit, as his biographer Ronald Harwood has noted, had none of Gielgud's graces:

Donald was always blinded to Gielgud's exceptional gifts – his superb voice, his grace of interpretation, his perceptive intelligence and, above all, a soulfulness that was capable of encompassing noble passion in the finest sense . . . as men, they had only their love of the theatre in common, and it would never be enough to form the foundation of anything more than chilly politeness, and sometimes not even that. Disagreements were plentiful and throughout his life, Wolfit would, at the very mention of Gielgud's name, inhale deeply and noisily through his nose, like an enraged bull, which was always his way of signifying enmity.

And there was yet another problem: Wolfit was virulently anti-homosexual, and already suspected John to be at the heart of a precious West End clique which would, as Donald saw it, be specifically determined to keep his old-fashioned barnstorming virility in a state of semi-unemployment.

The two men had of course already worked together on a couple of Sunday-night readings, and also in two or three productions at the Old Vic, but their tricky and volatile relationship made for some difficult rehearsals, followed by a curiously subdued first night, attended by few critics since it clashed with another major opening across town.

Yet *Richard of Bordeaux* was to be one of those plays that nobody liked except the public; the morning after it opened was so quiet at the box-office that the manager let his assistant go for a long lunch, only then to look through his window and see, to his utter amazement, a queue forming the length of St Martin's Lane. From that first matinée for the next fourteen months, there was scarcely a seat to be had.

Among those who now flocked to the play was the then Chancellor of the Exchequer, Stanley Baldwin, who wrote afterwards to John: 'I should like, if I may, to thank you and your admirable team for the delightful evening I spent on Saturday night in your theatre. I forgot all my own difficulties and became immersed in those of poor Richard. How little he realised the extraordinary times through which he was living, and how much you must have enjoyed working up the play.'

The actors Herbert Marshall and Edna Best wrote to John of 'a glorious evening and a superb play', while Hugh Walpole told him: 'I especially admired the way in which you never ceased to be Richard, even while taking your curtain call. This is great acting, and better still great poetic oration.' As for Ivor Novello: 'What is there to say? I am so grateful for your beauty, imagination and utterly touching loveableness.' And from the Shavian actor Esmé Percy: 'Having been born in an age that now seems legendary, my memory houses many splendours, but your Richard shall be added to my first sight of Henry Irving, to the sound of Bernhardt's voice, and Duse's extraordinary personality among the greatest and most poignant nights of my life.'

Clearly this was the most successful historical play since Bernard Shaw's *Saint Joan*, and, historically closer to the facts than was the Shakespeare, it remains an even more revealing assessment of the King's profligate character. Daviot's play starts with Richard at eighteen, an idealist poised for disaster, and then traces the course of his life, leading up to the late bitterness and defeat. As the critic Audrey Williamson was to write:

Dressed in cream or cloth of gold, the sculptured cheekbones and proud poise of his head nobly accentuated beneath his red-gold flame of hair, Gielgud was a royal figure with the hereditary Terry radiance. It was perhaps his romantic tenderness which consolidated his popularity with audiences, but the temper and irony were also superbly presented, his intelligence was never in doubt, and his playing of the last scenes showed a fine appreciation of the sharp springs of disillusion. His characterisation grew in strength with its bitter quietude, and if any one detail of the performance remains clearer than the rest, it is the simple one of Richard allowing his handkerchief to flutter to the ground like a dead leaf at the realisation of Anne's fatal illness. It was a key to the subtlety of his entire performance, one which dominates all memories of the play, and will become the Golden Legend of our age.

In later years, Gielgud was to be very dismissive of his original Old Vic *Richard II*. 'When I listen to the old recordings, they sound to me very voice-conscious, and I am rather ashamed to think that I was so contented with that kind of acting.' For *Richard of Bordeaux*, however, he found a kind of release into an altogether more contemporary style. The King in Gordon Daviot's play was less self-pitying, and had a sharper wit than in Shakespeare's, and when the critics did catch up with what was already a huge popular hit, they found in John a marvellous combination of vacillation, nobility and embittered disillusion. For Desmond MacCarthy of *The Times*, John was now 'right at the top of his profession, having acquired all the marks of the great actor'. For the *Daily Telegraph*, W.A. Darlington noted at the curtain fall 'a glorious, full-throated roar of approval, such as the West End seldom hears in these sophisticated days'.

But as so often, the most thoughtful review of both the play and the actor came in the *New Statesman*:

> When I first went to the play, historical drama was all the rage, from Lewis Waller to the endless revivals of *The Scarlet Pimpernel* by Fred Terry. But since the War, the high cost of productions has made pageantry impractical, while the popularity of new naturalistic plays has consigned the drama of swagger and duel to the shelf. Failing supply has accompanied diminished demand. But now, Mr Gielgud brings it all back. His Richard is quite remarkable; there is a morbid, feline elegance about his bearing and careful movements. He changes from the leader of a country in arms to a vain, selfish disillusioned man – an artist who has lost the desire to share delightful things, and can no longer put his faith in his friends. Mr Gielgud never allows pathos to sink into sentiment, and he triumphs with an economy of gesture. In my opinion he is now the first among English actors. Ours is far from being an age of great acting, but the range of his emotional scope, and the intelligence with which he conceives his role, put him right at the top of his profession. Mr Gielgud uniquely combines histrionic temperament with interpretative intelligence and that is very rare. Now his temptations will begin. He has the power to charm large audiences, but will he choose only plays which delight them?

Considering that on the first night the box-office takings were only £77, the immediate turn-around in the fortunes of *Richard of Bordeaux* was nothing short of a miracle. John himself, although he had characteristically turned down an offer to invest in the play, such was his terror of any business dealing, was now earning £100 per week, more than twice his most recent salary at the Vic.

The morning after *Richard of Bordeaux* opened, the director Victor Savile summoned John back to Lime Grove for retakes of some of the close-ups in *The Good Companions*: 'I congratulated him on the applause and extravagant praise, and all he said was, "What is the good of success in such an unhappy world?"' Even John now seemed to have awoken to the fact that, with the rise of Hitler and Mussolini, some kind of reality was about to invade his closed and closeted theatrical environment.

Still not yet thirty, John had, for the first time, become a star, as he explained to one of his many new friends: 'After the show every night I sit signing hundreds of post-cards in my costume as people come round backstage. Yes, I know it's vulgar, but I can't resist it. I am a star!' As Gordon Daviot was to write in her preface to the published edition, which is dedicated to John: 'I like to think that, in time to come, whenever *Richard of Bordeaux* is mentioned, it is your name that will spring to people's lips.'

Daviot's hope was to become more of a reality than even she could have wished. Although indeed the fame of her play was always linked to Gielgud's performance, it was effectively only to exist in London for the length of that first production. Although initially much revived and toured around the regions, the play (with Maurice Evans) only achieved a brief Broadway life, and has never been given a major post-war revival anywhere, perhaps because its unashamed, flamboyant, poetic sentimentality has never again suited the mood of the moment as it did so perfectly in 1933.

At this moment, a gossip writer in the *Evening News* began for the first time to profile John in some depth:

Inside the theatre he is always fiery, youthful and impetuous, a man of easy and gallant bearing, guaranteed to sweep even the most cynical and sophisticated modern girl right off her feet. Outside the theatre, however, he is just shy John, carefully signing autographs and warmly shaking every hand placed before him:

'These people are the galleryites and the pittites of the Old Vic, the kind of people whose support of Shakespeare makes you glad to be alive . . . they often send me lovely letters and presents of flowers and books. But I draw the line at any personal acquaintance. I do not believe in personal contact between an actor and his audience. The most difficult audiences are always the schoolchildren, but I usually go out first to explain to them that Shakespeare is really much more thrilling than Edgar Wallace. I also tell them not to giggle when two people kiss, or at any reference to magic and fairies. The other really difficult audience are the Old Vic veterans who hate anything fresh. They tell me that a part has always been played in a red wig, and how dare I now choose black?'

In the seventy years since Daviot's play first opened, only Maurice Evans seemed willing to challenge the memory of Gielgud, although towards the end of the run in London, and on the road, the future Stratford director, Glen Byam Shaw, often went on for him. On some nights, police had to be called to restrain the crowds at the stage door, while among the many celebrities who came backstage were the American star Alfred Lunt and his English-born wife Lynn Fontanne, who told John: 'You are a very strange and very beautiful actor, like a new-born colt, and I also adore your feet, which are the youngest I have ever seen on stage.'

By the end of the run, several members of the company, recognising perhaps that this was little more than a one-man show with extras, had gone off in search of more rewarding work, leading to yet another of John's foot-in-mouth curtain speeches: 'What a wonderful audience you have been, and some of you have come again and again, in spite of all the changes in the cast.'

Not until the Olivier-Richardson wartime seasons at this same New Theatre was any classical actor to take the town by any comparable kind of storm. *Richard of Bordeaux* was the making of John's career and also inevitably something of a millstone around his neck. Forty years later, when he was with some difficulty trying to move into the modern theatre of David Storey and Harold Pinter, he once said to me, rather sadly, about his older fans, 'If they had it their way, I would have gone on being Richard of Bordeaux for the rest of my life. And theirs.'

Even during the extended run of this first production, John rapidly tired of playing nothing but the homosexual, doomed King; over the next few months, while acting eight shows a week, he was to direct two other plays and make his first tentative stab at management. The first of the plays he directed was Somerset Maugham's *Sheppey*, for which he assembled a magical cast led by Ralph Richardson, Angela Baddeley and Eric Portman. Overawed by Maugham's presence at the later rehearsals, however, Gielgud declined to make any of the changes that could have solved the problems of *Sheppey*, which essentially were that the first act was a Pinero-like comedy, the second a Shavian kind of drama, and the third a flight of tragic fantasy. The result was not a success, although Maugham later dedicated the published text to John. 'I felt tremendously flattered by his [Maugham's] charming gesture, but I realised that I had found it very hard to get on intimate terms with any living playwright. I suppose my actor's egotism is to blame. I am not clever at drawing people out, and my friends tell me that I have no real interest in anyone but myself. I hope this is not the exact truth, but I rather fear that it may be.'

His relationship with Maugham was not helped by the fact that the novelist was already living on Cap Ferrat in the south of France, forced into exile by the fact that his lover, the American Gerald Haxton, had been declared an undesirable alien in Britain after several homosexual scandals. Maugham had, however, handed over all authority to John, as he wrote from the Villa Mauresque on 19 August:

> I am very glad indeed to hear that you want to produce my play. It needs to be done with a mixture of imagination and realism and I know no one who can do that better than you. I am not in the least sensitive about cuts, and I hope you will not hesitate to shorten wherever the play seems to you to drag, or wherever I have made a point at greater length than is needed to bring it home. I have a house full of guests, and do not see how I can abandon them to attend rehearsals. But please remember not to be too kind about firing people if they seem unsuitable when you start work. My own experience in the theatre was that people who are not right for their roles at once never really get any better, no matter how much time the producer devotes to them.

The other play that John directed during the run of *Richard of Bordeaux* was *Spring 1600* by the young Welsh actor and playwright whom he had first met at the Oxford Playhouse while he was still a star-struck undergraduate. In the intervening ten years, Emlyn Williams had begun to make his name as a somewhat sinister West End actor, notably in such thrillers as Edgar Wallace's *On the Spot*, and *The Case of the Frightened Lady*. This last play had taken him to New York, and while he was there Emlyn wrote *Spring 1600*, a swash-buckling backstage play about the Elizabethan world of such original Shakespearean actors as Richard Burbage and Will Kemp during their dress-rehearsals for the first-ever staging of *Twelfth Night*. In later years, Ned Sherrin and Caryl Brahms were also to explore this world in their *No Bed For Bacon*, but it wasn't until the late 1990s, with Nicholas Wright's play *Cressida* and, far more successfully, Tom Stoppard's *Shakespeare in Love*, that the idea really came to fruition. At the time of *Spring 1600*, Emlyn Williams was not yet thirty, and still two years away from his first great hit as an actor-dramatist with the thriller *Night Must Fall*.

So, although they were of an age, and to become lifelong friends with a good deal in common, not only a passion for all aspects of theatre, but also a cautious awareness that their homosexuality had still to be kept carefully hidden from their audiences, and even from some of their friends, John was still inclined to treat Williams with a tolerant patronage, insisting that if he was to direct *Spring 1600*, certain changes would have to be made. Accordingly, on his return from Broadway, Williams was summoned to a meeting:

At Number 7, Upper St Martin's Lane, I climbed the steep, narrow stairs to a top flat . . . Gielgud, on our occasional previous meet-ings, had seemed affable but a little haughty, and though he was less than two years older than me, I always felt in awe of him. I therefore expected, knowing of his fanatical dedication to his work, an impeccable room with perhaps one good painting, a classical bust and lofty talk about Shakespeare, with a couple of reverent acolytes hanging about . . . it was nothing of the sort, being unpretentiously small with good furniture and family pictures, comfortably lived in by the two bachelors who shared the flat. John Perry was my age, tall, gauntly handsome with thinning hair, and a mocking manner which contrived, as I later discovered, to hide a kind heart . . . it was all rather like being in digs on tour. Gielgud hurried in, bare-legged, in a shabby old dressing-gown, suggesting a toga.

In the years that followed, Williams was frequently to revisit the Perry/Gielgud flat, recalling: 'John G eating scrambled eggs before going off to another packed house, and the gramophone always playing Vivaldi. It was, in a way, like coming home. One evening, when I arrived, sitting having a drink was a tall, strikingly handsome boy who looked like an Oxford undergraduate, which is what he had been until very recently. But he had written a first play which was about to be produced in the West End, and from his pocket he gave me a throwaway postcard. It read "First Episode, by Terence Rattigan". On another occasion the three of us all changed in John's bedroom into hired Tyrolean outfits, with leather shorts, for the Chelsea Arts Ball.'

Rattigan now was a regular visitor, not only to the flat in St Martin's Lane, but also to the country cottage near Henley which the two Johns had rented for weekend house parties, as Rattigan's biographer Geoffrey Wansell notes:

There was poker and ping-pong, a great many famous faces and fre-quent Sunday lunches, as well as elegant and sometimes outrageous parties. This was the magical, star-studded world which Rattigan had longed to be part of. It was also a world of homosexuals, which the theatre accepted more readily and more consistently than any other profession. Gielgud's theatre company was certainly more welcoming to homosexuals than some of the more conventional managements and impresarios of that time; nevertheless, every homosexual knew only too well the dangers that confronted them if they dared to advertise their sexual appetites too brazenly. Any homosexual act between adults over the age of twenty-one was still punishable by months of imprisonment, while the punishment for an affair with a minor was even harsher – and Rattigan at this time was not even twenty-one . . . like every homosexual of his time, he was always on guard, preoccupied with preserving appearances at all costs, conscious of the need to protect his secret world. With Perry and

Gielgud however, he could relax in an atmosphere which delighted him and which he never really wanted to leave.

At 67 St Martin's Lane, not far from John's flat and almost opposite the New Theatre, the Motleys (who had taken their professional name from Jacques's line 'Motley's the only wear' in *As You Like It*) had by now set up their design business in a derelict third-floor studio, last used by the revue star Douglas Byng as a gay nightclub. It had also once been the workshop of Thomas Chippendale, and like him the Motleys now combined the studio with a kind of theatrical club where, as John recalled:

Guinness and Ashcroft and Guthrie and I would turn up most evenings, to drink their tea and gossip with George Devine who I remember looking very Bohemian, like an artist from the Latin Quarter with pipe and corduroys – always shock-headed, and twinkling and agreeable. I threw a first-night party for *Richard of Bordeaux* in the studio, and we managed to fuse all the lights by tampering with a very elaborate model theatre which George had just begun to build in one of the corners. Sometimes we would have all-white evenings – white food, white wine and the Motleys all in long white dresses. Their studio really became our powerhouse, where all the new plans were hatched out.

When Gielgud later took Devine into his Old Vic company, it was as much for his companionship as his talent.

Unlike the relationship with Devine, which had started very well at Oxford, John and Emlyn Williams failed to hit it off straight away. They had got off to a bad start, with John insisting on more and more changes to *Spring 1600*, and Williams torn between wanting to have his play directed by the hottest young theatre star in the business, while already being uneasily aware that not all John's changes were for the better. Under Gielgud's own management, no expense was to be spared. There were elaborate sets, designed of course by the Motleys, a large orchestra in the pit for the incidental music, a dozen madrigal singers and nearly twenty extras. Isabel Jeans, playing a wealthy patron of the Globe, had a negro attendant and a monkey which she carried on her shoulder, at least until it gave her a nasty bite. The budget was an almost unprecedented £4,000, most of which John had raised himself, but the first night ran nearly four hours and was, to say the least, not a great success.

John, of course, still playing *Richard of Bordeaux*, could not be there, and Williams was in such a high state of nerves in the dress-circle that he suddenly became convinced that he was in danger of imminently becoming the first playwright who had ever urinated over his own play.

His terror was needless, at least as far as some critics were concerned. Ivor Brown, for the *Observer*, wrote that: 'A world's great age begins anew, and we are all party to its pulsing life and the mood of the madrigal.' For the *Sunday Times*, James Agate labelled it 'choice entertainment for the fastidious', but there clearly were not enough of them, and despite some drastic cutting by the author and director on the second night, the production barely survived two weeks. The sets and costumes were sold off in job lots, and John wrote to Williams: 'Oh dear, I am so sad for you; we don't seem to have quite got away with it, all that work and love, and then it just evaporates.'

There had only been one terrible moment during the dress-rehearsal when, thinking that Williams was not present, John told the cast, through a megaphone from the stalls, 'This last act is very thin, but we must try to make the best of it.' A quiet voice at his elbow, that of the author, murmured, 'I think we all know the act is thin, John, but you need perhaps not have announced it to the entire cast. Why don't we just wait for the critics to do that?'

Unlike John, Williams had always been bisexual, and a few years later Gielgud was a principal guest at his wedding to the ex-wife of a barrister, Mary Carus-Wilson. 'I'm so glad for Emlyn,' John told her at the wedding. 'People keep telling me I ought to marry Peggy Ashcroft, but, much as we love each other, I don't think she'd have me; Gwen is such a darling, I suppose she might, at a pinch, but oh dear . . .' Lying behind this characteristically unfortunate summary was of course the fact that Peggy Ashcroft was hardly likely to settle for John as a husband, despite the fact that the *Evening Standard* announced their betrothal in 1935, while Gwen Ffrangcon-Davies was a lifelong lesbian. If John was drawn to women at this time, or ever, it was only really for the sake of his public image in a still intolerant world, and he was careful always to associate himself, both onstage and off, with precisely those actresses who were least likely to have any designs on him as a possible sexual or even marital partner.

From this very early stage, John was now beginning to direct as often as possible; he had realised, at the Old Vic, the immediate advantage of a semi-permanent group of actors who could start rehearsals over and over again, without the time-wasting need for constant introductions or allowances having to be made for often clashing temperaments:

> My greatest good fortune was that, over the years, I was able to bring together wonderful companies, part with them on excellent terms, and then a few years later come back to work with them again. I find myself so much at home that I can then start work much more quickly than if I have to break the ice with players I do not know at all, and in my first years as a director, I was lucky enough to have three or four elderly actors in minor roles who had started out with Tree, Benson, Fagan or Playfair. They obeyed me without question, and had beautiful manners; even if they were not very fond of each other, their discipline and good behaviour were unfailing. This meant that I was able, on the one hand, to have some highly experienced players and, on the other, to bring on some very enthusiastic young people like Anthony Quayle, Glen Byam Shaw, Alec Guinness, Harry Andrews, actors who were just beginning. The young people matched with their youthful enthusiasm what the older ones had in experience – it seemed to me an ideal situation.

Richard of Bordeaux came to the end of its long London run in the spring of 1934; but almost immediately it went out on the road, initially with John himself, and subsequently with Glen Byam Shaw, as John started preparations for what he hoped would be its triumphant sequel. Gordon Daviot had decided during the run that, having given John one of his greatest roles, it would now be only fair to try and do the same for his co-star Gwen Ffrangcon-Davies. *Queen of Scots* was therefore the story of the doomed Mary, and her affairs with Bothwell and Darnley. Strangely, although both Frederick Schiller and Robert Bolt scored considerable successes with this historical period, it proved somehow beyond the talents of Gordon Daviot, and *Queen of Scots* enjoyed only the briefest of West End runs.

Characteristically, by the time it closed, John was already into another and rather more promising project. He had discovered that just before Ronald Mackenzie had been killed in the car crash he had completed another play, this one called *The Maitlands*, which he had given to Komisarjevsky in the hope of repeating the success they had all enjoyed with *Musical Chairs*.

Thanks to that success it was now easier to assemble a strong cast, and joining Gielgud here were the young Jack Hawkins, the future Hollywood dowager May Whitty and the poet and actor Stephen Haggard, in whom many were already seeing a still younger Gielgud. The odds were now very high: Gielgud would be appearing in the West End for the first time since his triumph in *Bordeaux*. The first-night audience therefore expected to see him in another flamboyantly charismatic performance, and were thus somewhat shocked to find him in shabby modern dress, a moustache, and dressed for the carnival with which the play opened.

He was playing a schoolmaster, trying to bring a mentally disturbed young man (Stephen Haggard) back to health; May Whitty was the worried mother, and Jack Hawkins a flashy and heartless actor, brother to the schoolmaster.

The Maitlands was again a new play of some fascination, not only because Mackenzie pointed the way forward to such other 'lost' dramatists as Rodney Ackland and John Whiting, but also because of the violence with which it was greeted. Early in the first act, on the first night, voices from the gallery yelled 'Rubbish!' while others shouted 'Idiots!', leaving it unclear whether this referred to the characters on stage or the gallery first-nighters.

At the curtain call, the jeering from the gallery first-nighters persisted; John, aware that Mackenzie's widow was in the audience, stepped forward to make a speech referring to his recent death, whereupon, unsurprisingly, the jeers died rapidly away.

However, *The Maitlands* was doomed. James Agate accused the play of 'taking elegant umbrage at our crude world' and suggested that John was 'much too romantic an actor to be happy away from rhetoric and robes – if this fine actor must be modern, it should only be in a

Russian blouse. All that goes with a bowler hat utterly defeats him.' It was left to Ivor Brown alone, in the *Observer*, to mourn Mackenzie's early death and commend his 'new muscularity of attack'.

Chapter Eight

❧❦❧

THE READINESS IS ALL
(1934–1935)

*I was always being told by well-meaning friends (like Emlyn) how
jealous Larry was of me, but I could never quite understand why;
he had a great advantage over me in his commanding vitality,
striking looks, brilliant humour and passionate directness. When
we alternated as Romeo and Mercutio, he seemed to be holding all
the cards except one. I was of course the director.*

The *Maitlands*, largely because of the advance bookings that
had been made on John's name before the reviews came out,
staggered on at Wyndham's for nearly twelve weeks, and towards the end of the run Sir Bronson Albery, who owned that theatre
as well as a family chain of others, came backstage one night to offer
John the production he had really wanted all along. What Albery
suggested was a West End *Hamlet* which John could play and direct,
design with the Motleys, and on a budget far beyond the wildest
dreams of the *Hamlets* he had played at the Old Vic and the Court
in Sloane Square.

This was, in other words, to be the big one, and although initially
it was only meant to run six weeks, it in fact lasted more than six
months, to become one of the longest-running West End revivals
of Shakespeare at this time. To it, in what was then a generous
rehearsal period of four weeks, John brought all the influences that
had conditioned his early Shakespearean work. Not only the Motleys,
but a set heavily indebted to both Gordon Craig and Komisarjevsky,

and a production in which he would again try to combine the talents of a generation older than his with those of some very promising newcomers.

His Ophelia was to be the young Jessica Tandy; as Claudius and Gertrude, he had Frank Vosper and Laura Cowie, looking, he recalled, 'like two sleek, evil cats'. Jack Hawkins, soon to marry Jessica Tandy, was Horatio, Glen Byam Shaw was Laertes, and George Howe was Polonius. But perhaps the most intriguing member of this company was a young actor of twenty, who had been haunting Gielgud's stage door in the hope of an understudy job. Failing that, John offered him £20 to survive and a few weeks later, impressed by one student production, he offered Alec Guinness the role of Osric. Once again a long and loving friendship, which was to extend across the next sixty years, got off to a catastrophic start when early in rehearsal John decided he had made a terrible mistake.

Guinness's recollection of these early rehearsals is one of the best surviving records of John in action as a director at this time: '"Come on from the left. No! No! The other left – oh, someone make him understand! Why are you so stiff? Why don't you make me laugh? Motleys! Would it be pretty to paint the whole thing gold? Perhaps not. Don't fidget, Guinness; now you are gabbling. Now turn upstage. No, not you. You! Turn the other way. Oh, why can't you all act? Get someone to teach you how to act! Why is your voice so harsh? It really is quite ugly. Do just do something about it."'

And there was worse to come. Guinness, ten years younger than Gielgud, and on £7 per week, finally drove John to distraction: 'What on earth has happened to you? You were so good as a student. You're terrible. Do go away. I don't ever want to see you again.' But Guinness, who had already learned at least a little about the volatility of John's moods, knew enough to hang about until the end of that day's rehearsal. 'Excuse me, Mr Gielgud, but am I really fired?'

'No! Yes! No, of course not. But do go away. Come back in a week. Get someone to teach you how to act. Try Martita Hunt – she'll be glad of the money.'

In the event, Guinness decided not to go anywhere near Martita, whose teaching was to say the least a little eccentric, but instead to walk around London's parks for a week and then to report back to

Gielgud at the New. 'He seemed delighted to have me back, heaped praise on my Osric and laughed at everything I said. I couldn't swear that I was doing anything I had not done a week earlier. But suddenly and briefly I had become teacher's pet, and John told the Motleys that I should have a hat with a lot of feathers, just like the Duchess of Devonshire.'

Another member of this Hamlet company was Frith Banbury, later to become one of the most distinguished of West End directors and the one who first discovered such playwrights as Robert Bolt and N.C. Hunter: 'John was himself such a brilliant actor than he failed to understand those of us who were less good; he would sit with his feet on the railing of the dress-circle, yelling at us to be better in some way. I think that something about me always irritated him; I had only a very small part, but he kept taking lines away from me and giving them to Jack Hawkins. At the dress-rehearsal, I somehow missed an entrance, clambered over the bloody revolving stage, only to hear John scream, "Banbury, I don't mind you being late, but what I can't forgive is you standing about like that when you do arrive."' It was not so very long after this experience that Frith Banbury began to think about the possibilities of becoming a director.

During the run, Alec Guinness and Frith Banbury and the other younger members of cast would gather in the wings every night to watch what they seemed intuitively already to know was to be the *Hamlet* of their time. At Christmas, Gielgud gave Guinness a volume of Ellen Terry's letters, in which he inscribed what became Alec's lifelong motto: 'The Readiness Is All'. But even now, the critics were still divided. Several of them noticed how exhausted John G had become as actor and director, and Agate thought it was 'Everest only half-scaled'. In contrast, J.C. Trewin found it 'the key Shakespearean revival of its period', though Raymond Mortimer added, 'Hamlet attends the funeral of Ophelia in a sort of white fur coat, which as usual suits Gielgud, but not the scene.' In the view of the critic A.E. Wilson:

Mr Gielgud has many qualifications for Hamlet. He is an artist, he is intelligent, he is handsome. He still has the slim figure of youth and a romantic profile which he allows us frequent opportunities to admire. He has an agreeable voice with good lungs behind it, although under the stress of passion it becomes high and throaty instead of a full-throated roar. He has a personality which in young people seems to induce hero-worship. He speaks his lines with exceptional intelligence, his diction is elegant and his delivery is unexceptionable except when he falls sometimes into inaudibility. But, he lacks passion or any kind of real emotion. He seems aloof and abstracted from everyone and everything. He is no more excited after the Ghost has spoken to him than he was before; there is no bitterness in his disdain, no rage in his hatred, no affection in his friendship and no wildness in his melancholy.

For Audrey Williamson however:

Gielgud has always achieved his finest effects when surrounded by a cast of high distinction; his performances shine better for their setting. And though he always stressed the sensitivity of Hamlet, his range was remarkable. The mobile beauty of his hands and voice bespoke the prince and the poet; but there was a taut inner fibre in this *Hamlet*, expressed in sudden flashes of steel at moments of active crisis . . . There had been a gap of over a generation between Gielgud and the finest classical actors of the past, so audiences had never seen a young Hamlet. And the special charm of this one was that it welded together the best of the old and the new.

In these years, Shakespearean productions were not quite as academically humourless as they were later to become; John was a famous onstage giggler, never more so than on the night when Frank Vosper, as Claudius, had been chatting backstage to an old army friend. A few minutes later, coming on for the duel scene, instead of saying, 'Cousin Hamlet, you know the wager,' Vosper solemnly enquired, 'Cousin Hamlet, you know the Major?'

Looking back, John was to write that he had never been happier than during the run of this *Hamlet*. Not only was he playing, eight times a week, the role which alone would have justified his whole career, but he had made (largely from *Richard of Bordeaux* in London and on the road) enough money to buy, for £1,000, a little weekend cottage in Essex, near Finchingfield, where he and John Perry would often welcome such young homosexual friends as Terence Rattigan and Binkie Beaumont and Arthur Marshall.

The general critical enthusiasm for this production was reflected in hundreds of letters written to John at the theatre. From the novelist Rosamund Lehmann, whose actress sister Beatrix had already become a friend: 'Your scenes with Ophelia are a revelation, and I felt all through the production that this was exactly what Shakespeare would have wanted. For the first time I felt really satisfied by the play because your acting conveyed the sense of a colossal, overpowering Fate at the back of all the speculation and intellectual beating-about. I really was excited, and I never expect to see a better Hamlet – nor, for that matter, a better Ophelia or Polonius.' Emlyn Williams added: 'Last night was the best that I have ever spent in a theatre, and I hope you will not misunderstand me, when I say that I have never been less conscious of a great actor's interpretation, never more aware of the beauty and unity of the play.'

As for George Devine, newly down from Oxford and starting to make his own way in the theatre as an actor-director: 'I can't help feeling that most of the critics are men of a generation past. They keep comparing you to Irving, Tree, and Forbes-Robertson, whereas the whole point of your ideas and acting is surely that it is designed for a modern theatre audience with a much quicker perception. The general spread of culture and knowledge in our time makes it unnecessary for Hamlet to underline everything as he goes along. What you are doing is crediting us in the audience with a kind of intelligence and although I have some reservations about the other casting, I do think you have shown us the future for Shakespeare instead of, as usual, the past.'

Godfrey Tearle, always a rather more flamboyant player than most, sent John a telegram reading: 'Would I were Horatio, to support the finest Hamlet I have ever seen. May God in thy good cause make thee prosperous!'

The Queen Mother, then Duchess of York, sent a message via her lady-in-waiting noting how much she would have liked John to come to the royal box during the performance she and the future George VI attended; but, continued the letter, 'when she saw you had but one interval in such a long and exhausting evening, she thought it kinder to refrain'.

In addition to all the encouragement and praise from these letters, John also received thanks from within the cast. A particularly grateful member of the company was Alec Guinness, who wrote:

I could write you a very long letter thanking you not only for giving me a part, but also for your countless little kindnesses, which have made working with you so delightful, but I will spare you all that. It was very courageous of you to give an inexperienced person a part like Osric, and knowing how bad I was even at the end of the run, and how much you said I had improved, I shudder to think what I must have been like at the beginning. I suppose one never forgets one's first part – I certainly shall never forget how happy I have been during these last six months. I am not a very gay or happy person by nature, but I find the confidence you have in me a great source of happiness. I want to write this because it's one of those things which mean a lot to me, but I find very hard to speak.

In sharp contrast, an 'unknown fan', who declined to sign the letter, sent John a detailed, typewritten, four-page analysis of his current standing in the theatre which was an often devastatingly accurate review:

Most critics shower superlatives on you, and those who like to be different treat you as a mere matinée idol. I consider you one of the great hopes of the English theatre, but there are times when you simply don't quite come off. In the long run of *Richard of Bordeaux* your performance deteriorated badly, showing signs of wear and tear when you spoke too fast and too loud. In moments of strong emotion, something always goes wrong and you become unnatural. You tend to rant and cry far too often without much conviction. I felt that you were always terribly sorry for Hamlet, and you played it with a kind of self-pity which made the emotion ring false. In *The Maitlands* your mannerisms stuck out a mile, and there is always the problem of 'the Gielgud voice'. I suspect, although you often listen to it, that you have never really heard it. Listen next time, and you will hear the exaggerations. I am neither a schoolgirl nor a flapper, nor a fussy old lady. I don't want you to write back, but do please think about what I have to say, I am not alone.

In fact, with a budget of only £1,500 this *Hamlet* played to an average of £2,000 a week, and its eventual profit at the end of 155 performances, the longest London run of the play in sixty years, was just over £30,000. John himself was asked to explain his success:

There is plenty to account for it. For one thing, I notice that the audience is full of young people. Many of them have probably never seen the play, and they genuinely want to know how it ends. Another thing is that we have gone back to the old tradition of the actor who is also the producer. In this way, during the run of the play, I have been able continually to change and build up and improve the production in small details from night to night. The old school of actor-managers built up a company around them, who knew them and worked continually with them, and would do anything for them. But nowadays, when an outside producer comes in to direct the play, he does so and then goes away again. He usually only comes in once or twice later during the run and terrifies everybody; but there can be no sense of this continual and communal building up of a production.

As the run of *Hamlet* was coming to an end, the playwright Rodney Ackland (for whom John had directed *Strange Orchestra* a couple of years earlier) now brought him an adaptation of Hugh Walpole's bestselling novel, *The Old Ladies*. This was a macabre piece for four actresses, one of whom never spoke, and another of whom came to an ugly and unexpected death in what could be considered one of the first great psychological thrillers of this period. Gielgud assembled a magnificent cast (Edith Evans, Jean Cadell and Mary Jerrold) and devised, with the Motleys, a brilliant and radically new cutaway set in which the different bedrooms of a boarding-house, as well as the downstairs lounge, could all be seen and used simultaneously, like an exaggerated doll's-house.

Unfortunately however, the production clashed with King George V's Silver Jubilee celebrations of 1935, and the business suffered accordingly; but *The Old Ladies* has frequently been revived and owes a considerable debt to John's pioneering original production. Just when he had become the greatest Hamlet of his time, he also turned out to be a modernist stage director, far ahead of his contemporaries in realising that although he himself was still very unhappy with the new medium, some of the close-up techniques of cinema now needed to be borrowed back for the live theatre. And his unhappiness with the screen only affected him as an actor; it was around now that he began to develop the habit of going to the cinema once or twice a week, the only kind of regular relaxation he was to allow himself in a workaholic lifetime.

As Hugh Walpole himself wrote to John after the first night: 'You really have done a brilliant job, and I do congratulate you on your genius as a producer. Everything seems to have gone without a hitch, and the best thing is that the play seems to have fulfilled so many different tasks.'

John was also, at a time when the London theatre was still shamefully parochial, fascinated by the occasional visits of foreign companies. One of these, Michel St Denis's Compagnie des Quinze, had recently played London with André Obey's *Noah*, a biblical drama which intrigued John because it was produced in an endearing and stylised way, with animals portrayed by actors in exquisite masks, and all the sound effects performed by the company – in essence an amazing forerunner of the Théâtre de Complicité which was to take London by storm half a century later.

Pierre Fresnay had already taken *Noah* to Broadway, where it had enjoyed limited success, but John was still very eager to play it in London, under the direction of St Denis himself:

We did not really hit it off at first. Michel made me feel, in rehearsal, intensely lazy, ignorant and self-satisfied, and I in turn was terrified that perhaps he was right, and that my talents really were negligible . . . I was really very unhappy as Noah. I suddenly realised that the part really belonged to an actor like Charles Laughton or Cedric Hardwicke, and for some reason I was dressed in velveteen trousers and a fur cap, which made me look bizarrely like a jungle explorer who had suddenly arrived at the North Pole.

The critics as usual preferred it in the original French, and London audiences seemed embarrassed by our mixture of comedy, mime and religion. On the very last night of a rather brief run, the always purist St Denis came backstage to tell me that, at last, I was perhaps beginning to find a way of playing at least the very first scene.

Peggy Ashcroft, in the first of her many letters to John, wrote: 'I was so moved by your performance last night that I fear I did not make any sense in the dressing-room afterwards. It is very rare now to see a great performance such as yours, so big and moving and yet never breaking through to overbalance the production. I can't tell you how much I admire you for your courage in doing *Noah*, and I long to see it again.'

But the last word on this weird adventure should perhaps go to Ivor Brown in the *Observer*: 'Mr Gielgud plays Noah as a six-hundred-year-old man with a prodigious mixture of Lear, Job, Tolstoy and the Old Man of the Sea.'

Noah ran for only three months in a scorchingly hot summer that was an agony to the company, most of whom were heavily clothed; but thanks to Gielgud and St Denis, an amazing collection of young actors was here able to play some of their earliest roles. Among them were Jack Hawkins, Jessica Tandy, Marius Goring and (heavily disguised as wolves and sheep) Alec Guinness and his future wife Merula Salaman, while playing the Lion was Harry Andrews and, as John commented, 'obvious casting as a bear', George Devine.

It was Tyrone Guthrie who unfavourably contrasted this new production with the original by the Compagnie des Quinze: 'the magic somehow disappeared; originally the production was like a glamorous but rather passée woman in a big shady hat and heaps of tulle. The Gielgud version was the same lady but now in a cold, hard north-east light, a raincoat and no hat.' And, as Irving Wardle was later to note, what this venture proved was that there was going to be no grand alliance between the director and the star: 'For St Denis, it was a compromised excursion into alien boulevard territory; for Gielgud, it was an instructive digression from his natural line of work.

Temperamentally the two were as elementally opposed as earth and air. If Gielgud was a bird, St Denis was his cage. So although the two men were pushing for similar reforms, they retreated to their separate centres of power and viewed each other's work with respect but from a distance in future.'

Not content with being an actor, director and (in all but name) designer, John now decided to try his hand as a playwright; he had for some time been interested in the idea of a stage version of Dickens's *A Tale of Two Cities*, one that would allow John not only Sidney Carton's great guillotine speech about the 'far, far better thing', but also, in a typically Gielgud twist, the idea would be for him to double the wicked Marquis de St Evremonde. There were, however, initially two major problems. One was that the veteran Sir John Martin-Harvey, hearing of the plan, wrote Gielgud a sharp note to the effect that he was still on the road in his own version of the story, the long-running *The Only Way*, and would be therefore grateful if the young Gielgud would keep his hands off the property.

The second problem was that John was not really a dramatist at all, and for several months the project was also stalled by his simple inability to get on with it. Eventually, it was John Perry who thought of the solution. Terence Rattigan, a frequent weekend guest to whom they had both taken a considerable fancy, was a young dramatist looking for work, and he willingly went ahead unpaid with the actual writing of the adaptation, while John began to engage himself in a still more ambitious project.

The success that he had as Hamlet on Shaftesbury Avenue, following as it did hard upon both the Shakespeare and the Gordon Daviot *Richards*, clearly indicated that another glossy classic would be the obvious thing to do next. Ever since he had directed that first undergraduate *Romeo and Juliet* at Oxford, three years earlier with Peggy Ashcroft and Edith Evans, he had longed to direct them again in a professional production. He also now decided that rather than just play Romeo (as he had already done at the Old Vic and at the Coliseum), it might be rather more of a challenge to alternate Romeo and Mercutio with another star actor, night on, night off.

With this in mind, Gielgud approached one of his very few romantic rivals, Robert Donat, who had the characteristic grace to reply that he had in fact been planning his own *Romeo and Juliet*; this, he said, he was now willing to abandon in view of what he felt was Gielgud's innate superiority in Shakespeare, but he was still not prepared to alternate roles with John. It must have been the year of *Romeo*, because when John approached his second choice of a co-star, Laurence Olivier, it turned out that he too had been planning a production to star himself and his first wife, Jill Esmond. Ivor Novello was also thought to be in the running.

Olivier however was, unlike Donat, prepared to do the whole deal; he would abandon his own production and agree to alternate Romeo and Mercutio with John and, more importantly, under John's direction. There was still just one little calendar problem. John had already contracted to start making a film with Alfred Hitchcock, *The Secret Agent*, at the end of October, which left them by now barely three weeks to get *Romeo* up and running.

Again, John quickly resorted to the Motleys, who with their usual sense of theatrical economy even agreed to convert the sets they had designed for the currently abortive *Tale of Two Cities*, so that in some amazing way the scaffold for the guillotine now became Juliet's balcony. Always a great believer in relying on past strengths, John also repeated the scenic effect from *The Old Ladies* whereby a whole interior scene could be viewed by an audience through windows.

Because they were so tight for time, the production which brought together the two greatest stars of their century for the first and only time on stage got off to an uncertain and rather scrambled start. Years later, Gielgud was to reflect: 'Larry found me far too verse-conscious, and exhibitionist in my acting and directing Shakespeare . . . of course, he was a great exhibitionist himself, but in quite a different way – daring, flamboyant and iconoclastic.' For his part, Olivier admitted that he was 'constantly rebellious against John's power and gifts'. The conflict was understandable enough: Gielgud was only three years older than Olivier, but at this time he was the most famous and respected classical actor in England. Olivier, who had since his schooldays wanted 'to knock their bloody eyes out' with his acting, came from an altogether less theatrically privileged background. And although he, too, had already scored considerable hits at the Royal Court, in the West End, and on Broadway (in *Journey's End* and

The Rats of Norway and *Private Lives*, as well as the controversial closet-homosexual *Green Bay Tree*), he still regarded himself as the defiant outsider: 'I will show them, I will show them, I will show them . . . I'm going to be a simply smashing actor.'

This was not the first time that Olivier and John had worked together: Olivier had played the lover Bothwell in Gielgud's short-lived production of *Queen of Scots* in the previous year, but now, for the only time, they were face to face on stage, and the critics were less than enthusiastic. For the first six weeks Olivier was to play Romeo with John as Mercutio, and though the reviews were excellent for Peggy Ashcroft, Edith Evans and John, Larry's notices were scathing about his 'gabbling inexpertness' while many suggested that he had neither the lyrical voice nor the poetic diction required of a great Romeo.

Olivier's rage and depression at these reviews were such that he even threatened not to play the second night, a threat rapidly defused by Gielgud; but his ire was not assuaged by the knowledge that precisely those qualities he was being accused of lacking were the ones in which John most excelled, and in which he would soon be seen to advantage.

But nothing is ever that simple, and Olivier already had some influential admirers, not least the critic St John Ervine who wrote in the *Observer*: 'I have seen few sights so moving as the spectacle of Olivier's Romeo . . . an impetuous boy, struggling to be articulate. I think Shakespeare's eyes would have shone had he seen this Romeo, young, and ardent and full of clumsy grace.' J.C. Trewin also noted that: 'Olivier almost sprang on the stage, and I can still remember the gasps of admiration around me in the theatre.'

Most interestingly of all, those few American critics reviewing from London all recognised in Olivier the quality that was to ensure that in later years he, rather than Gielgud, had the majority of Broadway and Hollywood hits. Unlike more traditional and conservative local audiences, the Americans recognised that Olivier was emotionally accessible, and came across as a really passionate lover, in a way that Gielgud could never challenge. As for their respective talents, it was a comparatively neutral observer, Alec Guinness, who as usual got it right from the sidelines: 'Olivier did not have a bad way of reciting the verse, it was just a new and very different way to the one which Gielgud had made his own.'

'I wanted,' recalled Olivier, 'at that time to bring a new kind of

1930s reality and earthiness and immediacy to Shakespeare, regardless of the verse, but they all wanted still to hear it musically, and I felt that Johnnie was simply encouraging old-fashioned attitudes.'

Olivier, never the most generous of actors, husbands, fathers or men, was unwilling ever to forgive Gielgud this early, albeit unintentional, victory over him. 'John always had a preoccupation with the beautiful and the poetic at the expense of reality . . . he was always conscious of his gifts, of music and lyricism. At this time I was always the outsider, and John was always the jewel; everything and everybody was in his favour.'

For his part, John was always saddened by Olivier's often overt enmity, but could never really understand it; Gielgud was above all a company man who (while not averse to stardom) took the view that the production mattered rather more than the performance and there was, in his character, a genuine lack of envy or rivalry. Moreover, Shakespeare aside, Olivier and John were seldom up for the same roles, and although Gielgud certainly tired of endlessly being told that he was the best actor in the world from the neck up, and Olivier from the neck down, he genuinely wanted Olivier to succeed and always regretted his failures. The same could not be said in reverse, and indeed in Olivier's memoirs he cannot even bring himself to discuss Gielgud's performance, or his production, of their one great shared stage adventure.

In later years their relationship was to become still more tortured for other reasons. Olivier was never at his best in homosexual company, despite bizarre rumours of very brief backstage homosexual liaisons with the likes of Danny Kaye, and was nearly as quick as his definitive Richard III to believe that plots were being laid against him on all sides. In this instance, his second wife, Vivien Leigh, formed a near-lifelong attachment to Gielgud, and would use him as a refuge and as a sounding-board in the many bleak and black moments of that marriage. Olivier then decided, not perhaps entirely unnaturally, that not only was Gielgud a dangerous rival on stage, but that offstage he was threateningly close to his own troublesome and frequently manic-depressive wife.

These issues are never quite as clear-cut as they may seem, however. Laurence (Laurie) Evans, who was Olivier's production manager on the 1940s film of *Henry V* and then for nearly thirty years agent to both Olivier and John, recalls that Gielgud, too, could behave somewhat treacherously on occasion: 'I never saw evidence of Larry being in any way hostile to John, and he certainly had no problem with homosexuality, unlike Ralph Richardson, who until the 1970s always found John's private life a barrier to real friendship. When I later began negotiating for John, I found him often willing to go back on a deal, or to change his mind about playing a role when contracts were virtually signed. Larry, in my experience, never did that, and I think finally the truth is that Vivien [Leigh] loved John deeply, and that Larry didn't really feel that strongly about him either way.'

When it came time for them to switch the roles, John was just about to start filming for Hitchcock, but he was already more than familiar with Romeo, and Olivier seemed much happier as the boisterous Mercutio, all dash and swagger, and gave what he himself later called, 'a really good music-hall performance'. Indeed, his reviews now were the first really good ones he had ever received in Shakespeare, so good that while he was still playing the role he was invited to star as Orlando in Paul Czinner's film of *As You Like It*, thereby beating Gielgud to the Shakespearean film screen by fully twenty years.

This *Romeo and Juliet* broke all the play's box-office records by running at the New for 189 performances, and John was to recall happier times later in the run: 'Peggy and Larry, Glen [Byam Shaw] and I were always visiting each other's dressing-rooms or congregating in Edith's, which was the largest of them. She herself would sit in the middle of her sofa, dressed up in her voluminous padded garments as the Nurse, and wondering a little what sort of madhouse this was in which she had suddenly found herself.'

Perhaps the best summary of the difference between the two leading men came in retrospect from the critic Herbert Farjeon: 'As Romeo, Mr Olivier was about twenty times as much in love with Peggy Ashcroft's Juliet as Mr Gielgud was. But Mr Gielgud spoke most of the poetry far better than Mr Olivier. Yet, I must out with it, the fire of Mr Olivier's passion carried the play along in a way that Mr Gielgud's could never quite manage.'

The American critic and broadcaster Alexander Woollcott wrote to John:

I came last night to your *Romeo and Juliet*. At intervals, I have been going to see that lovelorn, tear-stained piece since long before you were so much as contemplated. Some of my first Romeos are now either dead, or shuffling, toothless gaffers. Come to think of it, many of them were when they played it. In my country, what usually happens is that some lovely actress suddenly gets the uncontrollable impulse to play Juliet. There is vast publicity, a hasty assemblage of scenery, and then someone remembers at the last moment that they have to have a Romeo, so some unlucky passer-by is flagged into the stage door and plays it as though he obviously had not been expecting to be called upon. One calamitous revival here was assembled rather too hastily by Ethel Barrymore, at a time when she had a vast bust. The public stayed away in droves. Rows and rows of orchestra seats gaped from the dusk of the auditorium. But, as I cruelly observed at the time, the balcony was full.

John's first drama teacher, Lady Benson, who had started her career as Juliet to Henry Irving's Romeo, wrote: 'for once the romance of the play came through perfectly. You are gifted with so beautiful a voice that the love notes are utterly charming. You are also unusually young in the part, and you deserve a high place in our theatre. I am so proud of having once taught you.'

Surprisingly, not only was this the only time in their long and often parallel careers that Olivier was to work with Gielgud on stage, it was also the only time that Olivier would appear in a play with Peggy Ashcroft. Their London run was followed by a long and triumphant tour, but John began to notice a new problem with his own performance: 'The curious thing is that, after you have played Hamlet, it is very hard to go back to Romeo, not only because he is supposed to be a boy of sixteen, which of course no actor ever manages, but also because the part is oddly badly placed within the play. The big banishment scene is inclined to go for nothing after Juliet with her Nurse, and the apothecary scene, in which Irving was always said to have made his name, comes immediately after the lamentation over Juliet's body. Irving, it was said, always cut back Juliet and the Nurse as far as he dared, but in our day the fashion was for restoring all the cuts.'

Intriguingly, some of Olivier's supporters in the great *Romeo* controversy were those who might temperamentally have been thought to side with Gielgud. Ralph Richardson wrote admiringly that: 'When Larry stood under the balcony you knew the whole character of Romeo in a moment, because the pose he took was so natural, so light, so animally correct that you just felt the whole quality of Italy, and of the character of Romeo, and of Shakespeare's impulse.' The director Tyrone Guthrie added that it didn't matter if Olivier never got the measure of the verse, because his performance had such terrific vitality, speed and intelligence, gusto and muscularity.

In the end, this double production did nothing but good for most of its cast, even though it could be argued that Peggy Ashcroft and Edith Evans got rather short critical shift, so eager were critics to compare and contrast the two men. Most importantly for Olivier, the word now spread that for the first time a real classical challenger had arrived on the Shakespearean scene to threaten John's hitherto undisputed lead; and Olivier himself grudgingly admitted, years later, that had it not been for Gielgud, he might never have become a classical actor. For him at least, the challenge was half the fun of the contest.

Ironically, John's new-found fame now meant another change in his private life: Upper St Martin's Lane had to be abandoned when too many autograph-hunters simply moved camp from the stage doors across the road, and John took refuge in the comparative tranquillity of a flat in St John's Wood.

Chapter Nine

❦❦

HAMLET GOES TO BROADWAY
(1935–1937)

By rights I should have been thrilled with the offer to take my Hamlet to Broadway. But my usual feelings of despair soon took over; I was certain that I should be a failure, and, what's more, extremely seasick on the voyage to New York.

N o sooner had an uneasy truce been established between Olivier and Gielgud backstage at the New Theatre, with John G safely back to his Romeo and Olivier cheerfully recast as the swashbuckling Mercutio, than John had to spend all his days honouring his contract to film for Alfred Hitchcock.

With the coming of talking pictures, Hitch had moved effortlessly from silents such as *The Lodger* through semi-talkies such as *Blackmail* to the full sound of *Rich and Strange*, and he was now riding high on the success of *The Thirty-Nine Steps* (1935). Looking for another thriller in this genre, he decided to merge two of Somerset Maugham's Ashenden adventure stories, originally entitled *The Traitor* and *The Hairless Mexican*.

Hitchcock had also developed, in these last years before going to Hollywood, a tradition of using London stage actors as often as possible, not least of course because for them the coming of sound presented no terrors. Thus, for instance, he had already cast Robert Donat (and indeed Peggy Ashcroft as the sinister crofter's wife), in his *The Thirty-Nine Steps*. For what was now to be called *The Secret Agent*, Hitch turned to John Gielgud, at the height of his Shakespearean fame, to play Ashenden himself, an intelligence agent who is assigned to Switzerland to kill a spy, and by mistake kills an innocent tourist instead. Robert Young, later to achieve considerable Hollywood stardom, played the real spy, but the picture was swiftly hijacked from them both by Peter Lorre, already internationally famous as the child-murderer of Fritz Lang's *M* (1931), and now beginning to develop a line of neurotic villains which would see him safely through to the end of his Hollywood career thirty years later.

Gielgud also had some small say in the casting of minor roles here, bringing in the director Michel St Denis to play a bystander and also the veteran Lady Tree, as well as one or two of the sword-carriers from his Old Vic days. This is also the film in which Lilli Palmer made her screen debut, albeit fleetingly.

But John was deeply unhappy with the shooting, as he frequently told two old Westminster schoolfriends, the producer Ivor Montagu and the writer Angus McPhail, both of whom were also now gainfully employed by Gaumont-British Studios at the time when the British film industry was entering one of its most active periods.

John worried that the character of Ashenden, complex and interesting in the Maugham stories, had been reduced to little more than a cypher. He was also terrified of his co-star Madeleine Carroll, who was a creature of film and therefore unlike most of the actresses he knew, and moreover one of those ice maidens always adored by their director. To make things worse, he had to contend with Peter Lorre, also a film animal, and readily experienced in the art of stealing every scene in which he appeared. John's characteristically nervous attempts to befriend Lorre were not made any easier by the fact that after almost every scene they shared, Lorre would rapidly vanish up on to the studio lighting grid, there to inject himself with the morphine to which he had already become deeply addicted.

And Lorre wasn't his only problem, as John explained to an interviewer on the set:

The trouble is, that I don't know the first thing about film acting, although I've always been a terrific film fan. In the days when no respectable people ever went to the pictures, I used to go regularly to that little cinema in Windmill Street, just behind Shaftesbury Avenue, to see all the German and Russian silents. My real problem is that on the stage you are part of a big and rather remote picture, and your defects can be hidden under make-up. You seem much more attractive and heroic than you really are. But on the screen you've got no alibis – every detail is in close-up and the more make-up you wear, the more you emphasise your own defects. Of course, the money is a great inducement; I can make more in six weeks on a film than I can in eighteen months on the stage. Real screen actors like Peter Lorre can come out at any time and joke to their hearts' content, or even make up some dialogue to fill an awkward moment, but we stage actors are terribly bad at doing anything impromptu. And we are so used to three or more weeks' rehearsal that doing something just once, for a take, and knowing it might be on the screen for ever, is really frightening.

But the stage is necessarily limited in scope, whereas film is so much more elastic. Can you imagine, for instance, how thrilled Shakespeare would have been if he could actually have filmed 'the vasty fields of France', instead of having to apologise to his theatre audience for having nothing more than 'this wooden O'? The problem with screen stories at present is that they are made by mass production, so the result is quantity but never quality. Meanwhile, our theatre is being sapped as both actors and writers go to Hollywood in search of better salaries. Producers over here only cast their artists from that very small group of us who have always played Shakespeare; surely they should now be looking at modern actors who may never have done it before, but might be much more interesting?

As for me, I have no wish to risk my stage Shakespearean reputation by appearing in what might be very unsatisfactory film versions of the same plays. I have occasionally had rather vague offers from Hollywood, but it's a long way to go if you are not sure of being successful. For instance, I cannot see how anybody would ever manage to make a totally satisfactory film of *Hamlet*.

Those who have seen the many subsequent attempts, from Olivier through Mel Gibson to Kenneth Branagh, might be inclined to agree. And however chary John might have been about film, he was among the very first stage stars to welcome radio, where he began now regularly to work in new and classic dramas, all the time of course encouraged by his brother Val who, from the very early 1930s, had begun to carve out a notable career as the first great BBC Radio drama director. John was frequently to be heard on the air in *Scenes from Shakespeare*, and then in 1932 he broadcast a two-hour *Othello*, with Peggy Ashcroft as Desdemona and Henry Ainley, one of John's greatest classical heroes, as Iago.

But then again, back at the film studios, Gielgud was not helped by Hitchcock deliberately casting the villain, Robert Young, as far more charming and amusing and attractive than the picture's moody and indecisive hero. Throughout the shooting, Gielgud was also made to feel thoroughly insecure by Hitchcock's usual chilliness on the set ('Actors are cattle,' the director once said, 'and should be treated as such'), and the realisation that with so many other stars around him, all of them more familiar with film, he was unlikely to make much of an impression: 'I also had to lie for several days under iron girders and rubbish for the scene of a train wreck. Another day I sat for hours before a blank screen, while a short length of Lake Como was unrolled before me in "back-projection" . . . a wonderful process, but utterly boring for actors to endure.'

As Hitchcock himself later noted: 'A comparative stranger to the screen, Gielgud was rather on the nervous side, but I think his performance is remarkable when you consider that throughout the whole production he was rushing away every evening to play in *Romeo and Juliet* – and declaiming Shakespeare on the stage is in direct contrast to playing such a matter-of-fact, natural part as that of Ashenden.'

John's recollections were mainly of sheer exhaustion:

While playing on stage every night I had to get up at dawn, and then was always fidgeting by five or six about getting away for the evening performance, which was how I grew so to dislike acting for the screen. Of course, I was paid much more money than in the theatre, but I had the feeling that no one thought I was sufficiently good-looking to be very successful. Hitchcock was naturally inclined to give Madeleine Carroll the best advantage of the camera, while I was seen mostly from the back of my head – which fortunately in those days still had some hair on it . . . Hitchcock was a great joker, and I don't think he had much confidence in my talent as a film actor. When I saw the film I thought I was rather poor, but at least I was not over-acting as grotesquely as I had been in my three or four silents.

At the time, neither Gielgud nor Hitchcock were in fact as generous about each other as in subsequent interviews. On the set, Gielgud once said, 'Hitchcock often makes me feel like a jelly, and I am sick with nervousness,' while Hitchcock responded, 'John's stage experience is of absolutely no use to him here. I have had to make him rub out everything and start again from scratch.'

Considering the tremendous success that another classical actor steeped in Shakespeare, Michael Redgrave, was to have in Hitchcock's *The Lady Vanishes* only two years later, there is no doubt that John missed an opportunity here; but so unhappy was the experience that he did not film again until 1940, and even then it was to be in the character role of Benjamin Disraeli.

As the filming of *The Secret Agent* and the London run of *Romeo and Juliet* were simultaneously coming to an end, in the late spring of 1936, John had a backstage visitor at the New: he was the American producer and director Guthrie McClintic, husband of the great American actress Katharine Cornell. Guthrie's idea was hugely welcome: that John should take his *Hamlet* to New York, with an otherwise all-Broadway supporting cast, among whom would be the Australian actress Judith Anderson and, as Ophelia, the great silent star Lillian Gish, whom Guthrie brought backstage with him:

Lillian was enchantingly dressed in a summer frock with short sleeves, her fair hair crowned with a big white straw hat with black velvet ribbons. When I saw her, I remembered the advertisements that I used to scan so eagerly on the Piccadilly Underground in the old days of silent films – the backs of two little girls, both wearing straw hats with velvet ribbons, and a big question-mark with an intriguing caption underneath: 'Two Little Strangers About Whom All The World Will Soon Be Talking'. When I mentioned this to Lillian at the first meeting, she said that she had been afraid that I would think her too old now for Ophelia, and had dressed the part to make a good impression on me. I felt sure at once that I should enjoy acting with her.

But before he set off for the New World, John had two last commitments to honour: a return to Oxford to direct the OUDS in
Richard II, and a production of *The Seagull* in which he would play
Trigorin under the direction of Komisarjevsky. The Oxford Richard
was to be David King-Wood, who had succeeded George Devine as
president of the OUDS, and the Motleys were again to design the sets,
but this college production was mainly notable for the young actress
whom John imported to play Richard's queen. She was Vivien Leigh,
then just twenty-three and at the start of the affair with Laurence
Olivier that was to end both their first marriages, and establish them
as the starriest couple of the mid-century British stage and screen. This
was also where John began a lifelong friendship with Vivien Leigh, one
that was to outlive her Olivier marriage; like Robert Helpmann and
Noël Coward, he was always to be there for her, even in the depths
of her many manic depressions.

This production was not as remarkable as John's 1932 OUDS *Romeo*,
not least because Vivien Leigh, for all her considerable charm, was no
Peggy Ashcroft, although Michael Denison, an undergraduate of the
time, recalled Leigh descending on Oxford like Zuleika Dobson:

> bringing ecstasy to those undergraduates whose invitations she accepted,
> and anguish to those whom, perforce, she had to refuse. It was in fact
> Glen Byam Shaw who did the donkey work of this production, while
> John, who was still alternating Romeo and Mercutio at the Vic, gave us
> all his Sundays and Mondays till mid-afternoon. What an introduction
> this was for me to the very best in the contemporary theatrical scene,
> and what a privilege to see such professionalism at work, and assess
> how far it all was from the carefree fun of the amateurs. My own share
> in this production was very small, a herald and two minor noblemen
> in unlikely beards, but I was sufficiently involved and exhilarated by
> all I saw around me to know that I need seek no further for a career.

The Times praised Vivien Leigh's stunning beauty, but thought her
'ill at ease with Shakespearean verse', while even the student critic of
Isis called her 'no more than adequate'. For John, the lasting memory
of this production was his decision to cast Max Beerbohm's wife, the
American actress Florence Kahn, as the Duchess of Gloucester: 'She

was a formidable lady, who played the Duchess with an old-fashioned declamatory passion. The unfortunate and very short young under-graduate who was playing John of Gaunt shrank back from her in dismay whenever she started to speak, and I can still see the incom-parable Max, in the wings, shaking with disloyal but irrepressible mirth.'

After these amateur shenanigans, John was able to return to the real theatrical world of *The Seagull*. He had been encouraged to take on the challenge of appearing in this, the first Chekhov ever performed in the West End, by having Komisarjevsky as designer as well as director, and by the granting of an unprecedented budget of £1,000 by their landlord and producer Bronson Albery, whom Komis referred to ever afterwards as 'that tradesman'. Nor did the director endear himself to the cast, on the first day of rehearsal, by delivering a lengthy speech about the dreadful state of the English theatre, with its appalling actors, so completely lacking in style compared to those he had known in Russia.

John, having already played Konstantin, was delighted now to be cast as the older Trigorin, with Stephen Haggard in his original role. He had also persuaded Komis to reassemble several of his *Romeo* company – Edith Evans would play Arcadina, and Peggy Ashcroft was to be Nina.

But this time the real triumph was to be Edith Evans'. 'She dressed the part,' John remembered, 'like a Parisienne, with a high, elegant coiffure, sweeping fashionable dresses, hats and scarves and parasols. On her first entrance she was all smiles and graciousness, but one could see from the angle of her head, as she sat with her back to the audience, watching Konstantin's play, that underneath all the sweetness she was a selfish woman in a very bad temper. Her per-formance was full of the most subtle touches of comedy, alternating with passages of romantic nostalgia.'

Given John's lifelong devotion to Komisarjevsky, and the gathering once again of all his classical clan (Martita Hunt was Masha, George Devine the bailiff and Alec Guinness the silent estate worker who operates Konstantin's curtain), this was a very happy production and most reviews were ecstatic.

Alan Dent wrote that 'Miss Ashcroft has never done anything quite so poignant as this,' while for *The Times* Charles Morgan added, 'Miss Ashcroft's Nina has an enchanting freshness in the early scenes, and her tragic return has the supreme quality not of the coming of a stranger, but the return of a girl we have known changed but not obliterated by suffering, so that what she was is visible always through what she has become.'

For John, the abiding memory of this *Seagull* was of watching Peggy Ashcroft 'with a shawl over her head, sitting alone offstage, working herself up for her entrance in the big hysterical scene at the end of the play'. But Komisarjevsky was at his most irritable, not only because Ashcroft had just left him, but also because he had discovered that she was now starting an affair with the twenty-one-year-old son of the bestselling novelist and author of *The Thirty-Nine Steps*, John Buchan.

In addition to this, there was a certain feeling that the production, although endlessly beautiful, was (in the words of the novelist Francis King) 'not quite naked enough, not quite passionate enough'. *The Times* disagreed: 'This is the first time that Chekhov has been produced on the grand scale. And everything is *de luxe*. People may not want to see this play, but they will want to see this cast, one which achieves an atmosphere of brooding melancholy, alleviated by gleams of humour.'

Another critic wrote of 'an exquisite exhibition of sensitive Gielgudry, his Trigorin pining after Nina as Dante did after Beatrice'. Bernard Shaw, however, remained deeply unimpressed: 'I went to *The Seagull* and disliked it extremely . . . Komisar has lost his old Russian touch. He filled the last act with pauses of the sort that are only bearable in a first act when there is no hurry, and the audience is willing to speculate a little on dumb shows. And anyhow, the dumb shows were unintelligible and uninteresting. Somehow it is all a little too careful, too elaborate, too beautiful. There is no waywardness, no rawness, nothing that is not competent and controlled.'

But for Ivor Brown in the *Observer*, what mattered here was 'the exquisite rhythm of Chekhov's laments for an old way of living, the pattern of the figures in their period clothes, and the tingling sense of a civilisation in its autumn mood, with the winds of winter at the door'.

For John's faithful chronicler Audrey Williamson, however:

> His Trigorin was remarkable, no longer the experienced seducer but a weak, impressionable character absorbed in his work, lazily acquiescent in his comfortable alliance with Arkadina, only to be jolted unexpectedly out of his groove by the fresh, abandoned intensity of Nina's flattering hero-worship . . . Gielgud subtly suggested the man's cultivated distinction, weak vanity and consciousness of being torn apart by forces suddenly outside his own control. His speaking of Trigorin's explanation of the professional life of the writer seemed new-minted from the brain, and in the scene where Arkardina persuades him not to leave her, a futile gesture of the hand illuminated the man's whole tragedy – his Trigorin was always clay in the hands of a stronger personality.

The directors Margaret Webster and Gordon Craig wrote John ecstatic letters about *The Seagull*, as did the actress Marie Tempest. As for Komisarjevsky, writing privately to John: 'I saw many of the early productions of *The Seagull* at the Moscow Art Theatre, and I can honestly say that yours is by far the best Trigorin. We still need to make some improvements in the pace, but when we have I think we will have achieved a perfect production, and I feel very happy to have been associated with you again – this is not flattery.'

Komis was also eager to clear himself of critical charges that he had made his production far too elegant: 'What do English critics know? I saw with my own eyes the original productions of the Moscow Art Theatre, and they were always very beautiful.' He was to comment rather more waspishly to a friend, 'Of course the trouble with John and Edith now is that they are so famous they only want to play themselves.'

Before starting to work on the Broadway *Hamlet*, John G and John Perry took a short holiday in the south of France. With John's lifelong aversion to driving, John Perry took the wheel as they went down towards Nice, and rented an old farmhouse with a vine-covered verandah and a swimming pool. There they were joined by Guthrie McClintic and his Broadway designer, Jo Mielziner. John was already eager to get as far away as possible from the memory of the last great

New York Hamlet, John Barrymore, almost a decade earlier, and they settled for the idea of scenery and costumes heavily influenced by Rembrandt.

John's holiday was however rather spoiled by the fact that he was already getting increasingly nervous about his first starring role in New York, especially because only Harry Andrews and Malcolm Keen were to join him in what would otherwise be, apart from Judith Anderson, an all-American cast. Keen had first played Claudius to John Barrymore's London Hamlet, and Harry Andrews was initially cast as Fortinbras, only to graduate to Horatio (and $10 more a week) when an American actor was fired early on the road.

John sailed over on the *Normandie*, and was immediately interviewed on the New York dockside by an alarmingly large number of reporters, sent there by McClintic to drum up some early *Hamlet* bookings:

They asked me at once what I thought of New York, and at the time, of course, I had almost nothing to say. But looking back I am still stimulated by the unpredictable, electric liveliness of the city, despite the extremes of heat and cold, cramped taxis and sweltering buses, the squalor of the subways, the steam-heat and air-conditioning, the friendliness and politeness and occasional rudeness, the foreignness, mixed with familiarity. I love the brilliant qualities of the New York lights, from twinkling towers as they begin to glitter on Central Park South round six o'clock on a winter evening, and the strip of sky which one can always see in four directions, even from the deep canyons of the Avenues. The vista of Fifth Avenue from St Patrick's Cathedral to the Plaza Hotel is to me one of the finest sights in the world . . . American theatres dismayed me at first, with their extreme width of auditorium and shallow stages – no bars or proper lounges (save for those cavernous, over-heated cellars with queues lining up for the single telephone in the intervals) and the very disagreeable men who tear up one's ticket as one passes through the doors in the narrow entrance-halls.

And yet, the sense of expectation in an American audience – especially at matinées when the women predominate, screaming and waving greetings across the aisles and wildly applauding every entrance and exit, song or dance – is wonderfully infectious and finally rewarding, both for actors and spectators alike, and infinitely preferable to the scene in London, where trays of tea are shuffled in and out over people's heads, and elderly ladies sit munching with dogged indifference, often slumbering and even snoring as the afternoon wears on.

Having only appeared once on Broadway (in the unsuccessful 1928 *The Patriot*), John was delighted to be back eight years later in considerably starrier and more luxurious circumstances. There was just one little problem: Leslie Howard, already a far bigger star than John on that side of the Atlantic, had also suddenly announced a forthcoming *Hamlet*, and at first John decided not to risk the competition. Howard had just filmed *Romeo and Juliet* opposite Norma Shearer (a role for which Gielgud had declined even to test, on the grounds that he could not leave the theatre for Hollywood) and although this had been disastrously reviewed by most critics, he had somehow managed to escape fairly lightly, not least because he had already established a strong Broadway career quite apart from such successful films as *Of Human Bondage*, *The Scarlet Pimpernel* and *The Petrified Forest*. Although the son of Hungarian immigrants, Howard was now known to stage and screen audiences on both sides of the Atlantic as the perfect English gentleman, and his profile was, even more than John's, classically well suited to the noble Prince.

But Gielgud was eventually persuaded by McClintic that Howard could still be successfully challenged when it came to Shakespearean intellect, knowledge and verse-speaking, and the reckoning was that the supposed rivalry might even be very good news at the box-office in terms of publicity. For a while, it looked as though Howard was going to withdraw from the race, but like John he was eventually persuaded by his managers to take up the challenge.

To calm John's considerable nervousness, McClintic had agreed to open their *Hamlet* in Toronto, thereby allowing Gielgud to play himself in somewhere safely removed from the New York critics. As so often with John, however, the first rehearsals had been something of a disaster. The formidable Judith Anderson, playing Gertrude, had gone to considerable trouble to have her hair elaborately dyed and styled for the role. 'Why not just wear a wig?' asked John, with his usual tact. 'It would look so much better, and be a lot less trouble.'

He spent the rest of the rehearsals desperately trying, first, not to put his foot in it again and, second, to adjust his performance until it matched those of the others who were, of course, considerably less experienced. There was also, as usual, the problem of John's fencing; he was arguably, and by his own admission, the worst fencer ever to play Shakespeare, and in London he had already managed to wound, quite seriously, Glen Byam Shaw in *Hamlet*, and Geoffrey Toone in *Romeo and Juliet*. In America, he was unwisely entrusted with a real Elizabethan sword, though on this occasion – for a change – it was he who sustained a nasty gash in his arm, thereby missing three or four days of rehearsal.

The Toronto try-out, in a climate far colder than any John had ever known, was, however, hugely successful, and it was here that the American critic Rosamund Gilder (long-time editor of the great *American Theatre Arts* magazine) first started to make the backstage notes that were to result in a book called *John Gielgud's Hamlet*, the first and one of the very few of its kind ever to be entirely devoted to a single production. Published in 1937 by the Oxford University Press, it takes us, across more than two hundred pages, scene by scene through the play, describing, in the most intimate and informed and intelligent and intricate detail, precisely where John stood on the stage at any moment, and exactly how he delivered the text. It is, perhaps, the most remarkably detailed account of any one actor in any one role that has ever been printed, and John himself added a lengthy, scholarly essay on the history of the play, commenting on other Hamlets that he had himself seen (such as those of Raymond Massey and Laurence Olivier), as well as delving back into his beloved theatre history to quote everyone from Sarah Bernhardt to Henry Irving on the trials and tribulations of this, the greatest of all classical roles.

It is of course to be regretted that (unsurprisingly in 1936) no film or radio record of this production was ever made, but the book, though shamefully out of print these many years, has detailed drawings and photographs, not just of the actors, but also of the sets and costumes. To read it is, even now, to come as close as has ever been possible to watching John at the height of his Shakespearean powers.

Another insight into John's character and spirit at this time comes from a series of long letters, hitherto unpublished, which he wrote from Canada to his mother, back in London:

We had two dress-rehearsals on Tuesday, with the usual hitches and disasters because the scenery was not ready . . . however the first night went very well, but last night I played abominably – bad anti-climax and exhausting in consequence. It is very difficult to judge the production now it is finished; I hate a lot of it, especially as they have no music at all. The Polonius is poor, and the Rosencrantz and Guildenstern rotten, Horatio only so-so, and the Sentinels and Fortinbras really terrible. This makes it all the harder for me, and what is maddening is that I know if I was the director, and had a few hours with them, I could bully them all into giving me something of what I want . . . outwardly I remain enthusiastic about everything and everybody, so that when I want my own way desperately about some scene, they all agree with a good grace. When McClintic has good actors (Gish, Anderson, and even old Malcolm Keen) he does very well by them, but of course the rest are cheap and inexperienced, and he hasn't the knowledge or experience to teach them how to speak Shakespeare . . . Toronto is a one-horse town, rather like the ones we used to see in early films; I keep expecting cowboys to ride past the theatre shooting their guns.

While they were still in Toronto, Leslie Howard opened his production in Boston, but as he had opted for a longer tour it was John who, by six weeks, was the first to open as Hamlet in New York. A decade or so earlier, John had in fact been briefly employed in London to understudy Howard in a revival of *Berkeley Square*, an assignment he rapidly quit in rehearsal, but now the two men were locked into what Broadway theatre columns eagerly called the Battle of the Hamlets, and John was only mildly amused to find cab drivers asking him, 'So, which Hamlet are you, buddy?'

Contrary to popular belief, John did not open to universally good reviews; Noël Coward led the cheers of the audience at a very glitzy first night, but the following morning the two most important papers at the time, the *New York Times* and *The New York Herald*, were surprisingly cool. McClintic had gone for a very traditional production, but John's view of the minor casting was less than flattering: 'They all seemed cheap and rather inexperienced, and I hadn't the heart to try and teach them how to do it. It would have made me seem so arrogant and English.' Nearly twenty years later, he was to make the same mistake during the filming of *Julius Caesar*, when although James Mason and Marlon Brando begged him to share his expertise, he was again too shy and embarrassed to do so for fear of seeming better at it than they were, which of course in this instance he was.

The word of mouth was initially much better than many of the *Hamlet* reviews, but it wasn't until Howard opened to a catastrophic press six weeks later that John's supremacy and success were finally confirmed, and he was seen to have won the battle. Indeed, at Christmas they even had to move from the Empire to a larger theatre (the St James's) to accommodate the crowds of people who were by now trying to get in. Old friends over from London and new friends from New York thronged John's dressing-room every night: among them Emlyn Williams, then also working on Broadway, and Mrs Patrick Campbell, who sent round a note before the performance reading: 'I am in front tonight. Give me the beauty I long for!' She was not, however, hugely impressed by the closet scene. As she told a somewhat abashed Judith Anderson, 'A great mistake to sit on the bed, dear. Only housemaids sit on beds.'

Comparing the two productions, the critic John Mason Brown felt that Howard had a better set, but that 'unlike Mr Gielgud's, Mr Howard's performance can scarcely be described as an interpretation – it avoids what lies behind the lines, where Mr Gielgud is always eager to let us see everything.'

Gielgud was now the toast of the town; Alexander Woollcott, who had given up his high-rated radio show a couple of years earlier, went back on the air for one night, expressly to enthuse about John, and other backstage visitors now included the Lunts, Helen Hayes, Ruth Gordon, Katharine Cornell, Burgess Meredith and the playwright Thornton Wilder (*Our Town*), whom John memorably described as 'a funny, little, nervous man, like a dentist turned professor, shy at first and then suddenly incoherently explosive, like a soda siphon'.

John had never known anything like this: the crowds at the stage door, the hundreds of fan letters and the applause whenever he went into a restaurant were something quite new to an actor who, in London, was already in some danger of being taken for granted. In New York he was not only the new boy in town, but also the greatest Shakespearean turn since Barrymore. As John wrote to his mother:

It is all very exhausting, but immensely gratifying. We are playing to new house records of $21,000 a week, and sometimes we have three hundred people standing, even at the matinées. I have had countless messages and backstage visitors – Mrs Pat, Helen Hayes, Stravinsky, Gloria Swanson, Dorothy Parker and Elsa Maxwell. Helen Hayes told Mrs Pat in my dressing-room that she wore her years like a crown, a compliment Mrs Pat as usual spoiled by asking, 'Is it on straight, dear?' I have really seen very little of New York, as whenever I am not playing I am trying to help Rosamund Gilder with her book which will, I think, be a really detailed account of my performance. A Negro has done a brilliant bust of me in the play, which I have bought – he only saw the play once and I only sat for ten minutes, but it is a really remarkable likeness. It is so good to have your letters and Father's and I really am enjoying myself, especially now that the gash in my arm has healed. I miss you all, and of course John [Perry] very much.

I see a lot of Emlyn (who is also playing here), with his wife and an enchanting new baby. Our flats, or apartments as they call them, all seem rather big and dark, but I keep being taken out to lunch, the other day by Maxwell Anderson, one of their most important authors out here, who wants me to do his new play about Rudolph of Austria; but it's all written in ponderous blank verse, so I am going to turn it down. The weather here is loathsome – warm and muggy and torrents of rain, and although I am longing for John P to come for Christmas I am already afraid of how homesick I shall feel when he leaves. Harry Andrews and I are both beginning to feel that we can't wait to come home, and in our spare time we have had to nurse Peggy through a very difficult first night.

Peggy Ashcroft was making her Broadway debut in Maxwell Anderson's *High Tor*, in which she was cast as a three-hundred-year-old Dutch ghost called Lisa, engaged in a somewhat tenuous love affair with a young landowner on a rock above the Hudson River. Ashcroft, characteristically, had started an immediate and tempestuous affair with her co-star Burgess Meredith, who later idly wondered whether, had he married her, he could have had a totally different career in the British theatre as 'Sir Burgess'. He was, however, at this time married to Paulette Goddard, and in order to keep their affair secret, Ashcroft took care to be photographed more often with John G than with her new lover. Unfortunately, these nights on the town with John led at least one New York showbiz columnist to announce that Gielgud was himself about to marry her.

This caused considerable surprise, not only to them, but also to Lilian Baylis, their Old Vic mentor back in London: 'I could not be more surprised,' declared Baylis, 'than if Oxford won the Boat Race.'

Perhaps trying to dampen any hopes his parents might have had in this area, John's letters home dealt only with Peggy Ashcroft's health, and that of his parents:

You don't say anything in your letters about how you are – I do hope you and Father are taking care of yourselves. Last weekend Peggy and I went to stay with the McClintics in their wonderful country house – in front of a log fire with the rain pouring down outside, we listened to the news from Europe about the Spanish situation [the Civil War], which nobody here, including me, seems to understand. I miss all the news from London, and have had to give up smoking and drinking as I have an awful cold, but I have been offered $1,000 to do a speech from *Hamlet* on the *Rudy Vallee Radio Hour*, all made up and dressed, in front of a studio audience, so naturally I turned it down. I hear, however, that Reggie Gardiner is doing a parody of me as Hamlet in the new Bea Lillie revue, and they tell me that is a sure sign that I have arrived. Poor Leslie Howard is really having a terrible time; one critic said he was 'more an antique Romeo than a Dane', and another said that I could cross the Giel out of my name and just be known as the 'Gud Hamlet'. The trouble is that I have so many English friends in his cast, that I suspect I may become very unpopular with them.

Whatever potential embarrassments this may have set in train, Gielgud

Family Album, 1912: Kate Gielgud with her four children,
Lewis (standing), Val (right), John and Eleanor (seated).

John feeding the chickens (1907); with his sister Eleanor in family charades (1912); and the four Gielgud children with their father Frank, and Lewis now in World War One uniform (1915)

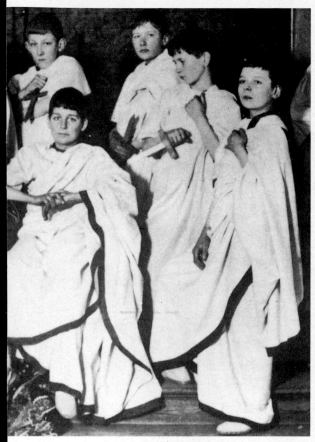

John (right) in his first major prep-school role as Mark Antony

John at 16 in an amateur open-air *As You Like It*

His great-aunt Ellen Terry circa 1890: 'with a family background like mine, I was hardly likely to go into the fish trade'

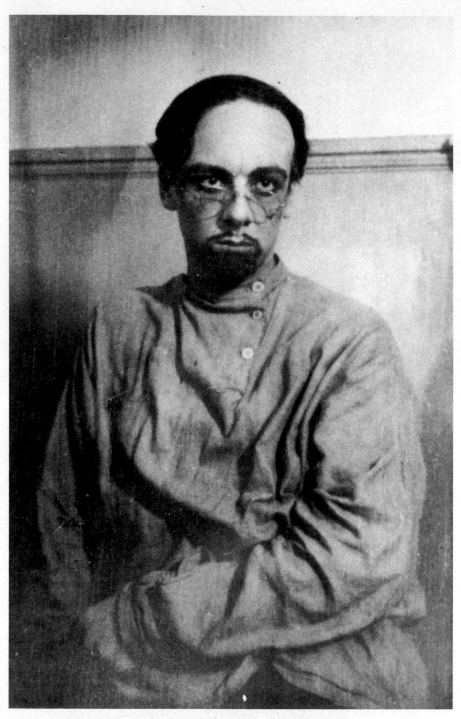

Trofimov in the 1925 Oxford Playhouse *The Cherry Orchard*,
made up to look strikingly like his brother Val.

Konstantin in *The Seagull*, Little Theatre 1925: 'I like to think I helped establish Chekhov for London audiences, who had hitherto found him foreign and somehow forbidding'

Replacing Noel Coward in *The Constant Nymph* in 1926, less than two years after he had understudied Coward in *The Vortex*

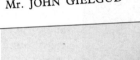

NOTICE

———

Owing to the sudden indisposition of

Mr. NOEL COWARD

the part of "Lewis Dodd" will be

played at this performance by

Mr. JOHN GIELGUD

'Baylis was a fearful old bat and often talked rubbish, but it was at her Old Vic that I really made my Shakespearian reputation as Romeo (with Adele Dixon as Juliet), Hamlet and Richard II, all for rather less than 25 pounds a week'

The Matinee Idol of the late 1920s and 1930s: 'I was photographed, painted, caricatured and interviewed: I signed my autograph a dozen times a day, with only close relatives to remind me that my walk was as bad as ever, and my diction both slovenly and affected'

Another of his signature roles: John Worthing, first played at the
Lyric Hammersmith in 1930

was to recall two mortifying backstage visits that actually occurred during the run. The first was the occasion Maria Ouspenskaya, the great Russian tragedienne who was now making a late-life Hollywood success, was announced at the stage door.

> She came into the dressing-room, a formidable and striking personality with a long cigarette holder in her hand, looking immensely distinguished and escorted by an elegant young man who leaned gracefully against the wall behind her. 'Oh, Madame Ouspenskaya,' I burst out, clutching my dressing-gown around me and wondering if I ought to kiss her hand, 'I am so sorry to think that you were in front tonight. I was dreadfully tired and I know I played so badly.' At this, Madame nodded her head twice, in profound agreement, turned around and left the room without a word.
>
> On another evening, Judith Anderson brought a friend of hers round to see me, a Swedish countess beautifully bejewelled and dressed. She seemed greatly moved by my performance, and as she was leaving, murmured, 'I would like to give you something in remembrance of this great experience.' At that, putting out her hand, she began to take off a most beautiful square-cut emerald ring that she was wearing. I, nervously, began to put out my own hand, but just as I did so, she hastily drew her ring back on to her finger and made a graceful exit.

Several local hostesses and theatre groups tried to bring Gielgud and Howard together while they were on Broadway, but they both behaved with admirable discretion, declining to see each other's productions and merely exchanging courteous first-night telegrams, as John wrote to his mother: 'Leslie Howard closed his *Hamlet* last night with his usual twenty-minute speech at the end, denouncing his critics. He has bluffed very cleverly, and appeared a great deal on the radio, and giving club lectures, which I am refusing to do. He has not been especially dignified over his failure, and I am glad to have avoided meeting him, though some people say he crept in to one of our matinées wearing dark glasses.'

By contrast, on 5 January 1937 John broke the Barrymore record of 101 performances, to become the all-time longest-running Broadway

Hamlet. On that night, for the very first time, he made a curtain speech. That record was to stand until 1964, when it was in its turn broken by Richard Burton, ironically in a production of which John was both the director and the Ghost. Gielgud himself was not to give up the role until well into the Second World War, and when he returned to London in 1937 to find Olivier playing it at the Vic, he went backstage to offer not only polite congratulations but also the sharp warning that 'This is still *my* role.'

At the end of the New York run, McClintic was eager to make some more money on the road, and John agreed to a brief tour, one that took him to Washington where they played before the President's wife, Mrs Eleanor Roosevelt, who seemed, thought John, 'gracious, if a bit vague – a very plain, keen-faced woman with a rather grating laugh'. On the road as in New York, Gielgud was getting almost a hundred fan letters every week, but one in Washington must have been especially welcome. It came from an old Catholic priest, Father Dawson Byrne:

> Before becoming a priest, I was an actor for more than forty years, playing over three hundred productions, all over America. In that time I played with many great actors and saw the best of them – Henry Irving, Tree, E.H. Sothern and John Barrymore. But never had I seen a real Hamlet until I saw yours this week. You were made for the part. You are ideal, and your acting excels all others. You are still very young, and I have in my mind the thought that Ellen Terry must have trained you from your infancy to play Hamlet, otherwise I cannot see how you could give such a reading of the part, but I advise you to take great care of your health: you put so much energy and emotion into the role that it must leave you totally exhausted. Thank you for the best performance of my long life.

The broadcaster Albert Payson Terhune wrote: 'My Hamlet memories go back to Edwin Booth, whom I often saw in the role. He played it with almost no make-up and wearing his own hair. Irving's Hamlet was more mannered and less tremendous than Booth's, although Irving's Shylock was infinitely better. Since then I have seen them all – Tree's, played in a yellow wig and beard, Sarah Bernhardt's, which was ghastly except in her scenes with Polonius, Barrymore's, Sothern's and Walter Hampden's. If a tired old man may say so without fulsomeness, yours turns all of theirs to water.'

Following this extraordinary reaction to his interpretation of Shakespeare, John suggested to McClintic that, after their triumph in *Hamlet*, it might be clever to go on to the *Richard II* which he had already made his own in London. McClintic was horrified: 'A pansy King will never go down well in America,' was his brief reply, before urging John to continue the *Hamlet* tour. In the event it was Maurice Evans who made his name on Broadway with *Richard II* and John, on his way home, crept into the back of the New York theatre feeling somewhat embittered as the cheering began to ring out.

In another of John's weekly letters home to his mother at this time, he wrote:

In what little spare time I have, I am reading a very technical but fascinating new book about acting by Stanislavsky. Like Komis and Michel [St Denis] and of course Uncle Ted [Gordon Craig], he really is trying to revolutionise the theatre, and I feel very proud that in some way I have been able to associate myself with what they are all attempting.

Yesterday I had lunch with Mrs Pat, who is, I fear, now very mad, living in Hollywood most of the time but grand and majestic as ever, and of course quarrelling with everyone as usual. Aleck Woollcott told me that she was like a sinking ship, firing on all her rescuers, which I thought very good. Everyone here is getting very hysterical about the Abdication crisis. I took Mrs Pat to see the Laughton film of *Rembrandt* on Friday, and afterwards we went to the Plaza Hotel and heard the King's farewell broadcast very distinctly. Mrs Pat kept saying it reminded her of *Antony and Cleopatra* but I just feel so sorry for the man and wonder what kind of life he will be able to lead. His frankness and obvious sincerity play very well over here, and it is a pity that the old men of the Church and state will now be crowing over their triumph. No wonder Edward was made bitter and cynical after going through the war and then finding that nothing had really changed. I don't think this business will send anyone flocking back to the Church.

Towards the end of the Broadway run there had been some good news from home. John had been attempting to sue Gaumont-British for an outstanding but disputed £500 in his contract for *The Secret Agent*, and the studio now settled out of court. When John heard of this, he wrote to his mother:

> This was an unexpected pleasure, so in a fit of extravagance I went out and bought a charming water-colour for myself by Dufy for £300. It is the square at Versailles, with the Roi Soleil on his horse in the foreground, and looks so well in my rented room. Dufy is thought a lot of just now, and his pictures are all the rage.
>
> A fat pianist called Copland, who looks like James Agate and plays Spanish music, gave a very good performance for me at a dinner party which had been especially arranged in my honour. On Sunday night there was another dinner in my honour at the Players' Club – delightful telegrams from Barrymore and Forbes-Robertson and wonderful speeches about me from the British consul and Maurice Evans and Cedric Hardwicke. It really was all very moving, and I wish you could have been here to see the love and respect in which they all hold our family. They really are mad about the British theatre, and seem to know as much about it as we do. John Barbirolli was also there, a nice little man, much thrilled by working with American orchestras.
>
> I have at last got rid of all my colds and am just beginning, now it almost time to leave, to appreciate New York – bridges, river, skyscrapers and sky just like the ones we have all seen in films. It is funny to meet film stars like Ruth Chatterton and Kay Francis in the flesh, though they are never as interesting as in their films. Mrs Pat came again to the play last night, and wanted to know afterwards why Hamlet had a Jewish mother with her bosoms falling out, which I don't think would have pleased Judith Anderson. I am sending you some photographs, which I hope give you some idea of the set and costumes.

This new-found, if rather belated, discovery of Manhattan social life led him to use his usually buried skills as a pianist to entertain fellow party-goers – something one associates more with Noël Coward than with John G: 'Just before we closed in New York Elsa Maxwell, the famous cosmopolitan party queen, gave a party – I went there and played jazz till nearly 3 a.m. by which time my thumbs were nearly scraped off. It was a thoroughly bizarre affair – we were told to come in barnyard fancy dress, and they had real animals, cows, sheep and goats, in cages around the ballroom. At midnight, six hogs rushed into the room, but I found it all rather unedifying.'

John was present when Coward played the piano on another occasion, but didn't enjoy that much, either. He was luckier with Coward's stage partner, Gertrude Lawrence, who was appearing with him on Broadway in the nine plays that made up Coward's *Tonight at 8.30*: 'I went to see Noël doing one of his midnight cabarets, but they were all songs I had heard before. On one spectacular night last week, for a charity pageant, Gertie Lawrence appeared as Day and I as Night, she on a white horse and I on a black. Amazingly, they behaved very well, and I just about managed not to fall off.'

John had an ambivalent approach to the festive season around Broadway, again best expressed in his letters home:

Christmas here was very strange and wonderful – the city very gay and pretty, but absurdly warm, like late spring. I have never seen such decorations – laurel wreaths with red ribbons on every door, and dozens of lighted Christmas trees in the windows of restaurants, hotels and churches. I can hardly move in my flat or dressing-room for the cards, flowers and presents – I shall need a crate to bring them all home, especially as I have been buying lots of records and books. This afternoon, Mrs Pat took me to see Edward Sheldon, who wrote one or two famous American plays before being stricken with blindness and an appalling, petrifying paralysis. All the well-known stage people go to see him and act scenes from plays for him. He lies on a bed like a catafalque, his head bent right back, unable to move his limbs, a black bandage over his eyes. But he is beautifully shaved, wears a collar and tie, and talks to you with consummate ease and charm, as if he had known you all your life. He has all the papers read to him, and knows everything about Broadway; he is entirely composed, alive, and yet removed from life, like some extraordinary human oracle. Though the spectacle is so painful and appalling, when you think of the incredible courage of it afterwards, the man himself is so magnificently powerful in his conquest that one longs to give him all the life and vitality he craves, and accept his philosophy and wisdom with wonder and awe. Like Mrs Pat, Helen Hayes, Kit Cornell and the others, I am going to read Shakespeare to him, as that seems to be what he likes best.

New Year's Eve, on the other hand, was perfectly horrible. Our theatre is on the main Broadway street, and the hooters and penny whistles began almost as soon as we were under way, and never stopped all evening – not a pleasant accompaniment for *Hamlet*. I have, however, survived very well, the only one of my company not to get 'flu. Yesterday Lillian Gish took me out to Helen Hayes' country place at Nyack. An amazing house with gold-encrusted pelmets, marble fireplaces and an extraordinary number of Renoirs and Vlamincks and Chiricos.

He was by now being inundated with offers to go to Hollywood at the height of the period when English actors were most in demand out there, not least for their voices and their ability to play something other than cowboys or criminals. But his experience with Hitchcock had so discouraged his hopes of ever becoming a film star anywhere that John swiftly ended the tour and returned to London, there to direct and star in a brand-new play, written especially for him by Emlyn Williams. It was, somewhat unfortunately for modern sensibilities – though not of course those of the time – to be called *He Was Born Gay*, a doubly tricky title considering the private lives of its two leading figures.

Chapter Ten

❧❦❧

GIELGUD AND COMPANY
(1937–1938)

My experiences at the Old Vic had already made me a firm
believer in the importance of a permanent company. The
only question in my mind was whether I could make it work
commercially in the West End.

He Was Born Gay dramatised the tragedy of the 'lost' son of
Louis XVI, supposedly brought up in England following the
French Revolution, only to come out of hiding at the time of
Waterloo, whereupon, disguised as a music teacher, he finds two other
men claiming to be him, both determined to prevent his return to a
reborn royalist France. John and Emlyn Williams co-directed, with
John as the real Dauphin, and Williams as one of the impostors. In
rehearsal, and even on the road, this looked promising enough, but
when it came in to the Queen's, they ran up against some savage
notices, not least from Charles Morgan on *The Times* who reviewed
it with 'an embarrassed, incredulous and uncomprehending blush.
What made Mr Williams write this play, or Mr Gielgud play it, will
never be understood.'

He Was Born Gay only survived twelve West End performances, and
Williams finally worked out what had gone so wrong: 'I had meant
it to be the study of a romantic, historical personage in very ordinary
circumstances, but he remained a character of tragedy, both vague and
unconvincing, while the people around him seemed to have stepped
out of a modern farce.'

John took this failure very hard, coming as it had so swiftly after

149

the greatest triumph of his life with the Broadway *Hamlet*; but the flop made him reconsider his whole career. He was now just thirty-three, and could be said to have achieved his initial ambition: he was beyond doubt the leading classical actor of his generation, and nothing that Olivier was still doing at the Vic had really threatened his leadership. But, with that leadership, there now came real problems; as Olivier and Redgrave and Richardson, his only real challengers, all began at relatively early ages to sign lucrative long-term film contracts with Alexander Korda, John remained convinced that option remained closed to him. What he wanted was quite simply to continue in stage classics, because his own experience with new plays, from *He Was Born Gay* back to *The Old Ladies* and *Noah*, had been far from happy.

On the other hand, the classics at this time were really only available to him if he returned to the Old Vic. And although money for himself was never an issue, he was painfully aware that the Waterloo Road budget would never allow him the freedom to develop his Shakespearean ideas any further. Like a student leaving college, Gielgud had now graduated from the Old Vic, and there was to be no going home.

In his private life, the relationship with John Perry, although still comfortable, had begun to lose any real sexual energy, while in his professional life he had reached a point where he had simply run out of mentors. With Gordon Craig maintaining a chilly distance, and Komisarjevsky now living in America, the great radical gurus of his earlier years had begun to fall away, and John was now too established to need the help of his original Old Vic teachers. At this precise moment he wrote to Harley Granville-Barker, now living and teaching in America but still the man who, with Bernard Shaw, had first revolutionised the Court, asking essentially how he could move not only his career but the whole idea of classical theatre forward in London.

Granville-Barker's characteristically thoughtful reply served to clarify at least some of the issues that John had raised:

> You are distracted by rival aims: one, which is really forced on you, has to do with your personal career; the other has to do with the establishing of the kind of theatre without which your career will not

be all you proudly wish it to be. This was Irving's dilemma; he clung on to one horn of it for many glorious years, then he was impaled on the other and it killed him. Beerbohm Tree would have died bankrupt had it not been for *Chu Chin Chow*. George Alexander felt that all he had achieved was paying salaries every Friday night without fail. The question is now, have times changed? Could you hope to establish, if not a blessed National Theatre (names mean nothing), at least a company like that of Stanislavsky or even Max Reinhardt? Could there be some kind of compromise? Everyone in England always likes this, just because they are English. All I can really tell you is this: don't expect to pick more than a few grapes from the thistles, and don't expect them always to be of the best quality.

While taking Barker's rather gloomy advice to heart, John realised now that if he was, with the Motleys, to progress his ideas as a director, and to play the rest of the great roles in the canon, he would have to form his own company on Shaftesbury Avenue. Accustomed as we now have become to forty years of the National Theatre and the Royal Shakespeare Company, it is almost impossible to conceive how revolutionary John's idea was for the West End of 1937, where there had simply been nothing like it since the heyday of Henry Irving and the actor-managers more than fifty years earlier. Certainly there had been, in the interim, modern companies run in their own theatres by the likes of Gerald du Maurier and Gladys Cooper, but these had seldom if ever focused on any kind of a classical repertoire, and the general feeling in these late 1930s was that this kind of highbrow thing was best left to occasional London visits by the Comédie Française from Paris.

The first issue to be resolved was that of the National Theatre itself. At the turn of the century a publisher called Effingham Wilson had begun to campaign for such a building, and several foundation stones had already been laid in various parts of west London, without, unfortunately, anything above them. In June 1937 Leon Quartermaine, who was to join John's first permanent company, had written urging him to open a National Theatre as 'the only member of our profession who could possibly do so'. That was easier said than done, and it was in fact to be almost another forty years before Olivier finally realised the dream. In the meantime, John published in the *Daily Telegraph* a kind of manifesto. 'Britain's National Theatre,' he wrote, 'should not waste money on a vast new building; it should not limit itself to just Shakespeare and popular hits, and, thirdly, it should unite Sadler's Wells, the Old Vic, and the Stratford Memorial Theatre as interchangeable companies, all of whom would form a part of the National.'

Surprisingly, there was already a National Theatre committee, made up of the great and the good, but as usual without many actual artists. This committee, which had so far failed to raise any kind of a budget or a building, now saw John as an awkward, external troublemaker, and published a reply demanding that the first priority should indeed be the building of a 'Temple of Drama'.

At that point the whole matter was returned to limbo and, seeing no action there, John decided to invest £5,000 of his own money, virtually all his New York profits from *Hamlet*, and another £5,000 of John Perry's family legacy in forming a company which would present four classical plays at the Queen's Theatre, each to be given an unprecedented seven to nine weeks of rehearsal. Peggy Ashcroft, with whom John had formed a firm offstage friendship the previous winter in New York, was to be the leading lady. Around them both, Gielgud managed to build a company of amazing strength, consisting very largely of people with whom he had already worked, and in some cases those he had actually discovered.

Alec Guinness was to be among them, and George Devine, Glen Byam Shaw, Harry Andrews, the young Michael Redgrave and Dennis Price; John was also careful once again also to include such comparatively veteran talents as those of Harcourt Williams and George Howe, and the budget would even allow for 'guest stars' such as Glen's wife Angela Baddeley and Gwen Ffrangcon-Davies to come in for one production only.

Having established his team, John decided they should play safe by opening with *Richard II*, though this was to be followed by *The School For Scandal*, *The Three Sisters*, and *The Merchant of Venice*. Rehearsals got off to a traditionally uneasy start when John was reminiscing about his triumphant New York *Hamlet* to the new company: 'Of course, I had a really terrible Horatio . . . Oh, it was you, Harry, isn't it wonderful how much better you've got since?' As Andrews had barely had time to come home, unpack and start with the new company, he was perhaps less than thrilled with Gielgud's attempted retrieval of yet another brick.

But there was now a great deal more at stake than just another opening of another Shakespearean show. John was betting his savings, and his reputation, on an ensemble the like of which had simply never been seen in the West End in the twentieth century. Each production was to run for between eight and ten weeks, and the team of directors was to include not only Gielgud himself but also Tyrone Guthrie and Michel St Denis, both of whom had already established their reputations as among the most adventurous and unpredictable directors in town. What the critic Harold Hobson was to call 'One of the rarest blazes of theatrical light this century' started with Peggy Ashcroft ('the Spring Queen of her time', as Anthony Quayle said) playing the Queen to John's Richard. And although he was the producer, director and star of this first production, he was now determined, because of his company ethic, to make this revival very different from the usual solo-star show it had been when he previously played the role in both its Shakespeare and Gordon Daviot interpretations.

Thus Michael Redgrave, who had only recently come into the theatre from being a public-schoolmaster, was encouraged to prove a formidable Bolingbroke:

> I felt proud to be a member of such a company; Gielgud himself was only three or four years my senior, but he had been a leading actor for more than a decade while I was still a newcomer. Indeed, when I played Richard at Stratford, fourteen years later, many critics thought they could find traces of Gielgud in my performance. I do not see how it could have been otherwise – if you have seen a performance which you consider definitive, you cannot help but be influenced by it. Even at the first reading, John was as near perfect as I could wish or imagine. Ninety per cent of the beauty of his acting was the beauty of his voice, and to this day I can see no way of improving on the dazzling virtuosity of the phrasing or breathing which was Gielgud's.

Ironically, while by night Redgrave was making his name as a comparatively junior member of Gielgud's company, by day he was doing precisely what John had a few years earlier so signally failed to manage – successfully working for Alfred Hitchcock in the thriller that was to make him a star, *The Lady Vanishes*.

But the whole survival of the new company was riding on this first production, and the reviews were not in fact as ecstatic as John could have wished. Perhaps because critics had now seen his Richard, both ancient and modern, so often, or perhaps because they were already growing weary of the Motleys' over-decorative sets, there was a slightly grudging reaction typified by Harley Granville-Barker, who sent a sharp note suggesting that John should play the lines and not between them. Others were however more enthusiastic; James Agate, after complaining that the set looked like a West End florist's shop, added: 'Gielgud's Richard has gained in depth, subtlety, insight and power since he first played it at the Old Vic eight years ago,' and Peter Fleming, for the *Spectator*, wrote the review that John must have been dreaming of: 'This might almost be a Russian company, so compact and smooth is the texture of a large cast, even in all the bad parts.'

The critic of the *Tatler* was in no doubt about the importance of this opening production: 'Mr Gielgud is always incomparable when handling neurosis and instability. What he gives us here is the idea of Richard as a young man bathed in luxury and preciosity, concerned not for his realm, but for the figure that he cuts in it. It is futile, at this time of day, to write of the rich range of melody in Mr Gielgud's voice, but his memorable performance now shares the limelight with half a dozen others that are nearly as satisfying. Mr Gielgud, having surrounded himself with a team of unusually expert actors, sees to it, as producer, that their roles are never whittled down to the advantage of his own.'

The second of the four plays at the Queen's was to be *The School For Scandal* and for this John brought in Tyrone Guthrie, a young director who was also still moonlighting as an actor; this presented several problems when Guthrie not only got a strong role in a Charles Laughton film called *The Beachcomber*, leaving John to take most of the rehearsals, but also had unexpectedly to return to the Old Vic, where the sudden death of Lilian Baylis had left the company in chaos. This was thus not the best time for the company to be starting on a Restoration comedy, considering how many of them (Gielgud, Redgrave, Guinness and Ashcroft) had all been deeply devoted to 'The Lady' who had given most of them their first real opportunities.

As Gielgud later noted:

I fear relations between Guthrie and me deteriorated rapidly, especially as he only gave us about six rehearsals. I also began to realise, here, the problems of having a repertory company of players, because many of them weren't in fact very well suited to the high comedy of *The School For Scandal*. I also found that Tony had devised some very gimmicky scenery, for instance playing the picture scene in a front cloth using the audience for the pictures – stunts like this I really didn't like at all, so in the end I just shut my eyes to his production, or lack of it, and tried to play my own part of Joseph as well as I could. I remember, typically, Guthrie taking great pains with a dance at the curtain calls. One critic wrote that the production really wasn't good enough, which must have been why at the end we all appeared to be going off to join the Russian Ballet. I learned there and then never again to do elaborate curtain calls.

An additional problem was that Guthrie's sets and costumes were characteristically anachronistic, and the third major difficulty was that when Guthrie did manage to spend some time with the cast, his main objective was to have several small-part players doing their own things in odd corners of the stage. John was thus not pleased, playing the relatively small role of Joseph Surface, to find that during his only good scene with Lady Sneerwell, a maid upstage was not only making a double bed, but then, for the wrong kind of laugh, clambering into it. In trying to get away from the mundane revivals of the past, Guthrie finished up with a manic farce, altogether too busy and contrived, although Laurence Olivier, in the first-night audience, was to recall John's Surface as 'the best light comedy performance I ever have, or ever shall, see'.

Two down, two to go. The next production at the Queen's was the one on which John was secretly banking all his hopes – a staging by Michel St Denis of *The Three Sisters*. With this, the company at last came into its own; as Herbert Farjeon wrote: 'If Mr Gielgud's season at the Queen's had produced nothing but this, it would have more than justified itself. There is a tenderness in the acting so exquisite that it is like the passing of light . . . Here in short is a production of the very first order, of one of the very great masterpieces of dramatic literature.'

But even this production was not without its problems in rehearsal. Michael Redgrave had wanted to play Andrei, the brother, but St Denis insisted on George Devine, relegating Redgrave to the Baron Tuzenbach, where he remained deeply unhappy, mumbling the lines, and casting envious glances at Devine.

In direct contrast to the careless Guthrie, St Denis arrived at the first rehearsal having already planned every move, every line, and every piece of stage business. John, although unhappy as Vershinin, the battery commander, was still delighted with the way in which the company now seemed at last to be coming together. And as the sisters of the title, Carol Goodner, Peggy Ashcroft and Gwen Ffrangcon-Davies all attracted brilliant reviews: 'they seem,' wrote the critic Lionel Hale, 'to have embraced their characters finally and naturally; they grow in them like flowers bedded in good earth.'

Yet below the surface the company was not in fact as happy as Gielgud could have wished, and the moment that *The Three Sisters* made way for *The Merchant of Venice* Redgrave left abruptly, and to Gielgud's great regret, to embark on a film career. But it was eventually Harold Hobson who understood why this *Three Sisters* made such a remarkable and lasting impression on anyone who saw it:

We should remember that at precisely this moment, at the very beginning of 1938, war with Hitler was becoming increasingly certain, despite all the attempts at appeasement. Michael Redgrave as Tuzenbach and Peggy Ashcroft as the youngest of the three sisters made a very poignant thing out of their shy, embarrassed parting on a note of forced cheerfulness in the last act, just before the duel; and the fading music of the marching regiment, dying away into silence at the end of the play, was a sadly sufficient comment on the vanishing hopes of the entire Russian bourgeoisie before their sky darkens into revolution. This was the last evening of tranquil beauty that the British theatre was to know for many years to come, if indeed it was ever to know such a thing again.

As for the translator, Constance Garnett, she wrote that ever since she had begun translating Chekhov, twenty years earlier, she had hoped, and longed for, an adequate production of his plays in Britain. At last, she told John, 'this has been achieved, and I just want to thank you for the great pleasure of seeing my dreams fulfilled'.

Tyrone Guthrie, still feeling somewhat ashamed of the shambles he had made of *School For Scandal*, wrote to John: 'This is the most articulate and accomplished Chekhov that I have ever seen. Naturally I don't agree with all of it – and I don't suppose you do. St Denis always overdoes his offstage noises, and all those bloody trilling birds and the wind simply take one's mind off the play. But the company is at its absolute best. Peggy is exquisitely moving and real, and Gwen really excellent. I am not sure the last act set is quite right, but Redgrave seems to me as near perfection as one has any right to expect and you are very distinguished, although some of your stuff in act two is a bit of a cliché.'

On the other hand, the poet Siegfried Sassoon wrote: 'to have given us such a performance, so flawless and superbly character-ised, is a magnificent thing for you to have done. Thank you for an evening I shall never forget.' So successful was this produc-tion that John borrowed an idea he had been much taken with on Broadway: that of a special midnight matinée at which actors from all the other West End productions could, if they wished, come to see this one, bringing with them members of their own companies. This resulted in more than a hundred letters written to John, some from actors who knew and had worked with him elsewhere, but many from those who had simply always been work-ing when he was, and therefore were now coming to Gielgud for the very first time. At the very end of the run, a 'tribute din-ner' was given by the Garrick Club, which John had only recently joined.

The repertory system, just as it meant advantageously that the company could move swiftly on from a poor *School For Scandal* to a great *Three Sisters*, also relentlessly meant that no sooner was this established but they all had to start work on the last production of the season, a revival of *The Merchant of Venice*.

John and Peggy Ashcroft were the only two leading players to appear in all four of the plays in Gielgud's season at the Queen's, and as she later noted: 'I had never before had such a long contract, and I feared that we might all get very stale, working together for almost a year, but in fact the reverse was true – it changed one's whole attitude to working in the theatre.'

After their triumph with *The Three Sisters*, however, the last of Gielgud's four chosen plays was to be something of an anticlimax. He was already feeling the strain of managing the season virtually unaided, and his production of *The Merchant of Venice* (in which he played Shylock to Ashcroft's Portia) was a considerable disappointment to critics, as indeed to John himself. At this historical time, given what was happening in Germany, audiences in London would probably have been happy to accept a heroic Shylock standing up for his Jewish race. Instead, John played him as a shuffling, morose and malignant outsider, ridiculous in his villainy. John's Shylock, wrote Ronald Hayman, 'was a Venetian ghetto-Jew, a mean little rat of a money-lender, lacking any dignity, a scavenger . . . this Shylock was a very strange shape, robes spreading like a gypsy's, hunching, crouching, lamenting and scrabbling about. Gielgud looked rather young, though almost bald, with straggling hair and beard, and a ring in his ear. In no characterisation since Noah had John got further away from his own personality.'

Some critics approved of this, but many felt that he had been unwise to direct and play Shylock, even though, as so often, he used Glen Byam Shaw as a kind of assistant director for those times when he had to be on stage himself. Some reviews indicated that John had simply miscast himself: 'He is,' wrote *The Times*, 'as incapable of portraying evil as he is of understanding it as a director.'

As this season came to its end, John began to have mixed feelings about the experiment. On the one hand it had come in fractionally under budget, with only *The Three Sisters* costing more than £2,000 to produce, and in critical terms two of the productions (*Richard II* and *The Three Sisters*) had achieved mostly good reviews, while even with the other two (*The School For Scandal* and *The Merchant of Venice*)

John had been applauded for the courage of the venture. He had also surrounded himself with most of the best classical and modern actors in the business, and shown them what it meant to be members of a permanent company. This was not an experience many of them would have again until the 1960s creation of resident companies first at Peter Hall's Royal Shakespeare Company, and then at the National Theatre. As Margaret Harris of the Motleys was later to remark:

> John's season changed the point of view by showing that the classics could be a box-office draw, that an identifiable team of actors could be held together in a freelance world, and that great plays repaid minute examination. John has never been given credit for what he did. He single-handedly put the English theatre back on the world map. He led Peggy into doing the sort of work she was best at; he found Olivier as a classical actor, and encouraged people like Alec Guinness, Harry Andrews and Anthony Quayle. He also encouraged George Devine and Glen Byam Shaw to find their way as directors. He really did the most amazing work, but because of his innate modesty, it was to be Olivier, after the war, who took all the credit for doing everything that John had done before it.

Not surprisingly, John had been depressed at the way in which some members of the company would drift off in mid-season as soon as a better or starrier offer came their way, and he was himself utterly exhausted by the strain of producing, directing, starring and generally acting as the company's only figurehead and driving force. More importantly still, he personally had made very little out of the venture and was therefore now easily tempted back on to the money-making side of Shaftesbury Avenue, first to direct *Spring Meeting*, a play by the Irish novelist Molly Keane (writing as M.J. Farrell) and his lover John Perry, and almost immediately after that to star with Marie Tempest in another new play, *Dear Octopus*, by Dodie Smith, today better remembered for creating *101 Dalmatians*.

Both these offers had come to him from Binkie Beaumont, the young Welsh producer who had by now taken over the running of H.M. Tennent, already the most successful of all West End theatrical managements.

Binkie was already forming the third corner of a triangular homo-sexual friendship involving Gielgud and Perry. He and John had first met when John had been acting in the Chekhov season at Barnes, and Beaumont just starting out as its business manager. But by now the balance of power had subtly shifted, and Beaumont, at the beginning of a long partnership with John which would stretch into the 1960s, was able not only to put regular work his way, but also from time to time to make it possible for him to pursue his lifelong desire for at least semi-permanent companies.

Yet it was to be a double-edged alliance: Binkie was not only to steal John's lover, he was also to keep him for the next thirty or so years on such an extremely tight salary that it wasn't until Gielgud first escaped to Hollywood in 1953 that he began to earn the kind of money which had years earlier been Olivier's and Richardson's and Redgrave's.

Binkie had however invested in the season at the Queen's, and while John was occupied day and night with its creation and management, his two backers found themselves falling in love. Away from the theatre, John Perry had rather more in common with Binkie than with John G: they both loved racing, gambling, visiting card clubs and casinos, and would happily spend whole nights playing bridge or poker with other card players. None of this had ever interested Gielgud, and it was perhaps not until John Perry actually moved out of their shared flat and into Binkie's in Piccadilly that John finally focused on what was happening in his private life.

Even then, he was remarkably forbearing; Binkie had already insinuated himself into the lives of the two Johns, and professionally Gielgud now saw him as his only regular employer. As the actor Keith Baxter explains:

John was clearly shocked by Perry moving in with Binkie, but it is possible that their relationship had not been sexual for some time; the theatre was always much more important to John G than any private relationship, and very soon he was able to restore his friendship with both the others, and would frequently go to stay with them at their weekend cottage. John Perry really was everything that Binkie was not – jovial, outgoing, always interested in something new. It was he who encouraged Binkie to take on much riskier plays in later years. And, until he was effectively banished from John G's life by his last lover Martin Hensler, Perry was to remain closer to John G than anybody else.

You have to remember also that John was always like a chameleon. He took on the character of whoever he was living with at the time, so when they moved from St John's Wood to Cowley Street it was like a very elegant theatrical lodging, whereas when, in much later life, he moved out to the country with Martin Hensler, the décor suddenly became almost Hungarian and Polish, to suit their family backgrounds. In fact, a little touch of the Austro-Hungarian empire, just outside Aylesbury.

Although John was to remain devoted to Cowley Street for the next thirty years, his enthusiasm was not shared by Noël Coward, to whom he offered board and lodging: 'I am not, repeat not, going to accept Johnny's sweet offer of his house to rent. It has no central heating and the bath and loo are on the top floor, above the main bedroom. It is all so terribly bijou that I should go mad in two days.'

Proving that there really were no hard feelings, John G continued all through their break-up to work for H.M. Tennent as both director and actor, starting with John Perry's own play.

Spring Meeting was a boisterous Irish farce about a family obsessed with racehorses, and although that milieu was very foreign to John G, he none the less delivered an immaculate production built around Margaret Rutherford, who made her name here as the eccentric spinster with a genius for backing winners. The play ran for over a year, during which time John Perry not only set up house with Binkie, but also became his partner in H.M. Tennent; as Bryan Forbes wittily once wrote: 'Perry thus became Mason to Binkie's Fortnum, purveyors of quality theatrical goods to the carriage trade.'

No sooner was *Spring Meeting* established than John G started rehearsals, under Glen Byam Shaw's direction, for Dodie Smith's *Dear Octopus*, a sentimental comedy about relatives gathering together to celebrate a golden wedding, at which the toast is 'to the family, that dear octopus from whose tentacles we never escape, nor ever really wish to'. Although it ran almost a year, *Dear Octopus* (like *Richard of Bordeaux*) was never really to achieve any kind of a post-war life; but at this moment of Munich and the approach of the Second World War, audiences in London (and around the country during its tour) found in Dodie Smith's domestic homilies something both touching and reassuring. If the middle classes were to have to go to war, this was precisely the world for which they would be fighting. John's role here was inevitably secondary to that of Dame Marie Tempest, and it may seem curious that he was willing to stay for so long in an admittedly triumphant but intellectually rather barren and even wooden characterisation.

One answer is that, at a time of considerable upheaval in his private life, he welcomed the relative security of the same dressing-room and eight performances a week, even if the play was being produced by the man for whom his long-time lover had just left him. Beyond this, John was also well aware that the Binkie Beaumont who had invested in his recent season of classics at the Queen's might well be persuaded to do so again, if John for his part proved amenable to Binkie's more commercial and pedestrian needs. Bridges were not to be burned, and if possible life was to continue on its usual course; in this last year of peace that was precisely what John most sought, at whatever cost to his pride or private emotions.

Chapter Eleven

❦❦❦

THE WEST END AT WAR
(1938–1940)

The outbreak of the Second War naturally transformed everything in the theatre. I was extremely lucky not to be called up, the authorities taking the view that I could do a better job by staying in the theatre. But I found myself living somewhat precariously, always moving from one production to another and never quite knowing what was going to happen next.

During the ten months that John played *Dear Octopus* through 1938 and into 1939, he and Binkie and John Perry were naturally concerned about what they should do next in an unusually volatile season. John's idea was that they should go for T.S. Eliot's *The Family Reunion*, a characteristically brave adventure which he even began to cast, with Sybil Thorndike, Martita Hunt and May Whitty. But both Binkie and John Perry were cautious in their enthusiasm for a verse drama several years ahead of its time, one that introduced the Eumenides into a modern family gathering, and the whole project came to a shuddering halt when John went out to lunch with the author at the Reform Club.

During an uneasy meal, Eliot made it clear that he would only allow his new play to be directed by Martin Browne, who had looked after his *Murder in the Cathedral* a few years earlier, and that he was extremely reluctant to answer any of John's questions about the real meaning of a family drama which brought the Greek fates into a latterday living-room. Soon afterwards, Eliot noted that as Gielgud clearly lacked faith in the play and the leading character of Harry Monchensey, he would rather take it elsewhere, which is what he duly did.

It was therefore with some relief that, as *Dear Octopus* closed, Binkie and John Perry persuaded John G to go back to a play and a role in which he had triumphed almost ten years earlier at the Lyric, Hammersmith. John now directed and starred in a series of eight charity matinées of *The Importance of Being Earnest*, so successfully that Binkie decided it should be their next West End project. Before that, however, there was to be another return to a safe harbour. During the previous summer, while Gielgud was otherwise occupied with *Dear Octopus*, but none the less furious at having missed the chance, Laurence Olivier had become the first British actor of modern times to take his *Hamlet* (directed by Tyrone Guthrie, with Vivien Leigh as Ophelia) home to the battlements of Elsinore itself. John was now determined to follow suit. For this production, which went into rehearsal as he was leaving *Dear Octopus*, John reassembled some familiar members of his old company, together with a few newcomers. Fay Compton was now his Ophelia, with Jack Hawkins and Laura Cowie as Claudius and Gertrude. George Howe, Glen Byam Shaw and Marius Goring were also in the cast, and the Motleys were again to design the sets.

These had to be suitable not only for the courtyard at Elsinore, but also for the Lyceum Theatre on the Strand where John had arranged a week of previews, just as the theatre itself was due for demolition. In fact it survived, only to be badly blitzed in the war a few years later; John's *Hamlet* was the last production to be seen there until the 1970s, when (after the building had been a Mecca dance-hall for years) Bill Bryden took his Miracle plays in from the National. For Gielgud, the real excitement of this production was the arrival in London of his old mentor Harley Granville-Barker, on a rare visit from America.

'He agreed to come to a run-through, on condition that there would not be any press or publicity. His name was not to be used in any way. We acted the whole play for him, and the following morning he sent for me to the Ritz Hotel. He sat on the sofa with a new edition of *Hamlet* in his hand, cutting the pages with a paper-knife as he went along, and giving me notes at a great rate. I scribbled away with all my might, determined not to let him get away until he had finished. The next day was a Sunday, but we spent all of it putting in his cuts and changes.'

Granville-Barker's main advice was that John should be stronger in the first half of the play, and then wilder and more despairing and disturbed after the killing of Polonius. He saw Fortinbras and Laertes as the twin poles of what Hamlet could have been, and he recommended an altogether leaner and less busy characterisation than John had hitherto opted for on stage.

Elsinore, however, was not a great success. The weather was stormy and terrible, audiences were duly deterred from sitting in the stone courtyard, and the hotel where the company stayed was already full of Nazi naval officers on leave. Marius Goring, to his credit, cut up all their swastika banners and flushed them down one of the hotel lavatories. By now the company had become somewhat hysterical, throwing each other into the sea and putting live chickens in each other's beds. The feeling was that with war due at any minute this was the end of an era, and John's 'regulars' were already aware that this was to be the last time for the foreseeable future that they would all be acting together as a unit. The Elsinore production was however to be the start of a lifelong friendship for John with the Baroness Blixen, better known as the author Isak Dinesen (*Out of Africa*).

Audrey Williamson, writing of this Elsinore revival, remembered: 'The unique quality of Gielgud's Hamlet has always been its radiant, nerve-tossed beauty. Fair and slender, it has the presence of a *roi soleil*; but the sun is always fitfully shadowed by the wings of demons . . . this is a fey, fairy prince hedged about with the powers of darkness, and Gielgud's performance has flashes of venom and bitter humour as well as sensitiveness and sweetness . . . this Hamlet cares not a jot for Ophelia or Yorick, but the distinctive features of Gielgud's Prince have always been intellect and poetry; there is music and cogency, and nobody has ever spoken the role so exquisitely.'

Back in London, John remained resolutely uninterested in the darkening skies; he seems to have believed that if he ignored the threat of war it might simply go away, and with the radio news from Germany getting worse by the hour, he went for a weekend to stay with the journalist and biographer Beverly Nichols: 'On the

Sunday morning, John walked into the village to get the papers and came back looking devastated. "Have they declared war yet?" I asked, nervously. "Oh, I don't know anything about that, but Gladys Cooper has just got the most terrible reviews!"'

The plan now was for John to stage his *The Importance of Being Earnest*, with Edith Evans as the definitive Lady Bracknell of her generation, and Angela Baddeley and Joyce Carey as Cecily and Gwendolen. Binkie spared no expense on lavish Motley sets and *The Times* went so far as to note that 'if the past theatrical decade had to be represented by a single production, then this is the one that a good many judges would choose.' The Motleys had moved the period forward to about 1906 from the original 1895, but this did not worry Lord Alfred Douglas who came backstage to tell Gielgud that he was the best John Worthing he had ever seen, and how Oscar would have approved. For Tyrone Guthrie, this was the staging 'which established the high-water mark in the production of artificial comedy in our epoch'.

Even though all those who could afford to were now starting to move out of London in fear of the bombing, *The Importance* sold out all through the summer of 1939, taking more than £2,000 a week at the box-office and confirming (as later did Coward with *Blithe Spirit*) that in time of crisis there is nothing audiences need more than to be taken out of themselves and to another time and place, one where they could, as both plays did, look death in the eye with nothing more threatening than a giggle. A few years later Edith Evans was to film her Lady Bracknell with Michael Redgrave and Michael Denison, but this was where her performance, with its cascading, multi-syllabic 'A handbag?', first began to be set in stone as the upper-class gorgon of all time. The role that was both to characterise and imprison Edith Evans had been played in John's first *Importance*, back in 1930, by his own aunt Mabel Terry, but as John admitted she was a lady remarkably lacking in a sense of humour, who would whisper under her breath to her nephew on stage, 'What is so funny about this play? Why are they all laughing at me?'

Edith Evans knew exactly, and it was her performance, built upon a lifetime's hatred of the *grandes dames* who had kept her mother's family in domestic service for so many years, rather than John's production that was to guarantee the success here. It was still running, to packed houses, when war was declared on 3 September; that Sunday morning, at a crisis meeting with Binkie and John Perry on stage, it was decided to close the production down.

The H.M. Tennent theatrical troops now began rapidly to disperse; Michel St Denis went home to fight for his native France; Coward went to Paris on a secret-service mission; Alec Guinness and Anthony Quayle and John Perry were among the many to enlist, and even Binkie now began to carry a gas mask around the office. Immediately following the declaration that morning, the first official wartime executive order had been that all cinemas and theatres in Britain should close for the duration, for fear of air-raids. But in the days that followed, there having been no raids of any kind, Binkie presented himself at Downing Street and won, within less than a week, a complete reversal of the order and the concession that theatres and cinemas could reopen in what were designated 'safe areas', though nobody specified precisely which these were.

John G and Binkie duly designated Golders Green in north London the first such 'safe' area, and reopened their *The Importance of Being Earnest* at the local Hippodrome only ten days after they had been forced to close it on Shaftesbury Avenue. One of John's most faithful chroniclers, Audrey Williamson, was in the audience: 'This was the first London theatre to reopen after the outbreak of war, and both audience and players felt terribly courageous, although of course there was really no immediate danger. Mutual admiration and sympathy nevertheless crackled across the footlights.'

After several more months on the road, they brought *The Importance* to the Globe on Shaftesbury Avenue where it ran happily into 1940. John meanwhile had decided that his contribution to the war would be a series of Shakespearean lectures, originally outlined by the critic Ivor Brown, in which he would talk about the major plays and perform extracts from the roles he had already made his own, from Richard II to Hamlet. These early and somewhat stilted talks still exist, on a series of shellac 78rpm recordings issued commercially early in the war and deeply loved by the poet Siegfried Sassoon, to whom John sent a set: 'Many thanks for the records, which do a vital service to poetry. The BBC has done a lot of harm in recent years by giving the public appalling broadcasts, such as the disastrous lecture of W.B. Yeats. What we need is a direct and clearly visualised poetry which would meet the listener more than halfway. My own poetry does that, but the BBC has ignored my existence for several years.' Ten or so years after the war, aided now no longer by Ivor Brown but by the Cambridge professor George 'Dadie' Rylands, John was to adapt these lectures into the more colloquial *The Ages of Man*, the most successful of all Shakespearean solo shows. Proceeds from these wartime lectures were equally divided between the Red Cross and the Polish Relief Fund, to which John felt a strong familial loyalty.

As soon as war was declared John, although thirty-five, volunteered for active service only to be told that his age group would not be called up for at least six months. For actors of his generation there was now something of a problem: they all wished to be seen to be doing their best for the war effort, despite official belief that in fact most actors would be far better employed playing to the troops than involving themselves in military activities for which they were mostly hopelessly ill-suited. There were of course exceptions: of John's 'regulars' Alec Guinness fought a brave war in the navy and Anthony Quayle was to play a crucial role with the Yugoslav resistance. But by and large the experience of actors in battledress was more akin to that of Laurence Olivier and Ralph Richardson who, after insisting on being called up to the Fleet Air Arm, were somewhat ignominiously sent back to the Old Vic, not least because so terrible was their sense of direction that they managed to crash several planes even before they were airborne, so careless was their runway technique.

As for John, the actual declaration of war found him not only playing in *The Importance* but also rehearsing for the stage the role that Olivier had just filmed as the sinister Maxim de Winter in Daphne du Maurier's *Rebecca*. But as Margaret Rutherford (implausibly now cast as the villainous Mrs Danvers) recalled, John immediately decided that this was altogether too lightweight a role in which to start the Second World War. Accordingly, he abandoned it to Owen Nares and, rather like Noël Coward, vowed that his wartime theatre engagements would be suitably solemn.

His next engagement, however, came from an unlikely and unexpected source. The conductor Rudolph Bing, then running the young Glyndebourne Festival for John Christie, wanted a London production of *The Beggar's Opera*, one for which he had already engaged Michael Redgrave as MacHeath and Christie's wife, Audrey Mildmay, as Polly Peachum. John, whose first production of an opera this was to be, brought in the Motleys as designers and decided to go for a very much more squalid and satirical staging than the classic and still familiar Nigel Playfair production at the Lyric, Hammersmith.

This *Beggar's Opera* did not, however, get off to a very good start, when Michael Redgrave lost his voice and John had to go on as a somewhat implausible MacHeath for four nerve-racked performances at which his singing had to be heard not to be believed. 'Someone,' as John ruefully told the *Daily Mail*, 'had to step in and play the part, and I'm afraid the someone had to be me.'

Redgrave rapidly recovered, but was to remain deeply unhappy throughout the run, not least with John's direction: 'I had been much too preoccupied with the problem of singing to lay the proper foundations for my character, and John had muddled me horribly in rehearsal, giving me one direction one day, and countermanding it the next . . . He also told Edith Evans' (with whom Redgrave – twenty years her junior – had now started a long affair) 'that my work was suffering, which was not exactly helpful. And my mood was not improved during an early matinée, when I came on for Act Two to hear a voice in the circle whisper loudly, "And who might this be?"'

Putting *The Beggar's Opera* swiftly behind him, John realised that the time had come to do something rather more serious for the war effort. He and Tyrone Guthrie now formed a plan to reopen the Old Vic with two productions, *King Lear* and *The Tempest*, for which, in what was still the 'phoney war', they were able to reassemble a strong team led by Jessica Tandy, her then husband Jack Hawkins, Fay Compton, Marius Goring, and such Old Vic veterans, all now too old to be called up, as Harcourt Williams, Lewis Casson and Nicholas Hannen.

John immediately went back to Harley Granville-Barker, living in a Paris not yet invaded by the Germans. Granville-Barker agreed to come to London, although again he insisted that his involvement should never be publicised. Lewis Casson was to co-direct this *Lear* with Guthrie, and the three men duly presented themselves at his hotel where they read through the play. Granville-Barker listened impassively until John got to the very end. 'You read exactly two lines correctly. Now we will begin to work. Your main trouble is that whereas Lear is an oak, you are an ash. We must see what we can do with you.'

From the very first rehearsal at the Vic, John remembered later, 'Barker inspired and dominated everyone like a master craftsman, and everybody in the theatre recognised this at once . . . He began to work with the actors, not using any notes, but sitting on the stage with his back to the footlights, a copy of the play in his hand, tortoiseshell spectacles well forward on his nose, dressed in a black business suit, his bushy red eyebrows jutting forward, quiet-voiced, seldom moving, coldly humorous, shrewdly observant, infinitely patient and persevering.'

Granville-Barker had long known precisely how he wanted this *Lear* to look and sound: not mad from the beginning, but gradually overtaken by events which he has set in motion and now cannot control. Granville-Barker also wanted the audience to understand the journey that Lear undertakes, and wanted him at the end of the play to revert to a kind of second childhood. Asked later to summarise the difference that Granville-Barker had made to this Gielgud *Lear*, John said, 'He encouraged me to characterise more, while being less declamatory, holding my emotional power in reserve for where it was needed.'

But Granville-Barker was still curiously determined not to be the director of record. Characteristically he abruptly returned to Paris the day of the first dress-rehearsal, leaving John only a brisk backstage note: 'My dear Gielgud, Lear is now in your grasp. Forget all the things I have bothered you about. Let your own now well self-disciplined instincts carry you along and up, while allowing the checks and changes to prevent your being carried away. I happily prophesy great things for you.'

Cathleen Nesbitt, whose life was to span a romantic pre-First World War affair with the poet Rupert Brooke through to the role of Rex Harrison's mother in *My Fair Lady*, and who had been Perdita for Granville-Barker as long ago as 1912, was cast here as Goneril, with Fay Compton as Regan and Jessica Tandy as Cordelia:

We were all being paid £10 a week, and John had a great deal to do with the atmosphere of harmony backstage. He was a wonderful person to be on stage with, less arrogant or egotistic than any actor of his stature that I have ever met. He and Granville-Barker had the same gift for making everyone seem equally important to the play . . . between them, in scene after scene, they achieved effects which were absorbing and moving to watch, night after night . . . I would stand in the wings watching John's *Lear*, its biting irony, its tender, moving gaiety, and a sense of grief too deep for tears.

But once again the critics were divided. 'We feel for the words Lear speaks,' wrote Herbert Farjeon, 'rather than for Lear himself,' while Desmond MacCarthy thought the role needed a voice of much greater compass than Gielgud's, and *The Times* added that John 'acts with a nervous force, but is inclined at times to fall something short on physical toughness'. During the run, John's backstage visitors included such admiring writers as Hugh Walpole and the poet Stephen Spender, who wrote afterwards: 'It seems to me that you have made such a profound study of the part that your acting transcends itself, so one forgets altogether the sense of a performance and has instead an impression of the poetry itself come to life. To me, this was something much more valuable than a star performer, because I now feel I understand the meaning of *Lear* so much better than from the many times I have read it.'

It was left to Audrey Williamson to sum up for the defence:

This was a Renaissance *King Lear*, but with enough barbaric force to make the action seem authentically placed in time . . . Gielgud's Lear on his first entrance was no senile, uncombed chieftain dressed in a nondescript nightgown, but a great King, still proud in person and mind, robed in blue satin and rich furs with white hair and carefully curled beard. The emphasis therefore was on an active octogenarian, rashly dividing his kingdom and divesting himself of the cares of state before he was ready to relinquish his authority. Gielgud's superb head, with its high marked cheekbones and forcible nose, had the regal poise of one accustomed to rule without question and the voice held possibilities of thunder . . . The scenery and costumes for this production were beautifully designed by Roger Furse and over and over again, during the performance, one felt the unseen impact of Granville-Barker's dramatic vision in gesture, pose and inflection.

Gielgud's Fool was Stephen Haggard, the actor whom he had first discovered in his undergraduate days at Oxford. Tragically, this was to be his last performance. A few months later he was killed on active service, having written a letter to his young sons headed by the last words he ever spoke on stage, the Fool's 'I'll go to bed at noon.'

As soon as they had opened this *King Lear*, John went into rehearsal for Prospero in *The Tempest*, another role he had first played when rather too young, a decade earlier. It was to be co-directed at the Vic by George Devine and Marius Goring, who persuaded John to get as far as possible away from the kind of manic conjuror he had first played in 1930. Oliver Messel, who had first attracted John as an Oxford undergraduate, was to be the designer, and according to *The Times*, John's Prospero was 'a scholarly Italian nobleman of middle age, lightly bearded and well-preserved, even though now accustomed to wearing spectacles . . . his voice is always attuned to the royal note of the verse, and he is never the preaching patriarch.'

Another critic added: 'Gielgud is a younger Prospero than most; he gives the character a certain wry humour and scholastic irony, and seems always surrounded by the invisible walls of his own enchantment.'

By the time this Old Vic season came to an end, on 22 June 1940, there was a plan to take both the productions to Paris; but the fall of France, coming as it did that very weekend, made that project untenable, and the Vic itself was now to go dark until it was hit by a bomb some months later and unable to reopen until well after the war.

It was now clear, even to John, that the war had become a reality, and that he should join several of his fellow actors on tours of military camps around the country. Shakespeare was hardly likely to be well-suited to audiences of soldiers, sailors and airmen, who might at any moment be ordered to the front, and he decided therefore to go for a couple of short comedies, *Fumed Oak* and *Hands Across the Sea*, both from Noël Coward's triumphant 1936 *Tonight at 8.30*, although he would add to them his own adaptation of Chekhov's *Swan Song*, the one about the old actor in a deserted theatre with only an equally ancient stage manager for company. While playing these every night at the head of a company which also starred the eccentric comedienne Bea Lillie, he also regularly repeated his Shakespearean lectures, now ending them topically enough with Henry V's 'Once more into the breach . . .'

The triple bill did not play well. John was never really at home in the brittle, comic dialogue of Coward, and Bea Lillie usually ended up having to retrieve the evening by leading the troops in mass singalongs of 'Keep the Home Fires Burning' and 'Lily of Laguna'. Matters were also not exactly helped by their having to share the bill with an American jazz band which the troops could not wait to hear. Bea Lillie, by now desperate to grab whatever attention she could, suddenly announced to one surprised audience, and John G's amazement, in the midst of one of the Coward plays, 'I shall now go to the piano and play Ravel's *Concerto for the Left Hand*, all the while smoking a cigarette with my right!' John was left watching gratefully from the side of the set.

While they were playing army camps in Scotland, John was offered the role of Disraeli in Thorold Dickinson's new film *The Prime Minister*, one of many being made at this early stage of the war not only for topical profit but also to remind cinema-goers of the highlights of the history of the nation for which they were now being asked to fight: Robert Donat's *Young Mr Pitt* and the Olivier/Leigh vehicle, *That Hamilton Woman*, about the romance between Nelson and Lady Hamilton, were other examples of the genre.

This was the first and indeed last time that Gielgud ever got to play the title role in a film, and it had been more than five years since his unhappy experience with Hitchcock on *The Secret Agent*. But now John was on very much more familiar territory, playing a character part that required him to age from thirty to seventy in a decidedly stagey House of Commons setting. Around him, Dickinson had gathered some strong support, not least from Diana Wynyard as his wife, but also from Fay Compton as Queen Victoria. Gielgud was here in fact challenging the memory of George Arliss who had twice filmed Disraeli's life, once as a silent in 1921, and then again in a more lavish

1929 talkie. John, working on a much more limited budget, managed however to be rather more convincing despite having to abandon the shooting for several days when a heavy make-up, consisting largely of fish paste, gave him a terrible skin rash. It is here for the first time, especially in the scenes when Disraeli is alone reading his wife's letters after her death, that Gielgud seems at last to be comfortable with the camera, though (apart from a couple of wartime shorts) it was to be another ten years before he filmed again.

Chapter Twelve

❦❧

WAR WEARY

(1940–1948)

I kept remembering how marvellous Du Maurier had been as the painter Dearth in the first 1917 production of Dear Brutus. *I could never touch him in the part.*

No sooner had John finished filming as Disraeli than he began to think about a production of *Macbeth*, another of those roles that he had first played when far too young, at the Old Vic, and which he now wanted to revisit. At first, it seemed that the new wartime climate was against any major full-length Shakespeare, especially as John's old enemy Donald Wolfit was now triumphing in a series of cut-down Shakespearean classics; these he would run for only an hour to lunch-time patrons who needed to get home well before the blackout, in a rough-and-ready Shakespearean equivalent of the Myra Hess wartime concerts at the National Gallery.

Casting around therefore for something rather lighter to appeal to audiences whose minds were often on something else, Gielgud now remembered a play he had first seen and greatly loved as a teenager in the First World War. This was *Dear Brutus*, by J.M. Barrie, a weird and whimsical variant of *A Midsummer Night's Dream*, in which characters wander into an enchanted wood, there to discover that they can, after all, achieve a second chance in life. Though it was never credited, *Dear Brutus* was really where, a few years after this revival, Alan J. Lerner and Frederick Loewe were, on Broadway, to get the idea for their first great musical, *Brigadoon*.

Gielgud as director and star now brought this back as a considerable hit, one that encouraged other theatre managers to light up Shaftesbury Avenue again if only for matinées, although John himself was always convinced that he had totally failed to capture Gerald du Maurier's original charm in the role of the lonely, failed, middle-aged artist. For the *New Statesman*, Desmond MacCarthy agreed: 'In the first act, Gielgud appears far too well pulled-together, too smart and attractive. In the scene in the wood between the painter and his dream daughter, his charm lacks the crispness of Gerald du Maurier's personality and acting, so necessary in counteracting the sentimentality.'

Yet this remained a clever choice in terms of wartime casting, in that there are very few leading male roles in *Dear Brutus*, but enough female parts to allow John a glamorous line-up: Zena Dare, Mary Jerrold, Margaret Rawlings, Nora Swinburne, Ursula Jeans and Muriel Pavlow, who made her name here as the young child. A four-month London run was followed by a two-month regional tour, during which other companies were forever meeting up in blackouts on Crewe Station on Sundays, as they criss-crossed the land. One especially dark evening, John opened a carriage only to see, through the gloom, that it was already occupied by Donald Wolfit. 'My God,' he told Zena Dare, 'the enemy has already landed.'

During the six-month run of *Dear Brutus*, John decided to tackle another play by the Irish writer Molly Keane (M.J. Farrell) and her partner John Perry, but lightning did not strike twice in that direction. The new play, *Ducks and Drakes*, lacked the innocent charm of *Spring Meeting*, and survived only very briefly at the Apollo.

As always, John was still finding precious little time for a private life, and his grasp of the unfolding events of the Second World War was to remain tenuous, to say the least; Alec Guinness once recalled walking with him over Waterloo Bridge and seeing a couple of barrage balloons, high above their heads. 'Oh!' said John. 'I do feel so sorry for those little men up there in the sky, with nothing to eat and no way of keeping warm!' It took Guinness some time to explain to John that by their very nature barrage balloons were always unmanned. But John continued, despite some distinguished war work, only really to consider the hostilities in the light of what they meant to him, and of course to the box-office receipts of wherever and whatever he was playing at the time. As he wrote in June 1942 to Lillian Gish in New York:

> I can't begin to tell you all that has happened here since the war began. It has been an extraordinary, timeless kind of nightmare. All one's friends scattered, and turning up again at odd times in uniform, and then gone again before there is any time to settle down and enjoy their company. I have been working continuously in London and on troop tours, where we always have to contend with illness and blitzes and German bombs, which they considerately only seem to drop towards the end of the evening. Everything is at sixes and sevens, and we have no idea when it will all come to an end. I so long to come back to America and see all my New York friends, but of course that is impossible, and sometimes I fear that I will never see any of you ever again. So please give everyone my love.

Since John Perry had moved in with Binkie, John lacked any real resident partner. In the meantime, he contented himself with occasional cottaging around the public conveniences of Chelsea and Westminster, depending as often as not on the kindness of strangers, and thereby falling into a sexual pattern which was, in barely ten years' time, to bring about the greatest crisis of his personal and professional life.

The critic Harold Hobson once told John that he had given himself to the theatre just as, in the Middle Ages, men and women gave themselves to monasteries and nunneries, and with something perhaps of the same reason. Monks and nuns were frequently people who had heard the voice of God summoning them to a life of remote piety. But often, too, the monastery or nunnery was a refuge for those who had no gift or dowry for marriage – people, that is, whose family had failed to provide a life for them: 'Gielgud's career has certainly been erratic; it could well have done with that bit of steadying and of common sense which a wife usually brings. He has reached tremendous heights more than once, and also fallen to some sickening depths. A touch of regularity would have saved him a lot of unhappiness.'

But for now John's thoughts were essentially on the *Macbeth* with which he firmly intended to reintroduce major full-length Shakespeare to wartime London, despite the fact that the murderous Scots thane had not proved one of his most natural roles. With the Old Vic now closed for the duration, and many of the younger members of his Queen's company already in uniform, Gielgud had to rely on a somewhat scratch cast, though he was able to reunite with Gwen Ffrangcon-Davies and to give a start to the young Alan Badel, not yet of military age.

John and Binkie, by now his regular manager, decided that they should open in a bitterly cold Manchester early in the January of 1942, prior to a long regional tour. In many ways this production was more notable for its backstage than onstage contributors: the music was by William Walton, and the sets and costumes, a deliberate mixture of Aubrey Beardsley and Burne-Jones, were co-designed by Michael Ayrton and another radical young artist of the period, John Minton. According to the critic Ronald Hayman: 'John devised a mask-like make-up for himself, with spidery eyebrows, derived partly from Alexander Nevsky in Eisenstein's film.'

But the alliance with Michael Ayrton, already one of England's finest painters and sculptors, was not an easy one, as Ayrton's biographer Justine Hopkins chronicles:

> Director and potential designer found themselves much in agreement over preliminary conceptions, and a contract was drawn up specifying that Ayrton should be paid £50 as an initial fee for costume drawings and set designs, with a further one per cent of the gross weekly box-office takings, up to a total of £150. At the time, this seemed like riches to the young designer, all too well aware of his inexperience and lowly status in the world of stage design; later, as costs snowballed and tempers flared, it was to be yet another bone of contention between himself and his harassed employer. It took only a few meetings to convince Michael that the burden of work and responsibility was too daunting to be borne alone, and less than a moment for him to fix on the ideal collaborator in John Minton.

Both Ayrton and Minton were however called up on active service during the run-up to this *Macbeth*, and although Gielgud secured

Ayrton's brief release from the RAF for the final rehearsals and tour, the strain was evident in Ayrton's behaviour backstage, at least according to an irate letter from John: 'Your ungraciousness of manner and lack of charm and generosity [is notable] toward the work people in every department . . . flinging up your hands at intervals, and announcing either that things have been done which you don't approve of and so you wash your hands of the whole thing, or else savagely resenting that there can possibly be still any improvements or adjustments to be made . . . if only you would appear more modest, you would find everyone ready to co-operate rather than oppose, to the great easing of every situation.'

By the time they opened on tour, John was still deeply unhappy not only with Ayrton's backstage behaviour but also his work on the scenic design:

> The surrealist things in the scenery are distracting, and must go. The hands on the throne, and the drapery in the trees . . . at the risk of you thinking me unpleasant, I must say I intend to carry out some changes whether you agree them or not . . . You will I am sure agree that I gave you as free a hand as possible in the beginning, and allowed you to finish in the theatre almost everything you had conceived. Now you must trust to my greater experience . . . If a man as experienced as Walton [the composer of incidental music for this production] can show such modesty, and collaborate with such complete unselfishness, I feel you should do the same, and I do deplore the fact that you haven't got on better with all the people you have come into contact with on this production, which has made the atmosphere sometimes lacking in constructiveness and ease. You will find if you want to go on working in the theatre (which perhaps you don't), that a capacity for extemporising in an emergency, tolerance and patience are three of the most essential qualities.
>
> After this somewhat disagreeable paragraph, I can only add that the big interiors and general atmosphere of the production are really a great success . . . and I am sure that if the changes are carried out, you will have a valuable and deserved success.

On the road, several of Gielgud's now-regular supporters (among them Alec Guinness, Tyrone Guthrie and the critics Ivor Brown and Alan Dent) all came backstage to offer often conflicting advice about a role in which John, by his very stage presence, was never going to be entirely happily cast.

The famous curse of *Macbeth* struck early when one of the witches (the veteran Beatrix Fielden-Kay) died during the first week of the tour, and as they trekked on through Scotland, England and Wales, they very often came up against schools or troop audiences who could hardly wait to either giggle or jeer at a sombre tragedy, not exactly designed as cheerful wartime entertainment. And there was worse to come. The actor playing Duncan, Marcus Barron, also died during the tour, while Milton Rosmer (playing Banquo) had to leave it due to ill health. But, when they finally reached the Piccadilly Theatre in June 1942 in some exhaustion, the reviews were surprisingly good. True, James Agate thought that both John and Gwen were deeply miscast, and W.A. Darlington thought that this Macbeth rated way below Hamlet in the hierarchy of Gielgud's Shakespeare, but another critic wrote of John's success in achieving 'the terrible feat of interpreting the most poetical of all murderers; Gielgud may not be bold or resolute, but he has a subtlety in Macbeth's quieter moments and an unusual sardonic intensity.'

'Though not as good as Olivier's pre-war *Macbeth*,' wrote Audrey Williamson, John's 'airborne dagger seared the eyeballs, and his imaginative impulse was never wholly lost until it dwindled into the yellow flicker of brief candle and the autumn sere. Surprisingly, our most lyrical actor caught the soldier and the murderer too; this was a lithe and virile figure, combining the mud-stained practicability of the warrior with the golden eloquence of the poet; a haunted and haunting performance, with a twilit bitterness at the last.'

It was, at this time, W.A. Darlington for the *Daily Telegraph* who made a useful list of Shakespearean roles that John should and should not tackle. On the forbidden list were Othello, Mark Antony and Richard III, while the list of desirables included Hamlet, Richard II, Coriolanus and King Lear. The critic of the *New Statesman*, however, thought that this Macbeth should be added to John's no-go areas: 'His voice is a magnificent organ, but he treats it here like a Wurlitzer, pulling out different stops for every other word. These ornamentations vulgarise the harmony, just as his pauses and syncopations wreck the melody. There is hardly a line in which the rise and fall of the verse are preserved, and never a passage in which an attempt is not made to improve upon Shakespeare's incomparably varied versifications. Mr Gielgud can, we know, speak blank verse very finely; but all too often in this production, one seemed to be listening to a cruel revue sketch about his mannerisms.'

As for the quarrels about the set, these seemed to calm down once the production reached London, and Ayrton was able to celebrate with a solo show of his paintings at the Leicester Gallery, including one of Gielgud as Macbeth, which the actor himself bought and cherished. The artist was however never again invited to design any Gielgud production, and John returned with a certain sense of relief to the comforting arms of the Motleys.

Despite its somewhat mixed reviews, *Macbeth* ran on in the West End until the beginning of October, whereupon, with only a week out, John went straight back into a short season of his ever-reliable *Importance of Being Earnest*, with Gwen Ffrangcon-Davies now replacing an otherwise occupied Edith Evans, thereby becoming the first actress to try to escape from Evans's all-dominating rendering of the handbag scene, not least by refusing to dwell on the word 'handbag' itself. No sooner had this revival come to an end, in early December, than John led a troop-concert tour, starting in Gibraltar and playing through Christmas to army camps all over the Rock.

Gielgud had by now begun to adapt himself to these uniformed audiences, who were so very different from those to which he had become accustomed at home, and this time he had strong support since his ENSA company now also included not only Bea Lillie but Edith Evans, Michael Wilding and the torch-singer Elisabeth Welch. John had opted for an incredibly mixed bill of songs, poems and extracts from *The Way of the World* and *The Importance of Being Earnest*; he also amazingly sang in a trio with Lillie and Wilding, and graciously allowed Lillie's manic sense of comedy to win over an audience who were not exactly his natural constituency.

Over the next four weeks they played two shows a day, including Sundays, not only in Gibraltar's hospitals and cinemas, but also on board the warships and aircraft carriers anchored in the harbour.

Though they never came under direct enemy attack, the dangers of their situation were brought home to the company when, during their season, the news came through that the plane carrying Leslie Howard had been shot down over the Bay of Biscay while returning from a somewhat mysterious propaganda visit to Portugal.

John was, throughout his career, always in awe of the way that Edith Evans could silence a large and initially hostile crowd by the strength of her personality, and the way in which Bea Lillie could do the same through laughter: 'I always envied stars who could suddenly walk out on to the stage quite alone and enrapture an audience by their sheer talent and originality. Somehow on these occasions my nerve always fails me. I need a set and costumes and other actors around me. I was never cut out for a variety bill.'

Gibraltar was to feature more than once on John's wartime tour itinerary, and for a very good reason. His old friend and lover John Perry, now known as Wingless Victory on account of his inability to learn how to fly, was stationed there as ADC to the governor. So whenever any of the old Tennent team were in the area, they could relay to him the latest West End gossip.

It was then with some relief that, back home and out of uniform, John answered, in March 1943, a panic call from one of the actresses to whom he was always closest and most devoted, Vivien Leigh. Two weeks earlier, she and the young Cyril Cusack had opened a triumphant revival of *The Doctor's Dilemma* at the Haymarket, but now Cusack had returned violently to the bottle, so disastrously that he had assaulted Vivien Leigh on stage one night, while quoting to the audience's amazement several speeches from an altogether different play, *The Playboy of the Western World*. This was clearly a sacking offence. Unfortunately, however, in wartime conditions there were not enough understudies and nobody, apart from Cusack himself, had actually learned the part. Olivier, on behalf of his wife Vivien Leigh, told Binkie that something drastic would have to be done, and thus it was that Gielgud, who managed to learn the long role over one weekend at Binkie's insistence, stepped into the breach for the two weeks that it took for Peter Glenville to be rehearsed into the part of the dying artist. All the same, during Louis Dubedat's long death scene, John kept a script in his lap for safety, concealing it under the rug which covered his knees in the wheelchair. As for Cusack, he returned to his native Ireland in considerable alcoholic disgrace, and did not return to the London stage for all of twenty years.

Once Gielgud had seen Peter Glenville, another old homosexual friend from Oxford, safely into the role, he embarked on a rather more ambitious project. There had been no London revival of Congreve's *Love For Love* for more than seventy years, but back in 1924 John had first played Valentine at the Oxford Playhouse and always longed to return to that role. Binkie, as always now, agreed to support him, although the casting was (as usual in wartime) somewhat problematic. Several actors, including Robert Morley, declined the crucial role of Tattle, which went eventually to Leslie Banks, and Gielgud only took over the production himself when his first choice of director, Leon Quartermaine, declared that he could never make it work.

Again, however, the female casting proved a great deal easier, and John managed to round up Yvonne Arnaud, Angela Baddeley and Rosalie Crutchley. After a five-week regional tour, they opened at the Phoenix to rave reviews, not least for the sets created by Rex Whistler, who was very soon to be killed on active service in France. The production then moved to the Haymarket where it ran on for over a year, during which time John managed to do a great deal of other work. With his brother Val now installed as head of BBC Radio Drama, John performed a broadcast of *Hamlet* and also a performance as Christian in a radio version of *The Pilgrim's Progress*. He also recorded the commentary for a wartime film, *Unfinished Journey*, about General Sikorski (the Polish general killed in a Gibraltar air crash, and later also to have been the subject of Rolf Hochhuth's controversial *Soldiers*), and then directed two short-lived new plays in the West End, *Landslide* and the Spanish *The Cradle Song* (with Wendy Hiller and Yvonne Mitchell), both of which rapidly came and went, to at best lukewarm reviews, during the run of *Love For Love*.

In spite of the uncertainties of war, the Gielgud family managed during the run one of their last great family gatherings, this to celebrate the golden wedding of Frank and Kate. All four of their children (Lewis at the War Office, Val at the BBC and Eleanor in the box-office at the Globe, where she would stay until becoming John's secretary a few years later) gave them a lunch which also included the dowager aunts and great-aunts Mabel Terry-Lewis and Julia Neilson.

It was also during the run of *Love For Love* that John made one of his greater mistakes. The movie mogul Alexander Korda and the director Gabriel Pascal now approached him to see whether, at Shaw's recommendation, John would consent to play the lead opposite Vivien Leigh in a film of *Caesar and Cleopatra*. 'I suppose,' reflected John, 'I should have taken this, and I did get quite excited when Shaw wrote to me saying that I'd be much better off playing his role "than a poor second-rate part in that eighteenth-century rubbish *Love For Love*".'

Unfortunately, when John met Pascal for the first time he so disliked the flamboyant Hungarian that he turned the film down, and the role eventually went to his old RADA tutor Claude Rains. Although John was in later life to play the Inquisitor in a film of *Saint Joan*, and also Shotover in a television production of *Heartbreak House*, his only real encounter with Shaw was the brief takeover in *The Doctor's Dilemma*. He even once refused an invitation to tea with Shaw at Ayot St Lawrence, on the grounds that he would have to be driven there and back by the somewhat overbearing Nancy Astor, and John simply chickened out of the long car journey.

He had by now moved, at least for the duration of the war, into the Park Lane flat where his former lover John Perry and Binkie Beaumont had set up as the resident couple, only to be joined by John in a distinctly curious but undoubtedly loving ménage à trois on those rare occasions when Perry came home on leave from Gibraltar.

Binkie, as always keeping a watchful eye on his box-office takings, now decided to subdivide his H.M. Tennent production company into a not-for-profit subsidiary called Tennent Productions to take advantage of a tax loophole applying to educational ventures. This was to cause considerable opposition from those rival West End managements who merely saw it as a clever tax dodge, a kind of shelter company within which Binkie could continue producing expensive, prestigious revivals on a much healthier and virtually tax-free basis. Lewis Casson, then heading CEMA (the Council for the Encouragement of Music and the Arts, essentially the forerunner of the Arts Council, and in receipt of a government grant of £150,000), also saw Binkie's diversionary tactic for what it was, and the subsequent argument spread to the House of Commons, where questions were soon being asked about the salaries that Binkie was paying, and the rather dubious nature of his theoretically tax-exempt second company.

John as usual kept well away from all this managerial bickering, central though it always was to the argument about funding for the arts. Casson was now automatically asked to serve on the advisory panel of any theatre requesting tax exemption, and although he came out firmly against *Love For Love*, Binkie still managed to get this set up on a tax-exempt basis, one with which he hoped to reinvent John's pre-war permanent company.

It was, however, John who for once recognised the immediate problems. First, he had already played, at least once, most of the major Shakespearean roles that really interested him, and was unlikely now to make a convincing Richard III or Antony or Othello; second, most of the pre-war company at the Queen's, in which he had his greatest triumphs, were otherwise engaged in the Second World War. However, having seen off the opposition from Lewis Casson, Binkie now insisted that John should set up a season of *Hamlet*, *A Midsummer Night's Dream* and Somerset Maugham's *The Circle*.

This was not a good time for John. His old rival Laurence Olivier was already filming *Henry V*, for which he had pointedly refused to offer John any of the numerous leading roles, including the Chorus that John ached to play and which went instead to Leslie Banks. Still worse, Olivier and Richardson were setting up their Old Vic company at the New, one from which John was again pointedly excluded by Olivier. Merely to return to Hamlet, a role he had already played in at least three major productions, would hardly prove an answer to the challenge that Olivier and Richardson now presented. Moreover, John's wayward decision to have two non-professional directors, the dons George Rylands and Nevill Coghill, direct in this season was nothing short of foolhardy.

And at last, with the war almost over, John was pressed into service as a firewatcher, which meant clambering on to the roof of the Haymarket and watching out for buzzbombs: 'I saw Garland's Hotel totally destroyed, and I dreaded that my beloved theatre, all made of wood and plaster, would also be destroyed, but happily it survived.'

The *Hamlet*, under Rylands's direction, soon fell apart, not least because he had always been accustomed to obedient students in his many Cambridge productions, and was thus totally unprepared for an intelligent, middle-aged company who challenged virtually his every decision. John therefore had to play peacemaker and go-between as well as the leading role, and, at almost forty, he was now having a certain amount of trouble with the student prince he had first played in his early twenties. His performance thus became a tired anthology of everything he had done in the past, and although this was where a young Richard Burton, on a school trip from Wales, first came into contact with the role he would one day make his own under Gielgud's direction, most of the reviews noted the difference between now and then. 'Not so much,' wrote Darlington in the *Telegraph*, 'a sensitive youth aghast at the wickedness of the world, this Hamlet now becomes a sophisticated man to whom wickedness was no surprise.'

None the less, some thought this was Gielgud's finest *Hamlet*, based as it was on fifteen years' experience in the role. It was Tyrone Guthrie (who had already directed the stage Hamlets of Laurence Olivier, Robert Helpmann and Alec Guinness) who now summed up: 'The new production is good, but curiously lacking in courage . . . it is a compromise in good taste . . . you stand quite alone, in my opinion, as a speaker of verse. Yours is a distinguished, sophisticated, masterful, gracious and imaginative performance of this majestic concerto. Your lack of youth is more than counterpoised by the new authority and sophistication of maturity, but I don't think you were sufficiently directed for mannerism of movement, and the funny bits are awfully unfunny.'

As touring was still a wartime priority, and the principal requirement of any not-for-profit company, John opened this *Hamlet* on the road, and then introduced a revival of *Love For Love*, before adding *A Midsummer Night's Dream*, coming in with all three to the Haymarket where the season was to be extended with new productions of Maugham's *The Circle*, Webster's *The Duchess of Malfi* and Wilde's *Lady Windermere's Fan*.

Amazingly, this was to be the first major revival of that play since Wilde's death, and it was also the production with which Binkie Beaumont was to celebrate the ending of the war; they opened at the Haymarket just two days after the atom bomb was dropped on Hiroshima, and as Binkie's biographer Richard Huggett has noted: 'The timing of this revival was suddenly perfect. After six years of war, Nissen huts, ARP, sandbags, gas masks, spam, fried eggs, clothes rationing, death, destruction, dreariness, discomfort and all the miseries of food shortages and the blackout, the theatre-going public was ripe and ready for a truly breathtaking visual experience.'

This experience came not in fact from John, or any of his very distinguished cast (Isabel Jeans, Dorothy Hyson, Athene Seyler and Griffith Jones), but from the newest celebrity in the Tennent circle, the designer Cecil Beaton. When they first opened on the road in Sheffield, a local critic wrote: 'the hero of this glorious evening is Mr Beaton, who has mounted the play in an Edwardian French set which surpasses the richest of period fantasies, while his costumes must be the most brilliant and striking that have been seen on the stage these many years.'

Not everything went according to plan, however. For Lord Darlington, John had wanted Rex Harrison, who at the last minute pulled out in favour of a film (*The Rake's Progress*), and his first replacement, Dennis Price, resigned after a week, saying that he could not deal with Gielgud's changeable and unpredictable methods of directing. The role was eventually played by Griffith Jones. John had further trouble with his old aunt, Mabel Terry-Lewis, whom he hoped to bring out of retirement to play the booming, dowager Duchess of Berwick. She found the part impossible to learn, sadly, and had to be replaced by Athene Seyler. Nor was John entirely happy with Beaton, who was clearly now about to usurp his own long-held place as Binkie's favourite. John recalled him as 'a terrible prima donna', and had been less than impressed when, meeting Cecil backstage, staggering under an armful of pink flowers for the set, he asked, 'Can I help at all, Cecil?' 'No, no!' replied Beaton. 'Just congratulate me!'

The Haymarket first night in August was a truly pre-war affair, attended by such ghosts of the Oscar Wilde past as his son, Vyvyan Holland, and the veteran Lady Alexander, widow of Wilde's most frequent producer, George Alexander. Of all the critics, only Philip Hope-Wallace, in the *Manchester Guardian*, thought that this *Lady Windermere's Fan* 'is just like a walk through a dusty old museum'.

The enthusiasm of all the others was such that the production was to run for almost five hundred performances, and Cecil Beaton, in his diaries, was to leave a detailed if characteristically waspish portrait of John at this time:

> In his appearance offstage, John Gielgud looks, at first glance, anything but an artist. But by degrees, one senses his poetic quality, his innate pathos. The large bulbous nose is a stage asset; the eyes, always tired, have a watery blue wistfulness that is in the Terry tradition of beauty. He is not altogether happy that he has inherited so many family characteristics, and praise of his mellifluous voice and superb diction always embarrasses him. But with the good manners that come from his true spirit, and not only on the stage, he has the grand manner. Unlike his rivals, he does not know the sensation of jealousy; he will always plan to do the best for the project as a whole, rather than as a means of shining brightly himself. This has often led him to obliging someone else, by doing the wrong thing for himself . . . something about John appeals very directly to one's sympathy. Often he appears to be deeply unhappy, and seems to make life hard for himself. Then one wonders if he does not take, from the parts he plays on the stage, the compensatory life he misses in private. One of his most disarming aspects is his knowledge and devilish enjoyment of his own shortcomings. 'I'm spoiled, I'm niggardly and I'm prissy. I come home in the evening and count the books on the shelf to see if one is missing.' John is the first to admit that actors are often vapid and stupid people, yet he spends most of his time, perfectly happily, retelling on the telephone unworthy Green Room gossip.

Beaton also recalled a memorable night on the last of John's wartime tours, when Gielgud found himself sharing a bedroom with both John Perry and Binkie. John G kept them awake until dawn talking about a prospective theatrical venture. When complete exhaustion ended the conversation, they managed a couple of hours' sleep, only to hear John again at daybreak, 'But who will do the wigs?'

The success of *Lady Windermere* luckily overshadowed the fact that the other productions in this Haymarket season did not work as well as they should have; although *The Circle* was strongly built around the high comedy of Yvonne Arnaud, and *The Duchess of Malfi* gave Peggy Ashcroft one of her greatest roles, *A Midsummer Night's Dream* was not helped by John as Oberon wearing a Greek helmet and bright green make-up – looking, said one critic, 'more like the ghost of Hamlet's father than the Prince of Fairies'. Once again, he was going back to a role that had suited him far better a few years earlier at the Old Vic, though this was when Edith Evans gave him one of the most useful backstage tips that he was ever to receive. 'If you were to cry less on stage, dear John,' Edith Evans wrote, 'you might find the audience cried rather more.' 'Oh yes,' replied John, 'I have always cried very easily, my Terry tears, you know; I cry for trumpets, I cry for Queens, oh dear, perhaps I should never have said that.'

Immediately after the war, Basil Dean's ENSA (irreverently known as Every Night Something Awful, but in fact the Entertainment National Services Association) was still required to provide touring entertainment for the many British troops who now remained stationed abroad on some kind of garrison or peace-keeping duties. John was duly commanded by Dean to take his *Hamlet* back on the road, but this time to alternate it with the role of Charles in Noël Coward's *Blithe Spirit*, for a little light relief. This tour, which occupied John all through the autumn and winter of 1945–6, was again not one of his finest hours. With John Perry now as the company manager, but the usual rather hit-and-miss touring cast, they opened in Cairo before moving on to Baghdad, Bombay, Madras, Colombo, Singapore, Saigon, Hong Kong, Rangoon and Karachi, closing back in Cairo early in February 1946. This was where John played his Hamlet for the very last time, and it was something of an anticlimax:

> It was a schools matinée, packed with children, and as we started the play, I thought, Well, this is the last time I shall ever play this wonderful part. I'm over forty, and it is high time to give it up. Early on in the performance, the unfortunate actor playing Horatio fell into my arms in an epileptic fit on the line 'My Lord, I think I saw him yesternight'. The audience was somewhat bewildered as I shouted rather crossly to the prompt corner, 'Drop the curtain. Put something between his teeth, and fetch the understudy.' The understudy, rescued from the bowels of the theatre, where he was making up for Guildenstern, did not know

a line of the other part. When he pointed to the Ghost and said, 'Look, my Lord, it comes,' I said, 'No, you bloody fool, the other side!' or words to that effect. Fortunately, the epileptic Horatio recovered the next day for *Blithe Spirit*, but I have never been able to forgive him for totally ruining my farewell appearance as Hamlet. I should probably have given up the role years earlier.

Nor had John been entirely thrilled, before leaving England, to receive a letter from a seventeen-year-old schoolboy, one Kenneth Tynan, suggesting that as Gielgud would doubtless need on tour to do a shortened version of *Hamlet*, he might like to use the cuts that Tynan had recently devised for a production of his own in Birmingham. Gielgud, ever courteous, wrote back that he had already chosen the version he was going to use, and did in fact already have a certain amount of experience of the play.

After giving up to eight performances a week in eighteen weeks around the Far East, John returned exhausted to London to start work on his first post-war project. This was to be his old friend Rodney Ackland's dramatisation of *Crime and Punishment*, and the first plan was that John should merely direct, with Robert Helpmann in the leading role. But before rehearsals could even begin, Helpmann was taken ill. John therefore agreed to play Raskolnikoff (with Edith Evans as Madame Marmaladoff and Peter Ustinov as the chief of police), and the ever-reliable Anthony Quayle now stepped in as director. This was in fact Ustinov's first encounter with Gielgud:

John is so contorted with shyness at first meetings that he makes someone like me feel brash and even boorish . . . and yet, despite his gossamer delicacy, an ego, totally invisible at first, imperceptibly takes over at the approach of an audience. He had been the idol of the drama students of my generation, and his single-mindedness has been constant, even when superficially challenged by the meteoric energies of Laurence Olivier, but Raskolnikoff was not his greatest role. His tremulous voice, so exquisite an instrument in illuminating classical texts with clarity and passion, seemed to me a little highly strung for the sly, down-to-earth subtleties of Dostoyevsky . . . One night I noticed he had left his small pink and white suitcase at the stage door, so I told him I would deliver it to his hotel bedroom. Unfortunately I got waylaid by the celebrated Jewish comic Max Bacon, and it wasn't therefore until about three in the morning that I remembered about the suitcase. Despite the lateness of the hour, I determined to try and deliver it. When I reached John's room I knocked with the greatest discretion. A voice both clear and brilliant rang out. 'Come In!' The door was on the latch. Because of the timbre of his voice, I did not so much enter the room as make an entrance into it. He was lying on his bed as though posing for a sacred picture by El Greco, naked and immobile. He put an end to my confusion by another ringing phrase, this time with a dying cadence and a throb of bitterness. 'My pyjamas,' he cried, 'are in that bag!' and immediately his eyes grew moist.

Playing a minor role in this *Crime and Punishment* was the actor Eric Holmes, currently Ackland's lover and the man with whom he would openly walk down the street hand in hand, hoping to shock conservative passers-by. This they abruptly ceased doing one morning when they boarded a bus, still hand in hand, and an old lady fondly enquired of Ackland, 'And how is your poor blind friend today?'

John was now back in New York, having been invited there to do a double revival of *The Importance of Being Earnest* and *Love For Love*. Alan Webb, still living at that time with Noël Coward, was instructed to take over in London a production which John had started to rehearse, and was amused to receive, within hours of Germany's surrender, the following cable from Gielgud: 'All those entering upstage right, now enter down left, and vice versa. Wonderful news. Love John.'

Always more concerned with his own life and problems than those of the world around him, Gielgud now, like many others at the end of hostilities, felt 'pretty well tired out. I had fulfilled so many of my youthful ambitions that I really did not know where to go. I had a fairly bad patch for a few years, when I seemed very bad at choosing new plays and was left reviving old Shakespearean hits which I really should have left alone. But I was already too old even for Raskolnikoff, and when the Americans invited me to New York to play a double of *The Importance* and *Love For Love*, it seemed somehow a safe thing to do, at a time when I really couldn't think of anything else. I felt empty of ideas and much more apprehensive of choosing badly.'

Predictably, the Americans took to *The Importance* (with Margaret Rutherford now graduating from Miss Prism to Lady Bracknell), but had very little interest in *Love For Love*, which they boycotted during a heatwave, thereby ensuring that the season ended on *The Importance* alone. Rutherford had scored a considerable success as Lady Bracknell, despite the fact that one night she managed to miss the last act altogether, having confused the second interval with the end of the play, only to rush back from the stage door in her street clothes when she discovered her mistake. *Time* magazine memorably noted: 'her nose is impertinent, her bulbous eyes swivel in a deep pouch, and her great jaw is buried in her jowls.'

What really mattered during this Broadway time, however, was John's discovery of the new energy and excitement of the post-war American theatre. Here and now, for the first time, he met Tennessee Williams and Gore Vidal and Elia Kazan and, away from the theatre, even the great Garbo herself: 'lovely, child-like expression and great sweetness – she never stopped talking, but to absolutely no purpose. She said her life was empty, aimless, and yet the time passed so quickly, one could never get anything done . . . I began to wonder whether her whole attitude was perhaps a terrific pose.'

By the time he returned to England there was yet more unwelcome news. Knighthoods had been announced for both Laurence Olivier and Ralph Richardson, and although they both wrote him letters of abject apology, indicating that they felt he should also have been so honoured, this was undoubtedly a considerable blow to his pride. The precise reasoning has never been clearly established; either the honours committee were nervous of his private life (no outwardly homosexual actor had ever yet received a knighthood) or, equally possibly, they felt that Olivier's war record as the director and star of *Henry V*, together with his directorship with Richardson of the post-war Old Vic, somehow made them both better qualified for honours as player-kings who had performed notable public service in wartime. True, Gielgud had undertaken long overseas troop tours, but then again so had such other leading actors of the time as Noël Coward.

As though drawing a line under his past, John returned to London invigorated by American energy and enterprise. He had already committed to returning to Broadway in October to direct and co-star, with Judith Anderson, in *Medea* and repeat his Raskolnikoff in *Crime and Punishment*. But now, realising that he badly needed a major new project at home, he and Binkie bought from the actor and manager Alec Clunes the West End rights in a play called *The Lady's Not For Burning*, written by a young Christopher Fry: 'Clunes had already produced and acted my play at the Arts Theatre, with some success, but generously he realised that only Binkie and Gielgud could now deliver a West End transfer. It was all very slow because we realised that we needed Pamela Brown to repeat her performance in the title role, but she was filming and would not be free again for almost a year.'

In the meantime, there was *Medea*: ever since, at drama school, John had been directed in scenes from the play by Sybil Thorndike, he had been determined to return to it, and, on Broadway, he was able to give Judith Anderson a considerable success while failing in his own mind to do quite enough with the role of Jason. Rehearsals had once again been fraught, not least because John had insisted on bringing in his old mentor Komisarjevsky, now rather down on his luck and running a drama school in Manhattan. Komis was however his old confrontational self, and after several major rows with both Judith Anderson and John, climaxing in a twenty-hour first dress-rehearsal, he was persuaded to leave the theatre, and John took over in the nick of time. On the first night, Komis returned to tell the assembled company that they were all rubbish, with the possible exception of Lillian Gish as Madame Marmaladoff.

During the subsequent run, Vladimir Sokoloff became the first of many actors to write (for the *New Yorker*) a detailed account of what it was like to work with John: 'We played *Crime and Punishment* for forty performances on Broadway, and each one was to me just like a first night. Gielgud is so flexible, so hospitable to each nuance that you give him, that there was always something new to find in what you yourself did. I enjoyed the way he would take it and answer it. In our three big scenes, I felt as though we were playing tennis with the audience, the ball going back to the audience and then back to the stage . . . We were playing doubles with the audience, and we always won. It was such bliss to act with a man like that.'

Gielgud had less happy memories, not only of having to go on to salary cuts when the box-office rapidly collapsed, but also of being so exhausted, by having to pacify all the people Komis had insulted backstage, that he was aware of having given a rather lacklustre first performance.

While he was in New York, John revived a pre-war friendship with the dramatist Terence Rattigan, who now paid him the tremendous honour of writing him not one but two new plays. This was the double bill of *Harlequinade* and *The Browning Version*, which would have allowed John to play not only a camp theatrical hysteric (in *Harlequinade*), but also the wonderful role of the old disillusioned schoolmaster, Andrew Crocker-Harris, in *The Browning Version*. Gielgud was the natural choice here, not least because the comedy of *Harlequinade* had in fact been based on Rattigan's own memory of his disastrous appearance as an undergraduate in Gielgud's *Romeo and Juliet*.

John did not take kindly to this, however, and although he recognised the brilliance of *The Browning Version* he decided that a double bill might be risky, especially given his lack of faith in the first half. Unfortunately he chose to tell Rattigan the bad news while they were strolling one spring afternoon in Central Park. 'You see,' John said, by way of explanation, 'I have to be very careful what I do next, and I can't afford to be seen in second-rate plays.'

Rattigan, hurt and for years unforgiving, took his plays back to London where, under the joint title *Playbill*, they scored a tremendous success with Eric Portman and Mary Ellis in the leading roles. Years later still, Michael Redgrave was to star heartbreakingly in the film version, and John had to be content with playing Crocker-Harris only on radio in 1957, and then two years later in his American television debut for the director John Frankenheimer.

Soon after Gielgud's refusal, Rattigan had written to the producer Binkie Beaumont in some fury: 'In future I am resolved to act firmly on the assumption that my plays will only be performed privately in the Colney Hatch mental home, whither the actor for whom they were written is plainly bound.'

Having, for neither the first nor the last time in his career, proved so totally inept at judging new plays on the page that he carelessly threw away precisely the West End and Broadway hit that would have given him what he now most needed, a new and successful start to the post-war years, John was to drift unhappily back to London, with no real idea of what to do next. His two greatest classical and modern rivals had just been knighted, the Old Vic company still apparently had no place for him, and in the West End Binkie and John Perry had now reverted to a general policy of safe old stars in safe old shows. It looked as though John's frustrated dreams of another permanent company, his inability to find film fame, and his general despair would add up to a total collapse in his fortunes, not only on stage, but also in his private life, where he had still not found any real successor to John Perry. Having survived the war, he was now to have real trouble surviving the peace.

Chapter Thirteen

❧

THE UNKINDNESS
OF STRANGERS

(1948–1949)

*The problem for any romantic actor, as his youth begins to
evaporate behind him, is what to do next.*

W hen *Crime and Punishment* closed on Broadway at the
beginning of 1948, it was to be the start of almost an entire
year in which John G did not act at all. One of the longest-
ever breaks in his acting career was brought about by his continuing
uneasiness about his place in the post-war theatre, as much as the
ongoing delay in the transfer of *The Lady's Not For Burning*. But
he was not exactly idle. He first took the chance to travel around
America, exploring it in a way that he had never been able to do
while on tour. Greatly impressed by a first meeting with Tennessee
Williams, he went to have a look at New Orleans and the Deep
South; equally impressed by the energy of post-war New York, he
also went to the ballets of Martha Graham, and began thinking about
the possibility of using her stylised movement and abstract settings
for Shakespeare, something he was first to achieve in 1955 with the
controversial Japanese *King Lear*.

He also realised that even the success in London of his *Lady
Windermere's Fan* had merely confirmed the feeling that he belonged
to a pre-war world, and that he was therefore going to have much more
trouble than Olivier, Richardson or Redgrave in rebuilding himself
for a drastically different audience. Almost inchoately, he seemed to
sense that the answer might well lie in America itself, as though that
country's theatre was the way ahead, and he must somehow separate

himself – at least for a while – from Wilde, Shakespeare and Chekhov, representatives all of the old Europe.

It was, curiously, Tennessee Williams who showed the way ahead. His first real success, *The Glass Menagerie*, had recently opened on Broadway, and Williams now suggested to John that he might like to direct it for London. John may have seemed an unlikely choice but Helen Hayes, who had agreed to star in London as Amanda, was already an old friend, and it was she who bullied John into overcoming his doubts. A London deal was duly struck with Binkie; Williams had just won the Pulitzer Prize, and was riding as high as he was ever to do. His arrival in London was celebrated by a lavish party, attended by the then young actress Maria Britneva, who as Lady St Just was later to become Tennessee's guardian angel and the dragon who was to stand at the gates of his posthumous estate. As a young actress, Britneva had already become a friend of John's, while playing small roles in Gielgud's last wartime tour of *Hamlet* and *Blithe Spirit*. John had then cast her as Edith Evans's daughter in *Crime and Punishment*, where they had confirmed their friendship in difficult conditions.

As Maria Britneva recalled:

Edith took an instant dislike to me on two counts: firstly, I was foreign and therefore unhealthy; secondly I was clearly becoming a close friend of John's. Every night, she used to give me a vicious slap before curtain up. As a Christian Scientist she took pains to point out that she had never had a cough in all her life; amazingly, however, she managed to cough loudly through all John's speeches in the play. John, as always too cowardly and too kind to say anything himself, asked me if I could do something about Edith's apparent choking fits. So I simply took a pillow and held it over her face on stage one night. The following morning I was sent for by Binkie Beaumont. 'My dear,' he said quietly, 'if we wish to get on in the English theatre, we do not smother our leading ladies. We take them cups of tea.'

At the party given by John were Laurence Olivier, Vivien Leigh and Noël Coward . . . I've no idea why I was invited. I'd borrowed a frock from somewhere. It was far too big for me, and I had to keep hiking the thing up. After a while, I noticed a little man sitting on a sofa. He was wearing a blue sock on one foot, and a red one on the other. He looked unassuming and vulnerable and no one was talking to him. I though he must be an understudy so I went up to him and asked if he would like another drink.

But if this first meeting between Williams and Maria Britneva was to condition the rest of their lives, things were not going so well between the playwright and his new director. Williams started referring to John in rehearsal as 'the old one', and was less than thrilled during the play's try-out in Brighton to have John refuse him a curtain call on the grounds that 'I don't want the beautiful effect of this play diminished by a perspiring little author with a wrinkled shirt and a messy dinner jacket coming up on stage.' The problem now was that despite earlier expectations, almost everything was to go wrong. Williams found London 'stuffy and full of middle-aged fags' and complained that only Christopher Isherwood and Gore Vidal ever spoke to him at all. Nor was Brighton a natural home for a play steeped in the Williams's family neuroses of life in the Deep South. It was already becoming clear that Helen Hayes, despite her life-long billing of 'first lady of American theatre', was not going to be able to live up to Laurette Taylor's searing creation of the role in New York. As Williams himself was to write in his memoirs: 'the great Gielgud has never been, I'd say, much of a director, but even so Helen Hayes should not have happened to him . . . At one of the last rehearsals she summoned John, me and the entire supporting cast to her dressing-room to announce that we were in for a tremendous disaster, as she could always feel that kind of thing in her bones.'

British audiences, after a long war, were looking to America for lighter and more escapist entertainment, in musicals as dynamic as *Oklahoma!*, and the all too realistic account of Williams's own brain-damaged sister was not something they were inclined to take to their hearts, even if they could find their way through the strong regional dialect on which John insisted. The first night at the Haymarket attracted a glittering audience, including Princess Margaret and Lady Colefax, but they again were not exactly Williams's natural constituency, and, unsurprisingly, *The Glass Menagerie* failed in London to live up to its original Broadway triumph. But the author himself was not among the first-night crowd. Depressed by the Brighton reaction, fearful of Helen Hayes's prediction and now convinced that Gielgud was making a mess of his play, and that he would therefore have a considerable disaster on his hands in the West End, Williams had fled to Paris, sending merely a telegram to his mother, Edwina, reading 'take a bow for me'.

A few days later, writing an apology for his absence to Helen Hayes, Williams explained that a condition of exhaustion, overwork, frayed nerves, emotional paralysis and constant heart palpitations had led to his abrupt departure. He added, in a terrible echo of what was to become his life's pattern, that to quiet his nerves he had taken an accidental overdose of the sedative Barbital, which had made him unconscious for six hours, thereby causing him to miss the London train. How much of this was genuine, and how much caused by his unhappiness at what John was doing to his play, remains unclear. About a week after the opening, Williams did overcome his unhappiness and took the young Gore Vidal, already an intimate friend, to a performance. 'It was just as bad as I had expected from the Brighton try-out. *Menagerie* cannot be tricked. It has to be honestly and more than competently performed and directed. There was no sign of this here, and to some extent that was all Gielgud's fault. He simply didn't understand the play.'

The two men did achieve, in later life, a kind of wary friendship, and the reviews were in fact nowhere near as bad as Williams had feared. Nevertheless, there lingered the feeling that John had not really come to terms with the world of Tennessee Williams, and it was with a kind of relief that he immediately went back to work on yet another *Medea*, this one designed for the Edinburgh Festival, with Eileen Herlie in the title role and Ralph Michael as Jason. John was against bringing this production into London, but Binkie insisted, only to have Gielgud proved right by a barrage of hostile reviews; it was Audrey Williamson who noted: 'This production fell well short of greatness, mainly because of the restrictions of an American translation of depressing colloquialism . . . John's direction could not overcome this handicap of prosaic flatness of speech, nor the limitations imposed by a weak and curiously stiff male cast; perhaps ours is not an age for tragedy.'

And there was yet worse to come. At the very end of this difficult year, John was persuaded by Binkie to return to the stage as an actor in a curious play called *The Return of the Prodigal*, by St John Hankin, who at the age of thirty-nine had drowned himself shortly after the original production in 1905. Lewis Casson had been an understudy in this, and he and Sybil Thorndike now begged John to bring it back to the West End as a lost classic. John was still really marking time, waiting to get back to *The Lady's Not For Burning;* but always reluctant to be out of work, he agreed to join a starry cast under the direction of Peter Glenville, one that would include Sybil Thorndike herself, Rachel Kempson, and three desperately over-decorated sets by Cecil Beaton.

The Times called the result 'the best dressed and best acted bad play in London', and several other reviewers noted that in his knicker-bockers and blond wig John bore an unfortunate resemblance to the American comic Danny Kaye, then having a huge success at the London Palladium.

One of the advantages, though, of John's reluctance ever to leave himself with even an offstage hour, was that he was able to put such disasters behind him, while racing on to a new project, and he was always unable to reject pleas for help. No sooner had he opened, in *Return of the Prodigal*, than Peggy Ashcroft and Ralph Richardson came to him in considerable despair. They were on the road with the British première of *The Heiress*, Ruth and Augustus Goetz's adaptation of Henry James's *Washington Square*, which had already triumphed on Broadway with Wendy Hiller and Basil Rathbone, and had both come to the reluctant conclusion that, with only five days to go before they were due to open at Brighton, they would have to fire John Burrell, a director of some standing, who had with Olivier and Richardson recently been one of the triumvirate running the Old Vic.

As a young member of the cast, Donald Sinden, recalls: 'There was obviously a terrible problem with the production, which we lesser mortals never knew about. At the Old Vic, Ralph and Larry would usually direct each other, and Burrell's job was just to make sure that the extras didn't get in their way. Ralph was also famously chilly towards directors. "I always say good morning to them, and ask if they have had a good breakfast." Anyway, on the Friday before we opened in Brighton, Burrell limped on to the stage and said, "Ladies and gentlemen, I am sorry to say that I am leaving the production, and John Gielgud will be taking over."' Burrell abruptly left not just the theatre, but England itself, to carve out a new career as a teacher and director in America.

The driving force behind the firing of Burrell by Binkie had come from Peggy Ashcroft, who felt that he was simply incapable of, as she put it, 'unknotting' the production; Ralph Richardson, uneasy about the insult to his Old Vic colleague, went around for days muttering, 'We have assisted at the murder of Julius Caesar!' which didn't make John's life any easier:

> I arrived to find that the furniture on the set was all in the wrong places, and the characters seemed to be standing around as if waiting for a train. Burrell's blocking really was appalling – the cast were strung out from side to side like a football team, and Ralph kept going upstage to look out through the door, as if to see whether the police were coming. I started changing the moves, and luckily the whole thing suddenly came to life. At first everyone in the cast was at daggers drawn, the play was nowhere near ready to open at Brighton, and the only thing the cast seemed agreed on was that nobody except Peggy wanted me to take over the direction, fearing that as usual I would immediately try to change everything, and the result would be chaos. Even Ralph had grave doubts about accepting me because I have such a reputation for altering things at every rehearsal. I do it because I believe actors have to try things, and then discard them and try others. I am very restless as a director and very apt to change my mind. I expect my actors to sift the wheat from the chaff, and to know when I suggest good ideas and more importantly how to discard my bad ones.

This last-minute rescue operation was a spectacular critical success, indeed the first that John had been able to enjoy in London since *Lady Windermere's Fan* four years earlier. The reviews were nothing short of ecstatic; Harold Hobson wrote of Richardson's 'relentless figure whose cruelty and restlessness were due to a great grief within'. As for Peggy Ashcroft, Hobson thought 'all superlatives are pale and feeble things. In her hands the exquisite tragedy of this unloved girl becomes one of the theatre's most moving experiences.'

Though Richardson had already filmed *The Heiress* with Olivia de Havilland, the play itself then disappeared for half a century or so; when it reappeared, with considerable success on Broadway in 1998, and then rather less successfully at the National Theatre with Alan Howard a couple of years later, this seemed to be a very creaky period piece about a dominating father proving that his daughter's lover is a wastrel. It was effectively an American version of *The Barretts of Wimpole Street*, which John himself was later to film, but clearly the original success depended crucially on the two central performances that John had teased out of Peggy Ashcroft and Ralph Richardson.

Things were definitely looking up. And now at last Pamela Brown had come free of her other commitments, so that, after a year-long wait, John could get down to the production of Christopher Fry's *The Lady's Not For Burning*.

Fry was now in his early forties; he had made his name just after the war with two plays (*A Phoenix Too Frequent* and *Thor With Angels*) but these, like T.S. Eliot's pre-war *Murder in the Cathedral*, had originally been designed for amateur players with a strong religious connection, and this was to be his West End debut, after the brief run of *The Lady's Not For Burning* at the Arts with Alec Clunes a year earlier.

Fry and Eliot were now to become the leaders (and virtually the only participants) in a movement of poetic drama which flourished very briefly at the end of the 1940s and early 1950s, only to disappear as rapidly as it had arrived, leaving remarkably little trace that it had ever existed. Nevertheless, for a few years it became the dominant and most discussed London theatrical form, hence John's determination to become associated with it at all costs.

Because of Fry's new-found fashionability, John assembled an amazing team. He would play opposite Pamela Brown in ravishing sets by Oliver Messel, with a supporting cast led by such veteran members of his pre-war companies as Harcourt Williams and Esmé Percy (who effectively also became John's assistant director), but more importantly by two hugely starry young players who had just begun to make their London names, Richard Burton and Claire Bloom.

Burton was an immensely good-looking Welsh actor who had already come to the notice of both Emlyn Williams and Peter Glenville while still an Oxford undergraduate; the two men and Gielgud now fell for his considerable charms. In the view of another contemporary, Frank Hauser: 'He already had the essential selfishness of the star actor, and a very attractive self. There is no doubt that the gay mafia around H.M. Tennent all fell for him, and although Richard was always resolutely heterosexual, I think he already knew how to play the gay game.'

The Lady's Not For Burning was set in the Middle Ages, and it told the story of a mercenary, back from seven years in the wars, and the young and beautiful witch who wants to be spared from death as eagerly as the soldier wishes to embrace it. Burton was hired at £10 a week to play the orphan clerk and John was always to retain a sharp impression of their first meeting:

> Richard did an immensely impressive audition and was marvellous at rehearsals. There was a true theatrical instinct and you only had to indicate something for him to get it and never change it. There was a moment when he had to scrub the floor while Pamela Brown and I were having a long and involved discussion upstage, and Alec Guinness told me that the audience never took its eyes off Burton. That particular, immediately unmistakable talent comes along very rarely, and of course it can be dangerous because it is so very difficult to control. But at this time Richard was very sunny, no vanity but so confident. He boasted now and then, but in a rather Welsh, pub way. He was a real pub boy, had a great stable of ladies. He was always very respectful to me but incredibly careless. At the very first morning of rehearsal he began to yawn and look at his watch, already eager to get back to the pub for a drink.

Characteristically it was in these rehearsals that Burton started an affair with Claire Bloom that was to carry over well into the 1950s, when they were to be reunited on film in *Look Back in Anger*, and on stage at the Old Vic in *Hamlet*.

As usual, wherever Gielgud was concerned, rehearsals were less than easy, as Claire Bloom recalled:

> John was anxious about this play, and desperately wanted it to be a success. He became more and more short-tempered with us all, until

one actor playing a small part contracted jaundice as a consequence of the pressure, and disappeared from the cast. I came in for a nice share of his disapproval, and he kept telling me to try to emulate Richard, for whom everything seemed to come easily. Burton's eyes on stage were mesmeric, giving him even in repose absolute command over an audience. In time I became envious of that control; he seemed to achieve it by doing nothing. At twenty-four he was recognisably a star, a fact that strangely enough no one in rehearsal seemed to question, not John and least of all Richard himself. Eventually I too collapsed with a kind of nervous strain, and took to my bed, convinced that John would use the opportunity, which I had now so conveniently given him, to fire me. However, when I came back to work, I met him at the stage door, where he simply raised his hat to me and said, 'I do hope you're feeling better. I am so glad you are back. We missed you.'

The Lady's Not For Burning went on a twelve-week regional tour before coming in, throughout which John, unable to remember Claire's name, would simply refer to her as 'that nice little girl upstairs', this being a reference to the height from the stage of her dressing-room. John, even though well aware of the importance to him of this production, and of the extreme difficulty of getting audiences around the country to tune themselves into Fry's quirky, evanescent verse, could nevertheless never lose his old workaholic habits. Thus, with *The Lady* still on the road, he agreed to direct Diana Wynyard and Anthony Quayle in the new Stratford season's opening production of *Much Ado About Nothing*, to which he would commute from wherever he was playing in *The Lady's Not For Burning*. During this frantic period John's father, who had been ailing for some months, died peacefully, leaving John all too little time to mourn him. He died, as he had lived, the unobtrusive member of the family, leaving John's mother to press on indomitably for several years to come.

Apart from Val, still at BBC Radio, and now using John whenever possible for broadcast drama, Gielgud's links with the rest of the family had become somewhat tenuous, although he was always to keep a careful eye on his mother. At this time, John still had no regular partner, but his life in London and Stratford was now made considerably easier by a genial American manservant called Bernie whom John had hired as a combination of cook and driver. He also now acquired a dresser, known only and always as Mac, who was to remain with him backstage for the next thirty years.

Perhaps because he had less time than usual to spend on the Stratford production, John's first *Much Ado* (for which Quayle, already the resident director at Stratford, clearly took care of much of the staging) was a critical and public triumph. This was where John first fell in love with a play to which he would frequently return, both as actor and director. And his initial success with it meant that he could return to the tour of *The Lady's Not For Burning* in considerably higher spirits.

That production came into the Globe Theatre on 12 May 1949 and although one or two critics thought that John lacked the masculinity for the bravura soldier Thomas Mendip, most others eagerly acclaimed the new verse drama, giving John the kind of social and professional success in London that he had not really enjoyed since his *Richard of Bordeaux* and *Hamlet* before the war. A junior member of that company was the actor and author Peter Bull who remembered that from the very beginning there were considerable doubts about 'a poetic drama about a witch who isn't a witch falling in love with a man who wants to be hanged, spending a night in jail, and being let off next morning. "Is there," an understandably nervous Binkie Beaumont once asked the author, "anything more to it than that?" "Oh yes," he replied, "there's an old rag-and-bone man called Skips, who comes on at the end, trailing a lot of cans, dead drunk and it's all marvellous and ends happily."'

It might even be possible to argue that in its own eccentric way *The Lady's Not For Burning* paved the audience's way for the *Waiting For Godot* seven years later, in which Bull was also to appear; though *The Lady* was somewhat more accessible, it too suggested to its audience a totally unfamiliar world to which they could only gain entrance by working rather harder than usual.

Bull recorded some bleakly funny moments on the tour, not least the night in Leeds when Esmé Percy's glass eye fell on to the set, only to be followed by its owner hissing at the rest of the cast, 'For God's sake don't step on it, it cost eight guineas!' before trying to get the play on track. In Northampton, they played a bleak Holy Week to small audiences in total silence, not helped by the fact that the front-of-house advertising was for a variety show due the following week, starring 'Real Frogmen in a Real Tank'. Halfway through *The Lady's Not For Burning* on the Monday night several of the audience stormed out, cursing that if real frogmen were advertised, they should at least have the grace to appear. Some nights even that would not have been surprising among the many confusions of the play. John was already tiring of the repetition, and one night told Bull to try coming on from the other side of the stage, which resulted in Peter walking straight into a cupboard while Burton, already on stage, dissolved into a fit of hopeless giggles: 'Sorry,' said John after the show that night. 'Better go back to doing it the other way.'

It was John himself who finally summarised the joys and the problems of directing *The Lady*:

> Since my return from America barely a year ago I have directed five plays: *Medea, Much Ado About Nothing, The Heiress, The Glass Menagerie* and *The Lady's Not For Burning*. Each play needed, to some extent, imaginative treatment, but each was utterly dissimilar in style, period and approach . . . *The Lady* was perhaps the most difficult task of the whole five. To begin with, I was to play the leading male part as well as direct, but the author gave me a very free hand, was entirely willing to make cuts, adjustments and a few additions to his already printed text, and I was fortunate to enlist Oliver Messel for the scenery and costumes. No play I have ever tackled demands more delicate handling; the lyric beauty of certain scenes and passages changes, almost violently from time to time, to modern idioms and phrases of wit and irony. The tone of the play is ironic but not bitter, tender yet never sentimental – the fantasy has something of *Alice in Wonderland*, the words have an Elizabethan boldness and splendour of imagery which must somehow be co-ordinated into an easy and fluent acting style. Comedy and movement must keep the stage alive without disturbing the concentration of the audience on the intricate pattern of the dialogue. I tried to get it played with the artless simplicity of children.

For Christopher Fry, the amazement of *The Lady* was the way in which it remained, for John, a kind of work in progress: 'The spate of his directorial inventiveness was sometimes difficult to check. Ideas came not as single spies but in battalions. Changes of moves and emphasis went on all the time . . . Pamela and John were always working to improve their performances and I was constantly struck by John's never-diminishing eagerness to learn his craft, as though he were always at the beginning of his career, and still seeing the fun of it all.'

When they finally settled down to a triumphant London reception, John immediately occupied himself with new projects, including a charity matinée revival of *Richard of Bordeaux*, for which he invited Bull to play the Archbishop of York. 'You see,' explained John to a somewhat crestfallen Bull, 'you can wear your *Lady's Not For Burning* costume, and that will save us having to hire one.' From there, Gielgud went back to Stratford on non-matinée days and Sundays to direct one of the few Shakespeares he had neither seen nor read, a *Love's Labours Lost*, of which his only recollection was 'a great lesson in how not to move actors around while they are speaking verse'. He also, back in the West End, directed another play by John Perry and his Irish collaborator Molly Keane (M.J. Farrell), called *Treasure Hunt*, in which Sybil Thorndike gave one of her greatest comic performances. At this moment, towards the end of 1949, John had no fewer than three productions running simultaneously in the West End: *Treasure Hunt*, *The Lady's Not For Burning*, and the still surviving *The Heiress*. He thus ended the 1940s in very much better professional shape than he could have imagined possible at any time since the end of the war.

Chapter Fourteen

❧❧❧

SHAKESPEARE AT STRATFORD

(1950–1951)

*In 1950, I had what amounted to a new beginning in a glorious
season at Stratford, playing four wonderful parts and meeting
the young Peter Brook, who really started me off on a totally
new line of work.*

I t was Anthony Quayle, the actor owing his own start to
Gielgud in his pre-war companies at the Queen's and the Old
Vic, who first had the idea of bringing John (who had become
available in the gap between the year-long London run of *The Lady's
Not For Burning* and its Broadway première) together with the young
director Peter Brook, who had made his name with Paul Scofield in
some early seasons at the Birmingham Rep.

On the face of it, this was not going to be a marriage made in
heaven. More than any other young director of his time, Brook, now
twenty-five, stood for everything that was hostile to John's lyrical,
poetic way of working. John had first met him while he was at Oxford,
living with Gavin Lambert, and had even lent him some old sets from
Love For Love with which Brook had made his first film, a version of
Sentimental Journey which he brought in on a budget of £250.

Already, Gielgud knew that Brook was going to be one of those rare
directors, like Komisarjevsky and Granville-Barker, from whom an old
dog could learn some new tricks. John was now nearly twice Brook's
age and, alongside Olivier, still the most famous Shakespearean in
the land. But from the first rehearsal of *Measure For Measure* Brook set

about deconstructing him, picking up on all his more facile vocal and emotional effects, and trying to remind a now somewhat mannered player king to go for the psychology of the man under the skin, rather than rely on a magnificent voice and some spectacular costumes.

Unlike some of his predecessors, however, Brook realised instantly that he was dealing with theatrical genius and was in no doubt that:

> John's highly developed sense of responsibility to an audience is greater than his responsibility to himself . . . Unlike a number of actors he will sacrifice not only himself but the reality of his own work, for the sake of not letting the audience down. The moment he hears a cough, he will sense that the house is restless and produce a brilliant but well-tried stage trick to catch the audience's attention. That's where his great professionalism and his enormous experience are both a virtue and a vice . . . What you do as a director is gradually build a glass wall around him, with an intense spotlight in the middle of it. When this spotlight of his own creativity turns inward on his own work, it has a shedding effect . . . he abandons the unimportant to get closer to the essential. Submerged in each of John's performances is a core which is pure, clear, strong, simple and utterly realistic . . . Where, historically, his Angelo in *Measure For Measure* seemed so striking was that there was more of the essential John in it than had been seen for a long time, and less of the superficial, extravagant and tricksy John that had been seen in plays where he had been concentrating on everything except his own inner work.

In other words, it was high time that John now found a director who was not himself, and in Peter Brook he was more than lucky. Brook went for the subtext of Angelo, having John play him not as the old evil sensualist whom Guthrie had found in Charles Laughton (the last famous Angelo in 1934), but instead a repressed Puritan, fervently trying to dampen down his own lust.

Brook's recollections of working with John are, as one would expect, particularly illuminating. First, there was the inevitable dropping of Gielgud bricks, in this case at the beginning of the first read-through of *Measure For Measure*, when everyone was understandably nervous, not least because of the awe in which the younger actors held John G:

To break the ice I made a short speech, then asked the actor playing the Duke to begin. He opened his text, waited for a moment, then boldly declaimed the first line: 'Escalus!' Gielgud listened attentively. 'My lord?' came the answer, and in those two words, hardly audible, one could hear the panic of a young actor, wishing for the ground to open and playing safe with a token murmur. 'Peter!' From John came an impulsive, agonised cry of alarm. 'He's not really going to say it like that, is he?' The words had flown out of John's mouth before he could stop them. But just as swiftly he sensed the dismay of his poor fellow actor, and immediately was contrite and confused. 'Oh, I'm so sorry, dear boy, do forgive me. I know, it'll be splendid. Sorry everybody, let's go on.'

Brook sympathised with Gielgud's notorious changeability in rehearsal, seeing him as 'an aircraft circling before it can land', and realising that although his approach could be maddening, it could also, with the right calibre of actors, bring out the best possible performances from them: 'His generosity toward them in performance comes from his need for quality, which has always been more important to him than his own personal success. When he directs, often he neglects his own performance and one has grown accustomed to seeing him in a leading role standing to the side, back turned to the audience, an observer, deeply involved in the work of others.'

This constant traffic-jam of ideas within Gielgud's mind, and the instant relay of his thoughts to his tongue, 'the sensitive instrument that captures the most delicate shades of feeling in his acting, and just as readily produces gaffes, indiscretions and outrageous puns', meant that, in Brook's opinion, he required strong direction, to remove the accumulated ideas of several weeks' rehearsals: 'He has too many ideas: they pile in so fast, hour after hour, day after day, that in the end the variation on top of variation, the detail added to details, all overload and clog his original impulses. When we worked together [on *Measure For Measure*], I found that the most important time was just before the first performance, when I had to help him ruthlessly to scrap ninety per cent of his over-rich material, and remind him of what he had himself discovered at the start.'

Brook and Anthony Quayle surrounded John with powerful support, including (as Isabella) a nineteen-year-old Barbara Jefford, along with Alan Badel and Harry Andrews. And it was the drama critic of the *New Statesman* who immediately recognised the importance of the change that was going on here: 'Gielgud has continually been haunted by his own Hamlet; he has never before entirely shed the last vestiges of that part, though not for want of trying. Now, with this Angelo, he makes a complete break with his past. In his thin, spinsterish characterisation there are no traces of romantic gestures, no echoes of the youthful tones. His Angelo is a bloodless civil servant hiding an ambivalent itch, and he cuts a clean swathe of sense through the play such as has not often been given to it.'

Apart from Laughton, Gielgud was the only star player until then who had ever agreed to take on Angelo, widely considered a character role. But his success gave him a new confidence with which he was easily able to go forward and become the leading actor and director of Anthony Quayle's first five years at Stratford.

After *Measure For Measure*, he stayed to direct a revival of the *Much Ado About Nothing* that he had first staged there in the previous year, with Quayle and Diana Wynyard. With Quayle's generous blessing, John himself now took over as Benedick and brought in Peggy Ashcroft to play Beatrice. This became another landmark production; John had not been on stage with Peggy Ashcroft for five years, and by the time they got together again both had acquired a kind of maturity.

As if to give himself a treat after the sombre psychiatric reality of Brook's *Measure For Measure*, this *Much Ado* was picturesque, opulent, formal and redolent of the High Renaissance. As usual, John's notes in rehearsal were not always exactly helpful: 'Come on with panache' was his chief instruction to a somewhat bewildered Ashcroft, and yet their partnership here was compared by one critic to the joy of listening to the finals in a verbal badminton championship. Ashcroft herself always said that her stage partnership with John was like ballroom dancing: 'It was like following your partner, never knowing quite which steps were to come next, but always knowing that you could instantly respond, because you were so in tune with him.'

But Peggy Ashcroft was determined to create her own Beatrice (a role that both Diana Wynyard and Margaret Leighton also played with

John), and to secure her own contrast with the lavish sets all around her. As a result, John found her performance 'a revelation – an impish, rather tactless girl with a curious resemblance to Beatrice Lillie', while a teenage Peter Hall first observed here her 'English containment and decency, contrasted with a wild passion'. Richard Findlater wrote of 'one of the most enjoyable evenings I have spent in any theatre, especially John's succession of remarkable hats: blancmange mould, florid cartwheel and even tarboosh, all worn with an air of amused disbelief'.

'I have now realised,' wrote Eleanor Farjeon to an old friend, 'that Henry Irving is only the second-best Benedick I have ever seen.'

John's third production this Stratford summer was to be a *Julius Caesar* co-directed by Quayle and Michael Langham, in which John first played the Cassius that he was famously to film with Brando three years later. With Quayle himself as Mark Antony and Harry Andrews as Brutus, rehearsals started in the only ever pitched battle between Gielgud and his old friend Quayle. Earlier in the season, Quayle had watched from the wings with delight at the changes Peter Brook had brought to bear on Gielgud's acting style, but to his horror John was now reverting to his old romantic ways, while Quayle was determined to have Cassius played as a tough and bitter soldier.

'Go down to Whitehall,' he told John, 'and look at the hard-bitten faces of men trained for action as they come out of the War Office. Cassius is a soldier, up against a better one in Caesar, and he is bitter like Iago because he too has been passed over. You should really be playing him with a clipped moustache.'

John remained unconvinced, but the critics were on Quayle's side, noting that they had never seen John play with such sustained vehemence. For J.C. Trewin, this was a production of 'passionate intensity, memorable force, reproachful nobility and flashing indignation – in the quarrel in the tent with Brutus, Gielgud has a questing, restless, impulsive, opportunistic discontent which I have never seen in him before.' For the second time this summer, John was learning the value of taking advice to heart from other directors and, in the view of *The Times*, 'Gielgud's burning sincerity makes Brutus and even Mark Antony seem puny by comparison.'

But Gielgud had saved for last the production he most wanted to do at Stratford, and as soon as *Caesar* was up and running, he co-directed with Quayle a *King Lear* in which for the third time he would be playing the title role.

This production, as John said in a curtain speech on the first night, was openly dedicated to the help that Harley Granville-Barker had given him when he had last played the role in 1940. Ten years on, this was to be for many critics and audiences the definitive Gielgud *Lear*. Around him he had gathered Peggy Ashcroft as Cordelia, Maxine Audley as Goneril and Gwen Ffrangcon-Davies as Regan, with Harry Andrews as Edgar, and Alan Badel now playing the Fool as a young boy in the only performance of the evening that radically differed from the rules laid down for the play by Granville-Barker.

To his credit Gielgud made no attempt to force Alan in other directions, once he realised that Badel was determined to go it alone. And John was especially thrilled by his mother, now eighty-two, writing after the first night: 'I can only be thankful that I have lived to see John so wholly master of his art and of his public – a great actor and a great artist. To have heard his voice break in "howl, howl, howl, howl" and die in infinite tenderness on a final "never" of utter desolation is to hold a memory unspeakably exquisite. Earlier, he is the primitive man at bay, opposed, frustrated, battered alike by the world and by the elements, forsaken by Cordelia, hounded adrift by his other daughters and their faction. His fight for power, for light itself, rises and falls like the force of a great tide against breakwaters.'

Critics however were not so sure; on the first night John had slightly lost his nerve and several reviews noted that his performance had not really developed since the Vic revival of 1940. But Anthony Quayle cleverly invited several of them to come back and take another look later in the season, by which time John had come into his own, and collected some glowing headlines – many of them, to John's delight, comparing him favourably with the last major *Lear*, the Olivier production at the New four years earlier.

As the season came to an end, Richard Findlater summed up: 'Gielgud has deepened and widened his acting range, ripening his fine sensibility, intelligence and skill; he seems to have renewed confidence in his powers, and a new awareness of his inner strengths and potential.'

The one thing that John had learned by the Avon was that he wanted to work with Peter Brook again as soon as possible ('He is so awfully good at knowing when I am false or bad, and unlike many directors he knows how to tell me so without making me lose my confidence'); and the opportunity arose very quickly with Brook's Festival of Britain production of *The Winter's Tale* early in the following year. Meanwhile he was gratified to learn from Quayle that the 1950 Stratford season had broken all the theatre's records, playing to a total of 350,000 people.

Before his reunion with Brook, however, there was still the Broadway transfer of *The Lady's Not For Burning* to be undertaken. This was not, by any standards, going to be easy. As one American seeing the play in London had remarked, 'Not only can I not understand the accents, I can't understand the language that it is written in.' Nevertheless the word of mouth spreading from London was to make this one of the first great post-war 'snob hits' on Broadway – the kind of play you had to see, even if you weren't entirely sure what it was about.

Pamela Brown and Peter Bull did not get off to the best of starts when they arrived at immigration with trunks entirely full, in Pamela Brown's case, of dead flowers and in Peter Bull's his large collection of teddy bears, plus several strings of pearls that were always worn by Esmé Percy, who had given them to him for safekeeping. The American customs officer decided he was dealing with lunatics, and redirected them straight to Boston, where the play was opening.

Boston went very well, and by the time they reached Broadway Bull noticed a curious phenomenon. They played the whole of the first night to a totally silent audience; the following morning, however, both the *New York Times* and the *New York Herald* announced that Christopher Fry was a brilliant new comic dramatist, and by the matinée that afternoon the theatre was entirely full of old ladies rolling about the aisles at every line. Gielgud gave his entire company tickets to a Christmas matinée of *Guys and Dolls*, and the play continued triumphantly at the Royale Theatre all through a bitter New York winter, even on the night when a confused black front-of-house commissionaire got lost backstage and appeared in his full uniform in the middle of the set. The play simply went on around him until he wandered off, leaving the audience rolling about at what they assumed was yet another Christopher Fry joke. The company also managed during the day to rehearse a radio version of *Hamlet*, not made any easier when John was told that in order to allow for the commercials, the running time could not be more than fifty-five minutes. This was by no means Gielgud's greatest radio *Hamlet*, but it was certainly his fastest.

After their Broadway run, John and his *Lady* company went on the road again, this time breaking all box-office records in Washington and Philadelphia. Then, after a short holiday, he returned to London and Peter Brook for the production of *The Winter's Tale* with which they were to mark the Festival of Britain.

Leontes, like Angelo in their earlier *Measure For Measure*, is one of the fundamentally unsympathetic Shakespearean roles that star players had traditionally avoided, but Brook saw that here too was a chance for John to surprise his critics by going deeply into the psychology of the character. Opening first at Brighton, then playing the Edinburgh Festival and finishing up at the Phoenix, this *Winter's Tale* was to run for a record-breaking 166 performances, the longest ever in Britain. As Peter Brook was later to write:

> Working with John Gielgud, first at Stratford in *Measure For Measure* and then a year later in London with *The Winter's Tale*, I was able to enter a unique and endlessly inventive mind, always open to change. As a director himself, John had acquired a notorious reputation for never knowing what he wanted, but I found this to be totally untrue. I felt very close to him and could easily follow his restless hesitations, as he had only one reference – his intuitive sense of quality. Everything that he questioned and discarded related to an impossible exacting standard that he could never reach. This indecision is far from the confusion that comes from weakness, for when John directed a company, the rejection of the mediocre, the constant demand to go further, to do better, and the sensitive awareness of every fine detail, always led to an impressive unity.

For the critics, T.C. Worsley summed up, in the *New Statesman*: 'Until Gielgud played Angelo in *Measure For Measure* at Stratford last year, he seemed unable to liberate himself from a certain softness which derived, I suspect, from the romantic actor's besetting fault of feeling it is always essential to win the sympathy of an audience. Freed by Peter Brook from that restriction, he is now discovering in himself new depths of feeling and ranges of voice which did not seem to be there before.'

As the run of *The Winter's Tale* came to its end, John decided to stay at the Phoenix and revive his *Much Ado About Nothing* from the previous season at Stratford. Peggy Ashcroft now being otherwise engaged, his new Beatrice was to be Diana Wynyard who had just been playing Hermione to his Leontes.

As Ronald Hayman has noted, there was no problem of rivalry here; Ashcroft and Wynyard had been at school together and remained best friends ever afterwards, even often playing Brutus and Cassius in a celebrated party piece at which they were already trying to point out how much better were the roles Shakespeare wrote for men than for women.

This revival of *Much Ado* was also notable for the casting of a twenty-one-year-old Dorothy Tutin as Hero, an equally young Robert Hardy as Claudio, and the veteran Lewis Casson as Leonato. By now, thought *The Times* critic, Gielgud 'has become adept at turning his minor failings as a tragedian, his natural hauteur and air of remoteness, into comic virtues'.

For Gielgud himself, 'Angelo and Leontes are both given wonderful scenes of repentance in which they are shamed, humiliated and at last forgiven. These later scenes give a fine opportunity for the actor to show both sides of the character.'

John still felt a considerable commitment to Anthony Quayle at Stratford, but this season, because of the long run of *The Winter's Tale*, his sole contribution was to be a somewhat disastrous production of *Macbeth*, starring Ralph Richardson. Relations between the two actors, so good before the war, had now become more than a little strained by what John saw as Richardson's rather threatening wartime alliance with Laurence Olivier, one that had led to their stunning success for the Old Vic at the New Theatre, at a time in the mid-1940s when John had felt at his most alone and unloved.

Moreover, even at this post-war moment, Richardson was still very uneasy about John's homosexuality; only a few seasons earlier, when Olivier had suggested that for their production of *Othello* it might be rather clever to play Iago homosexual, Richardson had simply and wordlessly left the theatre for two entire days, thereby conveying the unmistakeable message that he wasn't getting involved in anything like that, even on stage.

All the same, he now welcomed the chance to be again directed by John, albeit in a part at which John had himself spectacularly failed, and one that Richardson had never played. The critic Kenneth Tynan, already making his name as the brightest and most savage of the new generation, was to note that he had been 'unmoved to the point of paralysis by this production', coming as it did when Richardson had already had one disaster at Stratford that season with *Volpone*.

The *Macbeth* was to be not a lot better, and for years afterwards Richardson was to surprise young actors by going up to them in rehearsal and demanding £5 with the threat, 'If you don't give it to me, cocky, I shall put it about that you were in my *Macbeth*.'

The real problem here was twofold. John had never been entirely happy with the play, and Richardson could never convey characters who were the victim of blind passions. In a curious way he was just too ordinary, and although it was unfair of Tynan to complain that Richardson was 'sleepwalking through the role', there was no doubt that neither he nor Margaret Leighton were ever happy with a production for which John himself had designed sets consisting largely of black velvet drapes and very little else.

Chapter Fifteen

CASSIUS AND CALIFORNIA
(1952)

Joseph Mankiewicz's Julius Caesar *was the first film I really
enjoyed making, even though during the battle scenes, which we
shot in a great hurry in the Hollywood Bowl, I was nearly killed
by a horse leaping on top of me.*

Unlike all his Shakespearean star contemporaries from Redgrave to Richardson, who were now spending almost as
much time in movies as in plays, John was still seldom making
more than £75 a week; not only was that the going rate for leading
players at Stratford, but in London Binkie was still keeping him on
a very tight rein, having persuaded Gielgud that he never needed an
agent, and that simply by joining a loose alliance run by himself and
John Perry and termed the Company of Four (partly because they
reckoned that their theatrical ideal would be four weeks in rehearsal,
four on the road and then four in town, and partly because the original
managerial quartet was to feature Binkie, Tony Guthrie of the Vic,
Rudolph Bing of Glyndebourne and the regional theatre manager at
Cambridge, Norman Higgins), he would simply continue to be paid
at a minimal rate for whatever he did.

Binkie's best trick was to tell the ever-innocent John that if he really
wanted Peggy Ashcroft or Gwen Ffrangcon-Davies or lavish sets and
costumes, there would alas be very little left to pay him at anything
like the going rate. Whether John was really dumb enough to believe
this or, more likely, whether he had just decided as usual to keep his
head down and not makes waves, the fact remains that only with a

sudden offer from Hollywood, to play Cassius in *Julius Caesar* (his first since the one he had rejected long before the war, to play Romeo), did John even begin to think that it might be a good idea to have some sort of professional representation.

On his last visit to New York he had also been somewhat flabbergasted to meet Vivien Leigh at a party. As their conversation turned to the costs of living in New York during a long run 'on our kind of salaries', Vivien Leigh, in some amazement, told him she was having no trouble at all on her salary, since this was ten per cent of the gross. John, still on a 'friendly nation' deal whereby he was taking home at most $500 as against Leigh's $5,000 a week, began for the very first time to realise that there was something a little wrong with Binkie's mathematics. But he might well, even so, have done nothing about this, so paralysed with embarrassment and shyness did he become at any mention of cash or contracts until much later in his long life.

But John, with the Hollywood offer in his pocket, now went at Vivien Leigh's recommendation to see Laurie Evans, who having been Olivier's production manager on *Henry V* had now set up as an agent, and managed immediately to negotiate for John a contract on a sliding scale, up to $20,000 depending on the length of the shooting. For 1952, and an actor who had then no Hollywood profile of any kind, this was an amazingly good deal, as even John realised. Shortly afterwards, he asked Laurie to become his permanent agent, with only the proviso that Evans rather than Gielgud himself would have to break the news to an understandably irate Binkie, who took it as a gesture of deep disloyalty, despite the fact that he had cheerfully for almost fifteen years been paying everybody in and around Gielgud's companies, including himself and John Perry, vastly more money than was ever paid to John himself, without whom there would have been no such companies in the first place.

The Hollywood project was one of considerable fascination; with Joseph Mankiewicz as director, the producer was to be the John Houseman who had worked with Orson Welles on both *War of the Worlds* and *Citizen Kane*, and who was now retained by MGM as their producer in charge of culture, since the studio moguls had recognised that there was still something to be said for appeasing the critics as well as the public, as long as it didn't cost them too much. Houseman had also been, before the war, the director of the short-lived Leslie Howard *Hamlet* on Broadway, so Gielgud had always been in his sights; indeed he had unsuccessfully begged Howard not to open in New York until Gielgud had safely returned to London and there was no immediate danger of comparison.

So now, more than fifteen years later, it was Houseman's idea to bring John into the film that he was about to make:

> Against studio advice, I argued that the film should not be made in Europe, where at the time MGM did many of their pictures, but instead at their home base in Culver City, and with an even balance of actors from either side of the Atlantic. Our first casting was John Gielgud, in the role he had just played with success at Stratford-on-Avon, of Cassius. But to balance that, I wanted Louis Calhern for Caesar – an ageing, tired, nervous dictator, rather than the more usually triumphant one. For Brutus, we chose James Mason, now widely regarded as a Hollywood star, who although he had not appeared on stage in many years, had a classical training and the right quality for an honest, serious man torn between his republican ideals and his moral reluctance to shed blood. To play the wives, we used two MGM contract stars, both English-born but now generally accepted in American roles – Deborah Kerr as the devoted, fanatically loyal Portia, and Greer Garson as Caesar's neurotic and apprehensive mate, Calpurnia. For the small but crucial role of Casca, I chose Edmund O'Brien who was only cast now for detectives and crooked lawyers, but who I remembered as a young Shakespearean.

On his way to California John stopped over briefly in New York, where he noted, in a letter to his mother, a change in the Broadway climate.

> It is interesting how action has been stolen almost completely by the cinema nowadays and the American theatre is given over more and more to psychological exploitation with almost embarrassingly realistic dialogue and atmosphere and character taking the place of strong situations – not the long-winded perorations of Shaw and Ibsen but nostalgia mixed with violence, which seems to be so characteristic of

Tennessee Williams and other young writers . . . I am looking forward to getting out to Hollywood, especially as the plan we once had to do a *Julius Caesar* in London with Larry as Mark Antony and Ralph as Brutus seems to have disappeared . . . New York seems to me now like a gigantic monster waiting to swallow one up . . . traffic seems to drive right through one's bedroom and the noise on the streets is unbelievable . . . I find New York immensely stimulating, both in people and climate. The shops and streets are an endless kaleidoscope of colour and I seem to have made lots of friends here who are always glad to see me back. I rather fear we are never as hospitable to Americans in London as they are to us over here . . . I hope we manage to do *Julius Caesar* better than Orson's film of *Macbeth* which I have just seen – not uninteresting, but slow and dragged-out despite huge cuts and transpositions. The costumes are splendid, but the finer language is defeated by the limitations of the screen.

Houseman's careful casting still left him with one major gap: the actor who was to play the central role of Mark Antony. On a visit to London, he asked Gielgud for advice and John recommended the young Paul Scofield, who had just begun to make his name with Peter Brook at Stratford, and around whom John was soon to build his last resident company. But the Hollywood moguls weren't having any of that, and went instead for Houseman's second, and amazingly courageous, choice: Marlon Brando, who was just coming off his triumph as Stanley Kowalski in the stage and screen versions of *A Streetcar Named Desire*. Houseman knew, as most did not, that Brando was in fact capable of much more than just the slurred Polish rapist, and he invited Brando privately to make a tape of the 'Friends, Romans, Countrymen' speech, one that was in fact so impressive that Mankiewicz cast him right away, with only the provision (then unknown but later to become standard for 'serious' movies) that the entire cast should assemble for a three-week rehearsal period before any filming actually began.

As Houseman recalled:

Gielgud, from the first moment, set the tone. Not only was he already of course word-perfect and totally secure in the role of Cassius, but he seemed to inspire everyone in the cast, down to the smallest bit-player, with his own high sense of professional dedication. His perfectionism was apparent not only to his fellow actors but to everyone even remotely connected with the production. Hollywood technicians (a notoriously sceptical and bigoted lot) are men of great technical expertise, capable of recognising and appreciating such skills in others. Whenever Gielgud was working, our 'closed' set was invaded by grips, carpenters, electricians and sound men who left their own stages and dubbing rooms to come and admire the amazing skill of this English master of the spoken word, and to debate how such fluent speech could be transferred to film without loss of quality.

Houseman's budget was a mere $1.5 million, as against the $5 million that MGM had recently spent on *Quo Vadis*; but, again against advice from the moguls, he insisted on shooting in black and white, thereby preserving a grainy reality which brought back to audiences the wartime newsreels of the recent past, and even memories of *Citizen Kane*.

Gielgud at first kept his distance from Brando, determined not to seem the arrogant English classicist trying to teach the Hollywood natives correct styles of Shakespeare. His relationship with James Mason was of course much easier, in that John had given Mason one of his earliest breaks in the short-lived 1934 *Queen of Scots*. Mason had really been the idea of the director Joseph Mankiewicz: 'I knew he had once played Brutus in Ireland at a very early age, and he was precisely the one I wanted: very complex, and broody and unhappy, a man who looked as though he belonged on a lonely battlefield. I was very glad that Houseman had won the battle for black and white, because even though colour was then all the rage, I knew that the assassination scene would be nothing but a great bloody mess and the audience would be looking at the blood instead of the face of Brutus, which was really the heart of the film. There was always a romantic sadness about James, which was just perfect.'

As for John:

James had much more to teach me on that film than I ever had to teach him. I used to observe his technique in the close-ups, and saw how brilliantly he expressed his character's thoughts without making faces or grimacing. I thought his Brutus was underrated by most critics, since it is certainly the most difficult part in the play. He was extremely kind and generous to me, especially as I was still afraid they would all think I was this star actor from London who had come over to teach them how to do it. But I was surprised how much of my performance I was able to keep from the stage. It was only a question of modifying the volume and I was able to play it much faster, which I had always wanted to do in the theatre.

Even so, the first read-through was not easy, as Houseman recalled: 'Gielgud, justly celebrated as the finest reader of verse on the English-speaking stage, just sailed through the part of Cassius with terrifying bravura. Mason, both depressed and embarrassed by the brilliance of his compatriot, chose to read the entire role of Brutus with a pipe clenched firmly between his teeth.'

Meanwhile, MGM were taking no chances at the box-office: 'A Story Greater Even Than *Ivanhoe*' read the posters and for John G, on this first Hollywood assignment, the entire project was rich in local eccentricities. 'All right, kids,' he once heard an assistant director exhorting a crowd of recalcitrant American extras, just before the filming of the Forum scene. 'It's hot, it's Rome and here comes Julius!' On another occasion, Gielgud recalled, 'I was waiting to go on to the Rome street set with a whole menagerie of sheep, dogs and pigeons, which had been brought in to make the city look more lively . . . one of the pigeons left its perch and began walking around the floor of the studio, whereupon a hefty cowboy, who had evidently been hired to look after all the animals, dashed up and yelled at the bird, "Get back! Get back to your place! Don't you want to work tomorrow?"'

Altogether, the filming took very nearly four months; at first, John stayed at the luxurious Bel Air Hotel, but soon he moved into a little house on North Kentner Drive, owned by a doctor friend of the actress Merle Oberon's who was away in Europe for the summer. He rented John the house complete with a resident cook, and like so many English actors who had arrived and often settled there before him, John now began to understand the joys of the Californian life. Coming from a usually rain-soaked West End, where he had hardly even bothered to see daylight, the sudden availability of all that sunshine and sea and sand was not the only attraction: around such Anglophile directors as George Cukor, writers such as Christopher Isherwood and actors such as Roddy McDowall, there was already a strongly established homosexual community, one that was able to function in comparative freedom. The Hollywood press was still strictly controlled by the studios, and as long as one did not actually attract the attention of the local police, a discreet gay life was entirely possible. Moreover, if one went to the right dinner parties, handsome young men were often laid on to entertain the male guests afterwards, or later assignations could easily be arranged.

From the very beginning of the *Julius Caesar* shooting, John was much taken by Brando: 'a funny, intense, egocentric boy of twenty-seven with a flat nose and bullet head, huge arms and shoulders and yet giving the effect of a lean, Greenwich Village college student. He is very nervous indeed, muttering his lines and rehearsing by himself all day long. Very deferential to me, drags me off to record the speeches of Antony on to his tape machine where he also listens to his own voice, and studies recordings of Olivier, Barrymore and Maurice Evans, to improve his diction. I think his sincerity may bring him to an interesting performance; his English is not all that bad, but I fear he lacks humour.'

From the moment of his first arrival in Los Angeles, John wrote a series of weekly letters home to his mother in London, which can be read as a diary of that long, hot summer:

The sudden change is a bit bewildering, and I feel like a new boy at school. Luckily I have persuaded them not to make me wear a beard, but the general atmosphere of California is restless and ugly – like a poor copy of the worst of the south of France. Yet people are terribly kind to me; I had hardly unpacked before Danny Kaye rang up and sent his car to take me to his house for dinner – a very rich crowd and very nasty food, but everyone frightfully welcoming, the men in sports clothes and the women in deep evening dress. Los Angeles is really too hot for comfort, and the town is a horror of ugliness, as flat as your hand and crawling with cars. Nobody dreams of walking anywhere, and all the shops and houses are miles apart . . .

James Mason seems rather nasal as Brutus, and is playing him like a modern army officer but certainly much more intelligent than Harry Andrews in the role . . . Brando belongs to a student theatre in New York, but surprisingly the real star here at the moment is dear Richard Burton, having a huge success making Daphne du Maurier's *My Cousin Rachel*. Last night he drove me to Malibu Beach to dine with the Selznicks – she is Jennifer Jones. Chaplin was there, and I had a long and fascinating talk with him. He is prissy, weary and neat, with carefully waved white hair and wonderful little expressive hands. He alternates between rather pretentious philosophical generalities and sudden bursts of very natural sweetness and warmth. He has a funny, shy little young wife, the daughter of Eugene O'Neill, who obviously worships him. He talked to me with great nostalgia of his young days in London, and seeing from the gallery Beerbohm Tree and Eleanor Duse, of whom he can still do wonderful imitations, really brilliant.

Parties here are grand but clumsy – awful food, too much drink, too much noise and the weirdest mixture of clothes, but it is not difficult to pick out the people one really wants to talk to, and the other guests don't seem to trouble one, or expect one to trouble about them. I have hired a superb pale green Oldsmobile by the week, and drive to a little beach ten miles away, watching the enormous breakers. Conversations are always about local ambitions and disappointments, very like the West End, really, except for the fact that dining-room walls are hung with fabulous pictures by Matisse, Van Gogh, Daumier and Picasso. Sometimes one wall rises mysteriously into the air, complete with its paintings, and a film projector emerges to show us the latest films, all of which seem fairly terrible. Last night I went to the ballet in the Hollywood Bowl, and again it was amazing to be able to sit in the open air until nearly midnight, without a coat. The local houses and gardens are very artificial and over-elegant, usually imitation Tudor or American Colonial, and everyone looks very healthy. There is an extraordinary abundance of everything – fruit and flowers and vegetables laid out under the sky in the open-air markets, but in some curious way the whole of Los Angeles looks like an Ideal Home Exhibition at Olympia, which will all be taken down in a month or two and rebuilt for next year.

My Cassius is looking rather like the thirteenth apostle, but everyone seems very happy with it, and Brando and Mason are really going to be very good, although I fear Calhern is very hammy as Caesar, and both Deborah Kerr and Greer Garson simper horribly as the wives. Every night I get taken to a party, but some people are really intelligent and nice, and they love to display their elaborate homes, which are all like the sets for a play. At the studio, I have a dressing-room with a sofa, so that is lovely . . . We don't seem to get much news from England, though everyone here has been terribly shocked by the sudden death of Gertie Lawrence; like Ivor [Novello, who had died in March 1951], she really did go much too young . . . People seem delighted with the rushes, and Ethel Barrymore came regally to visit our set, wheezing heavily.

I spent Labour Day lying on the beach, and am hoping to visit San Francisco one weekend before I leave. The filming is getting rather dull, and I am now restless and eager to be home . . . I was taken to a dinner for Stravinsky, who seemed charming but rather vague, and I have begun already to make plans for a new season in London. I really have enjoyed being here, although the studio workers are really much more fun than the local high society, or all the English exiles who seem somehow vaguely disgruntled, trapped by the weather and the money but secretly yearning to be home. The last few days' shooting was the battle scene, which we had to do in the Hollywood Bowl under scorching sunlight and as usual I hated being on horseback, especially in the heat and dust. I have seen some early footage and think I am rather good in the tent scene, although I still blink and fidget far too much in the close-ups.

I have just been to see Charles Laughton, Charles Boyer, Cedric Hardwicke and Agnes Moorehead reading Shaw's *Don Juan in Hell*. As you know, I am no Shaw addict and it seemed to me a perfectly terrible exhibition of fake spontaneity and a terrific bore. As for the film, Calhern is dreadful as Caesar, and some of the sets are terribly over-decorated as regards furniture and accessories. Caesar's house is so full of statues and gongs and elephant tusks that you can hardly move, and at least one of the sets had been rebuilt from *Ben Hur*. I showed it to a knowledgeable friend, who pointed out quietly that all the statues were of emperors who had not yet been born, and one of the things that amuses me most is that the extras are paid different salaries, according to their looks – those closest to the camera are the ones with the most striking faces and the best salaries, while the ones at the back are allowed to keep their trousers on under their togas. But I have to admit that the plot comes over very clearly, and the poetry not at all badly.

As for Brando, already on twice John's salary and earning $40,000 for the film, he alone suggested that the word around the studio was that Gielgud was nervous at the possibility that his homosexuality might come across on the big screen. According to Brando, Gielgud had told the director that he was frightened of his mannerisms but as soon as he got into the armour of Cassius, Brando began to take a shine to him, especially when Gielgud offered him the chance to play Hamlet in London, one that Brando, perhaps wisely, declined.

Quite late in the filming, Brando, unaccustomed to the vocal disciplines of a long Shakespearean role, lost his voice completely, putting them four days behind schedule, but when he returned, recalled John, 'He never once seemed to lose his energy or concentration, and when he did falter he would stop, apologise gracefully, compose himself and start again.'

As for Joseph Mankiewicz, who was to return some ten years later to this Roman territory with the rather more epic and troublesome Burton/Taylor *Cleopatra*, the film was everything he hoped it would be, and when it opened a few months later Bosley Crowther for the *New York Times* wrote enthusiastically of the way in which 'he brings us so close to the characters that the very warmth of their body heat, and the intensity of their passions in thoughtful or violent moods, seems to come right out of the frame and create the dynamic of the picture.'

Mankiewicz memorably described his *Julius Caesar* as 'a good, rip-snorting piece of blood and thunder, coupled with eternally new and up-to-date characters'. As the years went by the rather cool initial critical reception began to change; although several critics still objected that the film lacked a central, organising principle (in, for instance, the way that Olivier's film of *Hamlet* a few years earlier had opened with his celebrated voice-over: 'This is the story of a man who could not make up his mind'), others began to feel that Hollywood could do no better with Shakespeare. Bennett Cerf called it 'the most impressive and exciting movie I have ever seen'. One or two other reviewers would have preferred Montgomery Clift as Cassius and again took the view that John was too stagey; but the film never takes too many liberties and John Houseman could proudly note that even though many studio moguls had originally wanted Richard Burton rather than Brando, Marlon's performance in the end justified the risk and even achieved heroic proportions.

During the last few weeks of the *Julius Caesar* filming, John had plenty of time to think, while sitting around on the set between shots, of what he would like to do when he got home to London in the autumn of 1952. He had decided, perhaps for the last time, to try yet again his luck as the star and director of a resident classical West End stage company. But this time, even his faithful Binkie was only prepared to finance him at the Lyric, Hammersmith, rather than, as previously, on Shaftesbury Avenue. Whether this could be considered an example of Binkie's usual economic caution, or more spitefully as revenge on Gielgud for having gone off to Hollywood and, far worse, acquired the services of an agent, remains unclear.

As 1952 ended, John took the train across America and sailed from New York for home, blissfully unaware of the tempest that was about to break over his head and all but finish his career.

Chapter Sixteen

❧❦❧

ANNUS HORRIBILIS
(1953)

You will leave this courtroom, and immediately seek
the help of your doctor.

The worst year in John G's life started harmlessly and happily enough; he was now home again, at the Lyric, Hammersmith, at the head of the first resident management he had achieved since the war. The disaster of the previous summer, his production of *Macbeth* at Stratford with Ralph Richardson, had already been forgotten, and the long stay in Hollywood, for the filming of *Julius Caesar*, had given him a certain amount of cash in the bank for the very first time in his life.

Writing at this time the first of his many Gielgud profiles, Kenneth Tynan noted:

Gielgud is not so much an actor as *the* actor . . . he is a theatrical possession, an inscription, a figurehead and a touchstone . . . he is the guarantee, rather than the product. The seal and signature rather than the proclamation . . . he lends dignity to the ramshackle business of stage pretence and he is always a tireless endorser – on a Broadway poster this season showing a gigantic, leggy picture of the coloured singer Eartha Kitt, there is the legend 'Just my cup of tea – John Gielgud' . . . his own style is eclectic – it is not wholly of its century but its stamp stays on the mind . . . it joins hands across epochs . . . his is a teacher's face, and the voice thrills like an arrow . . . even at his worst, Gielgud has a way of sanctifying everything that goes on in whatever theatre he occupies; he transforms play-goers into pilgrims.

Financially supported by H.M. Tennent's non-profit company, John had taken a six-month lease on the Lyric, Hammersmith with the idea of returning to a classical management, in many ways the only post-war forerunner (since Olivier's near-contemporary management of the St James's was always a much more commercial West End project) of what was to become the National Theatre a decade later, given that Stratford and the Old Vic were then purely Shakespearean. His repertoire was to consist of *Richard II*, Congreve's *The Way of the World* and Otway's then barely ever revived *Venice Preserv'd*. The arts diarist of *Vogue* could barely contain her anticipation: 'John Gielgud, the non-pareil, the cynosure of the theatre, is the flashing, sparkling mind behind this new season of infinite promise – he will direct all three plays and act himself in the second and third. Now his powers are at their greatest – sensibility, strength, imagination, wit, all combine to make him the true aristocrat of both tragedy and comedy.'

While he was setting up this season, John was introduced, by Cecil Beaton, to a flamboyant new figure on the West End scene, Kenneth Tynan, who had back in 1945 already been writing to John with suggestions as to how John might cut his *Hamlet*. Though not homosexual himself, at least not very often, Tynan's exotic theatricality and his extravagant reviewing style had already brought him considerable attention and as he now wrote to Beaton, Ken was basking in the starlight: 'John G, whom I had never met, suddenly asked me to supper and we talked until three, I coaxed into silence by his beauty, he garrulous and fluttering as a dove. What a possession he is for any theatre! It is irrelevant to say that he was fair in this part, good in that, brilliant in the other; Gielgud is more important than the sum of his parts, and any theatre that has him securely lashed to its mast will not steer dreadfully wrongly.'

Surprisingly, perhaps, the only leading role in this season that John was not playing was the one with which, Hamlet aside, the public still most identified him; but at forty-nine he had reluctantly decided that his years as Richard of Bordeaux were at last over, and his casting of

Paul Scofield, the young actor who in many ways most resembled him, was a torch being graciously passed on to the next generation. Scofield himself, then just thirty, found it somewhat uneasy being directed as Richard II by the man who above all others had made the role his own, especially as John was not above giving actual line-readings in rehearsal, and vaguely expecting Paul to recall precisely how his director had played the role, and exactly where on stage he had always stood for any one scene.

Nevertheless, the reviews were ecstatic, though John was perhaps less than thrilled to read in at least one of them that Scofield was now 'the true Richard' and less of a 'butterfly artist' than his director. No sooner had they opened than they were already in rehearsal for *The Way of the World*, John as both director and Mirabell, with Pamela Brown as his Millamant and Scofield rather less happy as the flashy Witwoud. This was the play that, with Edith Evans and Robert Loraine, had restored the always dodgy pre-war fortunes of the Lyric, Hammersmith, and there was the feeling that the role of Millamant still essentially belonged to Dame Edith, whom John had seen play it when he was just twenty. Once more, the general tenor of the reviews was ecstatic, not least perhaps because, at a less than wonderful time for Stratford or the Vic, critics were delighted to have a third classical company at their disposal. John had initially described his new company, in a wondrous word of his own invention, as the 'conglamouration of stars' and certainly this production, with not only himself and Scofield and Brown but also Margaret Rutherford in a rare classical appearance as Lady Wishfort, was glamorous and starry enough even for Tynan, who wrote in the *Observer* of Scofield's 'beautifully gaudy performance, pitched somewhere between Stan Laurel and Hermione Gingold'; of Rutherford he added, 'the soul of Cleopatra has become trapped in the corporate shape of an entire lacrosse team', and of the two principals: 'Mr Gielgud, an impeccable Mirabell in plum velvet, has Pamela Brown begging for mercy almost before their battle is even joined.'

It was left, unusually, to Brooks Atkinson of the *New York Times* to enter a more chilly verdict: 'As an exercise in stylisation the acting is immaculate, satirically mannered and accomplished, but in perfecting the style Mr Gielgud has omitted the life . . . both he and Miss Brown sacrifice the fun to the technique. His Mirabell is too scholarly, and her Millamant lacks force.'

But there was better to come: for the last play in the Hammersmith season, well into the spring of 1953, Gielgud had chosen Otway's *Venice Preserv'd*, the last great verse tragedy in the English language but at that time seen only once in the century, in a 1920 production at the Royalty with Cathleen Nesbitt, Ion Swinley and Balliol Holloway. But Gielgud had always known the play, and recognised its especial virtue: like *Othello* but almost no other classic it offered two virtually equal male roles, those in which he now cast himself and Scofield. Rather than direct the third play of the season himself, he brought in Peter Brook, then still two years away from his thirtieth birthday but already revered as the classical *wunderkind* of the decade for his early work with Gielgud and later Scofield at Stratford.

Brook now brought all of his beady, brooding intelligence to the major rediscovery of the Gielgud season and the London year: it was entirely because of this revival that *Venice Preserv'd* was brought back into the twentieth-century vision, and Brook's genius here lay, as one of the most reliable of all theatre historians, J.C. Trewin, observed, 'in neither forcing the tragedy, nor fussing nor pampering it as a fragile antique . . . even now I can recreate scene after scene, from the conspirators' heavy-arched cellar to the Senate, enthroned against the darkly glowing depths, the lagoon's sombre calm, the Execution scene suggested without some dolorous parade.'

This noble, romantic, morbid play gave Gielgud as Jaffeir, and Scofield as his friend and ally Pierre, the chance to play one of the great double acts of the classical decade, one that was only to be challenged three years later by Richard Burton and John Neville alternating Othello and Iago at the Vic, though Tynan was now less impressed: 'The play's major flaw is that Otway allows Jaffeir far too much self-pity, a mood of which John Gielgud as an actor is far too fond. The temptation sometimes proves too much for him: inhaling passionately through his nose, he administers to every line a tremendous parsonical quiver.'

Before the worst, the best was yet to come; both Ralph Richardson and Laurence Olivier were still feeling uneasy about the omission from any subsequent honours list of Gielgud, their contemporary, rival, sometime friend and (vocally at least) their superior, could they but admit it. Both actor-knights put the case to Churchill, who in 1953 overcame whatever official doubts there may have been about Gielgud's reasonably well-known, if still never publicly acknowledged, homosexuality. The case for knighting great actors with 'unusual' private lives was then a difficult one, best acknowledged by Gielgud himself in a flash of instant wit when, five years later, a still edgy Buckingham Palace agreed to the next great classical knighthood, the one awarded to Michael Redgrave. He too had an 'unusual' private life, one that had already combined marriage to Rachel Kempson and the fathering of Vanessa, Corin and Lynn with long homosexual friendships (notably the American producer Fred Sadoff) and a widely rumoured love of homosexual bondage. 'Ah,' said Gielgud, meeting Redgrave in the street a day or two after he had returned jubilant from the Palace, 'Sir Michael Redgrave, I'll be bound!'

But for now, Gielgud's own knighthood was a cause of considerable celebration; he received it in the Coronation Honours list of 1953, announced just twenty-four hours before the Queen came to be crowned, and man stood on Everest for the first time in a summer of general rejoicing. Indeed when John came out on stage in what the *Venice Preserv'd* cast irreverently referred to as their 'gondola garage' of a Venetian set, to speak Jaffeir's opening line, 'My lord, I am not that abject wretch you think me', the audience rose to cheer him as never before, as Paul Scofield recalls: 'The audience exploded into wild cheering and applause. When, a long time later, I came on, John's face was streaming with tears and the whole theatre was charged with high, emotional excitement. It seemed as if the whole world was glad for him, and he was overwhelmed by this quite unexpected and clamorous revelation of public affection. And it was his own humility and vulnerability that was most moving; it was also quite funny, because it wasn't easy after that to get on with the play.'

When, in July, the Hammersmith season had run its six-month course, John flew out to Africa, where his former lover John Perry was organising a Rhodes Festival for Bulawayo. Gielgud had decided, after handling the mantle of *Richard II* on to Scofield, that he would after all like to have one final crack at the role himself, a decision that he rapidly came to regret: 'on the verge of my fiftieth year I was simply too old for it, and all I really achieved was a rather poor imitation of the performance I had given in London sixteen years earlier.'

He had other reasons to dislike the Rhodes Festival: on the way out, his Comet had lost its undercarriage at Rome, only then to have to land in the midst of a sandstorm in Khartoum. The considerable delays meant even less rehearsal time than had originally been allocated, and John now also had to deal with a supporting cast that was distinctly patchy, since Perry had been unable to attract to the new festival any other stars or leading character players. But driving through Victoria Falls, he wrote to his mother in England of 'the most lovely light at every moment, two or three rainbows at a time spanning those great gorges where the vast heaps of water hurl themselves, while down below grey, heaving clouds of spray are like the bottom of a gigantic cauldron with rocks and slopes of trees that make the dramatic impact still finer'. The falls were clearly the highlight of the trip.

The theatre in Bulawayo was cold and vast, and a production that had been acclaimed only a few months earlier, with Scofield in the lead, now looked suddenly tired and dispirited: 'I was terribly disappointed to find that, contrary to all my expectations, it gave me no pleasure at all. I could only imitate the performance I gave when I was a young man, and the fact that I was older and wiser now didn't make me any better in the part; you can't imitate a young part with any kind of pleasure, and I realised I had done it so much better then. I should never have gone back to it.'

It was therefore an unusually and unduly depressed Gielgud who returned to England in the late summer of 1953; the joy he had felt at the knighthood and the triumph of his Hammersmith season, both critically and commercially, had abruptly vanished to be replaced with a deep sense of mourning over the death that summer of his beloved elder brother Lewis, and a strong feeling that he had failed, and failed badly, at the Rhodes Festival.

Not that his career prospects appeared any less golden than they had been a few months earlier. His plans now included another season at Hammersmith (this one to feature Trevor Howard and Gwen Ffrangcon-Davies in *The Cherry Orchard*), a commercial revival of *Charley's Aunt* to star John Mills, and the choice of two major new plays, both of which required him as director and star. The first of these was John Whiting's *Marching Song*, a strange, poetic piece which had been written specially for him by a dramatist still sadly overlooked today but who, in a brief period of 1950s glory (*A Penny For A Song*, *Saint's Day*), was reckoned to be among the major white hopes of the post-war theatre.

John announced to the theatre press that he would do *Marching Song* but then, and rather ashamedly, began to entertain serious doubts about its commercial chances in a West End still deeply in love with elegant revivals. These doubts were amply justified when the play was eventually staged without Gielgud's participation a year later, but it is arguable that Whiting never fully recovered from what he saw as the actor's betrayal of a promise, and it was a somewhat sheepish John who instead chose a vastly more commercial option.

This was to be N.C. Hunter's *A Day by the Sea*, reckoned by its admirers to be 'English seaside Chekhov' and by Kenneth Tynan to be 'an evening of unexampled triviality'. But Hunter had already enjoyed a huge Haymarket success with *Waters of the Moon*, and the plan by Binkie Beaumont of H.M. Tennent was once again to bring together an all-star cast (this time Ralph Richardson, Sybil Thorndike, Lewis Casson, Irene Worth and Megs Jenkins) in a production by Gielgud in which he would also star and which would safely and happily exemplify the Theatre Royal, Haymarket, at its most characteristically tea-matinée reassuring.

The play itself made few demands on John as either director or actor, since it was at best formulaic, and its merit can perhaps best be judged by the fact that it has never had a major London revival. But John now found himself in a deep conflict. On the one hand, the Hollywood filming of *Julius Caesar* and his first Hammersmith season, as well as the knighthood, all within the last twelve months, had represented new peaks in his career as actor and director, and his current dual engagement at the Haymarket was a reaffirmation of his standing in the commercial theatre as well as the classics.

But on the other hand, the death of his brother, the failure (in his own eyes, at least) of his farewell *Richard II* in Africa, and perhaps above all the feeling of personal inadequacy and shame that he had taken the soft option of *Day by the Sea* in lieu of Whiting's infinitely more risky but challenging *Marching Song*, all came together at a time of considerable personal and professional exhaustion to push him into the greatest tragedy of his life and one that to this day, some half a century later, still resonates throughout the sexual history of the British theatre.

It is difficult, in a new century after a Labour government has appointed an openly gay Minister for Arts and Heritage, and when their Tory predecessors knighted a crusading gay actor, Ian McKellen, in a deliberate attempt to allay accusations of sexual prejudice, to recall the precise social and sexual climate of Britain in Coronation year. The early 1950s were a quite remarkably intolerant time; the Lord Chamberlain, still the theatrical censor, was reacting unfavourably to any but the most coded suggestions of homosexuality on stage, and in private men were still committing suicide rather than live with any public knowledge of their homosexual lifestyles. In this summer of 1953 the most celebrated homosexual trial since that of Oscar Wilde in 1895 had started with two accusations by boy scouts that they had been sexually assaulted over a bank holiday weekend by Lord Montagu of Beaulieu and his friend, the assistant film director Kenneth Hume.

Montagu, who had just announced his engagement to Anne Gage, denied all charges and suggested that the scouts had stolen a camera from him and were now trying to cloud the issue of theft with one of homosexual rape. Both Hume and Montagu (who had courageously returned from France when it was clear the case was not going to slide away) were sent for trial, and on the very last day, when at Winchester Crown Court it looked as though the police were easily going to lose their case because of the unreliability and conflict of the scouts' testimony, the police introduced an altogether different charge, that of indecent assault on two airmen. This resulted in Montagu being jailed for a year, while two other men, the author and *Daily Mail* diplomatic correspondent Peter Wildeblood and Montagu's cousin Michael Pitt-Rivers, got eighteen months each for sexual offences. The magistrate, handing out what he called 'these lenient sentences' (the critic Kenneth Tynan had stood bail for Wildeblood, and nobody was expecting them to suffer anything worse than a heavy fine),

MARCH, 1933

Vol. XIX.—No. 98

THEATRE WORLD

THEATRE WORLD

SPECIAL SUPPLEMENT
"RICHARD OF BORDEAUX"

1/-

JOHN GIELGUD
PORTRAIT BY YVONNE GREGORY

West End stardom in March 1933: Vintage Bordeaux at £100 a week:
'Gielgud is now right at the top of his profession, having acquired all the
marks of the great actor' (*The Times*)

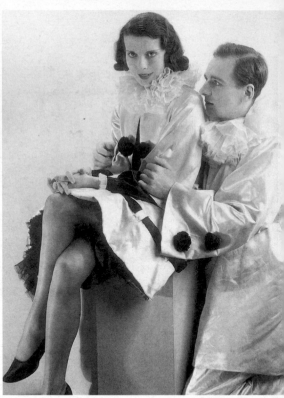

His first Prospero at the Old Vic; and with Adele Dixon, back in the West End for the play (and then the film) of Priestley's *The Good Companions*

His first *King Lear* at the Old Vic: John was just 27

'Even into the 1970s, there were audiences who wished I had never given up playing *Richard of Bordeaux*

The production that led John to the
creation of the first classical repertory
company in the West End; Jessica Tandy
was his Ophelia, and the company also
included her then husband Jack
Hawkins, George Devine, Glen Byam
Shaw, Anthony Quayle and a young Alec
Guinness

March 15

NEW THEATRE

ST. MARTIN'S LANE, W.C.2

Licensed by the Lord Chamberlain to HOWARD WYNDHAM

6D.

JOHN GIELGUD
as HAMLET

Lessees
THE WYNDHAM THEATRES, Ltd.

Managing Directors
HOWARD WYNDHAM and BRONSON ALBERY

John directing Laurence Olivier, Peggy Ashcroft and Edith Evans in the 1935 *Romeo and Juliet* for which Larry and John (below) alternated Mercutio and Romeo

Gielgud offstage (left), at the christening of Emlyn Williams' son Alan, with Emlyn himself and Noel Coward holding the baby

Gibraltar, Christmas 1942. (Back row) Hugh Beaumont, Edith Evans, Elizabeth Welch (middle row) John, Jeanne de Casalis, Michael Wilding, Cyril Baker (front) Phyllis Stanley, Beatrice Lillie

'A handbag?' John (again as John Worthing) with Edith Evans and Gwen Ffangcon-Davies in the definitive 1939 revival of *The Importance of Being Earnest*

Peter Lorre, John, Madeleine Carroll and Robert Young in Hitchcock's *The Secret Agent*, John's first major film but the one that convinced him he had no future as a screen star

'Blow winds, and crack your cheeks': John's second (1940) Old Vic *King Lear* and (below) showing the wig to his proud parents

solemnly advised all three to 'consult their doctors at the earliest opportunity'.

The witch-hunt which Harold Nicolson, himself a closet homosexual all his life, had first feared at the 1951 escape to Moscow of Burgess and Maclean, had taken a little longer than he forecast but there could be no doubt that by 1953 it was at full strength. For theatre people, still accustomed to a more lenient wartime sexual climate, this presented special problems; thousands believed that when, in 1944, Ivor Novello had been sentenced to two months in prison (a sentence which effectively led him to an early grave in 1951, so distraught was he made by it), his offence had to have been homosexuality. The fact that it was nothing of the kind, but a misdemeanour involving use of rationed petrol for private rather than wartime purposes, never somehow overcame the public perception, especially as it had been handed down by a notoriously anti-homosexual judge. Not entirely surprisingly, there were soon to be a number of celebrated British theatrical figures who found, in California and elsewhere, that life might be more sexually and financially beneficial the further they got from the West End after the war.

One of these was Noël Coward who, while never settling in either movies or Hollywood except for the briefest of visits, did now take up residence successively in Bermuda, Jamaica and eventually Switzerland. The prime reason, as he never tried to disguise, was that the tax situations overseas were vastly more beneficial to a man who, like Gielgud, had never somehow been able to build up any reserves of cash; but when you read between the lines of Coward's diaries, as of so many other exiled artists of the period, it becomes clear that just as important was a rebellion against the sexual and social repression of Little England which in the 1950s seemed somehow still to be worse at home than almost anywhere abroad. The spirit that had moved Auden and Isherwood and Benjamin Britten and Peter Pears to America at the beginning of the Second World War, and was to move such later artists as David Hockney and Tony Richardson to Los Angeles in these post-war years, was at least partially inspired by the sexual intolerance of their homeland.

If there should be any lingering doubt about British theatrical homophobia at this time, you have only to consider the writings of such respectable names as those of John Osborne ('The first thing that struck me about the London stage was its domination at every level by poufs; I have been hag-ridden by these monsters ever since') and the long-time drama critic of the *Spectator* in the 1950s and early 1960s, Kenneth Hurren:

> At the home of Hugh 'Binkie' Beaumont in Lord North Street, conveniently only just around the corner from where John Gielgud then lived in Cowley Street, parties were given at which there were more fag-ends walking around the rooms than in the ashtrays . . . a great deal of wrist-flapping went on, and it certainly wasn't only the girls who called each other 'darling' . . . the majority of actors and directors employed by Beaumont were homosexuals, and as he was the most powerful manager in London, that inevitably affected the climate of the West End . . . if you weren't that way inclined, you always tried to hide the unfortunate fact from Binkie, whose iron fist was wrapped in fifteen pastel-shaded velvet gloves . . . he would hold his auditions in Lord North Street, reclining in pastel pyjamas on black silk bed sheets, while young men would hopefully camp it up around him in search of a role.

John as usual failed to read the climate of the times. Much as he had enjoyed his recent stay in California for *Julius Caesar*, it had never for one moment occurred to him that he might find it safer to live there; for him, the only possible home had to be one within easy reach of the Old Vic, or the West End, or at a pinch Stratford. And it was not as though in the past his homosexuality had been a particular problem for him or for others; it had been a fact of his life since his very early twenties.

Like Noël Coward, John was however immensely discreet about his homosexual affairs, and happiest when in long-term relationships like the one through the late 1930s with John Perry or the one that he was to sustain for the last forty years of his life with Martin Hensler. Between these, he was certainly susceptible to more fleeting sexual affairs with other men such as the interior decorator Paul Anstee, but (again as with Coward) these were very often with young actors or other theatrical workers who had more to lose than to gain by posing any kind of public or private threat. Moreover, soon after John's trial, his sister Eleanor virtually took up residence in Cowley Street, not only to deal with his correspondence, but also to keep a beady eye out for anyone who was likely to get John into further homosexual trouble. The affair with Anstee therefore had to be pursued in other places and other times.

The London theatre was still, in these long pre-AIDS days, a very homosexual place to live and work, and there had seldom been any real sense of danger; indeed policemen around Shaftesbury Avenue were noted for their tolerance and, sometimes, their complicity. Yet there would be the occasional sudden and sharp attacks on homosexuals, all the more frightening because they were unpredictable.

There had, of course, been arrests and frequent convictions in the past, but these had seldom received the press attention that was now granted to them in the aftermath of the Montagu affair. Before the war, Lady Astor's son was found guilty of gross indecency with another man and sentenced to prison in 1931, while four years later the louche Labour MP Tom Driberg was charged with homosexual offences; neither of these cases was however reported in the press, thanks to the power of the Fleet Street censorship then wielded by Lady Astor and Driberg's great protector, Lord Beaverbrook. If Britain could be kept in the dark about an affair between its King and a married American, it certainly didn't need to know about a few homosexuals in high places.

Rather less fortunate, however, was Sir Paul Latham, an MP and former chairman of the Labour Party, who was amid much publicity sentenced to two years' imprisonment in 1941, having been found guilty of ten homosexual offences; a year later, the leading theatrical photographer of his time and a close friend of Gielgud's, Angus McBean, was sentenced to two years in gaol for similar offences, but that, if we accept the confusion over the Novello petrol affair, was the limit of the arrests visited on theatre people in Gielgud's circle prior to 1953. As a result the 'homosexual Mafia' headed by Gielgud and Coward and Binkie Beaumont and John Perry took it that, so long as they were reasonably discreet, and kept their liaisons well hidden within the theatrical community that they led, they would be unlikely to encounter any real public difficulty.

All that had abruptly changed, however, early in 1953 although John, wildly unworldly in non-theatrical matters, could hardly be expected to have noticed any cases not involving his immediate circle. The Montagu affair was hotly followed by another widely publicised arrest, that of the prolific author and biographer of Wilde's friend Lord Arthur Douglas, Rupert Croft-Cooke. On 4 October 1953 he came up before a viciously homophobic magistrate, R.E. Seaton, at the East Sussex Quarter Sessions, accused of having illicit homosexual sex with two adult sailors. Sir Compton Mackenzie and Lord Kinross both gave evidence for Croft-Cooke, being defended by one of the most able barristers of the day, G.D. 'Khaki' Roberts, who managed to prove that both sailors had frequently changed their stories, and almost certainly taken police immunity in return for telling their tales. Intriguingly, Roberts was himself homophobic and had been part of the prosecution team in the Montagu trial. He had also, a few years earlier, been fired for inadequacy from the British legal team at Nuremberg. On this occasion the police case was thoroughly shaky, but that did not deter the jury from finding Croft-Cooke guilty, or Seaton handing down a nine-month sentence; 'Your house has been a den of iniquity,' announced Seaton, 'and you are a menace to young men.' He added, however, just in case anyone might think him a shade prejudiced against homosexuals, that 'I know a waiter at my club who is a flaming pansy . . . I do not dislike him. I do not watch him. It is all right until you are caught.' In these pre-Wolfenden years, the issue was not one of age; two men could be 'caught', to echo Seaton's words, in the privacy of their own home and still be found guilty of homosexuality, though in most of the cases that now came to trial there was usually some element of soliciting. Young men in any kind of uniform were for some obscure reason considered especially vulnerable to such solicitation.

Anyone with even fractionally more public awareness or general common sense than John G would have realised that a pattern was being formed here, and an especially ugly one at that. In almost all the cases mentioned, house arrests were being made on Saturday mornings so that the police could obtain maximum coverage in such Sunday papers as the *News of the World*, famous for its front-page interest in sexual matters, preferably containing celebrities or vicars or, if at all possible, a combination of the two. Social and sexual historians of the period still seem divided as to whether what was happening in 1953 was the result of a co-ordinated police crackdown, or whether it was just the last, vicious, gasp of official puritanism. For Philip Larkin, sex may have started with the Beatles in 1963, but ten years earlier it was certainly stopping for a lot of people suddenly aware of a witch-hunt as potent as the one being contemporaneously waged on supposed Hollywood communists by the McCarthy tribunals in the USA.

With the wisdom of almost fifty years' hindsight, it can be reckoned that although there was no organised anti-homosexual British witch-hunt as such, a number of senior policemen and magistrates and even civil servants had decided that in this Coronation year, at the start of a new Elizabethan age, certain barriers did have to be repositioned if the country was not going to go to the dogs. As so often over here, this was not an especially organised or even sinister affair, merely the British in one of their periodic fits of hypocrisy.

Most high-ranking legal figures of the period had almost certainly gone to a public school of the 1920s, and would have been lucky to have escaped some form of buggery in the dormitory. But what was still perfectly acceptable at Eton and Harrow, and Oxford and Cambridge, was reckoned 'not a good thing' elsewhere, rather on the principle of Mrs Patrick Campbell's celebrated dictum that she never cared what anyone did sexually 'so long as they don't do it in the street and frighten the horses'. Several people now seemed to think that altogether too many horses were being frightened for the public good, and that, in another celebrated English phrase, 'Something must be done'.

What, precisely, was never made clear, and certainly not in time to save Gielgud from the worst night of his life, and the greatest public and private humiliation of his career. On the evening of 21 October 1953, with rehearsals for *A Day by the Sea* coming to the end, and an opening on tour planned for the following week, John was arrested in a public lavatory in Chelsea for soliciting.

The lavatory had long been staked out by police as one much used for 'cottaging' (casual homosexual pick-ups involving strangers), and there is considerable evidence that Gielgud had been there several times in the last few weeks as, without a steady boyfriend, worried about the new play and exhausted from the various ventures of the last few months, all of which had crowded in on him at an unhappy and insecure time in his life, he sought some form of physical relief among strangers – anonymous strangers – in the night. It was even suggested, though without any very solid proof, that charitable detectives, those who disliked the task of lurking around in plain clothes in underground gentlemen's lavatories hoping to secure a conviction, had actually warned Gielgud off, telling him that now he had the knighthood he really should be more circumspect, but that if he was ever to get caught he was to be sure to give a false name. That way, it was said, the charge sheet could be effectively 'doctored' overnight and there would be no danger of a public court appearance in the morning.

If that was the police plan or intention, it backfired badly. John, caught by a police decoy he had propositioned, remembered something about not giving his real name, and therefore announced that he was Arthur rather than John Gielgud when questioned at the local Chelsea police station to which he had been immediately taken. In truth he had of course been christened Arthur John Gielgud, but as it was the surname that the friendly police were trying to avoid having to inscribe on the public register, the reversion to his first Christian name was of remarkably little advantage in the crisis. John had by now well and truly lost the plot.

His temporary loss of all common sense and any personal security could not have come at any worse time in the entire century. What Coward was to call 'that deafening Kinsey Report' into sexuality had just been published in America, thereby giving an eager British press some legitimate excuse, however hazy, to put sex at the top of their headline agenda. Added to that, 1953 had already also seen the start of the debate over whether or not the newly crowned Queen's sister was to be allowed to marry 'a divorced man', Group Captain Peter Townsend, and the Church of England, as if aware of moral ground now fast slipping away beneath its feet, had just successfully demanded the imposition of a Press Council to control the greater sexual excesses and liberties of a newly liberated Fleet Street. The old Victorian order was at last ending, but there was no agreement as to what should take its place as the standard of public or even private morality.

None of this, of course, would John have noticed in any of his rare breaks from rehearsal; and when Gielgud was arrested his only words to the decoy policeman were, 'I am so terribly sorry.' An hour or two later, at Chelsea Police Station, he pleaded guilty to the charge of importuning, but rallied sufficiently to give what he thought was a suitably false name and to describe himself as 'a clerk earning £1,000 a year'.

He was bound over by an Inspector Puckey to reappear at Chelsea Magistrates' Court at 10.30 a.m. the following morning. The actor who had been a Knight Bachelor for barely three months then returned home to Cowley Street to consider his options. Forty years later, I asked him what these had been:

Suicide, for a start; I thought about that a lot for an hour or two, and for the first and last time in my life. But even then, it seemed somehow ridiculously melodramatic even to me, and besides I hadn't the faintest idea how one would go about it. What I should have done, of course, was to telephone Binkie who was always said to be incredibly well-connected, and might well have known someone high enough up in Scotland Yard to help. He also had a wonderfully secretive press secretary called Vivienne Byerley; she was known in the business as 'no news is good news' and ever afterwards Emlyn Williams always mischievously said that if I had simply told her, nobody would ever have found out.

So why didn't I call on Binkie's help? For all kinds of reasons, none of them perhaps good enough. I was thoroughly ashamed, not of what I had done but of being caught, and I couldn't bear to hear the anger or disappointment in Binkie's voice. Then again, I had some vague Westminster schoolboy idea that when you were in trouble you had to stand on your own two feet, and 'take it like a man'.

He stayed awake all night, and soon after eight next morning heard the phone ring. A desk sergeant coming on duty at Chelsea Police Station had been reading the overnight log and realised the worst had now happened. Gielgud, drunk and confused, had given his real surname and nothing could be done to get his name off the arrest register, even by a policeman considerably more liberal than the one who had entrapped him.

But the desk sergeant had an idea that all might still not be totally lost. If he could get one of the duty magistrates to come in thirty or so minutes earlier than usual, before the official opening of the Chelsea Police Court at 10 a.m., then it was just about possible that Gielgud could be heard, fined and got safely away before any members of the press arrived to report the business of the day.

A resident magistrate, E.R. Guest, proved grumpily willing to start his court's proceedings at 9.30 a.m., and Gielgud was now telephoned to attend. In the dock, he merely repeated his statement of the previous night, adding only, 'I cannot imagine how I could have been so stupid; I was very tired, and had a few drinks. I was not responsible for my action.'

Guest was mercifully not of the hanging or flogging persuasion, and showed no sign that he had ever heard of the man who had been brought up before him. He merely fined John the standard £10, solemnly adding the instruction: 'You are to see your doctor the moment you leave this court, and tell him exactly what you have done. If he has any advice to offer, you are to take it, because this conduct is dangerous to other men, particularly young men, and it is a particular scourge in this neighbourhood.' On the very same day, Douglas Byng, a notoriously camp cabaret star, was fined a mere £7 for driving without due care and attention.

Precisely what medical cure Guest had in mind is unclear, nor can one tell what evidence he had for the belief that Chelsea had suddenly and uniquely fallen victim to a 'scourge' of homosexual, middle-aged actors importuning plain-clothes policemen in public lavatories.

By now it was already too late. A Fleet Street police reporter, on his way to some altogether different courtroom, had suddenly heard the most distinctive voice in British theatre and had rapidly alerted his colleagues. As the press box filled up with hacks who could not believe their luck that morning, the magistrate rose to his theme: 'I hear something like six hundred of these cases every year,' he announced, more in sorrow than in anger, 'and I begin to think that they ought to be sent to prison . . . I suppose on this occasion

I can treat you as a bad case of drunk and disorderly, and fine you accordingly, but nobody will ever do that again.'

And nor, of course, would John. He slunk back to rehearsal, only to find that the early edition of the *Evening Standard* already had him on its front page. His company, with only the rather puritanical exception of one wardrobe mistress, was solidly behind him and yet deeply embarrassed, though no more so than John himself. After a terrible pause as he came on from the wings to start the afternoon rehearsal, it was left to the veteran Dame Sybil Thorndike, herself no stranger to police courts where she had frequently made personal appearances before and during the First World War as a leading suffragette, to break the silence with the most brilliant phrase that had perhaps ever occurred to her. 'Well, John,' she murmured, 'what a very silly bugger you have been.' Her support for John, in this terrible time, was remarkable; she even arranged at the stage door to have the hate mail addressed to him redirected to her, whereupon she would write to all the correspondents, asking them 'to extend Christian charity to somebody who was different'.

By that evening the story was of course all over London; Kenneth Williams wrote in his diary next day: 'It appears from the papers that Sir John Gielgud has been arrested on a charge of homosexual importuning. He described himself on the charge sheet as "a clerk of Cowley Street, with an income of £1,000 a year". Why tell these kinds of lies? Of course, this is clearly a case of persecution. Poor fellow.'

During the afternoon, John had been able to bury himself in the final rehearsals of *A Day by the Sea*. But that night, in the private sanctuary of the house that Binkie Beaumont and John Perry shared in Lord North Street, just behind Westminster School, there was the inevitable crisis meeting. John, ever the man to do the right thing when his limited social skills enabled him to work out just what that might be, at once tendered his resignation as star and director of the production. This, however, was easier said than done, it now being late on Wednesday night and the play due to open the following Monday at the Royal Court in Liverpool, at the start of its pre-London tour.

It was hardly likely that a leading actor/director could be found to replace him in less than four days, and the concept of simply not opening on the Monday night was one in those far-off days still totally unfamiliar. The show must indeed go on regardless. Besides, Binkie Beaumont, by now the most powerful theatrical manager in the whole post-war history of the British theatre, was a treacherous and cunning bugger, to use an unusually literal expression. He had no choice but to play for time. John would have to open in Liverpool as planned, and it would then be up to the great British public. If they showed no sign of undue offence, and more important still exhibited no dangerous tendency towards withdrawing support from Gielgud's box-office on the road, then John could remain assured of his patronage and friendship. But if, though this was nowhere written nor even hazarded during Binkie's lifetime, the tour had noticeably suffered through John's unfortunate indiscretion, then it would not perhaps be beyond the bounds of possibility to attract another actor and director to the project before the play had eventually to open in town.

There is no doubt that John's career really did now hang in the balance; to the crisis meeting at Lord North Street, Binkie had summoned Glen Byam Shaw and his wife Angela Baddeley, Laurence Olivier and Vivien Leigh, and Ralph Richardson and his wife Meriel Forbes. All but one of those present agreed that it would be fatal, not only to John's career, but possibly to John himself, if he were not to be allowed to open in Liverpool. The one dissenting voice was that of Olivier, never one of John's greatest supporters, who now saw the chance to do his old rival down. He suggested that the production should be postponed for at least three months, whereupon his own wife, Vivien Leigh, turned on him in a savage outburst, pointing out that Olivier had always been jealous of John and that his view should therefore be totally discounted by the meeting, which indeed it was.

And now, another voice was heard. John's brother Val was no longer especially close to him, and, as a man who was to marry a total of five different wives, he had little or no understanding of John's homosexuality. He was however still his elder brother, and felt now that as their mother was distinctly aged, he should stand in loco parentis for John. What Val now did had a kind of Machiavellian brilliance. He presented himself at Binkie's home with a direct threat. If, said Val, Binkie or his friends did anything to destabilise John's position in the theatre as a result of the arrest, Val would simply go public with the names of all those actors, directors, designers and playwrights who were within Binkie's homosexual circle of friends and employees – including Binkie and John Perry themselves.

Luckily for John, Binkie's resolve never had to be tested. What happened over the next weekend was that the company travelled to Liverpool, and prepared for their opening night almost as if nothing untoward had happened to their director and star. 'Almost' because Binkie had taken the precaution of hiring extra security men to make sure that no enraged anti-homosexual Liverpudlians, or worse still journalists, could get past the stage door. Then came the Monday first night, as described by the theatre historian and Beaumont's biographer, Richard Huggett:

It is unlikely that there was ever a Tennent first night filled with such tension and gloomy foreboding. Gielgud's first entrance, as Julian Anson, the diplomat, was a quarter-hour into the first act, probably the longest and most crucifying fifteen minutes of his life. When the moment came, he could not enter: he was paralysed and shaking with fear. Once again, it was Sybil Thorndike who came to the rescue. She was on stage, having just completed a short scene with Irene Worth. When Gielgud failed to appear she could see him in the wings, knew what was the trouble and what had to be done. She walked off through the French windows, grabbed him and whispered fiercely, 'Come on, John darling, they won't boo me,' and led him firmly on to the stage. To everybody's astonishment, and indescribable relief, the audience gave him a standing ovation. They cheered, they applauded, they shouted. The message was quite clear. The English public had always been loyal to its favourites, and this was their chance to show that they didn't care about what he had done in his private life, he was still their adored leading actor, still a star, still their own, their very own John Gielgud, and that they loved and respected him dearly. It was a moment never to be forgotten by those who witnessed it, Sybil Thorndike hugging him and smiling with unmistakable defiance at the audience, as if to say 'I don't think it matters, do you?' and Gielgud, the famous Terry tears visibly running down his cheeks, unable to speak. It was a long time before he could stammer out his first line, one of delicious triviality: 'Oh dear, I'd forgotten we had all those azaleas', which, at a moment of such cosmic significance, was greeted by a roar of laughter and renewed applause.

There was a certain irony in the fact that John played his first post-trial performance at Liverpool, since it was there, just after the war, that Alec Guinness, while a member of the local rep, was himself picked up for homosexual soliciting. This never came out in Guinness's lifetime because, unlike John, he did remain alert enough to give the police a totally false name; the one he chose, Herbert Pocket, was of course from Dickens's *Great Expectations*, a role he had already played on stage and was soon to film. Luckily for him, Dickens appears not to have been required reading at the Liverpool Police Headquarters and Pocket's name is still solemnly inscribed in the list of offenders.

In more senses than one, they were up and running and the tour continued in a triumph only to be repeated, albeit a little less vociferously, on the London first night at the Haymarket. Binkie, still nervous of some kind of counter-demonstration, had carefully arranged to have John exit through the front of house after the show, thereby avoiding the stage-door crowds. 'Nonsense,' announced John, who had by now found his own voice again. 'I shall leave through the stage door like any other actor.' And he did, to renewed applause from the faithful.

Yet it would be wrong to suggest that all had ended anything like happily. The price John paid for his Chelsea indiscretion was considerable and very long-lasting – arguably, indeed, until the very end of his long life, nearly half a century later. In immediate terms, rumours that his knighthood could be withdrawn were immediately discounted; even when, thirty years later, Sir Anthony Blunt had his taken away, it was because of his treachery as a Soviet spy rather than his homosexuality.

As against that, however, the Garrick Club, dominated then (as for so many years to come) by some extremely right-wing lawyers and judges with remarkably old-fashioned and intolerant views, seriously debated behind closed doors the removal of John's membership; by the time the club got round to honouring Sir John with a lunch to celebrate his Order of Merit in 1997, it was fervently hoped that if any of those who had threatened him in 1953 were still alive, they would at least have the grace to stay away from that celebration.

Feelings also ran high backstage, ranging from the fearful sympathy of many other leading homosexual actors to a vicious whispering campaign which climaxed in a petition sent anonymously to all stage doors demanding Gielgud's resignation from Equity. The organiser of this petition was the character actor Edward Chapman who ironically, a few years later, was to turn up as the mad Marquess of Queensbury in the Robert Morley film of *Oscar Wilde*. But so loved was John within the profession that Chapman found very few signatories and when the petition appeared on the stage-door bulletin board of the Arts Theatre, the then director Alec Clunes commendably called his company together on stage to announce that anyone who signed it would be immediately fired. This was a gesture of especial generosity considering that less than two years earlier John had effectively hijacked *The Lady's Not For Burning* from Clunes, who had first produced the play and played its leading role.

I also have here to admit, with some residual familial shame, that my grandfather Herbert Buckmaster, who had been married to two actresses (Gladys Cooper and Nellie Taylor), wrote to the *Evening Standard* at this time: 'If the public refrained from going to theatres where actors with queer habits were employed, managements would not be so anxious to engage them. In older days actor-managers like Sir Charles Hawtrey would never have one of them in his theatre.' In Buck's defence, some forty years after his death, I can only add that he was a compulsive letters-to-the-editor writer on a vast range of topics, and that his opinions often changed sharply during a single day. He had several gay friends in a long life, but conceivably felt that the predominantly military members of the Buck's Club he had founded just after the First World War would expect some sort of harrumphing response from their leader.

And there were other, much more serious consequences. The United States, then still in the grip of its McCarthy intolerance, had a 'moral turpitude' clause in its entry visas which meant that in the following year, when Gielgud was invited to lead the Stratford Memorial Company to New York as Prospero in *The Tempest*, the British Embassy in Washington had regretfully if perhaps over-cautiously to advise cancellation lest John's presence should prove to be 'an embarrassment' in view of the local press comment that might occur. It was to be almost four years before he played the United States again.

But that was still not all; the after-effects of the Gielgud trial were being felt around the world. In Jamaica, Noël Coward wrote a diary entry which was virtually the only one of major significance which his editors (Graham Payn and I) decided, in deference to Gielgud's wishes, not to publish in his lifetime. Published now for the first time, it reads:

> Poor, silly, idiotic, foolish, careless John. Of course I feel very sorry for him in what must be an agonising time, but did he not even for a moment think about what trouble his little indiscretion would cause the rest of us? England, my England, has always been full of intolerance and bigotry. Just when things might have started to improve for us all, John goes and does something so utterly careless that it will do us harm for years to come, at least among those who still think that our private sex lives are any of their bloody business. And to do this within months of a knighthood, which made it seem as though at long, long last things might have been beginning ever so slowly to change . . . how could he, how could he, have been stupid and so selfish?

Noël Coward did not get his own knighthood until 1970, fully seventeen years later, and it could well be argued that Gielgud was very largely to blame for the long wait. But Coward was concerned with more than just his own rehabilitation or return to English orthodoxy: always an astute social observer of the seismic shifts in the popular taste of his beloved countrymen, even when viewed through the long telescope of a Jamaican exile, he had realised that the issue here was still greater than the career of one man, however exalted.

That issue was also the concern of an Australian journalist, Donald Horne, writing in the *Sydney Sunday Telegraph* of 25 October 1953, four days after John had appeared in court. It was Horne who first formulated, at least in print, the still-contested notion that there was an official witch-hunt against celebrated homosexuals in the years

1953–4. This is a theory shared by such later biographers as Humphrey Carpenter on Benjamin Britten, Margaret Drabble on Angus Wilson, and Alan Hodges on Alan Turing, all of whom were in some form of homosexual troubles at the time, but it is equally strongly contested by the historian Patrick Higgins, who points out that there were in fact fewer homosexual arrests in these two years than those immediately before.

Nevertheless, for Horne at least, the message was clear:

> The sensational charges made this week, against Lord Montagu of Beaulieu and actor Sir John Gielgud, are the result of a Scotland Yard plan to smash homosexuality in London. The plan originated after strong United States advice to Britain to weed out homosexuals, as hopeless security risks, from important government jobs. One of the Yard's top-rankers, Commander E.A. Cole, recently spent three months in America consulting with the FBI officials in putting finishing touches to the plan, one which was extended to a war on all vice when Sir John Nott-Bower took over as the new Commissioner at Scotland Yard in August (1953).
>
> Sir John swore he would rip the cover off all London's filth spots. Montagu and Gielgud were the latest accused in his drive against the shocking crime of male vice which is now linked with drives on call-girl rackets, obscene postcards and the widespread vice trade. Under laxer police methods before the US-inspired plan began, and Sir John moved to the top job at the Yard as a man with a mission, Montagu and his film-director friend might never have been charged with grave offences with Boy Scouts. This week's conviction of Gielgud for persistently importuning also sprang from increased police vigilance.

The conspiracy theory is at first sight an attractive one, especially when linked to America in one of its periodic fits of social and sexual paranoia. But the evidence is seriously shaky here, and it could even be argued that the Gielgud arrest was, on the contrary, the start of a considerable liberalisation of the laws governing homosexuality. Within a few days of his story breaking in the press, the *New Statesman* and the *Observer*, both publications of considerably more influence then than now, were calling for law reform to bring Britian into line with France and several other European countries where homosexual acts in private between consenting adults were considered in no way criminal. True, this would not have helped John's case since his act was not committed in private, nor could soliciting be considered in quite the same light as consenting. Nevertheless, for the first time since the death of Oscar Wilde in 1900, the debate had now been formally reopened in print, and the Home Office was soon forced to include homosexuality within the remit of the report it had long promised on female prostitution, the two issues then being considered of a similarly scandalous nature.

Gielgud still had ferocious enemies, not least one of Beaverbrook's leading editors, the deeply reactionary John Gordon of the *Sunday Express* who wrote in his column on the Sunday following the court appearance:

> Sir John Gielgud should consider himself a very lucky man to have met such a gentle magistrate. I am loath to make his punishment heavier by provoking a wider discussion of his delinquency, but the moral rot in the charge against him of 'persistently importuning male persons' menaces the nation much more than most people realise. Because the offence to which Gielgud pleaded guilty, with the excuse that he had been drinking, is repulsive to all normal people, a hush-hush tends to be built up around it. Sensitive people shrink from discussing it. Newspapers are disinclined to switch on the searchlight of public exposure, regarding it as a peculiarly unsavoury subject. What have been the consequences of that delicacy? The rot has flourished behind the protective veil until it is now a widespread disease. It has penetrated every phase of life. It infects politics, literature, the stage, the Church and youth movements, as the criminal courts regularly reveal to us. In the exotic world of international politics, it seems at times to be an occupational disease.
>
> It is not purely a West End plague: it is often pleaded, on behalf of these human dregs, that they are artistic or ineffectual creatures, who because of their special qualities should have special freedoms. This is not so; the vice is as prominent among lowbrows as it is among highbrows, and the suggestion that peculiar people should be

allowed peculiar privileges is arrant nonsense. The equally familiar plea that these pests are purely pathological cases, and should be pampered instead of punished, is almost as rubbishy. It is time our community decided to sanitise itself, for if we do not root out this moral rot it will bring us down, as inevitably it has brought down every nation in history that has become affected by it. There must be sharp and severe punishment; but more than that, we must get the social conscience of the nation so raised that such people are made into social lepers. Decent people should neither encourage them nor support them, and it is utterly wrong that men who corrupt and befoul other men should strut in the public eye, enjoying adulation and applause however great their genius. And I would suggest that in future the nation might suitably mark its abhorrence of this type of depravity by stripping from men involved in such cases any honours that have been bestowed upon them.

Gordon's hysterical, homophobic rant was in fact the only call in print for John to be stripped of his new knighthood; but before we dismiss it from the infinitely safer and more comfortable standpoint of a new century, it is worth recalling that Gordon was writing for some twelve million readers, at the height of the *Sunday Express*'s power and influence, and could have proved an extremely dangerous enemy had he not been happy to set off the following Sunday on some equally manic tirade aimed elsewhere.

Other journalists were now inclined to leave the Gielgud case alone, not so much out of some new-found sense of probity or shame, but rather because the mass adulation that had swept across the footlights towards him on stage was a pretty fair indication of the way the public wind was blowing in his favour, and astute newsmen saw no good reason to challenge so open and vociferous a gesture of forgiveness, in Liverpool as in London.

Gordon was later to return to the fray, congratulating himself on having 'taken the opportunity provided by the case of Sir John Gielgud to draw attention to this male perversion menace' and later still, in an increasingly desperate attempt to get him stripped of the knighthood, adding, 'These men have earned social criticism and they should get it, whatever the nation may have conferred on them; for while they remain public idols, it demonstrates to all that fame not shame have been the fruits of their depravity, and they draw other men into the depths with them.'

No barrister at the Wilde trials could have put the case for the prosecution more forcibly, but Gordon was immediately accused by such other Sunday editors as David Astor of the *Observer* of writing 'in the most rabble-rousing tones of the witch-hunt', and already the word was coming over from America that, on reflection, just possibly witch-hunts weren't such a good idea after all.

The debate ended up where such British debates almost always do, in the correspondence columns of the *Daily Telegraph*, where the row rumbled on for several weeks between liberals supporting continental tolerance and irate colonels demanding that anti-homosexuality laws should be printed as posters, akin to Keep Death Off The Roads.

For a while, the more that liberal journalists demanded a relaxation of the laws, the more the judiciary hardened its view to the contrary, yet again all too eager to demonstrate that they weren't about to have their minds changed by columnists whom they dismissed as left-wing, and suspected of harbouring abnormal sexual desires into the bargain. The fact that large numbers of judges were only really happy when dressed in long robes and wigs was thought too sensitive to mention, even in the *New Statesman*. After the Liberace case of 1959, in which the columnist Bill Connor (writing as Cassandra) was fined a then unprecedented £8,000 for suggesting that the pianist eventually to die of AIDS was a 'deadly, winking, sniggering, chromium-plated, scent-impregnated, luminous, quivering, giggling, fruit-flavoured, mincing, ice-covered heap of mother-love', matters were finally allowed to rest until the Wolfenden Report's recommendations, made in 1957, were finally passed into law in 1967, belatedly bringing Britain nearer its continental neighbours' tolerance of consenting homosexual relationships.

Peter Wildeblood, who had been charged with Lord Montagu, wrote a memoir called *Against the Law* soon after his release from gaol, reminding readers that 'In most other countries, the behaviour of consenting adults in private is now considered a matter for themselves alone. Britain and America are almost the only countries left in which such behaviour constitutes an offence . . . Most people, if they were asked to define the crime of Oscar Wilde, would still imagine that he was an effeminate poseur who lusted after small boys, whereas in fact he was a married man with two children who was found guilty of homosexual acts committed in private with male prostitutes whom he certainly did not corrupt, and who lied on oath to clear themselves of other charges . . . the Prosecution never attempted to prove that he had done any harm by his actions.'

This case, and that of Gielgud, were undoubtedly the most famous gay trials since that of Wilde himself, who had of course given from beyond the grave one of John's greatest successes in *The Importance of Being Earnest* where, as Oscar's grandson Merlin Holland now suggests, the line about 'all women take after their mothers, that is their tragedy; no man does, that is his' could be seen as yet another coded plea, this one for men in Victorian society to be allowed to exhibit more of the female side of their nature without fear of arrest.

Be that as it may, fully forty years after his own trial Gielgud himself was still refusing to make any public comment of any kind about his own sexuality. In this, of course, he was not alone: Alan Bennett once replied to Sir Ian McKellen (who was suggesting that he should 'come out' with a precise declaration of his sexuality) that it was 'like asking a man, crawling across the Sahara Desert, whether he would prefer Evian or Perrier'. Sir Nigel Hawthorne was famously only 'outed' by an American journalist at the time of his Oscar, and there are still many actors for whom, as for John, the subject remains just too painful or too personal to allow of any public comment.

A few months after Gielgud's court case he suffered a delayed nervous breakdown which caused him to withdraw, temporarily and very uncharacteristically, from both *A Day by the Sea* and his rehearsals for the Trevor Howard/Ffrangcon-Davies *Cherry Orchard*. In the years that followed, John was ever careful about where and to whom he would give press or broadcast interviews, choosing wherever possible those he could trust not to enquire deeply, or at all, about his private life.

Perhaps the most enduring tragedy of the Gielgud trial is that had John been able to come to any real terms with his own sexual identity, he could into his nineties have taken some pride and pleasure in the eventual outcome of his arrest, which was essentially to pave the way for a vastly more tolerant attitude towards homosexuality in this country. But precisely because he himself came from the far side of the 1953 divide, he was never able to understand the change that he himself had wrought, and his terror of being outed was to reach such ludicrous proportions that, appearing at a celebrated literary festival some six months after his death, I was solemnly asked not to bring any of this up, as 'there are those who still find the whole thing distasteful'. Admittedly, it was Cheltenham.

But John was, in one way, very fortunate. The publicity surrounding the 1953 case meant that very few writers could be totally unaware that he had suffered and survived some kind of sexual scandal, and that it was more than likely to have been of a homosexual nature. In none of his own many volumes of stage and personal memoirs, nor in any biography published in his lifetime, nor in any of his numerous autobiographical radio and television broadcasts, has the case ever been mentioned, and as John grew in distinction and fragility to his late-life status as our greatest living actor, it would somehow have been unusually churlish to bring it up. Somerset Maugham and Terence Rattigan and Noël Coward and Michael Redgrave and Emlyn Williams and Binkie himself and even Dirk Bogarde had by then all managed to escape any 'outing' in their lifetimes, not least because the laws of libel could have been invoked on their behalf, so professionally damaging was the suggestion of homosexuality still believed to be, even into the mid-1990s.

But the scars of John's court appearance never truly healed; until the very end of his life, almost fifty years later, he was never openly to support any of his theatrical colleagues who felt it important for leading homosexual actors to declare themselves as such. Nor would he join the many hitherto silent gays who in 1991 signed a letter to the *Guardian* protesting at Derek Jarman's vilification of McKellen for accepting a knighthood from what many then considered a virulently anti-gay Thatcher administration. Gielgud went to his grave believing, as Coward wrote in his last full-length play *A Song at Twilight* (1968), that 'even when the actual law ceases to exist, there will still be a stigma attached to "the love that dares not speak its name" in the minds of millions of people for generations to come. It takes more than a few outspoken books, and plays, and speeches in Parliament to uproot moral prejudice from the Anglo-Saxon mind.'

And in 1953 the law did of course still exist; as a result, although in private he was to receive dozens of letters of support and love, in public ranks were now being closed, and the homosexual community decided that although they would do what they could for John behind closed doors, in public they would do nothing to support him that might endanger their own still precarious position. Typical of the private response was the letter that John received from the playwright Dodie Smith, for whom he had directed the triumphant *Dear Octopus* a few years earlier. 'This damnable business will be forgotten in a few weeks, whereas the fact that you are the greatest figure in the present English theatre will remain unchanged . . . we think the world of you, and always shall.'

Dodie also took the trouble to write to John's mother Kate: 'Dear Mrs G, I find myself longing to send you our sympathy about John's misfortune. His magnificent achievements will never fade, and no one in the theatre is more loved and admired.' Some indication of John's family's feeling about the crisis can be gathered from Mrs Gielgud's brisk reply to Dodie: 'Thank you for your kind letter. John has nothing to his discredit, save one drink too many at a Chelsea party.'

Others concurred, although some with rather more reservations: 'I do wish,' as Christopher Isherwood wrote to Dodie from the comparative homosexual safety of California, 'that we had a better issue to join battle on than Gielgud's stupid indiscretion.'

And yet, John's case, taken together with that of Lord Montagu, did begin to mark the shift in public opinion and the start of the long road to the reform that came about with the Sexual Offences Act of 1967. For all those who still believed that homosexuals should be, if not actually hanged or flogged, nevertheless sent to prison, regardless of the fact that they would there find themselves in the kind of all-male community specifically designed to encourage precisely the kind of sexual behaviour for which they were supposedly being punished, there were faint signs of a new orthodoxy. The *Sunday Times* of 28 March 1954, less than six months after Gielgud's arrest, published an editorial which read, in part: 'The case for the reform of the law as to acts committed in private between adults is very strong. The case for an authoritative enquiry into it is overwhelming.' At precisely this time, the Church of England's Moral Welfare Committee published a report concluding that such behaviour, although sinful, should now no longer be treated as a crime, doubtless much to the relief of several hundred homosexual clergymen. In the House of Commons the MP Robert Boothby, now deeply in debt to the Kray brothers (the leading East End gangsters of the day) and himself a lifelong bisexual who had recently won £40,000 in damages from the *Daily Mirror*, for suggesting (rightly) that he had criminal connections, now urged Parliament to set up a Royal Commission, pointing out that the law as it stood led to many cases of blackmail and was being unfairly invoked around the country, depending on the sexual beliefs of the various magistrates concerned.

But still the government of the day hesitated. In the House of Lords, Earl Winterton initiated the first ever debate there about homosexuality by announcing for the prosecution that it was a 'filthy, disgusting and unnatural vice'. Several younger peers pointed out that blackmail was surely the greater evil here, although the Bishop of Southall memorably remarked, 'Once a people lets its ultimate convictions go, there can be no stopping halfway, and the moral bottom is in danger of falling out of Society.'

Matters were rapidly becoming farcical; when at the end of 1954 Sir John Wolfenden, vice-chancellor of Reading University, was finally charged by a reluctant Home Secretary (the reactionary David Maxwell Fyfe) with leading a commission of enquiry, the first thing Wolfenden did was to write to his homosexual son Jeremy: 'I have only two requests to make of you at the moment. One, that we stay out of each other's way for the time being, and two, that you wear rather less make-up.'

Soon after the Committee on Homosexual Offences and Prostitution (the title alone suggested what was then public thinking on the issue) had begun to meet, a number of high-profile, non-homosexual figures such as the columnist Lord Arran (less formally known as Boofy Gore, and a Wodehousian figure around Fleet Street) came out in favour of reform, as of course did such homosexual MPs as Tom Driberg and Robert Boothby. But that reform came very slowly:

in 1955, as Norman Lebrecht notes in his critical history of Covent Garden,

The *People* ran a headline 'Music Chief leads big campaign against Vice', and the story that followed was as explicit as the times and libel laws permitted: 'A campaign against homosexuality in British music is to be launched by Sir Steuart Wilson, until last month deputy general administrator of the Royal Opera House, Covent Garden. Sir Steuart, 66, told the *People* last night: "The influence of perverts in the world of music has grown beyond all measure. If it is not curbed soon, Covent Garden and other precious musical heritages could suffer irreparable harm . . . Many people in the profession are worried. There is a kind of agreement among homosexuals which results in their keeping jobs for the boys." ' The *People* cast around for men of substance to authenticate its scoop. Mr Walford Haydn, 'the famous composer and conductor' said, 'Homosexuals are damaging music and all the other arts. I am sorry for those born that way, but many acquire it – and for them I have nothing but contempt. Singers who are perverted often get work simply because of this. And new works by composers are given preference by some people if the writer is perverted' . . . Wilson's target was unmistakable, and the report must have struck terror into (the general administrator) David Webster, coming as it did in the midst of a police crackdown on homosexual men. On a 1953 tour of Rhodesia, Webster was reportedly seen in the sauna with other white men and black boys 'red all over and looking like a boiled lobster'. According to rumour, he so injured an African boy in the act of love that the victim was rushed to hospital, and Webster had to be hustled out on the next flight . . . most of his team at Covent Garden were lifelong bachelors. Christopher West was professedly gay; Morris Smith and John Sullivan were avowedly religious and hostile to women. 'Nobody asked if they were gay,' said stage manager Elizabeth Latham, 'one was very careful what one said and did in those days.'

In the next year or so two MPs, William Field and Ian Harvey, both had their careers ruined by prosecution for importuning, and it wasn't until 1958 that a first shift was detectable, in the Lord Chamberlain's decision no longer to ban overtly homosexual characters from the London stage. Three years later, in 1961, Dirk Bogarde (himself a life-long but very closeted gay) courageously persuaded a very reluctant Rank Organisation to make a film called *Victim*, entirely about the blackmailing of a married but homosexual barrister. In this same year, there were to be no fewer than two films about the Oscar Wilde trial (one starring Peter Finch, the other Robert Morley), and the actor Murray Melvin played the first overtly homosexual character on the West End stage in Shelagh Delaney's hit *A Taste of Honey*.

During the 1960s the climate finally began to change for ever; even the television hit *Z Cars* dealt with the blackmailing of homosexual couples, and on radio Barry Took and Marty Feldman for *Round the Horne* invented the outrageously camp couple Julian and Sandy, immortally played for many years by Kenneth Williams and Hugh Paddick. Even so, the Sexual Offences Act was not introduced into Parliament until 1967, more than ten years after the Wolfenden Committee had begun to meet. Under the new rules, homosexual male sex now became a non-criminal offence provided that it was committed in private by not more than two people, and that both of them were twenty-one years of age. By 1975 a rally in Trafalgar Square brought together what the press described as the largest ever public gathering of homosexuals – 2,500 in all. By the early 1990s Gay Pride rallies attracted more than 300,000. Yet it was not until 1998 that the House of Commons voted on whether the age of consent should be lowered to seventeen or even sixteen, an argument that persists to this day, alongside the dispute over Clause 28 in a Local Authority Bill, forbidding the 'promotion' of the homosexual lifestyle.

All these changes were however to come too late for John. The events of 1953 were to leave him utterly unable to come to any real terms with the slow liberalisation of British attitudes to homosexuality, although towards the very end of his life some forty years later he did grudgingly admit in a television interview, when asked why he went on working so very hard well into his nineties, 'The man I live with has expensive tastes.'

The Gielgud case was to find its way to a kind of immortality at the roots of the play that his old friend and occasional lover Terence Rattigan was now writing. Although in its final draft *Separate*

Tables has no really homosexual theme at all, in the first version the protagonists of the first play were to have been two men, while the offence committed in the second play, by the Major, was to have been that of touching up young men rather than women in the local cinema. As Rattigan later explained, 'John had enough courage to go and open his play only a few days after the trial, and that Liverpool audience had enough grace and sympathy to accept him purely as an actor . . . the acceptance by those very ordinary people of something about which they had very little understanding, I found very moving.' In fact, as Geoffrey Wansell adds: '*Separate Tables* is really about the two themes that have always preoccupied Rattigan – the suppression of emotion, and the difficulty the English have always found in accepting sexual deviance. As someone says in the play, "You know what the real *vice anglais* is? Not flagellation, or pederasty, or whatever the French think it is, but the inability to express emotion."'

And it all could, just about, have been worse; when Lord Montagu was sent down, a few months after John's arrest (following one aborted trial), for a year in prison, one of the first letters of sympathy he received was from Gielgud. 'There,' wrote John, 'but for the grace of God . . .'

Chapter Seventeen

❧❦

KING LEAR GOES TO JAPAN
(1954–1955)

I made one great mistake with the Japanese King Lear, *and it was purely technical. Noguchi, who is a sculptor, designed some brilliant sets, but no one had ever told me that he didn't also do costumes.*

As 1954 began, John was still reeling from the shock of his arrest. Luckily, he had eight shows a week to play with a friendly and highly sympathetic cast in *A Day by the Sea*, but away from the theatre he was now very reluctant to go to the parties he used once so to love. Embarrassed beyond belief by what had happened, his natural good manners also made sure that he would at no time give anybody else any cause for uneasiness.

At this time he was still living alone at 16 Cowley Street, and it is of course quite possible that, if he had had a partner in residence, none of the events of the past October would have taken place. But Bernie, the burly American he had originally hired in New York some years earlier as a kind of chauffeur and secretary, and who had joined him in London where their relationship became that of lovers, had now tired of the West End life which he could never really fathom and gone back home to New York, suffering from the cancer that would soon kill him.

John's affair with the interior decorator Paul Anstee was still something less than a total commitment for either of them, and at this crucial time he was unable to look for too much support from Binkie or John Perry, as their relationship had now gone into a crisis of its own. Soon after the war, Binkie and John had taken into their Tennent management a young and very striking American, the manager and actor Toby Rowland who was later to produce John in one of his greatest late-life hits, the 1968 *Forty Years On*. Although Rowland was already married, he had first come to England as a lover of the actor Alan Webb and was therefore soon to find himself at the heart of the H.M. Tennent coterie.

Within a few months he was to leave Alan Webb for John Perry, an affair that only came to Binkie's attention when Noël Coward inadvertently let slip the news that Rowland was in Paris at precisely the same time that – as Binkie knew – John Perry was. The affair finally hit the fan one weekend at Knots Fosse, Binkie and John's country cottage, when, in the presence of Keith Baxter and several others, Binkie told John Perry that he was to decide there and then between him and Rowland. Perry went to the phone, and came back to announce to the somewhat startled dinner party that his affair with Rowland was at an end. It was then Binkie's turn to leave the table; he phoned his manager Barney Gordon to instruct him to remove any trace of Rowland from the London office, and to fire him immediately as an associate producer of H.M. Tennent. It was, as Rowland's widow Millie recalls, only to be in the very last months of Binkie's life, almost twenty years later, that he and Rowland ever spoke again.

Back at the Haymarket, the continuing success of *A Day by the Sea* was a considerable relief. It was Milton Shulman who had perceptively noted in the *Evening Standard* that John's opening night performance was played 'on a note of nervous tension that almost shrieked', but the other critics seemed not to have noticed anything adrift, and the play ran for eighteen months on the strength of glowing reviews and its all-star cast, one in which only Ralph Richardson still seemed to have any difficulty in coming to terms with the truth about John's private life.

John's high level of stress, however, his ongoing conviction that he had let down both friends and family (especially his now elderly mother) very badly indeed, and that he might well have done his future career considerable damage, led him five months into the run towards a nervous breakdown. By now he was not only still playing eight shows a week at the Haymarket but also directing the long-delayed *Cherry Orchard* with Trevor Howard and Gwen Ffrangcon-Davies, which he had been planning at the time of his arrest. The breakdown finally manifested itself as double vision, and John had to take to his bed for a couple of weeks.

Not everyone had been ecstatic about *A Day by the Sea*; for the *Manchester Guardian* Philip Hope-Wallace wrote that 'with so many big guns on the stage, there is some wonder that the explosions are not louder', and Kenneth Tynan for the *Observer* thought the cast were wasting their time on 'an evening of unexampled triviality . . . it was like watching a flock of eagles and macaws of magnificent plumage jammed for two hours into a suburban birdcage.'

It was Irene Worth (another of the all-star cast) who alone noted that something special was now beginning to happen onstage between Gielgud and Richardson. 'They began,' she recalled, 'to spar with each other, trying to keep one another on his toes and under all this was the marvellous respect those two men had for each other. There seemed no rivalry or bitterness, but a sharpness with their ripostes; I had never seen anything like it in my life, and it was electric for the audience.' Offstage, however, there was still some tension, especially when Richardson was sent a radical new play by Samuel Beckett called *Waiting For Godot* which, it was hoped, Richardson would play with Alec Guinness under the direction of Peter Glenville. Richardson was totally bemused by it, and gave it to other members of the company to read. Predictably, the intellectual Irene Worth told Richardson he would be mad not to do it; Gielgud on the other hand announced that it was all new-fangled rubbish, and should not be touched with a bargepole, and when Beckett himself refused to answer any of Richardson's questions (a five-page list starting 'Who is Pozzo?'), Richardson turned the job down and regretted it for the rest of his life.

Despite John's illness, the production of *The Cherry Orchard* which he directed during the Haymarket run was a considerable success, both for Trevor Howard and Gwen Ffrangcon-Davies. As Noël Coward wrote in his diary: 'a magical evening in the theatre, every part subtly and perfectly played, and a beautiful production by John, so integrated and timed that the heart melted. I came away prancing on my toes, and very proud that I belonged to the same theatre as John.'

As for Trevor Howard, John himself wrote: 'I loved working with him, and he gave a brilliant performance in the part of Lopahin. But he was always really a film actor, and the discipline of playing eight times a week seemed to be too much for him. To my great regret, he only managed to last five weeks.'

Towards the end of their time together at the Haymarket, both Richardson and John were asked by Olivier to join him in the film of *Richard III* of which Olivier was now planning to be the director and star. But whereas Richardson got what was effectively the second lead, as the Duke of Buckingham, all that Olivier could bring himself to offer John was the Duke of Clarence, who is so swiftly drowned in a butt of Malmsey within the first twenty minutes of the picture. This was to be John's first film since *Julius Caesar* and although his recollections of the shooting were pleasant enough, he remained firmly convinced that Olivier, as well as the King he was playing, were both keen to see him dispatched as swiftly as possible.

Whatever the continuing unhappiness he experienced at this time, and several close friends acknowledged that he seemed to have grown older and wearier than usual as a result of the court case, John was still determined to keep working as hard as possible, as if only by doing so could he overcome a feeling of internal despair. Thus during the run of *A Day by the Sea* he also directed a brisk revival of *Charley's Aunt* with John Mills, before setting his sights on the forthcoming 1955 season at Stratford, where Anthony Quayle had once again offered him a summer home.

The plan was for two productions: John would open the season by directing Laurence Olivier and Vivien Leigh in a starry *Twelfth Night*, and would then close it by playing and directing *King Lear* in a radical new setting with the scenery (and supposedly costumes) of the great Japanese designer Isamu Noguchi.

Rehearsals for *Twelfth Night* got off to a thoroughly uneasy start. Olivier was unusually exhausted from the strain of his *Richard III* movie, Vivien Leigh had just emerged from one of her frequent nervous breakdowns, this one so severe that she had been given electric-shock treatment, and Gielgud himself was still only really just getting over the trauma of his arrest. As if that were not enough, the Oliviers' marriage had barely recovered from Olivier's unsuccessful attempt to drag his wife away from Peter Finch during the Ceylon filming of *Elephant Walk*, where she had had to be replaced by Elizabeth Taylor, and also from a disappointing Coronation staging of Rattigan's *The Sleeping Prince*, which Olivier had now decided (to Leigh's understandable jealousy and rage) that he would film with Marilyn Monroe.

In addition to all this, a new and major problem had arisen: Olivier, always a master of disguise, had decided before rehearsals began that he would play Malvolio with a pointed nose, thick and crinkly hair, and the general demeanour of an outrageously camp, lisping hairdresser. Not surprisingly, Gielgud treated this as a personal insult. He and Olivier had not worked together (apart from the *Richard III* filming) for fully twenty years, not since they had alternated Romeo and Mercutio, and Olivier was not about to submit again to his direction without a fight. Nor was he exactly thrilled to discover that Peter Finch had moved into a nearby hotel to pursue his affair with Vivien Leigh, and the unhappiness of their marriage spread through rehearsals like a cancer. 'The best you could say,' recalled the American novelist Elaine Dundy, then married to Kenneth Tynan, 'about Vivien and Peter's affair was also the worst thing you could say about it – they did nothing behind Olivier's back.'

From the very first rehearsal, this *Twelfth Night* was clearly going to be more of a nightmare than a dream; on the very first morning, John G announced that he would like the cast to read through the play without any interruption from him. The Australian actor Keith Michell, cast as Orsino, duly began the opening speech, 'If music be the food . . .' but got no further as John came racing down the aisle, screaming, 'No, no, no, no, no! Not like that at all!'

At one point during rehearsals, relations between Olivier and John reached such a crisis that Olivier turned to his director saying, 'Darling John, please go for a long walk by the river and let us just get on with it.' John, brooding on the problem of Olivier's Malvolio, and unable to sleep, rang his old rival at two the next morning. As Olivier sleepily answered the phone, John said, 'I've got it, darling boy, just play him very, very Jewish.' Olivier uttered a stream of invective about the time of night and the general idiocy of the suggestion, at the end of which John just said, 'Oh, all right then, play him very, very not Jewish,' and put the phone down. Olivier, whose nights and weekends at the nearby Notley Abbey were not being made any easier by the presence of Finch, and who was also trying to learn *Macbeth* for the next production of the season, eventually opened *Twelfth Night* with no reference to Gielgud whatsoever.

'In rehearsal as in performance,' John said later, 'I thought Larry's Malvolio terribly vulgar – he strongly resented my criticisms and although I thought Vivien was delightful as Viola I suspected that she was torn between my attempts at directing her and Larry's views of how she should play the part, which were different from mine, but of course influenced her strongly.' This was in fact a very bad time for John: banned from rehearsals, torn between Olivier and Vivien Leigh, still bruised badly by the court case of nearly two years ago, he became increasingly confused and disheartened.

Critics in general soon echoed John's uncertainty. Olivier was generally thought to be vulgar and over the top, while Vivien Leigh, although as always described as 'graceful and pretty', was reckoned to be speaking so quickly that she lost all the poetry of the role. As W.A. Darlington wrote in the *Daily Telegraph*: 'What might have been a great occasion became merely a fairly good one.' As Vivien's biographer, Alexander Walker, has noted: 'By temperament as well as by technique, Viven was always closer to Gielgud than to her own husband. She enjoyed Gielgud's intellectual playfulness, his pouncing on an apt word, his love of poetry, his wide reading, and his knowledge of some of the most eminent players to whom he was related by blood. Both of them were sprinters on the middle track, unshaped for the gruelling marathons in which Olivier always entered himself. Vivien and John shared a quizzical, well-mannered, amused social assuredness – polishing the apples on the applecart, not upsetting it.'

Another problem here was pinpointed by John Barber, writing in the *Daily Express*: 'I hate the phrase "The Oliviers", which kow-tows to the pair royally known as Larry-and-Viv. Look beyond the gloss. Olivier was a great actor. But since his gleaming, viperish Richard III and his fiery Hamlet he has lost his way. Now, at forty-eight, he is an ageing matinée idol desperately fighting to win back his old reputation while she, at forty-two, is still a great beauty, but as an actress only good in a dainty, waspish way that seldom touches the heart.' There was worse to come; when, a few weeks later, the Oliviers opened under Glen Byam Shaw's direction in *Macbeth*, Kenneth Tynan wrote: 'Olivier shakes hands with greatness here, but Vivien Leigh's Lady Macbeth is more niminy-piminy than thundery-blundery . . . still quite competent in its small way.'

Unsurprisingly Vivien Leigh moved that summer towards one of her worst nervous breakdowns, one that John could do little to tranquillise in the face of the constantly savage onslaughts of Kenneth Tynan. Writing of her Lavinia in *Titus Andronicus* (the third of the Oliviers' Shakespeares that Stratford season) Tynan added: 'Vivien Leigh receives the news that she is about to be ravished on her husband's corpse with little more than the mild annoyance of one who would have preferred foam rubber.'

Another major problem with their *Twelfth Night* was a set by Malcolm Pride which had very difficult sight lines, and a decision by John to play all the comedy upstage behind a box hedge. As for Vivien Leigh, John could not understand why she did not dissolve into tears as Viola: 'All my leading ladies always cry,' he told her after the first night. 'Oh, I do,' replied Vivien, 'but only when I have to go home to Notley with Larry afterwards.'

By now, the Oliviers' marital collapse was obvious to everyone who called in at their dressing-rooms by the Avon: 'Their life together is really hideous,' wrote Coward at this time, 'as they are trapped by their own public acclaim, and have to scrabble about in the cold ashes of a physical passion that burnt itself out years ago.'

As for Olivier, he found himself one afternoon describing the plot of *Macbeth* to Tynan in terms that clearly referred to his own marriage: '*Macbeth* is a domestic tragedy, the passage of two people; one going up and one going down. And there comes a moment in the play when he looks at her and realises that she can't take it any more. He goes on, and she stops.' For John, this Stratford summer should have been a tranquil time for the preparation of his long-awaited *King Lear*; instead he found himself increasingly caught up in the still greater real-life drama of the Oliviers in meltdown.

Now he was forming, for the first time, an 'away' Stratford company which would tour abroad through the late summer and autumn of

1955, only returning to their Stratford base at the end of November. John's company was to be headed by himself, and such old Gielgud regulars as Peggy Ashcroft and George Devine. They were to present two plays, *Much Ado About Nothing* and *King Lear*, and the touring schedule (at a time when the Stratford company still very rarely played away from home) was nothing if not ambitious. Opening in Brighton, they were to play Vienna, Zurich, the Hague, Amsterdam and Rotterdam, before coming home to four weeks at the Palace in London and then going on to Berlin, Hanover, Bremen, Hamburg, Copenhagen, Oslo, Newcastle, Edinburgh, Glasgow, Manchester and Liverpool before finishing up, exhausted, at Stratford, where they played most of December.

The two productions were wildly different. *Much Ado About Nothing*, which John again directed and played opposite Peggy Ashcroft, was the familiar old vehicle in which they had been totally at home for several seasons. *King Lear*, however, was to be designed by the Japanese-American artist Isamu Noguchi, who had done the dance sets for Balanchine's *Orpheus* and Martha Graham's *Appalachian Spring*, but never yet for a play, with an equally radical 'sound-score' by the avant-garde composer Roberto Gerhard. The idea here was clearly to prove to audiences at home and abroad that Stratford was not just in the business of elegant museum pieces, as John's programme note now explained: 'Our object in this production has been to find a setting and costumes free of all historical and decorative associations, so that the timeless, universal and mythical quality of the story may be clear in a simple and basic manner; so the play comes to life through words and acting and nothing else.'

That may well have been the intention, and a worthy one, but it was not designed to appeal to the critics. J.C. Trewin, usually an admirer of Gielgud, reported that John now came on stage 'with around his face a vast, drooping circlet of white horse-hair, on his head what seemed to be an inverted hatstand, and in his grasp a decorated lavatory brush'. For the *Tatler*, Anthony Cookman found Goneril and Regan like 'sinister geishas from *The Tea House of the August Moon*', while the critic of *Punch* found 'women hideously wrapped up, while the men wear cellular bath-mats over space-suits in heavy leather. No wonder Lear is eager to leave a palace in which he has to sit side-saddle on an abstract horse.' As for his throne, noted the usually respectful Harold Hobson, this most closely resembled the seat of a golden metaphysical lavatory. Other critics were all too eager to quote Lear's 'I do not like the fashion of your garments' while Gielgud's Lear was elsewhere more flatteringly described as a great oak struck by lightning.

John was given no credit at all for the courage of this experiment, and indeed many critics thought that the sets and costumes had simply 'got him down'.

Although Peter Brook was later to acknowledge this production as the starting point for his triumphant Paul Scofield *Lear* of eight years later, John himself was in no doubt about the scale of the disaster:

I made one great mistake with the Japanese *King Lear*, and it was purely technical. Noguchi, who is a sculptor, designed some brilliant sets, but no one had told me that he didn't also do costumes. So he arrived with no costumes at all, designed them very hastily, and left again before he had even seen the fittings. Nor was he at the dress-rehearsal, or even the first night. I remember suggesting then to the director George Devine that we simply abandon all the costumes, and play in nondescript black cloaks. This might just have worked, but we hadn't the courage to make such a drastic alteration at the last minute, and we went through with it because I felt that Noguchi was too individual and brilliant a designer to throw overboard completely.

For John, on the long pre-Stratford tour, there were one or two consolations, not least while in Berlin the chance to see Brecht's own production of *The Recruiting Officer*: 'A strange propaganda version,' he wrote to his mother, 'with a rather indifferent company but very attractive décor . . . I found Brecht's presentation very interesting, though I resented his twisting of a light comedy into a savage attack on the British army.'

Brecht himself, who could have been expected to be deeply unimpressed with Gielgud's traditional approach to Shakespeare, was in fact amazingly enthusiastic, to such an extent that he commanded his Berliner Ensemble to hasten along and catch John while they could.

In Vienna, the army had to be called out to control a stage-door crowd of several hundred, and in Germany the applause every night was timed at thirty minutes. Obviously Noguchi was rather more accessible to European audiences than he was to those at home, who still expected their Shakespeare at Stratford to be a more traditional and familiar affair.

This *Lear* was in fact to be George Devine's last production as a classical Stratford director. By now he and John had lost all the intimacy of their early years together at Oxford and the Old Vic; Devine had long since gone off to manage companies of his own, leaving John feeling vaguely bereft, and the *Lear* which brought them together again was so dominated by Noguchi that neither of them could really claim the production as his own.

Devine already regarded the Shakespeare Memorial Theatre as 'a death trap – there it is, that great lump of masonry standing on the river bank, imposing itself on everyone who has to work there'. Devine's hope had been that Noguchi would dynamite all that, but in fact they were simply out of the frying pan and into the fire. In later years Gielgud himself never flinched from calling the production 'a disaster', and Devine was so horrified by it all that he increasingly retreated into his own performance as Gloucester. For Peggy Ashcroft, who was playing Cordelia while trying to sustain yet another tumultuous backstage affair, this one with Tony Britton, it was 'a matter of awful despair. With those clothes I didn't see how anybody could act . . . the intention was that they should be totally negative, but they were in fact the most positive thing on the stage. You simply couldn't get over them.'

Peggy Ashcroft was therefore not entirely sorry to give up her Cordelia to Claire Bloom when the production eventually returned to Stratford; she had not been happy during the tour but, as so often in a Gielgud company, a kind of greatness was to be plucked from disaster. Waiting in the wings one night in Berlin, George Devine happened to ask her if she might be interested in playing Brecht's *The Good Woman of Setzuan* for a new company he was thinking of forming in the following year at the Royal Court. This was to be the English Stage Society, and within a few months of *Setzuan* they were to have their first real hit – John Osborne's *Look Back in Anger*, the play that was to put an end to the kind of theatre in which John had starred for almost forty years.

Chapter Eighteen

❦❧

BACK ON THE AVENUE

(1956–1957)

I act these plays – I never understand them.

As the ill-fated Noguchi *Lear* ground to a halt at Stratford just before Christmas 1955, John decided once again that it was time to get back to Binkie and the commercial theatre of the West End. What was on offer now was a new play by Enid Bagnold, a formidable novelist and dramatist of the period, whose reputation also rested on her having once had an affair with Frank Harris (of Oscar Wilde fame), and a long marriage to Sir Roderick Jones, the chief of Reuter's.

The Chalk Garden was, depending on which critic you read, either an autumnal comedy or a Chekhovian thriller. It turned on an eccentric dowager hiring a governess for her wayward granddaughter, only to discover, over an uneasy lunch with a neighbouring judge, that the woman has in fact recently completed a prison term for murder. The play had already opened with considerable success on Broadway, though rehearsals had not been easy. In addition to Bagnold, in the leading role was Gladys Cooper and the producer was the equally formidable Irene Mayer Selznick, recently divorced from the maker of *Gone with the Wind* and herself also the daughter of Louis B. Mayer of MGM.

These three determined dowagers were more than a match for any male director, and George Cukor indeed left the production on tour, feeling distinctly henpecked. Nor were relations much better between the author and the star. 'Before the first rehearsal,' wrote Bagnold, 'Gladys always called me Enid. After the first rehearsal she called me Miss Bagnold, and after the first night she called me Lady Jones. Gladys was an old hand; she had run her own theatre in management, and I think she regarded me as a rather silly society outsider. We were about the same age and very positive characters, and we both annoyed each other from the start.'

Nevertheless, by the time they reached Broadway, *The Chalk Garden* was the hit of the season, and Binkie Beaumont (despite his initial doubts about the play) immediately decided on a London production. This would need an entirely new cast, under John's direction, and the two men decided to play safe: they would try to get Edith Evans for the dotty dowager, and Peggy Ashcroft for the sinister governess.

This they duly did, and it could be argued that in the year that was to see the creation of George Devine's Royal Court and the confirmation of Joan Littlewood's Stratford East, *The Chalk Garden* was the final flourish of the old guard at the Haymarket – the last truly all-star, elegant, country-house party on stage. It was Kenneth Tynan who noted: 'at least the West End cavalry is going out with a flourish, its banners resplendent in the last rays of the dying sun.'

In fact, there is a good deal more than that going on beneath the soil of *The Chalk Garden*. Reviewers at the time referred it back to both Pirandello and Ronald Firbank as well as to Chekhov, and the play's enduring power lies in its ability to counterweight an Agatha Christie kind of murder mystery with strange, surreal dialogue, heightened in language, affected certainly, but also curiously poetic.

During the Haymarket run, Peggy Ashcroft was awarded both her DBE and a Best Actress award from the *Evening Standard*, although it was always largely Edith Evans's evening, from her wondrous first offstage line: 'Where are my teeth?' Tynan went as far as to call *The Chalk Garden* 'the finest artificial comedy to have flowed from an English pen since the death of Congreve', and Gielgud as director knew enough not to get in the way of any of that, but simply to give his two favourite actresses their heads, and arrange the rest of the cast tactfully upstage.

However, he had decided that the Broadway original was about twenty minutes too long, and therefore put in some useful cuts; these would not have been a problem, had it not been that about nine months into the run Dame Edith suddenly collapsed on stage with an intestinal complaint, which her fervent belief in Christian Science had led her to ignore for far too long. By apparent good fortune, the Saturday night on which she collapsed was also the closing night of *The Chalk Garden* on Broadway. Binkie duly telephoned Gladys Cooper, demanding that she spend Sunday on a plane and open at the Haymarket in place of Edith on the Monday night. This she duly did, unaware of the difference in the London production, so for the next few nights Gladys Cooper played the Broadway version while Peggy Ashcroft and the rest of the London cast persevered with the London text, only occasionally meeting somewhere mid-stage in a state of mutual confusion.

Gladys Cooper was subsequently heartbroken to lose the film of *The Chalk Garden* to Edith Evans, but by any standards the play did nothing but good for all of those involved on either side of the Atlantic. Curiously it had originally been turned down by local managements, including Binkie's, and it wasn't until Gladys Cooper's Broadway success that he realised what he had so nearly missed. John meanwhile, as soon as the show was open, picked up a role from Noël Coward, the first time the two men had worked together since *The Constant Nymph* exactly thirty years earlier.

Admittedly, this new play was not one of Coward's best, and John was by no means his first choice of either star or director. *Nude With Violin* was, not unlike Yasmina Reza's *Art* some forty years later, a satire about perceptions of modern art. Its central character was an all-knowing valet whom Coward had originally written for Rex Harrison and, on his refusal, turned into a housekeeper for Yvonne Arnaud. When she, too, turned it down, Coward turned the character back into a man and would have played it himself (as he did subsequently on Broadway) had it not been that he had just entered into a controversial and highly publicised tax exile which meant that only in Dublin could he get to see the play, let alone appear in it.

From the very start John had his doubts; as he wrote to his mother: 'it is very broad and a bit vulgar, but full of some surefire situations, and Noel's plays are usually quite successful, so I think I shall do it, while taking great care not to give just another imitation of him.'

Noël Coward was now at his most unpopular. The British press, headed by Beaverbrook's *Daily Express*, vilified him not only as one of

Britain's very first tax exiles but one who, in plays such as *Cavalcade* and films such as *In Which We Serve*, had set himself up as the kind of patriot who should not now be resident abroad. But as Coward himself explained, 'I am not a businessman; I have never made real money, my brain is my only fortune, and at fifty-six I have got to tread pretty carefully.'

The plan was that although John would of course direct the play, Coward himself would supervise it during the Dublin try-out. He duly arrived in Ireland to a storm of tabloid indignation, and a full programme's discussion on ITV as to whether or not he had the right to live how and where he chose. This row completely overshadowed *Nude With Violin*, not a bad thing considering that Coward himself was by now having premonitions of disaster:

> I do not think John is anything like ideal for the part, but he is such a wonderful man of the theatre that I am sure that it is all being done with taste and dignity . . . he really is rather better than I expected, looks fine, and although not yet comedically very sure, he is neither embarrassing nor mannered in the role, both of which I dreaded. There are still a few ringing Terry tones in his voice, but I am hoping to eliminate those before London. The rest of the cast are fairly terrible, especially David Horne, hopelessly miscast and bellowing like a mad water-buffalo . . . The set by Paul Anstee [John's current lover] is very good, but the lighting far too dim and John has directed everyone with so much fussy business that all my best lines are getting lost. The actors get up, sit down, carry trays, change places and move around so incessantly that I am nearly going out of my mind . . . it is extraordinary that so fine a director as Johnny, who has done *The Cherry Orchard* definitively, could have gone so very far wrong with me. I can only conclude that it is all about over-anxiety.

Coward's doubts were unfortunately all too accurate; although the Inland Revenue did grant him ten London days to see the play at the Lyric ('I am staying,' he told the *Evening Standard*, 'in the Oliver Messel suite at the Dorchester; all that luxury is not really me, but doubtless I shall be able to rise above it; thanks to the vilifications of the *Daily Express* I am now nearly as famous as Debbie Reynolds, which I find most gratifying'), he could not do very much to rescue a play which, said one critic, 'started as a farce and ended as a corpse'. Kenneth Tynan also put the boot in for the *Observer*: 'Sir John never acts seriously in modern dress; it is the lounging attire in which he relaxes between classical bookings, and his present performance as a simpering valet is carried out with extreme elegance but the general aspect of a tight, smart, walking umbrella.' Yet despite that very hostile press, it is some tribute to the enduring box-office power of Coward and Gielgud (fully thirty years after they had first worked together) that the play ran on Shaftesbury Avenue for more than twelve months, during which time Gielgud was replaced first by a wildly unhappy, stammering Michael Wilding, and then rather more successfully by Robert Helpmann. As for Gielgud, 'I really only took it on because I was longing to do something frivolous, and I wanted to see if I could do a Coward play without giving an imitation of its author. I think I managed, but only just.'

Indeed, when Coward himself came to play the role in America, a year later, he had rather less success than John had enjoyed in London.

During the nine months that John played Sebastien in *Nude With Violin*, he was frenetically otherwise engaged on day jobs. There were two films: first a cameo appearance, again with Noël Coward, in Mike Todd's all-star *Around the World in Eighty Days* (in which he has one memorable scene as a tearful valet fired by David Niven as Phineas Fogg), and then a rather more serious role as the forbidding father in *The Barretts of Wimpole Street*.

This was of course the role that Cedric Hardwicke on stage and Charles Laughton on film had made their own well before the war, and the only possible alibi for the remake was the coming of CinemaScope and the need of MGM to complete a three-picture deal with Jennifer Jones. Bill Travers was cast as the young Robert Browning, and the result was predictably dire. Even CinemaScope didn't help because, as Keith Baxter (then a drama school student, later to become a lifelong friend of John's) was to observe, the screen was now so wide that those like him in minor roles tended to disappear off the sides of it. John's role consisted mainly of appearing at inopportune moments to interrupt the romance, though there was a good giggle to be had when he comes in to find his cherished daughter helping the hated suitor on with his uniform: 'Since when,' he asks her, 'has it been your custom to button on his accoutrements?'

Keith also recalled lunching with John and Maxine Audley in the studio canteen, and to his horror hearing John complain that as he had no other work on offer, he was having to do a not very strong new play (*Nude With Violin*) from Noël Coward. 'At that moment John's eyes suddenly lit up as into the canteen strode Yul Brynner, dressed in his full glory for *Anastasia* which was being shot on a nearby sound stage. "Isn't he gorgeous?" John whispered. Maxine asked if Gielgud would like to meet him. Thinking she knew him, John eagerly agreed. What Maxine then did was simply to stick out her leg so that Brynner would fall, literally into John's lap. It was a splendid introduction, but I don't think it led to anything very much. All I can recall is the shocked realisation that if John in all his eminence was still scratching around for work, my own life in the theatre was unlikely to be any easier.'

Apart from these two films, which did more for John's still shaky bank balance than for his reputation, his other project during the run of *Nude With Violin* was altogether more ambitious, and some might say even foolhardy. At the suggestion of David Webster, he was invited to direct at Covent Garden the first uncut version ever performed anywhere of Berlioz's *The Trojans*. This had normally either been heavily cut or performed in two quite separate parts (*The Fall of Troy* and *The Trojans at Carthage*). Not only was this to be the first complete version, but it was also to be John's first-ever opera, one that would involve five Irish wolfhounds, a chorus of 180, forty extras, twenty-two principals and two entire orchestras.

Faced with this vast multitude, John decided to borrow the system pioneered by Noël Coward while directing his equally epic *Cavalcade* at Drury Lane back in 1930. The cast was therefore divided into teams bearing placards carrying their respective numbers, and John took to blowing a whistle and shouting from the stalls when he wanted any of the groups to move anywhere. His plan worked well enough at the early rehearsals, but once the orchestra arrived it was inclined to drown out the sound of the Gielgud whistle; by the final dress-rehearsal he was more than frantic, and seen by the surprised conductor Georg Solti rushing down the aisle shouting at the orchestra, 'Do stop making that terrible noise and give me time to think!'

The end result was somewhat catastrophic, not least because Amy Shuard as Cassandra politely declined to make any of Gielgud's moves, on the grounds that only if she stayed close to the prompter could she get any assistance with the lines should she dry up during an aria. One critic complained of the costumes that 'the Trojans are all dressed as jesters, while the Carthaginians all look like chefs'. John himself was not greatly thrilled when his now eighty-eight-year-old mother mistook the Trojan Horse for a ship in full sail, and all in all the experience was not inclined to endear him to a life at Covent Garden. All the same, when the production came back in 1960 he seemed a little happier:

> I was always totally bewildered by the volume of noise; I never knew how to stop the chorus and if I ever succeeded, I could never get them started again. They kept having half-hour breaks in which they seemed to do a great deal of knitting, and I was also amazed by the way that, unlike actors, singers never wait behind after a performance for production notes. We would have a dress-rehearsal, and by the time I got up on to the stage at the end they had all left the building. They seemed to expect my notes to come from my secretary, but the trouble was that I didn't have one. And just when I got everybody finally in the right place, the chorus master would suddenly rearrange my moves because he had to have all the tenors on the same side of the stage. None of the chorus seemed to have the faintest interest in the scenes, and all I could do was try not to treat them like cattle. I think I failed.

John's connection to Covent Garden was not only through the homosexual network that existed backstage. All through his career he had taken a passionate interest in music, not only going to concerts, operas and ballets at home and abroad whenever he had a rare evening off but also, where possible, giving as much importance to background music as to sets and costumes. In productions such as *Much Ado* and *The School For Scandal*, he had insisted on very melodic scores:

> It is a pity theatres no longer have live orchestras. In the old days if

a play was rather thin, orchestral interludes brightened things up a little, even though all too often what you got was a little palm court orchestra sawing away at tea-shop music between the acts. During the war I managed to persuade William Walton to write a complete score for *Macbeth* which we recorded up at Maida Vale with a vast orchestra. It was immensely expensive, and at the end of the overtime session I found myself signing mad cheques like Ludwig of Bavaria, but the score was one of the best things about the production, and having had to pay for it Binkie Beaumont was determined not to waste it, so it turned up rather surprisingly some years later as the score for Thornton Wilder's *The Skin of Our Teeth*.

Relieved to have escaped more or less intact from Covent Garden and the long run of *Nude With Violin*, John now planned to return to Stratford for the 1957 season, solely to play Prospero in a Peter Brook *Tempest* but with the understanding that they would take it into Drury Lane for Christmas, as the theatre was unexpectedly vacant, awaiting the arrival of Rex Harrison in *My Fair Lady*. This *Tempest* was to be entirely Peter Brook's, in that he not only directed and designed all the sets and costumes but also composed a musique-concrète score. With Alec Clunes as Caliban and Patrick Wymark as Stephano, the Ariel was to be a young newcomer from drama school, Brian Bedford, whose looks, charm and passion for theatre had already enabled him to move into Gielgud's backstage circle and had also much impressed Peter Brook. It was Brook, giving Bedford *The Tempest* to read, who invited him to choose himself a role; Bedford unerringly went for Ariel, and managed in rehearsal and performance to stay closely by Gielgud's side, learning everything he could and noting with some surprise that the great actor was far more giggly and light-hearted than he had somehow expected:

John struck me at first as a nervous kind of thoroughbred, and there was one of his characteristic bricks when, leaving rehearsal one afternoon, he suddenly looked at me and said, 'Tell me, is it difficult being so short?' As I was only four inches shorter than him, that seemed a little harsh, but all through my early career he was just wonderfully helpful. Once, when I was playing Hamlet in the regional theatre, he sent me fourteen pages of notes in his minute, extraordinary handwriting, advising me to look up Granville-Barker on the subject.

Another time, when he invited me to lunch, I asked him what I should wear, and his reply was, 'Nothing beaded'. But all through *The Tempest* I shadowed him, and perhaps the most important thing he taught me was that Shakespearean speeches are like trains – you have to run with them right to the end of the track, keeping up your energy for the whole journey. When Brook first cast me as Ariel I'd had hardly any experience at all of speaking Shakespearean verse, and so while John was in Noël's *Nude With Violin* I used to go along every Wednesday and Saturday to his dressing-room after the matinée for master-classes in verse speaking. As I got to know him better, John used to invite me to wonderfully theatrical dinners at his house in Cowley Street, where everywhere you looked, everything was absolutely exquisite, taste and beauty all over the place, and everything in the right place. All the same, I fear he was not terribly impressed by my Ariel. All he could bring himself to say at the end of the Drury Lane run was, 'I met a man in the Burlington Arcade today, who thought you were really quite good.'

In fact, John had been rather more impressed, on and off stage, by Bedford than he cared to admit, and it was because of John that Brian soon got his first real West End break in modern dress, although even this came to him in a somewhat grudging way. 'I have,' John told him at dinner one night, 'been reading this new play by someone called Peter Shaffer. I fear it is dreadfully suburban, but maybe it would suit you.' The play was *Five Finger Exercise*, which Bedford was to play for almost three years in London and then on Broadway, at the start of his long American and Canadian acting life.

John's Prospero was his third in thirty years, but at Brook's insistence he was determined to do away with the turbaned conjuror of 1931 and the angry old man of 1941. This Prospero was to be a kind of biblical hermit in a magnificent blue robe, black skull cap and coronet. As John said, 'I tried to play it this time with strength and passion, as a kind of Jacobean revenge drama. The whole action of the play is Prospero growing to the final understanding that hatred and revenge are useless – all he has left is agony.'

Prospero now became the last great Shakespearean figure of John's life; he was to play the role once more on stage (at the National Theatre in 1974) and finally in his long-desired film, although as this was directed by Peter Greenaway in 1991 it was sadly not quite the more orthodox *Tempest* on which he would have wanted to go out.

As for the Peter Brook production, *The Times* found that 'Gielgud takes little joy in Prospero's magic powers. He is an angry and embittered aristocrat speaking his tortured thoughts as though they disgusted him. Clean-shaven with the grizzled hair of virile middle age, and half-bare to the waist, he looked like a workman about to strike the anvil . . . his speeches of harsh intemperance work better than those which give rein to parental and human tenderness.'

Eileen Atkins was one of the child-like nymphs in this production, and Brook said that he had been trying for 'a mescalin world of sound and light', but this hint of a drugged dream was not pursued far by Gielgud, who relied yet again on all the majesty of his magnifi-cently poetic voice. As Ralph Richardson wrote in a backstage note: 'magnificent, I felt I was back with giants, the best Shakespearean acting I have ever seen, and I am sure that WS would have been delighted.' Ronald Hayman noted that this was more than generous, considering that when a few years earlier Gielgud had gone backstage after Richardson's Prospero, it was only to say, 'I think I hated you more in the first half than I did in the second.' Unwisely, Richardson asked why. 'Because there is more of you in the first half.'

When they reached Drury Lane, which had seen no Shakespeare since Ivor Novello in *Henry V* in 1938, the reviews improved con-siderably. This was where Tynan wrote of John G as 'the finest actor, from the neck up, in the world today' and he went on to add: 'his face is all rigour and pain, his voice all cello and woodwind. The rest of him may be totem-pole but he speaks the great passages perfectly, and always looks full of thinking. Prospero demands no more.' For Derek Granger in the *Financial Times*: 'Gielgud, of course, has all the qualities for Prospero. He is, above all else, the speaking poet of our theatre and here, appearing in the handsome stamp of an Old Testament prophet in the wilderness, he speaks the poetry with an enthralling appreciation for its sense and music.' For the *Sunday Times*, Harold Hobson wrote: 'Gielgud comes to Drury Lane at one of the triumphant points of his career . . . his reading of Prospero is darker than that of most actors. He does not offer us a well-meaning old bore, ready with a few tricks like a conjuror at a Christmas party. The night hangs over his whole performance, a night that is lit by dazzling and magic stars. The sternness in it is inescapable, and so is its incredible and sinister beauty. By subduing all gentleness, Gielgud unites the twin aspects of Prospero and creates a nobly isolated figure whose resolution is taxed only by the inner battle caused by relinquishing his cherished magical powers.'

Towards the end of this *Tempest* John, at the request of the British Council, was given two nights' leave to slip over to Paris and present a recital of Shakespearean verse, the kind of thing that he had been doing occasionally at troop concerts during the war, but which he was now (with the considerable help of his friend, the Cambridge don George Rylands) to reshape into what was soon to become his *Ages of Man*, the most successful solo Shakespeare show of the entire twentieth century in Britain and all over the world.

While he was still playing Prospero at the Lane, John also agreed to take up the challenge of a new play by Graham Greene. This was *The Potting Shed*, which he had originally rejected as being altogether too poetic and difficult to understand. As a result, the play had first opened in New York with his old friends Robert Flemyng, Lewis Casson and Sybil Thorndike in the central roles. By now, this had become the snob hit of the Broadway season, and its success encouraged John to think again about playing it in the West End.

Greene's play, as the critic Robert Tanitch has noted, is a spiritual detective story in which a Nottingham journalist, trying to uncover the source of his own mid-life crisis, discovers instead that at the age of fourteen he has in fact hanged himself in the garden shed of the title, only to have been raised from the dead by the Roman Catholic priest who is also the boy's uncle. In some ways the best part was that of the priest, who in order to get the boy back has to lose his own faith; but an immensely strong cast (Irene Worth, Gwen Ffrangcon-Davies, Lockwood West and Redmond Phillips) got the play off to an impressive London start, although the run had to be curtailed because, characteristically not confident of a success here, John had already committed himself to playing Cardinal Wolsey in an Old Vic *Henry VIII*.

The reviews for *The Potting Shed* were bemused but generally respectful: Milton Shulman thought that the play would soon acquire the fashionable status of something you had to see, even if you weren't very likely to enjoy or even fully comprehend it. For the *Observer* Kenneth Tynan wrote a brilliant parody of Greene's usual Catholic despair, noting that Gielgud always talked to other members of his company 'as though he were about to tip them'. He also decided that this was not so much a whodunnit as a Goddunnit, and was amazed to find beside him in the audience row after row of rapt, attentive faces who were actually taking this play seriously, 'and there, suddenly, in a blaze of darkness, I knew that my faith in the theatre and the people who attend it had been withdrawn from me.' Others were however more enthusiastic. 'His playing,' wrote Derek Granger, 'suggested a convulsive inner struggle kept under rigid control; nothing he does is without a sense of tautness and strain,' while for the *Daily Mail*, Cecil Wilson wrote: 'Gielgud's ability to cry genuine tears as the hero's uncle, yet another of Graham Greene's shambling whisky priests, lays bare his whole dread childhood secret. He only has to make himself look as insignificant as possible to mesmerise his audience.'

Harold Hobson, reflecting years later on *The Potting Shed*, wrote:

John played the part of a man who, without knowing it, had been raised from the dead. I found his performance of the resurrected boy masterly, especially as I knew that personally he did not believe in the resurrection of this boy, or of Christ, or of anyone else. If ever, I felt, there could be presented on the stage a good man from whom God has removed his presence, then in this play Sir John presented him, with cheekbones sharp under shaven flesh, looking like a man carrying within him a world of Polar ice. The poignancy of this performance lay in Gielgud's capacity to suggest ice which even at its thickest yearns for the sun . . . This is why Gielgud, though an unbeliever, could always play expositions of belief. There are two things in the theatre which exalt me – faith, which Gielgud can always arouse, and love . . . He has not the tremendous self-confidence of an Olivier, but always seeks guidance and advice. He found help chiefly in Granville-Barker and once described a rehearsal with him as like being at a masseuse's – you felt bruised and broken, but with muscles functioning that you never even suspected of being there.

All through his non-Shakespearean career, John was to make a habit of appearing in 'difficult' modern work, from André Obey's *Noah* in the 1930s through Christopher Fry's *The Lady's Not For Burning* and Greene's *The Potting Shed*, all the way up to Albee's 1960s *Tiny Alice* and Harold Pinter's *No Man's Land*. However, friends and fans alike had long since learned not to go backstage to John for any enlightenment. On one famous occasion Gielgud irritably retorted, 'I merely act these plays; I am not supposed to understand them.'

His courage in going after new work did still have certain strict limits; at this time, while his old friend and director George Devine was setting up the Royal Court, it was mooted that John might like to open a season there as Hamm in Samuel Beckett's *Endgame*. But Gielgud, having already firmly discouraged both Alec Guinness and Ralph Richardson from playing in Beckett's *Waiting For Godot*, was not now about to change his mind. 'When I saw *Godot*, I felt there was no communal experience at all. The audience was glum, and miserable, while in *Endgame* there is nothing but loneliness and despair.' He still had within him just enough of the old-fashioned showman to delay his crossover to the Royal Court for another twelve years.

Even by his standards, John was now moving into a period of intense activity: while playing eight times a week in *The Potting Shed*, he was also now planning to direct the première of a new Terence Rattigan drama (*Variation on a Theme*), and continuing to work with George Rylands on the solo *Ages of Man* recital which he would open in America and Canada towards the end of 1958; meanwhile, there was still an Old Vic *Henry VIII* in which he was about to play Wolsey and, added to all of that, a few weeks' filming as the Earl of Warwick in Otto Preminger's screen version of Bernard Shaw's *Saint Joan*.

With a screenplay by Graham Greene, sets by Roger Furse and a starry cast (Richard Widmark, Richard Todd, Kenneth Haigh, Anton Walbrook, Felix Aylmer and Harry Andrews) this should have been a success, but in the title role Preminger had cast an eighteen-year-old unknown girl from Iowa, Jean Seberg, who (as John noted) was sadly inexperienced for the role:

> Having chosen her but then decided it was a mistake, Preminger was utterly horrible to her on the set and I desperately wanted to help in any way I could. There wasn't an unkind bone in her body, but she was desperately insecure about everything and when one day I gave her a cup and saucer that had belonged to my great-aunt Ellen Terry, she simply broke down in tears. She didn't know anything about phrasing or pacing or climax – all the things the part needed – but she was desperately eager to learn, and we became great friends. The next time she was in London she rang to say she was with Gary Cooper, and would I like to join them for dinner? I had never seen quite so many flash photographers and for once I felt terribly important. What was so lovely about Jean was that she learned how to be a star long before she learned how to be an actress.

When the film came out, it was to very tepid reviews, although John's Warwick was applauded for its chilly, icy malevolence. As for Jean Seberg, after several suicide attempts she was found dead in her car in the back streets of Paris early in 1979; she was just forty-one.

Chapter Nineteen

THE AGES OF MAN
(1958–1960)

I toured the Ages of Man *for so many years that I began to fear I would be out of practice when it came to acting again with other people. Also, eight performances a week, all by myself, and sitting alone in a dressing-room during the interval, was a very lonely and sometimes depressing business.*

In the closing weeks of *The Potting Shed*, in which he had somehow failed to repeat the success that Robert Flemyng had had in the play on Broadway, John agreed to direct for Binkie what must have seemed another of their really safe bets: a new play by Terence Rattigan, *Variation on a Theme*. However, this was Rattigan in a newly liberated form; in the past there had always been the suggestion that *Separate Tables* and even *The Deep Blue Sea* were coded homosexual dramas, in which the sex of the leading character had simply been changed from a man to a woman in order to satisfy the Lord Chamberlain. But now the Wolfenden Report had just been published, and *Variation on a Theme* was to some extent intended as Rattigan's response. Loosely derived from Dumas's *La Dame Aux Camélias* (hence the *Variation*), it was to be the story of Rose Fish, a wealthy, much-married, middle-aged woman falling in love with a homosexual ballet dancer – an affair that ends (like *La Dame Aux Camélias* and the subsequent Garbo *Camille*) with Rose coughing herself to death of consumption.

But as with Noël Coward's *Song at Twilight*, written a decade later, there was all manner of reality lurking just below the greasepaint of an apparently conventional Shaftesbury Avenue drama. Many saw the character of Rose as being Rattigan in disguise, with his current real-life lover Ron Vale as the young dancer. Then again, Margaret Leighton, a lifelong friend of Rattigan's for whom the play was written, had also just married a much younger man, the actor Laurence Harvey, a Lithuanian who (again like Ron Vale) had anglicised his name and had famously had a long homosexual affair with the film producer James Woolf, who was later to commit suicide, many believed as a result of Harvey's having left him for Leighton. So the coded messages here threatened to overbalance what was in truth far from one of Rattigan's best plays. Its moral was intended to be of the tragedy that lies in store when rich and older people fall in love with feckless opportunists, whose sexuality has always been their calling-card to both men and women alike. Margaret Leighton and Vivien Leigh (soon to star in a very similar script, Tennessee Williams's *The Roman Spring of Mrs Stone*) were both famous for having built up networks of homosexual friends to whom they could turn in their serial moments of marital despair. Rattigan had already had one homosexual lover (Kenneth Morgan) commit suicide at the end of their affair, the producer Binkie Beaumont was still living with the John Perry he had stolen from John G, and Gielgud was far from totally able, even now, to banish the shadows of his court case five years earlier.

All in all, therefore, this was going to be a rough emotional ride for all the principals concerned, and it failed to get off to the best of starts when Laurence Harvey turned down the role of the young dancer, which went first to the actor Tim Seely, to whom Binkie Beaumont had taken a considerable fancy when he had recently played the boy in *Tea and Sympathy*. It was however to prove an unhappy choice as Seely recalled: 'I was entirely heterosexual, which didn't help much in that company, and I was pitifully inexperienced and lacking in confidence. I also couldn't cope with all those famous people, or with Gielgud's habit of changing everything a dozen times in rehearsal. "For Christ's sake!" I shouted at John one afternoon. "Can't you ever make up your fucking mind?"'

Not entirely surprisingly, Seely was fired at the end of the tour and replaced by a young Jeremy Brett, who was about to marry Anna

Massey, the daughter of Adrianne Allen, and therefore to join, at least as an in-law, the charmed and often closed circle of the H.M. Tennent backstage family.

But the central problem with *Variation on a Theme* was that although it appeared to be topical, in allowing for almost the first time an overtly homosexual leading character on stage, in truth it creaked along on the tracks laid down by Dumas a century earlier; and critics who might have been charitable, two years after *Look Back in Anger*, to Rattigan's apparently new-found courage of exposure were turned off by a pallid script. A number of them instantly realised the problem he had faced in keeping this modern Camille figure female rather than male; as Alan Brien wrote in the *Spectator*: 'the subject of Rattigan's play should be a homosexual relationship between a bored and ageing "rentier" and a sharp, oily male tart.' Harold Hobson also thought he was being asked to review a play which was really about something that was not its ostensible subject, while Tynan put the boot in by accusing Rattigan of clumsily disguising a blatantly homosexual theme in a pathetic attempt to stay on the right side of his own traditional Aunt Edna audiences, and of course of the Lord Chamberlain, who was still then in charge of censoring West End plays.

In Rattigan's defence, his old friend the critic T.C. Worsley in the *Financial Times* attacked any suggestion of a covert homosexual theme as 'a seamy line of personal smear', but as he was known to be both homosexual and a close friend of the author, this defence did the play, author and critic rather more harm than good.

Rattigan himself resented the attacks, maintaining that he had purposely tried to show the reality behind the apparently romantic characters in *La Dame Aux Camélias*, but the play only achieved lasting fame for what it inadvertently led to: a teenage schoolgirl called Shelagh Delaney had been in the audience at a matinée during the Manchester try-out of *Variation on a Theme*, and went home convinced that, even though she had never written anything in her life (apart from school essays), even she could do better than that. Within a few months she had written *A Taste of Honey*, which ran in the West End for altogether two years as against the barely four months that *Variation on a Theme* was to last.

In many ways the failure of *Variation on a Theme*, despite the involvement of Rattigan, Gielgud, Leighton and Binkie Beaumont, was the wake-up call that John G should have heard whenever he was tempted to go back to the Shaftesbury Avenue of his earlier years. As for Rattigan, his biographer Michael Darlow pinpoints the problem that now faced all homosexual writers in rapidly changing theatrical times:

> Until the late 1950s, Rattigan's art as a dramatist depended upon the oblique, the implicit, the struggle of frightened, damaged people to find self-expression and fulfilment in a society whose strict moral codes had always inhibited them. But once those moral codes began to be relaxed, Rattigan was not only out of fashion, he was stranded. Not only his technique as a writer, but his background and lifetime's conditioning, meant that however passionately he resented the old hypocrisies, he was not equipped to make do without them. The result was that when he tried to confront sex, however frankly and sincerely, in the permissive atmosphere of the post-Osborne theatre he always seemed evasive, insincere and sometimes actually embarrassing.

No sooner had *Variation on a Theme* opened on Shaftesbury Avenue than John went back to the Old Vic, for his only post-war appearance there before it became the first home of the National Theatre. *Henry VIII* was also to mark the climax of the Vic's Five-Year Plan for which, under the overall direction of Michael Benthall, all thirty-six Shakespearean First Folio plays had now been produced. To close that marathon project Harry Andrews was cast in the title role, with John as an unusually lean and unpadded Wolsey. Inevitably, during rehearsal, Gielgud felt occasionally obliged to make a few suggestions; when Harry Andrews objected to yet one more of these at the dress-rehearsal, John merely murmured: 'Oh, yes, of course, I always forget, Harry, that you really are very slow. All right then, just do it your way.'

Edith Evans was playing Queen Katharine but even so John remained unhappy, not so much with Benthall's production as with the play itself, which he found episodic and unsatisfactory: 'I was not even now sufficiently confident to try and change the character to accord with my own style, although after the first night I did pad out my clothes and changed my make-up altogether.'

Edith Evans's biographer Bryan Forbes was to recall this production for its quality of stillness: 'There were moments that made me regret that Edith and Gielgud had never established a more permanent company together. Their partnerships were always made in heaven, whether Edith was acting alongside John or being directed by him. So different in temperament – John gregarious and volatile, working with a sentimental intensity of emotion to gain his ends; Edith withdrawn, feeling her way by instinct – they were yet ideally suited, and on those few occasions when they found the right vehicle, they complemented each other superbly.'

The young John Mortimer, just beginning to turn from the law towards the theatre, found Gielgud's Wolsey 'wearing an expression of pained disgust, rather like a clergyman who shrewdly suspects that someone is frying fish in the vestry . . . in his farewell, however, he produces a brilliant study of the bitter but noble resignation of a man who could never be likeable and will always be greater in failure than success – a performance the more to be respected, in that it never plays for sympathy or easy emotion.'

The Vic's Five-Year Plan went out on a note of triumph with *Henry VIII* playing a gala season in Paris, while the last London performance was marked by a mass visit from the actors of the Moscow Art Theatre, who were themselves on a gala season in London. As this short run was coming to its end, John focused all his attention on a project that had been at the back of his mind for all of ten years: a version of the solo Shakespearean recitals which he had tentatively and hesitantly started on some of his wartime troop tours. Although originally the critic Ivor Brown had been responsible for putting these together with Gielgud, the actor now turned to his old friend the Cambridge don George Rylands, who had just published a Shakespearean anthology under the title *The Ages of Man*. As John was to recall:

This was meant to be for people who had not seen me in my early days . . . it needed a totally different technique, the use of my voice which I had learned from radio and early recordings, and then carefully planted moments of Leontes, Richard II and Lear full out . . . I kept changing the order every night, to get the contrasts and balances in the right spaces. That's where the sonnets were so useful; I used them to leaven the mixture, rather like a cheese sandwich.

Of all the times I played it over the next nine years, at home and abroad, the only time *The Ages of Man* recital was not a success was when Binkie Beaumont suggested that, as I'd had such a success touring Shakespeare around the provinces before the war, I should go back to Edinburgh, Liverpool, Cambridge and Brighton. At Liverpool no one would come near it, and Edinburgh was also very hard. When I got to Brighton, the houses were so terrible for the first three nights that Godfrey Winn and Alan Melville both wrote letters to the local paper saying it was an outrage that I was not a success. The theatre was packed for the rest of the week, but I found it somewhat humiliating having to write and thank them. Audiences outside London seemed to be suspicious of a one-man show, perhaps because they felt they were not getting their money's worth. I toured *Ages of Man* for so many years that I feared I would be out of practice when it came to acting again with other people. Also, eight performances a week, all by myself, sitting alone in the dressing-room during the interval, was a very lonely and sometimes depressing business.

Here again, in fact, John was merely reverting to family type: Ellen Terry had toured a solo recital called *Shakespeare's Heroines* all through her later years, and as a boy John had seen it at the Haymarket, where she would link the excerpts together with a personal narrative spoken intimately to the audience. It was precisely this technique that John now adopted and adapted, having also seen his old friend Emlyn Williams in his solo Dickens recitals which had brought this format back to popularity all around the world early in the 1950s. John however remained extremely chary of performing for any kind of a run a classical anthology that was still work in progress, and although he played it for one night in Bath immediately after the Old Vic *Henry VIII*, he did not bring it into the West End until the following June.

Although the brief English tour of *Ages of Man* would not prove entirely triumphant, John was now tempted by an attractive amount of dollars to take his recital all over America, through the autumn and winter of 1958. Before that, however, he had to honour a promise to Binkie and Brian Bedford that he would direct Peter Shaffer's first play, *Five Finger Exercise*, for which he now also cast Roland Culver, Adrianne Allen, John Mills's elder daughter Juliet, and an equally young and untried Michael Bryant.

The play itself was, in many respects, the most immediately contemporary that John had tackled since his pre-war work with Rodney Ackland and Ronald Mackenzie. It told the relatively simple story of a young Austrian tutor (Bryant) coming to stay with a hidebound English family, and subtly changing all their lives, not always for the better.

In rehearsal, John was his usual indecisive self, on one occasion telling Michael Bryant, 'Oh, it is so boring to have you just come down the staircase. Why not come in through the French windows?' Bryant politely explained that, as he had gone upstairs in a previous scene, this would look somewhat odd. 'Or have I,' Bryant enquired, 'climbed down a drainpipe? And if so, why?' 'Oh, Michael,' was John's only reply, 'do stop being so drearily practical.'

On the road there was considerable doubt, shared by John and Binkie, as to whether this somewhat downbeat, domestic, psychological drama was really going to work in the West End, and although they had shored it up as far as possible for Shaftesbury Avenue with two well-established character players of the period, Roland Culver and Adrianne Allen, the rest of the cast were as unknown and untried as their author. It was therefore with some surprise as well as relief that they opened to ecstatic reviews and played to packed houses for fourteen months. The story did not, though, have an altogether happy ending: there was the offer of Broadway and a long American tour to follow, but Binkie and John decided that to make this work they would need at least one American star for the posters. Accordingly, Jessica Tandy (in fact, of course, English by birth but by now long resident in America and married to Hume Cronyn) was hired, but neither Gielgud nor Beaumont could find the courage to tell their old friend Adrianne Allen that she alone would not be crossing the Atlantic with all the rest of the cast. When she did find out, largely by accident, Adrianne was so hurt by what she saw as a total betrayal that, on the last night of the London run, she abruptly gave up acting after a thirty-year career, leaving not just the theatre but England itself, to spend the rest of her life in a Swiss exile, separated angrily not only from her children, Anna and Daniel Massey, but also from Binkie and John, to neither of whom she ever spoke again. 'It all might,' noted Anna Massey later, 'have been more tactfully managed.'

This had only been Bryant's second London engagement after several years in regional repertory companies; John had seen him in *The Iceman Cometh* at the Arts, and offered him the role of the tutor:

I remember having to audition with a young friend of John's, a young friend of Binkie's and a young friend of John Perry's, all of whom I was convinced were going to get the role instead of me, because this was still a very homosexual time in the West End, and I was already married. But to my amazement they all agreed they wanted me, and except for John's incredible indecisiveness in rehearsal it was a lovely engagement, nearly a year in London and then another year in New York, but of course without Adrianne. John handled all that very badly; he really wasn't good in a crisis, and this was at least for her a real crisis. She took it very badly.

I realised, very quickly in rehearsal, that I had to be very careful with adopting John's suggestions; I'd already worked with some really terrible directors in the regions, and I knew how they could mess you up. I had to stand up for what I believed about the character, and John wasn't always very used to that. I remember he tried to make me cut a wonderful speech beginning, 'My father was a Nazi'. John kept telling me how boring I was and to cut it, and finally I told him that he could cut it if he liked, but I certainly wasn't going to do any such thing; I think he suddenly realised he was dealing with a new generation of actors, who did a little thinking for themselves and guarded their own backs, and that seemed to unnerve him. Another speech he wanted me to cut was the one about the tutor having slept with a girl, and finding next morning at the wash-basin nothing had really changed. John was convinced the audience would think he was going to wash his private parts, and somehow found it all terribly embarrassing, but I stuck to it.

In all fairness, neither he nor Binkie nor anyone ever tried anything on with me, and at the first-night party all John said was that I had been right to reject his cuts. But then a very funny thing happened: I started getting letters from old colonels and admirals in the audience, saying that their wives were away for the weekend and would I like to come down for a little shooting or sailing? I realised at last what was going on, and insisted that in the programme the management should explain that I was married, whereupon all the letters stopped. I steered well clear of the H.M. Tennent world, though Brian Bedford was right in the middle of it and so was Keith Baxter; I was a jobbing, ambitious young actor, and I didn't want to get caught up in that very closeted little community. By now the Royal Court had started up, and I knew there was something out there beyond Shaftesbury Avenue and the Haymarket.

With *Five Finger Exercise* now safely installed in the West End, for the rest of 1958 and well into 1959 John toured *The Ages of Man* through no fewer than sixty American and Canadian cities, finally arriving at a unique format, in which as his old friend and mentor Michel St Denis noted: 'John devised a programme in which he could present himself in three ways – as an actor, as a director indicating how these various roles ought to be played, and as a man talking directly to the audience between excerpts.'

Just before the start of the coast-to-coast American tour, there had however been one great sadness. In August 1958 John's mother, Kate, died at eighty-nine. In all the letters that John wrote her it is eminently clear that, since Lewis's early death, John had replaced him as her favourite son, although she was to remain until the very end sharply critical of those occasions on which she felt he was failing to live up to Terry family standards. All through the aftermath of his 1953 trial she had remained rock-solid, maintaining that it had all been a drunken escapade, and refusing to allow herself to hear any of the malicious gossip which at that time surrounded her son. Her daughter Eleanor had been working as John's unofficial secretary until now, but, with a deep dislike of flying, she opted to stay behind and sort out Kate's effects, leaving John on the road in America with an even greater than usual feeling of backstage isolation.

But this long tour, the start of what really could be considered John's greatest Shakespearean achievement, almost failed to happen at all. Because he had originally performed it under the auspices of the British Council, they still had a certain interest in the production, and this would be the first time that John had gone back to work in America since his trial for homosexuality. Although at home he had managed to overcome this with remarkable speed, at least on the surface, the case and its publicity had not been forgotten by an official of the British Council in Washington, who solemnly wrote a report back to headquarters in London suggesting that *The Ages of Man* tour should not be allowed to go ahead, in view of the very real danger that John might be refused a work permit for America on the grounds that his police record made him 'an undesirable alien'.

How much of this ever got back to John is unclear; happily the official was overruled by the British Council's headquarters in London, and throughout the tour no reference was ever made in the American press to John's arrest.

In the event, this six-month North American tour of *The Ages of Man* was utterly triumphant, as John himself later recalled:

Beginning in Stratford, Ontario, and ending in Tallahassee, Florida, I travelled eighteen thousand miles, giving eighty-one performances in sixty different towns and cities. I motored and flew everywhere in small cars and aeroplanes, never knowing from one day to another whether I was going to appear in theatres, stadiums, chapels or schools, or if the audience would be two thousand or two hundred. I never had the chance of staying more than one or two days in each place, so I saw the whole of America, but have very little recollection of any of it. It was all motels and travelling . . . Of course I enjoyed working on my performance, and although at first I had no real plan of doing it in London or New York, towards the end of the tour the recital began to be such a success that I felt at last I had found the way to present it in its best possible shape. I certainly owed the eventual success of the recital to that long tour.

The Ages of Man was divided into three sections, the first referring to youth, the second to manhood and the third to old age. The stage was hung with red velvet curtains, but there were no other props or costumes save for a downstage lectern containing the script. John would occasionally move across to this and turn over a page or two, but it was obvious from the very first performance that he had in fact learned it all by heart – speeches from *Hamlet*, *Richard II*, *Macbeth*, *Julius Caesar*, *Romeo and Juliet* and *King Lear*, all of which he had of course already played in context, and mostly more than once. But this recital format also allowed him speeches from plays he had never performed, among them *Othello* and *Henry VI*.

By the very end of the tour, John had agreed to play a limited six-week season at the Forty-Sixth Street Theatre on Broadway, although this almost failed to start on time. Having only a few days' holiday between the end of a gruelling road tour and Broadway, John, with uncharacteristic traveller's courage, had decided to explore Havana, Cuba. He arrived at his hotel to find the city unusually and ominously quiet. The following morning the Castro revolution broke out, and John spent several nervous hours trying to get an exit visa at the now rebel-occupied airport. In the end, he made it back to New York with only hours to spare before the first Broadway night, a gala affair with Marlene Dietrich, Lauren Bacall and Lillian Gish among the audience.

The following morning it was announced that the season would be extended by three more weeks; John's good fortune, which had threatened to run out on him in Cuba, now kicked back in with a vengeance. The day after his New York opening was the first in which newspapers were back on the streets after a six-week strike, so the reviews for *The Ages of Man*, all ecstatic, were the first to have been seen in print for over a month.

Immediately after the Broadway run of *The Ages of Man*, he was invited by CBS to make his television debut, ironically in a role that had been written for him but that he had declined to play on stage, that of the failed schoolmaster with the unfaithful wife in Rattigan's *The Browning Version*. The director was to be John Frankenheimer, later a celebrated maker of Hollywood movies, and his co-star, as the chilly, resentful wife, was to be his old friend Margaret Leighton. Gielgud did not take easily to the new medium, however, and found the proximity of the camera more than a little off-putting; but as always he learned quickly, and the broadcast was acclaimed not only by all the American television critics, many of whom described John's as the performance of the year, but also – and far more importantly to John – in a rare letter of praise from Laurence Olivier who, filming in Hollywood, admitted somewhat ruefully that it had been a much greater success than his own recent American television debut is *John Gabriel Borkman*: 'Your old friend was bursting with pride and admiration. Your performance was quite flawless and dreadfully moving, it haunts me still. Bravo, dearest Johnny, it's just fascinating and most inspiring, the way you seem still to find room for improvement all the time.'

Having suddenly thus discovered that he could manage television, John was eager to try it again on home territory, and as soon as he got back to London in the spring of 1959, at the time of his fifty-fifth birthday, he agreed to star on ITV for 'Binkievision' (a television offshoot of the H.M. Tennent management) in the play he had opened at the Haymarket during his term of trial six years earlier, N.C. Hunter's *A Day by the Sea*. Gladys Cooper now flew home from California to play the Sybil Thorndike part, and although it went out to an audience of many millions, the result was not entirely successful, largely because this was an ensemble play that had now to be shot in a series of disconnected close-ups.

Immediately after his live television debut at home, John went back to work in the theatre for H.M. Tennent, this time directing rather than starring in another play by Graham Greene. If his previous venture into Greeneland, *The Potting Shed*, had been considered somewhat obscure, *The Complaisant Lover* was altogether more user-friendly. In it, Ralph Richardson played a suburban dentist whose wife (Phyllis Calvert) is having an affair with a local bookseller, Paul Scofield. All three decide, rather as though they were in Coward's *Design For Living*, that a triangular affair might be the best way forward. And Gielgud now understood that, with Greene at least, less was more – he did not so much direct the play as arrange it neatly for an audience, allowing Richardson to do his own thing, and the other actors merely to settle down around him. During the run Richardson was also filming Graham Greene's *Our Man in Havana* by day, with Noël Coward now playing the role of the master spy which John had rather unwisely rejected.

He was however now beginning to realise that if he was ever to make any real money he would have to cease turning his back on the world of film, and he therefore instructed his agent Laurie Evans to pick up within reason any movie offers that were to come his way. Laurie did not always find this easy, as John was perfectly capable of abandoning a film, even after he had signed a contract, if something theatrical were to come along. He still regarded the cinema as essentially a secondary medium, and was not for several more years to bring to it or television any of the selfless dedication he brought to his work both onstage and backstage; the shadow of Alfred Hitchcock and his unhappy time in *The Secret Agent* still seemed to hang over John in the cinema more than a quarter of a century later.

A few weeks later Gielgud took his *Ages of Man* to the Spoleto Festival in Italy, the first of many such festive engagements, and then early in June he brought it for the first time to the West End, thereby reopening the Queen's Theatre on Shaftesbury Avenue, which had lain in ruins since its 1940 bombing, and was now the first new theatre to open in the West End for twenty-eight years.

From the romantic youth of Roméo, through the tragedy of *King Lear* to Prospero's fond farewell to the magic of his art, this was, as Philip Hope-Wallace wrote:

> one of the most memorable evenings I have ever spent in a theatre. I find it hard to think that any other living actor could so deliver Clarence's dream speech – this was like great singing, paradoxically not to be analysed in words . . . even after more than two hours of concentrated attention on an unusually hot night, there was not a stir in the house . . . without forcing his voice, Sir John managed to bring into it every kind of cadence. He was born, he grew up, he was even funny, and he died under our eyes. The anthology is sometimes a dangerous form, but I have seldom heard speaking which impelled us to listen so intently. Standing slim and erect in a dinner suit, he ranged in age and mood without any sense of strain – he appeared as fresh at the end of the recital as he was at its beginning.

Not everyone however was equally impressed: 'Went to John G's opening in his solo Shakespeare show,' records Noël Coward's diary. 'He was superb in his quiet moments, but not so good when he wept and roared.'

During the London run, John gave a very rare interview (to *The*

Times) in which he analysed, in some detail, his own development as an actor:

> When I was young, I enjoyed colouring the words . . . now, I try to shut the phrases, so to speak, in rat traps. I try not to sing, not to elongate syllables or vowels . . . I try now to exert a rigid discipline, and above all not to indulge. As Leontes or Wolsey, I weep at the same point for exactly the same amount of time each night, and no longer. When I hold any mood or tone for too long, I am aware of the fact and try to change it. Poetry has a beginning, middle and end, held in a kind of arc which must not be broken, although inside it there can be many variations. Like a Gothic arch, within it there can be elaborations, but the arch remains intact.

As soon as *The Ages of Man* closed its first West End season, John returned to America, first to revive the recital at an alfresco summer festival in a huge tent outside Boston, and then to open his third *Much Ado About Nothing* there, at the start of an American tour. Among the cast was Barry Ingham, who remembers John G as being 'unkind in rehearsals, at one point saying, in exasperation, "Barry! Why did on earth did I bring you out here? You're terrible." ' Ingham also remembers a culture clash between Gielgud's approach to acting and that of the local American Method School:

> He told the young American actors, on for just a scene or two as extras, to 'Walk like lords'. One young, cocky guy asked John what a lord was. John replied, 'A great English gentleman. A powerful man. Walk like one, come on the stage, go to the altar, cross yourself then come back and stand with your hand on your hilt, as if you own the stage.' The boy swaggered across the stage to the altar, said, 'Hi, God!' then came back down to the front to await John's reaction. 'No! No!' said John, 'that's not it at all. Walk as if you're a lord, a great English gentleman.' The boy continued to play up: 'But, Sir Gielgud, if I'm going to walk like this guy Lord, I need to know something about him. Who am I? Where do I come from?' John, having got the measure of him, shot back, 'Oh, you silly, silly boy! You come from offstage, of course!' When we eventually reached New York my first-night present

from John was a book, inscribed: 'To dear Barry, in remembrance of your New York debut and laboursome struggles with the elusive and difficult Claudio. John Gielgud'.

After Peggy Ashcroft and Diana Wynyard, Margaret Leighton was now his third Beatrice, but their initial experience at the Cambridge summer festival tent near Boston was, as John later wrote, far from happy:

> First of all a bulldozer broke through the pipe laid on for our water supply, so we could neither drink nor wash off our make-up . . . Before the matinée, I was asked to sign autographs for a party of blind people, who were the only ones who had bothered to turn up in an otherwise empty house. For some reason they got to their seats late, helped or hindered by usherettes who then sank exhausted into the chairs nearest the stage, and, yawning heavily, started to buff their nails and chew gum directly beneath our feet. People whose seats were in the direct rays of the sun kept moving their canvas chairs to get into the shade, and in the interval some of the cast went outside to the river bank to gasp for air, thereby missing several entrances. One local actress outraged me by trying to photograph the production in all the scenes she wasn't actually in. During the last act a cloudburst meant that not a single word could be heard, because of the noise of the rain hitting the canvas roof. By now the aisles were running with water and the audience sat with their feet tucked under them, preparing to plunge out at the earliest possible opportunity, umbrellas at the ready.

After that unhappy start, things did not get much better when *Much Ado* reached Broadway, where a number of critics pointed out that, despite the arrival of Margaret Leighton, this was still essentially the production that John had opened at Stratford-on-Avon ten years earlier, and was now looking a little the worse for wear. But John also had the Broadway transfer of *Five Finger Exercise* to occupy him, and when that repeated its London success, he returned home for Christmas to consider the possibility of a new play by Enid Bagnold, which Glen Byam Shaw was to direct for Binkie Beaumont.

The Last Joke had an extraordinary cast, including Ralph Richardson,

Anna Massey, Ernest Thesiger and Robert Flemyng. It was however to prove such a fiasco that John did not do another new play for five years (and even then he was to have not much better luck with Edward Albee's *Tiny Alice*), while for the Tennent management it was almost the final straw: if Ralph Richardson and John could only survive two weeks in a play written by the author of *The Chalk Garden*, and directed by Glen Byam Shaw, the recently retired head of the Shakespeare Memorial Theatre, then clearly the revolutionaries who had taken over the Royal Court in Chelsea four years earlier were now moving up west. After *The Last Joke*, the old Shaftesbury Avenue empire of Binkie Beaumont was really and truly finished. Bagnold, however, was more inclined to blame the two knights: Richardson had missed the first week of rehearsal because a film overran in Cyprus and John, claiming he couldn't really understand any of it, allowed Shaw to change several speeches on the grounds that 'I had to be saved from myself'.

Gielgud was cast here as a Romanian prince, while Richardson appeared as a Levantine millionaire, and both knew almost at once that they had made a terrible mistake. One reporter even rang Bagnold the morning after the first night to ask what total failure really felt like. The savagery of these reviews stunned both Richardson and John, who had not appeared on stage together since before the war. The *Sunday Despatch* recorded 'a meaningless jumble of pretentious whimsy, preposterous melodrama and laboured poet symbols', the *Daily Mail* found it 'a perfectly dreadful charade, both baffling and boring,' and Milton Shulman for the *Evening Standard* wrote: 'It is a long time since such a caravan of overblown nonsense has rolled into the West End, masquerading as a serious vehicle for some of our best actors.' Harold Hobson, usually among John's and Richardson's greatest fans, added: 'At the opening night everything came out of the top drawer. The dresses were by Balmain, the acting by Gielgud, Richardson, Flemyng and Massey, the guns by Bapti and the apathy and boredom by an audience of rank and beauty.' The sheer mind-boggling awfulness of *The Last Joke* even defeated Richardson's and John's usual supporters; the old actor Charles Doran, who had given Richardson his start, went backstage, by now well over ninety, and was only able to mutter: 'It's quite a good wig!'

The moment they closed after only two deeply unhappy weeks, Richardson fled to America to film *Long Day's Journey Into Night*, while John stayed in London where, although his professional life had taken a considerable beating, his private life had suddenly begun to look up. A chance meeting in the Tate Gallery had brought him into contact with a very good-looking but somewhat mysterious Hungarian exile, Martin Hensler, with whom he tentatively began the affair that was in fact to last for the rest of both their lives.

Hensler was strikingly elegant, and in many ways precisely what John had always wanted: someone to take care of him and his house, someone to love, but above all someone so discreet and private and low-maintenance that there was never any fear of another homosexual outing.

There were those who believed that Martin had once had a wife and even possibly a child; others maintained that he had always been homosexual, and eventually there was some agreement that he had probably fled Hungary at the time of the 1956 uprising; he himself always divulged so little of his past, and so frequently changed his stories of it, that in the end he went to his grave keeping almost all of his pre-Gielgud secrets intact.

None of this is to suggest that Martin was always undemanding in his relationship with John. He had, perhaps because of an obscure but possibly somewhat aristocratic background, expensive tastes and every good taste; he therefore always encouraged John to work, so that their lifestyle in Cowley Street could be maintained, and made sure that, with the help of housekeepers, the place always looked immaculate. He had, however, unlike John, a certain taste for gardening and the countryside, and began now to work on his new partner in the hope that Gielgud might eventually be persuaded to quit his beloved London and settle somewhere rather more rural.

As Keith Baxter, the actor who perhaps was closest to John towards the end of his life, explains:

Martin could be very cruel. I remember driving them both down to the country one night around this time and Martin screaming from the back seat, 'John, you terrible actor. You always terrible.' John amazingly seemed to take all this without complaint, but you have to understand the nature of their relationship, and John's sexuality. Like Noël Coward, he was not especially highly sexed, and took a rather schoolboyish view of the whole thing, forming crushes on often very unsuitable people. Ever since his arrest, he had been traumatised by the possibility of it happening again. His sister Eleanor had by now moved into his life as a mixture of secretary and gatekeeper, and she made sure that at Cowley Street young men were not encouraged to stay the night. So John's early meetings with Hensler were almost furtive; at weekends when John Perry was in the country with Binkie they would take over his rather small flat in Pimlico, and I can still see them there sitting up in bed sharing a cup of tea.

Some people had this fantasy of Binkie and John Perry running a kind of male brothel at Knots Fosse, the weekend cottage they had bought in Essex, but having stayed there a great deal I know it wasn't like that at all. Binkie had an Italian couple looking after the house, the sheets on the beds were frequently darned, and Binkie could be seen in Viyella pyjamas. It was more old English village life than gay theatrical, and there were always women like Vivien Leigh and Margaret Leighton down for the weekend.

Speaking again of Hensler and John's home life, Keith Baxter recalls:

Martin always had three opening questions for any newcomer he met. Are you rich? Are you famous? Are you homosexual? And depending on the answers he got, he would then carry on the conversation. At first, he always seemed to be wearing the same clothes, so he must somehow have washed them every night, as he appeared tremendously chic but something of a trial for all John's other friends, who had to keep bringing him into conversations about the theatre, of which he seemed to know little and care less.

He was strikingly tall, and I would guess in his early or middle thirties when they had first met. But, as Orson Welles once said, if you have a Hungarian for a friend, you don't need enemies, and certainly there was something very uneasy, always, about Martin. His constant rudeness, his savage attacks on John's talent, and his refusal ever to join anyone for meals suggested that here must have been a very unhappy man, working out some of his Hungarian background by taking it out on others. On the other hand, John was absolutely devoted to him, came more and more to rely on him, and we eventually all came to realise that Martin was the price we had to pay for maintaining any kind of relationship with John.

Hungarians can be hell. If you are happy, they tell you you have no right to be, and if you are sad, they keep telling you to cheer up. His English was always heavily accented, as though he had never bothered to learn how to speak it properly. And there is always, in the theatre, something especially terrible about the civilian partner who wants to tell you what he or she thinks is wrong with what you are doing; the chances are you already know, and don't want to hear it – least of all from them. But Martin became especially tiresome at this, increasingly voicing his own uninformed, incoherent and often unintelligible suggestions, which John just accepted with a weary smile, so as not to provoke Hensler's terrible temper. There was also an appalling occasion when the two Johns and Martin were all in New York, and Martin was lecturing John G as to how he was far too gentle and submissive with the management of *Ages of Man*, and how John should lay in to the producer Alexander Cohen and threaten not to appear unless he was treated better by him. Finally Perry let rip at Martin, telling him that it was none of his business, and that he had not the faintest idea of the relationship between a star and a producer, least of all on Broadway. Martin simply left the room, but it was John Perry who was then banned from Gielgud's company, by Martin, for the next thirty years.

Chapter Twenty

❧❧

OTHELLO'S REPUTATION GONE
(1961–1964)

I have neither the voice nor the power for Othello,
and I should simply never have attempted it.

W hile John was thus reorganising his private life, and still reeling from the shock collapse of *The Last Joke*, he began to pick up whatever work he could, sometimes for his brother Val in BBC Radio drama, but then most happily in a return to the world of opera. Early in 1961, again at Covent Garden, with Georg Solti conducting, and some brilliant designs by John Piper, Gielgud directed the first London performance of Benjamin Britten's *A Midsummer Night's Dream* to considerable acclaim. After the difficult time he'd had with *The Trojans* three years earlier, he was relieved to find that now, because he knew the play so well, he was on much more familiar territory with the opera. His success was more than welcome after *The Last Joke*, but it was to prove a false dawn: 1961 was to be yet another distinctly uneven year, though it concluded with John finally retrieving his reputation, in the nick of time, with a memorable Gaev for the newly formed Royal Shakespeare Company at their Aldwych home.

The first project for the new year was to be the Broadway première of a new play by one of John's many New York friends, the London-born American dramatist Hugh Wheeler, who was to achieve considerable success in later years as Stephen Sondheim's librettist on *A Little Night Music*, *Pacific Overtures* and *Sweeney Todd*. But *Big Fish, Little Fish* was in fact his first play, and for it the Broadway management had assembled a starry cast led by Jason Robards, George Grizzard and Hume Cronyn, whose diary of the production suggests that John's technique as a director had not changed much over the years:

> February 7th: Rehearsals begin. No introductions, no explanation, just 'Shall we read it?' Everybody stiff and nervous, until halfway through Act I someone lets go with an uninhibited fart. Everyone seems relieved.
>
> February 8th: Johnny G seems to have sixteen new ideas a minute. I write and erase, write and erase. Script now covered with lunatic markings.
>
> February 28th: John expects his actors to do a great deal of work for themselves, which is perhaps a reflection of his own superb powers as an actor. At the same time, he is better able to do those things for an actor that no actor can be expected to do for himself, and that lie purely within the realm of direction, than any other director I have ever worked for. John expects everyone to act as well as he does, which is of course an impossible order to fill, and his machine-gun delivery of instructions always makes me feel that I am going to bump into myself either coming or going: 'Hume, cross left on that line . . . No, quite wrong. Go to the sofa . . . try it there . . . No, that's terrible, cross right . . . No! No! You just came from there, so try standing still.' Despite my extravagant admiration for John as actor and director, I somehow feel I am never able to please him, and always I know that whatever he tells me to do, he could do so much better himself. I ask him if he always changes everything every day to make it better, or simply because he is bored of all of us, and in truth he never really replies.

Nevertheless, *Big Fish, Little Fish* opened to some rave reviews ('Mr Cronyn is so good it hurts,' *New York Times*) and John was soon to be the proud holder of two Broadway Tony awards, neither in fact for his acting, but for the directing of first *Five Finger Exercise*, and then *Big Fish, Little Fish*.

John's good fortune, however, was to prove only Broadway-bound; back home in London, amazingly enough, he still seemed to have not entirely learned the lesson of *The Last Joke*, which was basically that whatever had worked in the West End before 1956 was highly

- unlikely to work there after it. Out of his extraordinary long-lasting loyalty to Binkie, and to John Perry, he now agreed to direct the last of Perry's collaborations with Molly Keane, yet another Irish country-house comedy, this one rather misleadingly entitled *Dazzling Prospect*. Despite a cast headed by Margaret Rutherford and the young Sarah Miles, with sets and costumes by the ever-faithful Motleys, it barely survived two weeks at the Globe, although it did allow John to bring the already eccentric Sarah into his circle of friends: 'I always had a great deal of time for John – such dapper style and inborn good manners. Genuine humility, too, so rare among directors . . . each morning he would come into rehearsal at the Globe and say, "Good morning, everyone, you are all going to have to be very patient with me today, I'm afraid. Because I really want to start again from scratch. I really am most terribly sorry."'

John now decided, for what in fact was to be the last time, that he would like to go back to the Shakespeare Memorial Theatre in Stratford, the scene of so many of his classical successes. But the theatre by the Avon to which he now returned was very different; both Anthony Quayle and Glen Byam Shaw had given up their management in the late 1950s, and Stratford was now being run by a young twenty-five-year-old director, Peter Hall, whose ambition it was to establish a permanent company, not only by the Avon but also at the Aldwych in London, one that was about to become known as the Royal Shakespeare Company.

Hall knew that he would have to find something very tempting to bring John back to the home where he no longer felt himself to be so closely allied to the directorate, and in due course he found it. The Italian director Franco Zeffirelli had recently made his name in London, not only in opera but also with a stunning Old Vic *Romeo and Juliet*, and he was now keen to direct *Othello* at Stratford with an all-star cast including Peggy Ashcroft as Emilia, Dorothy Tutin as Desdemona and the young Ian Bannen as Iago. Peter Hall himself takes up the story of the nightmare that was to come:

> Franco had designed realistic Italian sets, more suited to Verdi than to Shakespeare, which took forever to change. I sat with him in the auditorium all through one night until six the next morning, trying

unsuccessfully to get him to cut some of the scenery. It was clear to me that if things were left as they were, the interval was going to last some forty minutes. Franco took the view that audiences would not mind the wait if what they saw, finally, was beautiful. I told him nothing could be that beautiful. Also, I was desperately worried that the full sexuality Gielgud had found in previous years, in his tortured Angelo, his jealous Leontes, and his questing Hamlet, were eluding him as he came to the simple naïveté of Othello. He was unhappy and uncertain, and appeared swamped in the enormous, misplaced splendour of the production. The setting was so dark that against it Gielgud's darkened face all but disappeared, added to which Zeffirelli made the fatal mistake of dressing John in Venetian robes – so he looked, as many critics said, like an Indian civil servant having a bad day.

On the first night, monumental stone-like pillars swayed whenever John leaned against them, and Ian Bannen, uncertain of his lines, pluckily improvised Iago to disastrous effect. It was one of those nightmare evenings when everything went wrong – a famous catastrophe, as much talked about as any of our successes. I felt very responsible for John's failure in the part. After all, I had listened when he and Franco had said they wanted to do the play. It had seemed to me, given the extraordinary sweetness and innocence of one side of Gielgud's personality, that he could create the trusting Moor, but he was never the soldier; the poetry was extraordinary, but the animal wasn't there.

Yet one more problem was John's apparent inability to register any kind of jealousy, as Peggy Ashcroft recalled: 'In desperation one morning I said, "Surely, John, you must have been jealous of something or somebody in your life." John thought for a long time then said, "Well, I did cry once when Larry had his big success as Hamlet."'

Hall's verdict was one with which the critics could only agree. The production had probably been doomed from the very beginning, not least because, as is indicated by a series of letters to Hall from John, the final casting bore almost no resemblance to the initial hopes. Having failed to interest Peter Brook, John had gone to Zeffirelli suggesting that Peter O'Toole should play his Iago. When he proved unavailable, John drew up an amazing list of alternatives, led by Rex Harrison, Peter Finch, John Mills, Robert Shaw, Alan Badel, Robert Stephens, Albert Finney, Jack Hawkins, Maurice Evans and John Clements, all of whom proved otherwise engaged, leaving the comparatively inexperienced Ian Bannen to carry the ultimate catastrophe alongside John.

Zeffirelli himself, never given to understatement onstage or off, later said that the opening night was the most disastrous and ill-fated in the whole history of English, and possibly world, theatre. This was conceivably an exaggeration, but not a very great one; it ran for over four hours, at the end of which Ian Bannen as Iago was heard to announce, 'Cassio is dead, er, I mean he must be almost dead.' John's beard kept coming astray, thereby causing the critic Michael Billington to note that if *Hamlet* was the tragedy of a man who could not make up his mind, *Othello* was here the tragedy of a man who could not make up his beard. Proceedings were not helped by a wall which mysteriously flew upwards in Act Two, taking with it several surprised actors who happened to be sitting on it at the time.

After that, anything the critics had to say proved almost an anticlimax. Tynan merely noted that Bannen was 'all warts and no face', and that Gielgud was simply 'overparted'. Intriguingly, during the endless search for a Iago, Zeffirelli said to Peter Hall, 'I see him as very young, with a baby face, and always smiling. But behind that young, round, smiling face, is a heart of steel. By the way, Mr Hall, do you act at all?'

Peggy Ashcroft, whose memories of *Othello* went back thirty years to her own Desdemona opposite Paul Robeson, always maintained that John was on the verge of giving a great performance which was then totally destroyed by Zeffirelli's scenery. But in fact Hall got closer to the truth: Gielgud was simply not now, or ever, going to be a plausible Othello either vocally or physically. Like Richard III and Henry V, this was always going to be one of the great Olivier roles which John could never attempt to make his own.

Luckily, both John and Peggy Ashcroft were able, immediately afterwards, to retrieve their reputations in John's own adaptation of *The Cherry Orchard*, one that went into production at the Aldwych for Peter Hall's new company, with Michel St Denis directing, immediately after the rapid withdrawal of *Othello* from the repertoire. For this they were allowed a full eight weeks of rehearsal, twice the usual length.

Even so, some critics had reservations about St Denis's production, one that featured not only Gielgud and Ashcroft but also Judi Dench, Dorothy Tutin, Ian Holm and Patience Collier in the first great takeover by the RSC of the Aldwych. It was heavily, some thought perhaps too heavily, influenced by the recent visit to London of the Moscow Art Theatre players. John, given his Russian ancestry and the fact that they were using his own adaptation, was unusually at home from the very beginning, and the production generally caught what Michael Billington called 'the essential point about Chekhov, which is that his plays are a collision of solitudes, in which people marooned in their own private worlds are brought into social contact to act out their inner lives, in a way that is both farcical and sad'.

As for Michel St Denis: 'When one sees Gielgud, it does not take long to discover that he is restless, anxious, nervous and impressionable. He is not over-confident in himself. His restlessness goes with a tendency to be dissatisfied. Therefore he works out more and more plans, more and more ideas, rejecting one for another, working all the time from instinct rather than from careful study.'

Robert Muller, for the *Daily Express*, noted: 'Gielgud makes of the monumental bore, Gaev, a more endearing individual than I would ever have thought possible. His silences are pregnant with memories; time passes visibly behind his closed eyelids; there is no more use for the Gaevs of this world, and he knows it and suffers accordingly.' Alan Brien found John 'wearing an elaborate outfit of petty, potty mannerisms with the superb comical unself-consciousness of an ex-King receiving courtiers in his pyjamas. I have never seen that brief role count for so much.' As for J.C. Trewin, John's Gaev was 'the most extraordinary piece of creative acting I have ever seen . . . He has, in his very bearing, the great poetry of the dying life of the aristocracy, and yet whatever is in his mind reaches us as the sentimental or the trivial . . . behind all is the wistfulness of a weak man who has betrayed his trust and can now only move himself by his own speeches.' Kenneth Tynan simply found John 'just right – elegant and gravely foolish, lost in thought, and leaning on a bookcase being solemnly dusted by Firs, the butler, as if he were a piece of furniture'.

But sadly, having retrieved his classical reputation with this considerable Aldwych success, John was now to move into another two lean years, propped up only by revivals of his *Ages of Man*, and even they were beginning to suffer from the law of diminishing returns. The recital had simply been seen already by most of Gielgud's faithful audiences.

His first project after *The Cherry Orchard* was to direct his old friend Ralph Richardson in a glossily old-fashioned H.M. Tennent revival of *The School For Scandal*, with a cast that also featured John Neville, Margaret Rutherford and Anna and Daniel Massey. The initial reviews here were far from glorious, but the combination of Gielgud and Richardson and Richard Brinsley Sheridan was enough to carry a somewhat dull production through to a new box-office record at the Haymarket, where it took just over £5,500 in the first week. During the run, there were considerable cast changes: John himself took over from John Neville as Joseph Surface, the role he had played triumphantly in 1937, Gwen Ffrangcon-Davies came in for Margaret Rutherford, and Geraldine McEwan replaced Anna Massey. The production, thus heavily recast, went on a long American tour and then to Broadway, where Walter Kerr for the *New York Times* thought 'the staging has a convalescent air about it, as though the entire population of eighteenth-century London was just getting over bad colds and couldn't possibly think of going out for a couple of days.'

Others however were more impressed. For the *New York World*, Norman Nadel noted: 'by slightly raising a corner of his mouth, and distending the left nostril, Gielgud can express a cargo of contempt better than other actors can in fifty lines.' But John had arrived at yet another dangerous corner: his choice of new plays was still almost unerringly terrible, at Stratford Peter Hall had effectively hijacked his scheme for a permanent company, at the Old Vic the rebirth brought about by the National Theatre was still several years off, and the prospect of returning to a freelance life as a jobbing actor and director was somehow not how Gielgud had hoped or expected to enter his fifth decade as an actor, nor indeed his sixth in real life.

Nevertheless, he did not have much other choice. He lacked the financial resources to set up yet another company, and was effectively

therefore at the mercy of whatever projects were on offer. Unfortunately, the next of these was to be Jerome Kilty's dramatisation of
Thornton Wilder's *The Ides of March*, an imaginary correspondence
between Caesar and Cleopatra, which required John to appear in
modern dress as the Roman dictator. Gielgud took on what must have
seemed even to him a dodgy project, something halfway between a
recital and a drama, because Kilty had recently enjoyed a major
worldwide hit with *Dear Liar*, based on the letters of Bernard Shaw
and Mrs Patrick Campbell. The thinking here seems to have been that
lightning might strike twice at the Post Office, but in fact it was to be
another thirty years before A.R. Gurney's *Love Letters* was once again
to breathe life of a kind into a deadly, static, epistolary format.

Long before they opened at the Haymarket John knew they were in
trouble, not least because, bizarrely wearing a laurel leaf and a toga
over his lounge suit, he felt distinctly uneasy having to read out of
an old paperback the account by Suetonius of Caesar's death at the
Capitol. This considerable fiasco was best summed up for *Punch* by
Gerald Barry: 'Here is an SOS. Will Sir John Gielgud, now believed to
be wasting his great talent at the Haymarket, kindly return at once to
the theatre of Shakespeare where his admirers are getting dangerously
restive?'

The only good thing to have emerged from *The Ides of March* was
John's new-found fascination with presenting the classics in modern
dress, one that was to lead him a year later, rather more successfully,
back to Broadway with a Richard Burton *Hamlet* set entirely in a
contemporary rehearsal room.

Before that, however, he managed to reactivate his long-dormant
movie career with an appearance in the minor but flashy role of Louis
VII of France in the film of Anouilh's *Becket*, which Richard Burton
and Peter O'Toole were now shooting for Peter Glenville, the director
whom John had first encountered as one of many good-looking homosexual undergraduates around the Oxford University quadrangles
when he was there in 1932 directing *Romeo and Juliet*. The importance
of this *Becket* was considerable and long-lasting; for the very first time
it established John as a useful character player who could bring his
unrivalled theatrical dignity to bear on roles and films that often did
not deserve it, but were nevertheless greatly enhanced by it. On this

occasion it was Richard Burton who wrote, from the set: 'John is the only actor I've met who makes me feel slightly uncomfortable with awe. In truth, from my earliest years, I modelled my acting on Gielgud's, though, because of our vast differences in temperament, voice and body, nobody has ever remarked on it.'

Glenville took considerable pride in what *Becket* was to achieve for John: 'I think this was the first time in his later years that he realised films didn't have to be rubbish, and I was very careful in trying to show him how to tone down his staginess for the camera. I think it also helped that we had known each other for so long, and that as I had always been a stage director he trusted me much more than some of his other film people. You could actually see John, in the few short weeks we filmed his role, learning how best to do it for the camera, and I would go as far as to suggest that his whole late-life and very profitable career as a film actor really starts with *Becket*.'

It was also the filming of *Becket* that led on to John's last Shakespearean production as a director. On the set, he had renewed the acquaintance with Burton which went back to *The Lady's Not For Burning* fifteen years earlier. Burton now was at the very height of his considerable fame, just coming off the filming of *Cleopatra* and about to embark on the marriage to Elizabeth Taylor which would condition virtually the whole of the rest of their lives.

In the breaks between camera set-ups, Burton noticed that his old mentor was unusually depressed. With Olivier already installed at Chichester and soon to form the first National Theatre company, Stratford Shakespeare having moved into an era of realism and youth, and the West End still shell-shocked by the Royal Court revolution, John seemed literally to have no home except of course the one made for him by Martin Hensler, who had now moved into Cowley Street as lover, friend and housekeeper, thereby replacing Eleanor, who went back to working in the box-office of the Theatre Royal, Haymarket.

True, he could go on slogging around the world playing his *Ages of Man* in ever smaller and remoter venues, but the prospect was not exactly cheering. Even the faithful Binkie had begun to abandon major classical revivals on the grounds of cost alone, and John's famous ineptitude at finding the right new plays for himself meant that Shaftesbury Avenue had also become a cul-de-sac.

The men who had always advised him, notably Binkie and John Perry, were now themselves beginning gently to wind down their management, having realised however reluctantly that the 1960s was a decade for much younger men and fresh theatrical visions, while the new directors and playwrights of this period were either nervous of approaching John, or else convinced, however wrongly, that his melodious Terry elegance could not possibly suit the modern British theatre.

So, back on the set of *Becket*, it was essentially in an effort to cheer up the man who had given him his first real break that Burton genially asked one morning what were John's plans for the forthcoming Shakespeare quatercentenary in 1964. Discovering to his amazement that Gielgud had none, and that nobody had approached the greatest Shakespearean of his time with even the suggestion of a celebration season, Burton wondered idly whether John might like to direct him in the modern-dress *Hamlet* he now wished to play on Broadway, if only to maintain his classical status at a time when he was chiefly known as the Lothario who had just stolen Elizabeth Taylor from her husband Eddie Fisher.

Gielgud agreed with alacrity, even though he still had certain reservations about Burton's suggestion that they should work in modern dress; Gielgud had seen Burton's Old Vic *Hamlet*, and knew that the talent was all there. What he had failed to take into account, however, was the hysteria surrounding the Welsh actor who actually married Taylor during the pre-Broadway tour, thereby ensuring that the production, for better or worse, would be totally overshadowed by the publicity accorded to the most famous couple in the world.

During the winter, John carefully assembled a strong American cast to support Burton: Eileen Herlie was to play Gertrude, Alfred Drake was Claudius, John himself would play the Ghost in sound only, and Hume Cronyn was to play Polonius. Two entire books have been written about this production, both by players of its minor roles: Richard Sterne, cast as 'a gentleman', published one volume (*John Gielgud Directs Richard Burton in Hamlet*), while the other (*Letters from an Actor*) was written by William Redfield, who had been cast as Guildenstern. What emerges from them both is, once again, an account of John uncertain in rehearsal, frequently changing his mind and having considerable problems in dealing with Burton, who, having already triumphed in the role at the Vic in 1953, now had some equally strong ideas about how the role should be played. In order to achieve his book, Sterne actually hid a sizeable tape recorder in his briefcase which he then left in the rehearsal room to capture every one of Gielgud's comments – a breach of rehearsal confidentiality for which he was later castigated in the trade press.

Where Redfield's book focuses on the difference in temperament, ambition and training between British and American actors, Sterne's is a blow-by-blow description of work in progress towards what was to be at best a theatrical curiosity. 'The whole of the rehearsals,' writes Sterne, 'were a brilliant, butterfly-brained lecture by Gielgud on *Hamlet*, Shakespeare, Forbes-Robertson, John Barrymore, Alec Guinness, Paul Scofield, Laurence Olivier and an actor John had once seen play Hamlet in Inverness in 1928, but now alas could not recall by name . . . What was chiefly fascinating here were the gymnastics and scattered scholarship of John's remarkable mind.' As Burton himself later added:

> We talked endlessly about how to make the impact of the play as modern as possible without destroying the essential beauty of its line. And we both agreed that very often the final run-through of a show, before the costumes start to entrammel the actors, seems more exciting than the final thing . . . We wanted our production to look deliberately unfinished, so each actor was allowed to choose the clothes he felt most comfortable in, though we ruled out pyjamas and bikinis. I wanted above all for people to feel that they were seeing the play for the first time, and if that meant that the verse had to be mauled and brutalised a little, then mauling and brutalising should go on, although John, the most mellifluous verse speaker of our time, never approved of some of my more horrendous line readings.

As for Hume Cronyn, now more acclimatised to John's way of working:

> The entire production was a replay of the hysteria which I had first encountered in Rome the previous year during the filming of

Cleopatra. The world press was obsessed by the Burton-Taylor romance, especially as they actually married in Montreal during the *Hamlet* tour. I have never in my life been frightened by a crowd, but I was every time I went out of the stage door with Richard. You had to make your way through a gauntlet of snatching hands, cheers, jeers, and waving autograph books . . . teenagers would risk their lives by climbing on to the roof of Richard's car, and what I remember best is Elizabeth, inside the car, sweetly smiling and waving like royalty while silently mouthing, 'Fuck you – and you – and you over there – and you too, dear.' Somewhere inside of all this madness there was a play to do, with rehearsals and opening nights and reviews, by no means all of them very good. Although this production of *Hamlet* was to break every known record in terms of its length of run and box-office receipts, I wish I could say this was Shakespeare's triumph, or the collective effort of a hard-working company, or even a discriminating audience starved for classical theatre and given by us a rare opportunity to see a production of one of the greatest plays of all time. Sadly, it was to be none of the above, but rather a triumph of publicity and curiosity . . . Sometimes I felt I was the only member of the company reasonably content, although I cannot tell you how intimidating it is to rehearse a play when the director knows every word of it without reference to the text. That was perhaps our main problem – American actors in general do not have the classical background of the best of English actors, and the occasional gulf between our company and our director was largely attributable to our company's inexperience . . . Of course, John had certain idiosyncrasies as a director that were easy to mock – he believed in trial and error, and moved so quickly that the actors sometimes felt they were trapped by his indecision. He also never hesitated to read a line for an actor, or to demonstrate a move he thought might be helpful – a practice some American actors find reprehensible and even downright insulting . . . On one occasion, I remember sitting in my dressing-room, hearing Phil Coolidge, a bony-faced New England actor of considerable experience, being directed as Voltemand by an increasingly frantic John: 'No, no, no! You are absolutely terrible! Why not try wearing a hat?'

Reviews, on the road as in New York, were mixed to chilly. The *Toronto*

Star wrote of 'An unmitigated disaster', and even on Broadway several weeks later there was the feeling that somehow this whole production had failed to come together. As Walter Kerr wrote for the *New York Herald Tribune*: 'Richard Burton is one of the most magnificently equipped actors alive today. He places on open display not only all of his own reverberating resources, but also all the myriad qualities which the man Hamlet requires. All except one. Mr Burton is totally without feeling.'

This *Hamlet* lives on for one of John's most celebrated bricks. Struggling backstage through the Broadway first-night crowds and what seemed like several thousand Burton-Taylor freaks, he finally reached Burton's dressing-room door, only to find his star still in costume. What John meant to say was that he would return when Burton was ready to go out to dinner; what he actually said, once again giving unfortunate voice to his current thinking, was, 'I'll come back when you're better.'

By now, the New York police were having to close off the whole street so that Burton and Taylor could reach the safety of their limousine after the show. Burton, still relatively inexperienced in these matters, once asked his wife the reason for such crowds. 'Basically,' explained Taylor after years of Hollywood experience, 'they are frustrated sex maniacs, and we are their favourite sinners and freaks.'

During the run, John did himself get to star in one special performance, that of the opening of the John F. Kennedy Centre for the Performing Arts in Washington, where during the inauguration ceremony led by President Lyndon Johnson he read some Shakespearean sonnets, thereby becoming the first actor to work at the new arts palace by the Potomac.

This new *Hamlet* ran for 138 Broadway performances, four more than John himself had achieved there back in 1936. During the run, as Daniel Rosenthal writes, Burton arranged for a unique record of this production to be made:

Three performances were recorded through a revolutionary process called Electronovision, which used five small electronic cameras that could deliver for the first time adequate picture quality using only the available stage lighting. The result, said *Variety*, was 'distressingly dark' . . . apart from Burton and Cronyn, the rest of the largely American cast seem terribly wooden. Alfred Drake's Claudius, unwisely kitted out in cosy slacks and cardigan, is more a self-satisfied Manhattan executive than a ruthless killer . . . Burton insisted that this *Hamlet* could only be shown for two days in cinemas, but it was seen by an estimated five million people and netted Burton about $500,000 – perhaps $5 million today. The deal also required that all prints should then be destroyed, but in 1991 Burton's widow Sally discovered three rusty cans of film at their Swiss home, which, carefully restored, have enabled a whole new generation to discover Burton's *Hamlet* on video.

Watching it at the time, Gielgud was horrified by how much broader Burton's performance had become during the run. This was to be John's last-ever *Hamlet*, and he never managed to disguise the fact that it had always remained vaguely unsatisfactory, not least because Burton, despite a wonderful Welsh sense of the poetry, could never quite achieve the princely bearing that John thought the role demanded:

In directing Burton, I tried to show him how the more relaxed scenes were placed, so that for instance he need not tear himself to shreds in the ghost scene, or other passages between the big emotional climaxes. But he never seemed to want to work with me alone. And eventually I was reduced to writing long notes, which I would leave in his dressing-room before the evening performance. He would then read them through very quickly, discard most of my suggestions, but use three or four of them during that same evening's performance, without even rehearsing them. All the same, he was very often instinctively right, and he was shrewd, generous, intelligent and co-operative. I grew very fond of him, but I felt he was, finally, something of a 'Shropshire Lad' as Hamlet, and I would rather have had the opportunity of working with him as either Macbeth or Coriolanus. It would have been much better for us both if we had come to *Hamlet* absolutely fresh.

Chapter Twenty-one

❧❧

ALL'S WELLES
(1964–1967)

I don't think any of us understood what the last act of Tiny
Alice *was about, and as Edward Albee would never discuss the
play with me, I never really could find any indication of what he
wanted me to do with it.*

W hile he was still in New York, fighting his way nightly
through the Burton-Taylor crowds to try and keep *Hamlet*
roughly on the rails, John was asked by Tony Richardson
if he would like to fly out to California to play Sir Francis Hinsley in
Evelyn Waugh's memorable Hollywood parody of the American way
of death, *The Loved One*.

In the original novella, Hinsley is clearly modelled on Sir C. Aubrey
Smith, the crusty doyen of the Hollywood Raj of veteran British actors
in California, who suddenly finds himself fired by the studios where
he has worked for forty years. It could have been a wonderful role,
but Richardson was so intent on unnecessarily updating the story,
and generally camping it up and messing it around, that Gielgud,
like so many others in the cast, including Robert Morley and Margaret
Leighton, found his part cut to shreds. *The Loved One* had been through
several hands before it reached those of Tony Richardson, himself now
starting a long Hollywood exile. Evelyn Waugh had originally hoped
for Alec Guinness, and noted in his diary: 'The film has now been sold
to a mad Mexican, who will doubtless sell it on to Hollywood, where
they will produce an elaborate and tasteless travesty – no redress.' 'The

Mad Mexican' turned out to be Luis Buñuel, but Waugh's gloomy prediction came all too true. By the time the film fell into Richardson's hands, he and Christopher Isherwood, another Hollywood exile who should have known better, made the fatal mistake of trying to update it to the 1960s, complete with bodies flying around in outer space.

What might have been a brilliant period gem became instead a neurotic travesty billed desperately as 'The motion picture with something to offend everyone'. 'A spineless farrago of collegiate gags,' thought Pauline Kael for the *New Yorker*, 'this sinking ship only makes it to port because everyone on board is too giddy and self-obsessed to panic.' But for John, if for no one else, *The Loved One* was to have a happy outcome: four years later, as if by way of apology, Richardson gave him one of his finest movie roles as the benignly dotty Lord Raglan in *The Charge of the Light Brigade*.

By now, the two men had established a firm friendship, as Richardson recalled:

John is, quite simply, the nicest, most human actor I've ever worked with. And, together with Jack Nicholson, the most intelligent. John adores the theatre, theatre gossip, actors, actresses – he is steeped in them – but he equally adores books, poetry, music, films and travel. What he likes delights him, and he can delight you with his delight. And what he loathes, he can amuse you with. He is a constant responder, a constant enjoyer. That is what has kept him so perpetually young, and perhaps is why he has outlasted so many of his great contemporaries who have fallen by the wayside.

After the filming, John packed his *Ages of Man* suitcase yet again, this time taking the recital to Ireland, Russia, Finland, Poland, Sweden and Denmark, and then set off for Spain on one of the greatest movie adventures of his life.

This was to be Orson Welles's long-planned filming of *Chimes at Midnight*, the Falstaff anthology from the two parts of Shakespeare's *Henry IV* which he had already staged in Dublin and was now determined to commit to film.

Relations between John and Welles had not been entirely tranquil since the occasion when the two of them, and Ralph Richardson, had been working for a day on an unintentionally hilarious recording of some *Sherlock Holmes* stories for long-playing records. In the early part of the recording, Welles makes a fine Moriarty, with John as Holmes and Richardson as the faithful Dr Watson, but on the second side of the old LP his performance seems to tail off somewhat abruptly, and I once asked John if he knew why this was: 'Oh yes, I'm afraid it was all my fault. During the lunch break I asked Orson what he was planning to do next, and when he said, *"King Lear"*, before I could stop myself I replied, "Not in London, surely?" whereupon he sulked for the rest of the afternoon's recording.'.

But all that was now forgotten, as Welles begged John to come out to Spain and play the dying King Henry IV, a role that he had always longed to try at the Old Vic with Richardson as Falstaff, a plan always stymied by Richardson's reluctance to go back to a role he had somehow never enjoyed. Now Welles himself was to be Falstaff, with an amazing supporting cast led by Margaret Rutherford as Mistress Quickly, Jeanne Moreau as Doll Tearsheet and Keith Baxter as Prince Hal. As Gielgud himself later recalled:

Like most of Orson's films, it was full of very fascinating things, but did not work as a whole, though it did have a real Shakespearean feeling. Orson was splendid to work with, although he was always pressed for money and usually in rather poor health. Having engaged a very fine company, he could never afford to keep us all permanently employed, so we each did our parts in separate weeks and he only did his own scenes at the very end, by which time he was exhausted, and there was nobody left for him to act with. I never even saw him in character as Falstaff until the film was released. But he had found a marvellous setting, a great empty building in the hills above Barcelona, which had once been a prison, and had a huge hall with a stone floor. However, there was no glass in the windows, and the cold November air poured in. I was wearing tights and a dressing-gown, but practically nothing else for my death scene. I would sit on my throne with a tiny electric fire to warm my feet, while Orson spent his last pesetas sending out for brandy to keep me going . . . The organisation was chaotic, but I was lost in admiration for Orson's unfailing flair in choosing camera set-ups, encouraging me with an extremely perceptive appreciation of the Shakespearean text, and managing fifty or so Spanish extras who spoke no English and were always wandering about demanding money. There were no kind of sanitary facilities on the premises, so the results were apt to be unsightly and demoralising to say the least. Orson was suffering from eczema, and worrying about two other unfinished films, *Treasure Island* and *Don Quixote*, on which he had already started sporadic work in various other parts of Spain.

Because John was himself already committed to starring in a new Edward Albee play on Broadway, all his scenes had to be shot out of sequence, and usually in tight close-up as Welles had yet again run out of money for any other actors. As with so much of his post-*Citizen Kane* work, the result was a mixture of major weaknesses combined with some brilliant moments. Jeanne Moreau was, to say the least, an implausible Doll Tearsheet, and much of the dubbing and post-synchronisation proved incomprehensible, but as the Welles biographer Frank Brady notes: 'aside from the temporary difficulties of understanding some of his lines, there was the sheer presence of the hippopotamic Orson looking like a figure from a Reubens painting, or an early Victorian Christmas card picture of Santa Claus. In the role of his life, Orson duels, dances, drinks and revels through the night. A greatly articulated Falstaff, he was filled with relish and tenderness, first as the self-destructive roisterer and anti-King, and then with expert balance as the self-pitying exile poisoned by unendurable melancholy for the loss of his old friend Hal. In the last scene, of rejection, it is hard to tell where Falstaff begins and Welles ends.'

When the film eventually reached art-house cinemas on a very limited release, several European critics realised that Welles and Falstaff had much in common: never the King, always the clown; and as Welles himself once told Kenneth Tynan, 'I see Falstaff like a Christmas tree, decorated with vices.' Sadly, however, the film initially reached such limited audiences that a couple of years later a Hollywood studio chief wrote quite seriously to Welles, asking if he had ever thought of playing Falstaff on film. As Welles told Frank Brady, 'What is a man to do but weep – you make the greatest film of your life, and nobody in your own country even bothers to go see it.'

Years later, John was making similarly frustrated attempts to film

The Tempest and suggested that Welles might be a perfect Caliban. Sadly, that idea never even reached any kind of studio. At the time they were shooting, Gielgud found Welles's hit-and-miss techniques rather unnerving, and was not best pleased to find himself doing his final scenes in close proximity to a sound recordist with appalling flatulence. 'I don't mind,' John told Welles, 'handing the crown over to Keith Baxter, and I don't even mind dying, but does it have to be in a gas chamber?' Welles eventually ran into such economic difficulties that when Norman Rodway came to film his Hotspur scenes they couldn't even afford a horse for him to ride into battle, so he had to sit on the shoulders of two sturdy extras who jiggled him as he spoke. Keith Baxter found himself in long shots also standing in for Justice Silence, and Margaret Rutherford is often represented, again from a distance, by a male assistant director, wearing her clothes.

But, as so often with the films of Orson Welles, distance has lent enchantment. The film, upwardly revalued these last ten years or so, regularly features in Welles retrospectives and has gradually grown in stature, until now it is widely recognised as one of the best, albeit most eccentric, of all Shakespearean movies. Several critics have found traces here of both *Citizen Kane* and *The Magnificent Ambersons*, but as David Thomson, another Welles biographer, has noted: '*Chimes at Midnight* is an unlikely epiphany; it bespeaks an extraordinary act of will, not to mention the idealism that saw such a thing might be . . . if Welles had only ever made *Chimes at Midnight*, I suspect I would know it as a footprint of genius.'

The play for which John had to leave *Chimes at Midnight* was Albee's *Tiny Alice*. Although at this time there were still those who seemed to find Albee's *Who's Afraid of Virginia Woolf?* hard to fathom, that apparent obscurity was as nothing compared with *Tiny Alice*. Asked, in some desperation, by John and his co-star, the faithful Irene Worth, what the play was about Albee simply replied, 'Forget about the meaning of the play, just play the meaning of the characters,' which was not, perhaps, the answer they were looking for. The director Alan Schneider did his best to bridge the gap between author and star, writing afterwards to John: 'I have simply never met an actor like you – all I can do is thank you for your willingness, your trust and your understanding.'

As Albee's biographer Mel Gussow has noted:

> The first choice for the role of Brother Julian was Albert Finney . . .
> Albee never formally objected to the casting, but in retrospect he
> revealed his hesitation: 'It wasn't my idea to have somebody whose
> sexual fires were dampened. I remember I wanted somebody younger
> and more sexual. But when John became available, I guess I was talked
> into it; what thirty-five-year-old playwright is going to turn down John
> Gielgud for a leading role?' . . . In contrast to Gielgud, Irene Worth [in
> fact John's idea] loved the play. That is not to say that she understood
> it much more than John or anyone else did, but from the beginning she
> seemed to have a greater feeling for its mystery and an enthusiasm
> for its subject matter . . . Alan Schneider agreed to direct the play
> although he, too, had serious reservations about it and felt that it
> became 'murkier and murkier, ending in a scene I had difficulty in
> believing on any level' . . . He was also disturbed by the idea of
> Gielgud playing such a young innocent, a role he thought was better
> suited to Marlon Brando or Montgomery Clift.

As Schneider was to write in his autobiography: 'Gielgud wanted
to withdraw almost every day, and was sustained mainly by post-
rehearsal brandy and Irene's good-natured joshing. Pleas to Edward to
rewrite and clear up at least some of the confusion went unanswered.
I don't think he knew what to do either.' At one point somebody
backstage asked John if he was embarrassed by the seduction scene.
'Oh, no,' he replied. 'I just think to myself, thank God it's only dear
old Irene.'

So hot was Albee on the back of *Virginia Woolf* that despite very
mixed reviews and audiences who booed virtually every night, they
in fact ran two hundred performances on Broadway with John as the
lay priest who has lost his faith and Irene as the richest woman in the
world, prepared to pay him for sexual favours. All three of the leading
Broadway critics cheerfully admitted that they couldn't understand a
word of it, though one did add how lucky it was that Gielgud could
convey such religious belief: 'He is the master of tensile wonder,
uniquely equipped to skim delicately over surfaces while sinking
slowly into the depths. His arms and legs never seem to know

quite where his head is leading him, but he is a spirit vibrating in repose, sighing at the edge of the world.' Others, however, were less impressed: John Chapman for the *Daily News* reckoned 'there is even less to this than meets the eye', while the critic of the *Journal American* wrote of 'a wildly abstruse and unfathomable three hours, impossible to explain but full of elaborate symbolism concerning mysticism, faith and worldliness in contemporary society'.

Tiny Alice marked the start of Broadway's determination now to turn its back on Albee, sending him into a critical exile from which he was not totally to emerge until the coming of *Three Tall Women*, thirty years later. In the meantime, in conversation with Albee, John began to talk about his early thoughts on the play:

> Of course I was very frightened, especially by the scene in which I am seduced onstage, because I really thought I had passed the age limit for all that, but I was enormously flattered by the idea that this play was actually written for me. None of the young English avant-garde playwrights has dreamed of writing me a part, and I've always had the feeling that the 'kitchen sink' school in London despises me as being a part of the Establishment and a bit snooty. In fact, one longs to create a new part more than anything else in the theatre. And although to me it's often very depressing to go to a contemporary play and see completely gloomy and sub-human characters in despair, I think that is something to do with my generation and the war. Young people today don't seem to mind that so much. And as for the critics, it is very rare that you get the reviews you want. I don't think many interesting actors or good plays are ever really ignored or dismissed, but critics see too many bad plays and always have to write in a hurry. If they are proud of their craft, they get more interested in their own writing style than what they are supposed to be writing about. That's why Shaw and Beerbohm were so wonderful – they only worked as full-time critics for a year or two.

Ever since he had begun starring in the plays of André Obey and Christopher Fry, John had become well accustomed to playing leading roles in scripts that he never fully understood; as he always admitted, sometimes with pride, his secondary education had been minimal. He was inclined entirely to trust his own theatrical instincts, rather than his intelligence. As Albee had virtually requested, he now played the part rather than the play. It was his co-star Irene Worth, on one of the very rare occasions when she agreed to talk about John, who perhaps expressed this best:

> John practises and performs his roles by the rules of classical discipline, and these have made him a romantic actor of such unique spirit . . . once when we were doing a Shakespeare recital together, I asked him how he made poetry so accessible. 'I just follow the beat,' he said. 'It may be obscure, but the rhythm makes it clear.' . . . His mind works at lightning speed, his energy is positive, he relies on his strength. He is never idle, never ill. He is prompt. He replies to all letters, has time for everything and learns his roles by writing them out in his fine, nearly illegible longhand.
>
> John has an undiminished curiosity and interest in the theatre, in new actors, writers, directors; he searches them out like truffles, and remembers the names of all his colleagues from time immemorial . . . He has reserves of commitment and fairness, patience and equilibrium and endurance. His agreeable nature and his humility give him resilience. He is a radiant man and a rare friend.

Their friendship survived *Tiny Alice* and became one of the most important of John's life, though the rehearsals had been somewhat nightmarish. Shortly before the first night, John told Albee that there would have to be some cuts in his closing ten-minute monologue, especially as he was supposed to be delivering it flat on his back, dying from a bullet in the belly. As Albee recalls, 'This gave me a certain dilemma: I could fire John, which would have been unusually stupid; I could have him do the first half of the monologue, or the second half, or the monologue's greatest hits. In the end we did the greatest hits and got it down to about six minutes. Nobody except me missed the other four, and when, some years later, in another production, I put them back, it was only to realise how utterly right John had been – his instincts were always impeccable.'

As Noël Coward wrote in his diary: 'The first act of *Tiny Alice* was hopeful, but after that a chaotic mess of sex and symbolism.

Beautifully directed and acted except for poor Johnny G, who was strained and unconvincing. Altogether a maddening evening in the theatre, so nearly good and yet so bloody pretentious.'

For the critic Stanley Kauffmann:

throughout the evening, Gielgud and his colleagues had done their best with this spurious work, but had progressively lost the audience, some of whom started to boo. Then he was left alone (deserted one could say) to finish, in a torrent of fevered rhetoric, a play that had long ceased to matter. The audience continued to murmur and rustle their programmes as he kept on and on. The buzz swelled a bit, punctuated now by giggles. Toward the end, Gielgud seemed utterly isolated, separated by an invisible wall of protest. I was filled with admiration, not because of any 'show must go on' hokum, but at his powers of concentration, his inner ear. He had kept his own music going, against a hostile chorus.

Irene Worth was to repeat her performance in the London première of *Tiny Alice* a few months later, with David Warner in the Gielgud role; it did not achieve much greater success, and perhaps the whole experience was best summarised by a *New Yorker* cartoon showing a middle-aged couple in bed, the husband sound asleep and the wife suddenly alert: 'Hayden!' she says. 'Wake up at once! The meaning of *Tiny Alice* just came to me!'

After struggling with the still-obscure symbolism of *Tiny Alice* for almost six months on Broadway, it was with some relief that John went back to his *Ages of Man*, taking it this time all over the Far East and Australasia. When he got to Auckland he was contending not with the hostile audiences of *Tiny Alice* but, and possibly still worse, the noise of a nearby nightclub belting out pop tunes for teenagers. 'I just dread going on each night,' said John. 'Those guitars can penetrate through any walls.' The nightclub owner proved unrelenting: 'Ask most New Zealanders whether they prefer the Top Twenty or Shakespeare, and I think you would get a swift answer.'

By the summer of 1965 John was home in England and still in a career crisis as he embarked on his sixties; Olivier had now established his National Theatre company at the Old Vic, and was conspicuously failing to invite Gielgud anywhere near it, as actor or director. At Stratford Peter Hall, perhaps also remembering the fiasco of the Zeffirelli *Othello*, also had no other offers to make, and John's recent unhappiness on Broadway in *Tiny Alice* had not exactly encouraged him to go on seeking out new plays. As for the West End, H.M. Tennent was still being managed by Binkie Beaumont and John Perry, but they too had nothing to offer John, and all he could find for the time being was a rather unhappy television version of Anouilh's *The Rehearsal*, which again failed to convince him that his future lay in that new medium.

During this fallow period he began to work on his second Chekhovian adaptation, this one of *Ivanov*, which he himself now proposed to direct at the Phoenix, playing the title role opposite Claire Bloom as Sasha. Although this was (amazingly) to be the play's first full-scale commercial production in the West End, John had known it since 1925, when he had first seen the Komisarjevsky production at Barnes. The critics were divided, some taking the view that John had neglected his own performance in order to draw fine ones not only from Claire Bloom, but also from a starry supporting cast led by Roland Culver, Yvonne Mitchell, Angela Baddeley and the young Richard Pasco.

On the other hand, for the *Sunday Times*, J.W. Lambert thought John's Ivanov ranked with his Hamlet and Richard II among his three best performances, and the run was extended by six weeks before they took it on a long American road tour (for which Yvonne Mitchell was replaced by Vivien Leigh) and then a rather brief Broadway run, at a time when most critics wished that Gielgud and Leigh could have come back to them in one of Chekhov's rather more familiar dramas.

At the time of the London opening of *Ivanov*, Ronald Bryden wrote for the *New Statesman* an intriguing summary of Gielgud's stage status at this time:

> For a decade or more, new movements in British drama have driven Gielgud from the London stage . . . not that he is blameless in the matter, of course. His published statements on the post-war theatre have not shown a notably keen or receptive intellect. And it is partly his fault if he has not been offered the kind of opportunity that Olivier

seized in *The Entertainer*, or become the kind of national figure that
Jean-Louis Barrault cuts in France . . . Gielgud is the least showy actor
in the world. He has always confined himself to a coinage of classically
simple physical signs – the hands outstretched in gentle eagerness or
clenched in pained nobility; the profile turning with a hint of slyness
and vanity, or straining aside in wincing self-contempt . . . The heart
of his acting is vocal and internal. Its richness lies in the infinitely
expressive range of his voice, the clarity with which it is sustained
by every turn of thought and emotion. His style may seem glassy,
but through that glass you read the darting of motives, watch the
tick of the heart, and see the intelligence perform like a stripped-down
motor . . . He sees himself as the champion of old theatrical virtues
(good speaking, graceful movement, style) against the anarchy of The
Method . . . in consequence he has never become a character actor.
He has never won the ability to impersonate like Olivier, building
a characterisation up from the rich, coarse soil of mimicry. He has
never learned the Brechtian trick of presenting someone other than
himself – his Lear was the imagination of Gielgud old, his Leontes
the imagination of Gielgud jealous. His is an art we have come to
undervalue, associating the technical name of 'romantic' acting with
the fustian age of the actor-managers in the pre-war West End.

As if in response to Bryden, Gielgud now gave a fifty-minute BBC
television interview to Derek Hart for the *Great Acting* series, in which
he unusually allowed himself considerable licence to consider his own
character in public:

I'm a terrible escapist in life, and it has always given me great pleasure
to go to a theatre, shut myself up in a dressing-room and come out
as somebody else. I have always tried to live in a fantasy world . . .
Nowadays I think we have lost an enormous stage public to television
and the movies, but I hope that if you can retain vitality and keep your
balance between the old and the new, then you can still go on being of
some use to your art and your craft. If not I think you ought to stop.
Now I would be quite prepared to play smaller roles, provided that
I could find things that I really thought I could do, in my own way,
better than anyone else. I would love to direct a musical, as they seem

to be so profitable, and I would like to take my *Ages of Man* to the few countries I have never visited, like Turkey and Greece. I don't really want to fling myself into violent action again, but nor do I want to retire or slacken off. I would just like to be what Ellen Terry always called 'a useful actor' for the rest of my life.

Before leaving *Ivanov*, John played the role in a rather unsatisfactory television adaptation and then took on an altogether more intriguing small-screen project which, although this was scarcely noticed at the time, was in fact the role that first released him into a whole late-life career of eccentric comedy. John had by now become painfully aware that he was missing out on an entire generation of new young writers, who somehow regarded him still as a poetically pre-war dinosaur. As he wrote at this time in a letter to Lillian Gish: 'I have just met Harold Pinter for the first time, and he really is surprisingly nice – not nearly as gloomy as his plays.' Another group of newcomers of whom he had become an eager fan were the four young Oxford and Cambridge postgraduates who had revolutionised revue with *Beyond the Fringe* (Jonathan Miller, Dudley Moore, Peter Cook and Alan Bennett). In later years he was to work with both Moore and Bennett, and it was Dudley who asked him for a letter of introduction when *Beyond the Fringe* was going to New York in 1965, because as Dud remarked, unlike the other three, he knew absolutely nobody on the other side of the Atlantic. John duly obliged, giving Moore an envelope addressed To Whom It May Concern. John had, however, failed to seal it, and Dud, sitting on a long transatlantic plane journey without anything else to read, decided to find out what the great classical tragedian had said about him by way of introduction to America and Americans. 'This,' said the letter, 'is to introduce my new friend, a brilliant comic pianist called Stanley Moon. Please be very nice to him.' Dud spent several of his early weeks on Broadway having to pretend, in order to get into parties, that Moore was only his stage name.

But now, it was another of the Fringe quartet who came into John's life. Jonathan Miller was about to make a television version of *Alice in Wonderland* and had the characteristically eccentric notion that the Mock Turtle (played by John G) and the Gryphon (played by Malcolm Muggeridge) should be seen as a couple of lackadaisical Victorian uncles, still clinging to private incomes, but having totally lost the meaning of their lives in late middle age, and having nothing left to do but reminisce about their schooldays.

John was thus to be found walking along a beach singing 'Will you walk a little faster?' and although it was only a brief appearance (in an all-star cast featuring Peter Sellers, Peter Cook, Leo McKern, Michael Redgrave and Wilfrid Lawson), he collected the best of the reviews, and suggested for the first time a late-life talent for eccentric comedy which was to stand him in very good stead over the next thirty years.

John's next television appearance was however somewhat more classical: again for Jonathan Miller, he played Chekhov in an anthology of the great playwright's letters which also starred Peggy Ashcroft, Wendy Hiller and Dorothy Tutin.

Chapter Twenty-two

❦❦❦

INTO THE VALLEY OF DEATH
(1967–1969)

*The physical discomforts of filming do not worry me unduly . . . I
find I am rather good at quietly doing my crossword and watching
other people's scenes. One does, after all, have plenty of spare time
to think about one's part, gossip with one's colleagues, and have
fun . . . It is no good being hysterical or highly strung in movies;
at the same time, you need to have all your energy ready, coiled
up inside you, awaiting the next take.*

John now occupied himself in London and New York with a
couple of new television plays (*The Love Song of Barney Kempinski*
and *The Mayfly and the Frog*), neither of great distinction, before
yet again touring his *Ages of Man* around America, finishing up this
time back in Hollywood, only returning home to turn up in a minor
thriller (*Assignment to Kill*), as well as narrating a couple of television
documentaries about the Spanish Civil War (*To Die in Madrid*) and the
early days of Lenin (*October Revolution*).

He was really marking time, waiting for something interesting
to come along, which it did, in the summer of 1967. The offer
was to spend almost three months in Turkey, playing Lord Raglan,
commander-in-chief of the allied forces in the Crimea, for Tony
Richardson's *Charge of the Light Brigade*.

With a script by John Osborne, based on Cecil Woodham-Smith's
The Reason Why, this had been a work in progress for several years.
The playwright Charles Wood had also developed the screenplay, but

337

it looked for a while as though the film would never get made, not least because the actor Laurence Harvey, hoping to make a rival version, had tied the project up in several lawsuits. These were finally resolved, however, and all that Richardson had to deal with was a recalcitrant Turkish government and a powerful cast (Trevor Howard, David Hemmings, Vanessa Redgrave, Jill Bennett, Harry Andrews), none of whom was especially happy with the location conditions outside Ankara.

But for John, this was still a rare chance to make his mark on the screen and he delivered a wonderfully cynical, jokey performance as the gently eccentric Raglan, a forerunner to his notable headmaster in Alan Bennett's *Forty Years On*. By now, Gielgud was learning how to establish himself in relatively minor screen roles, as one who could give to often badly underwritten roles a curiously distant, starry theatrical dignity which was also often self-parodic. He seemed to bring all of his past performances and memories on to the location like a suitcase, and indeed during this long summer's filming he happily performed his *Ages of Man* for the film unit at the local opera house in Ankara.

Like *Chimes at Midnight*, *The Charge of the Light Brigade* is another of those movies which, after initially somewhat hostile reviews, have grown considerably in stature over the last thirty years. John's performance as the sublimely vague Raglan, always unable to separate the enemy from his own allies, was hailed by *Variety* as 'a gem of a performance – Gielgud's polite, foolish, foppish old gentleman with fading memory and vapid, outworn ideas might have sprung straight from Lewis Carroll'. Given a screenplay credited to Charles Wood from the Osborne original, it was hardly surprising that, unlike the previous Errol Flynn 1936 Hollywood version, the remake would be considerably more subversive, intent on ridiculing the class attitudes and bigotry of the mid-nineteenth-century British army and the futility of the Crimean War as a whole.

A year before Attenborough's film of *Oh! What A Lovely War* (in which Gielgud was also to feature), Richardson's *Light Brigade* also ends on a note of bitter irony, with the generals standing on a corpse-strewn battlefield, heatedly passing the buck as quickly from hand to hand as if it were a bomb about to explode. The film is a scathing indictment of war, but Gielgud's performance has a lightness of touch and a wonderful kind of fey grandeur which give his scenes an altogether different and sometimes almost surreal dimension.

The shooting did not, however, get off to a very good start; John, as ever deeply afraid of having to ride a horse, was put on one which promptly bolted, throwing him to the ground only an hour or two into his first scene. He was not, luckily, badly hurt, and from then on Richardson made sure that John's reins were secured by extras standing just out of sight on either side of him, to keep his mount reasonably stationary.

When Tony Richardson died, far too early, in 1991, John wrote: 'He was one of the first directors who really managed to persuade me to overcome my former dislike of filming.'

For David Hemmings, the memories of John on this long location were of:

> an immensely witty man, deeply talented of course but imbued with a natural sense of humour that forced one to smile when in his company. He was also, as always, an incorrigible gossip, spreading the rumour that Jill Bennett was having an affair with our director, although none us ever really established the truth of that one. He amazed us all by having *The Times* sent out from England and then finishing the crossword in record time, folding up the paper with the long-suffering look of one who has been presented with a task too belittling to be contemplated. The rest of us, when we could get hold of the paper, would struggle on for hours, until finally it dawned on us that John was not completing it at all; he would merely answer the clues he could and then fill in all the remaining spaces with totally random letters, but appeared not at all put out when we remarked rather unkindly that anyone could do *The Times* crossword that swiftly if they cheated.

Unlike Guinness or Olivier, John never really disguised himself on screen, and made no attempt to modify his golden voice with any kind of accent; he was simply there to add dignity and sometimes a wry, cynical humour to whatever film was currently on offer. In it unashamedly for the money rather than the glory, he yet found, from now on, in film studios and exterior locations all over the world, a kind of clubby companionship, a world of egos and gossip, of love and loyalty and betrayal, which to a certain extent made up for what he now most missed: the life of a resident theatrical company. Just as he had come inevitably to be an outsider at Peter Hall's Stratford or Olivier's National Theatre, he now found himself an insider in movies, which was just as well, for in his private life the partnership with Martin Hensler had now, in a curious way, begun to alienate many of John's best friends.

When he was not working, John and Martin began to search for a country house where Martin's passion for gardening and especially bonsai-tree-growing could be satisfied. The search was to take several years, during which time they remained at 16 Cowley Street, though they were not exactly thrilled by a 1967 robbery in which thieves got away with a Sickert portrait of John himself, one that was never recovered. Their desire to leave London eventually took them to the south wing of an amazing country house at Wotton Underwood, just outside Aylesbury, which was now to become their home for the last thirty years of their lives.

Here, John began to live in a kind of exile from the West End that had for so long been his personal fiefdom; even in the country Martin was both cranky and shy, unhappy with having to share John, and even such old friends as John Perry stayed out in the cold, only really able to see John on his increasingly rare visits to London when he was usually on his own.

As a result, film and theatre jobs became all-important to Gielgud, not merely to finance the very considerable cost of restoring the country house that he had bought from the historian, Sir Arthur Bryant, but also because only when he was working could John sustain contact with all his old friends even while making new ones. Martin was by contrast always something of a recluse, and John, utterly devoted to his last life partner, went along with his increasing need for almost total privacy.

True, a few old friends such as the Denisons (who lived nearby), and Laurie Evans's wife Mary, and John and Mary Mills usually managed to break through the Martin barrier, as did some younger players such as Keith Baxter, journalist-interviewers such as the faithful John Miller, and old friends such as Alec Guinness and his wife Merula, but only by taking care to befriend Martin and deal with his eccentricities, in much the same way that they had first dealt with those of John himself. Other visitors to Wotton Underwood were first vetted by Martin, and subsequently often vetoed by him. There is no doubt that Martin took great and loving care of John's creature comforts, but unlike all his earlier lovers Hensler had no real interest in John's work, and very seldom travelled with him on location or tours.

John thus began now to lead a double life: when working, or on the telephone as he was for hours a day, he was still fascinated by the backstage sagas of the stars and their supporting casts; at home, however, he led a rather more solitary life, over which Martin hovered as lover and housekeeper. Hensler would, visitors reported, seldom if ever sit down for meals, remaining detached somewhere halfway between kitchen and dining-room, as if always somehow uncertain of the precise role he was supposed to be playing in John's life.

Returning home from Turkey after *The Charge of the Light Brigade*, John was drawn back to the West End by the offer to direct what seemed like a sure-fire commercial hit: a new play by Peter Ustinov, *Halfway up the Tree*. This was a brittle, quirky comedy of modern manners chiefly concerned with General Sir Mallalieu FitzButtress, who returns from military duties in Malaysia to find that his beatnik son has been sent down from university, and that his daughter has become pregnant by an unknown lover. The general's reaction is to climb a walnut tree in his garden, from where he makes occasional descents in full hippy gear himself, to hold forth to his amazed family on the changing times.

With Robert Morley in the role to which Gielgud had originally hoped to attract his old friend Ralph Richardson, and a strong supporting cast led by Morley's frequent stage partner Ambrosine Phillpotts and Jonathan Cecil (as a manic scoutmaster), this should have been the dream ticket, but all did not go smoothly in rehearsals. 'Trying to direct your father,' as Sir John said to me later, 'was about as useful as trying to change the sequence on a set of traffic lights. He knew what he wanted to do and did it regardless of all other suggestions.' Luckily, Ustinov himself was otherwise engaged, and on very strong reviews the play lasted a year at the Queen's Theatre. Towards the end of its run Ustinov finally caught up with it, letting out, as he said, 'little whoops of joy when I occasionally heard one of my own original phrases, as so many others had long since disappeared from the script'. Peter did, however, venture to suggest that John might have made one of the younger actresses in the cast somewhat more assertive. 'You're absolutely right,' mused Gielgud. 'I should have had her wear a hat.'

During the run it was announced that John would at last be joining Olivier's National Theatre company at the Old Vic for a sequence of three productions in the 1967–8 season. The first of these was to have been Ibsen's *The Pretenders*, in which Olivier and John were scheduled to co-star, until the sudden onset of Olivier's long and near-terminal illness meant that it had to be abandoned. That left just two productions, Molière's *Tartuffe* (in which John was to play Orgon opposite Robert Stephens in the title role), and then an eagerly awaited Peter Brook *Oedipus*, in which John was to play the title role opposite Irene Worth as Jocasta, in a new translation of Seneca's play by the poet Ted Hughes.

But although John's arrival at the National should have been a happy homecoming to the kind of resident company which could not have existed had it not been for his pioneering work on Shaftesbury Avenue in the 1930s, this in fact was to prove a curiously unhappy time for him. With Olivier ailing and already feeling too insecure to give John any proper support, both productions were something of a disappointment. Tyrone Guthrie's *Tartuffe* was characteristically eccentric, turning the title character into a shabby mummerset country boy, and thereby making it hard to believe that John's Orgon could ever have been taken in by him. Just before the opening night, Gielgud gave an unusually open interview to *The Times* about the current state of his career:

I began the 1950s feeling rather disappointed that my production of *A Day by the Sea*, though very successful, was written off by the critics as a Chekhovian pastiche and not held to be a text of much importance. Later, I think I did myself a great deal of harm by giving interviews expressing lack of sympathy with all the new writers. Larry has been much wiser in doing *The Entertainer* and *Rhinoceros*, and has always remained in the vanguard, while I myself could not really do a play like *Endgame*, which I was once offered but had no feeling for. Even *Tiny Alice* I never really understood, and refused to do over here. Of course, I am now very lucky to have my *Ages of Man* recital to fall back on – when I was younger, I was appalled at the thought of having to recite at parties, and always felt very self-conscious about it, although now I find I enjoy it very much indeed . . . at this juncture, the problem for me is to find the right point at which to discard the things about my style that have become old-fashioned, while retaining the essential qualities that make me the particular actor I am.

Tartuffe had a very rocky first night at the Old Vic, and such good reviews as there were went almost entirely to Joan Plowright as the pert young maid. But if that had proved a disappointing experience, it was as nothing compared with the Peter Brook *Oedipus*, on which John immediately went to work. Brook was no longer the amenable ally of their previous relationship on *Measure For Measure*. His status now as a world-class theatrical guru meant that he allowed very little interference in his working methods, which included three whole weeks of body movement and vocal exercise before even starting on the text.

This had never been John's favourite method of working, and some of the improvisations were going on right up to the week of dress-rehearsals and previews. One morning, around this time, Brook asked each member of his *Oedipus* cast to come downstage in turn and state the most frightening thing they could possibly imagine; when it came to Gielgud's turn, he simply murmured, 'We open on Thursday.' Nor was he much helped by a set dominated by a vast golden phallus, one that was greeted from the stalls on the first night by a piercing whisper from Coral Browne: 'Nobody we know, ducky.'

In rather more serious vein, Irene Worth tells the story of those fraught *Oedipus* rehearsals: 'John was really at his humblest and deepest, breaking right away from his classical training of being totally in command of his material . . . the old technical skills and the old tricks were no use. There was one session when John and Peter and I were in that filthy Old Vic rehearsal room for six hours while Peter tried to help John to achieve a certain note of pain, to make a real spring of truth for the speech. John tried and tried and tried. I've never seen an actor go through so much breaking down. He was like a loaf of bread being broken into small pieces.'

But however hard he tried, John never really came to terms with this production, not least perhaps because he was now playing a role in which Olivier had once triumphed; the first night was not helped by a blazing row between Brook and Olivier, who now threatened to cancel the entire production, so horrified was Olivier by the golden phallus and the way in which Brook had roped several of his actors to pillars in the stalls. As Ronald Bryden noted for the *Observer*: 'Brook has turned the Old Vic into a kind of cathedral laboratory of the twenty-first century, a wind-tunnel designed to contain a hurricane of human emotions.' Other critical reaction was deeply divided between those who saw Brook as a genius who could do no wrong, those who wished that Gielgud had not been so totally deconstructed by the production, and those who wished they could put the clock back twenty years to the comparative simplicity of the Olivier version for the Old Vic in exile.

John's reaction was as usual twofold. On the one hand he was justifiably proud that he'd had the courage to throw himself into Brook's now rather alien rehearsal methods, and on the other he wanted, as soon as possible after the first night, to make his way back on to safer theatrical shores.

It had been those rehearsal methods, and Brook's general attitude to his actors, that John had found most disturbing. His recollection of the experience, and his defensive self-deprecation, suggests that he found Brook's methods autocratic and unpleasant:

Peter enjoys his authority: he would walk into the rehearsal room and say curtly, 'No newspapers!' and every morning the whole cast had to do exercises. It was rather like being in the army and I dreaded it; but at the same time, I wanted to be part of such an experiment. Peter battered me down to my lowest ebb during the rehearsals, saying, 'You can't do that, it's awfully false and theatrical,' and giving me extraordinarily difficult things to do.

In the big scene where Oedipus realises he has killed his father and married his mother, I had to deliver a highly emotional speech kneeling on the ground, then get up quietly and go to sit at the side of the stage . . . while the messenger came on and described me putting my eyes out. At the end of his ten-minute monologue, I then had to get up from my stool and go into the voice and manner of the blinded Oedipus, trying to produce my voice in a strange, strangled tone which Peter had invented at rehearsal with endless experiment. It was one of the most difficult things that I have ever done in my life – but very good, I suppose, for my ego.

Olivier had nothing else to offer him at the National, and once the relatively short season of *Oedipus* and *Tartuffe* was over, he went back with some relief to a range of random assignments, none of which had the distinction of Brook's *Oedipus*, in which Irving Wardle, for *The Times*, had found him 'dispensing honeyed cadences amid the carnage, and registering blood-freezing discoveries with a testy frown, as though only marginally in contact with the show'.

By now, the death of Vivien Leigh and of Olivier's best friend and manager Cecil Tennent, who had crashed his car on the way back from her funeral, together with Olivier's own increasing illness, had cast a long and dark shadow backstage at the National. Tynan alone, as literary manager, still wanted to keep Gielgud with them and had been making all kinds of random suggestions, including the intriguing one that Olivier and John might now like to alternate as Lear and Gloucester, just as they had thirty years earlier as Romeo and Mercutio. Olivier however was not up for that one at all, and in July 1967 Tynan wrote to John suggesting that he might like to do either a revival of Anouilh's *The Rehearsal*, or the first stage production of Beckett's *All That Fall*, or, still more intriguingly, three short farces by John Maddison Morton, a nineteenth-century comic dramatist whom Tynan was ever eager to promote, but with no success at all.

Instead, what came now, in quick succession, were well-paid cameo roles in two major movies, *The Shoes of the Fisherman*, in which John played his first of several Popes, and then Richard Attenborough's first feature, *Oh! What A Lovely War*, in which he was cast as Count Leopold von Berchtold, the inept Austrian Foreign Minister at the outbreak of the First World War, memorably described by one historian as being 'outstanding for the vacuity of his mind, and the snobbishness of his character'.

Having now acquired the taste for these brief screen cameos, he also played the Inquisitor (heavily cut) in a BBC television production of Shaw's *Saint Joan*, before going back to the world of opera for the last time. He had been invited to mark the arrival of Sadler's Wells Opera at their new base in the London Coliseum with a production of Mozart's *Don Giovanni*, which attracted rather lukewarm reviews ('Gielgud's handling of the singers is mainly conventional, safe but dull,' *The Times*). However, Gielgud was to establish yet one more career here: as his designer, he had courageously chosen a twenty-five-year-old artist who was soon to make his mark as one of the outstanding talents of his generation, Derek Jarman, whose décor combined pop techniques with eighteenth-century pyramids. The critic Rodney Milnes was less than impressed: 'It is understandable for the management to seek out celebrity names for so auspicious an occasion, but surely an opera director and designer would have been a better idea.'

Gielgud remained unrepentant about Jarman: 'I was so glad to have chosen him – he taught me more things than I knew myself about the world of opera.'

It wasn't until the autumn of 1968 that John got the offer of the play that was finally to establish his late-life career, and introduce him into a whole new world of satirical comedy. *Forty Years On* had begun its life as a series of separate parodies of such disparate literary figures as Oscar Wilde, T.E. Lawrence and Virginia Woolf.

Gradually, however, the dramatist Alan Bennett had come to realise that these could be combined into a script which traced the history of twentieth-century Britain through the frame of an end-of-term school play at a minor public school, Albion House, where the headmaster is about to give way to an unwelcome new world. Bennett, whose first play this was, had not thought of offering it to Gielgud, but Patrick Garland, who was to direct, insisted that he would be perfect casting. Despite considerable initial doubts, John finally came to see that in this very loose metaphor for England he would have a wonderful chance to display the line of eccentric comedy that he had recently begun to develop for Tony Richardson in the films of *The Loved One* and *The Charge of the Light Brigade*.

What makes *Forty Years On*, in my view at any rate, one of the greatest plays of the century is its mixture of snobbery with violence; the play is at the same time a savage attack on the class structure and general upper-class idiocy of a dying Britain (hence the school name, Albion House) as well as an achingly nostalgic attempt to get back to the world it is even now sending up rotten. As Bennett himself has noted, the play is full of terrible jokes: 'Thirty years ago today, Tupper, the Germans marched into Poland, and you are picking your nose.' Later, in a John Buchan parody, someone announces, 'Sandy will accompany you, disguised as a waiter. That should at least secure you the entrée.' One of the schoolboys is given the surname Lord, purely to allow a master to instruct him 'Lord, take this cup from me.' And in one of the early sequences, sadly lost on the pre-London tour, there is the suggestion of a ballet jointly written by Nijinsky and Sir Arthur Conan Doyle.

'It was,' Bennett recalled, 'the only detective story in ballet, and it was to be called *The Inspectre de la Rose*. The choreography was by Fokine, but not up to much; the usual Fokine rubbish, in fact.'

Forty Years On came at an utterly perfect theatrical and historical moment: the office of the Lord Chamberlain, as theatrical censor, had just been abolished, thereby allowing all kinds of jokes to get by; the recently published diaries of Chips Channon and Harold Nicolson had rekindled public interest in the period just before the Second World War, and perhaps above all, as for some of Bennett's sketches in the recent *Beyond the Fringe*, there had suddenly arrived a West End audience keen for mockery and parody of what had until now been untouchable monuments of the old empire.

Bennett developed here a unique form of mangled memory: 'They are rolling up the maps all over Europe, we shall not see them lit again in our lifetime.' Gielgud however now found himself in something of a backstage quandary; in putting himself into the hands of Alan Bennett and Patrick Garland he was working, unusually, in a contemporary play with a relatively untried director and dramatist. Much of his role consisted of long speeches to the audience, in most of which he was being asked to send up rotten the Edwardian world of the Sitwells and the elegant country-house parties where, like Noël Coward, he had found some of his first homes. To his still somewhat old-fashioned aesthetic, Bennett's waspish parodies of people he either did or easily might have actually known ('there were the Berlins, Irving and Isaiah, and there was George Rylands, down from Cambridge for the all-in wrestling at Finsbury Park') seemed wildly tasteless, and yet, from the very first weeks on tour, he realised that they were on to something, despite the fact that in Manchester and Brighton some older and unreconstructed members of the audience had stormed out in disgust.

There was also the little matter of the schoolboys; since this was to be a school play, there had to be a good many of them, and on one occasion, during Garland's early staging, John found himself not only surrounded by them, but forced by their sheer numbers to the very back of the set. Finally, he could stand it no longer: 'Patrick!' came a querulous voice from way upstage. 'I am not terribly happy here.' 'No, no, Sir John,' said Garland, ever eager to appease his star. 'Where would you like to be?' 'Well,' said John G thoughtfully, 'I think downstage, in the middle, under a light, and on something.' Seldom has stardom been better defined. Among the schoolboys were Anthony Andrews, later to star with John in *Brideshead Revisited*, and the composer George Fenton.

Bennett's rehearsal diary indicates John's constant uneasiness about some of the liberties taken with people he once revered, but the script led him to remember other stories of the period, such as Emerald Cunard summoning him to dinner at the Dorchester during the Blitz, and demanding butter from the butler: 'Regrettably, Your Ladyship,' says the butler, 'there is no butter.' 'No butter?' echoes Lady Cunard in a voice worthy of Lady Bracknell. 'What does the merchant navy think it is doing?'

At one stage, Gielgud decided that all they were missing was a Noël Coward parody, and commanded Bennett to write one instantly. When Alan demurred, saying that his talents were not quite up to this, John announced dismissively, 'Nonsense! Noël Coward dialogue is perfectly easy to write. Noël does it all the time.'

Alan's diary continues:

John treats the production as a kind of open dress-rehearsal, his theory being that any audiences coming this early deserve everything they get, or don't get. But gradually the show is being carved into a slimmer, simpler shape. Gielgud is a very humble man. He can be wayward, obstinate and maddeningly changeable, but one can forgive all this because he sets so little store by his own reputation. He is entirely without malice or *amour propre*, and in a succession of gruelling rehearsals, he never once loses his composure. Today I find myself telling him how to deliver a line in order to get a laugh, and I begin to apologise, but he pooh-poohs the apology and begs me to go on. He will not be shielded by his own reputation, or allow it to intrude between him and his fellow actors.

As John grew more comfortable in this kind of anti-*Cavalcade*, he began to dominate its complex structure much after the fashion of the leader of a seaside concert party, moving swiftly through the century until he reached the heart-breaking final speech: 'The hedges come down from the silent fields. The lease is out on the corner site. A butterfly is an event . . . Once we had a romantic and old-fashioned conception of honour, of patriotism, chivalry and duty. But it was a duty which didn't have much to do with justice, with social justice anyway, and in default of that justice, and in pursuit of it, that was how the great words came to be cancelled out. The crowd has found the door into the secret garden. Now they will tear up the flowers by the roots, strip the borders and strew them with paper and broken bottles.'

During the run of *Forty Years On*, John gave one of the longest and most revealing interviews of his career thus far to Katharine Brisbane of the *Guardian*:

It's a funny thing, but suddenly I've become very much more recognised. I suppose because I've done television and films a bit, people seem to know me in the street, which never really happened to me when I was at Stratford or the Old Vic. Now, the most extraordinary people come up to me in St James's Park, which is very sweet of them; I have lived in London all my life, and I am frightfully nostalgic about its past. I adored this city when I was young, and the thrill of playing on Shaftesbury Avenue for the first time, and going to the Vic, but now I'm about to start a new life in the country, and I feel I've done all those things and I had better not appear too often, or they'll get bored of me. A lot of us older actors are not working at the moment

– Scofield, Redgrave, Dame Edith – and Peggy is only playing in some short Pinter plays, which really isn't very much. I think we all feel we are in some danger of being left behind; I often think I should have played the father in *Look Back in Anger*, because that was a rebellious kind of play, and it might have made me look as though I wasn't just part of a forgotten establishment. The British theatre has in the past ten years become a director's theatre, no longer ideal for people like me, and although I love Chekhov and Shakespeare, I really wonder if there's anything major left for me to do. At sixty-five it is quite hard to keep your ambition going. The last war really changed everything, and the craftsmen have all gone . . . Having beautiful clothes and shoes specially made, beautiful food and a wonderful staff of servants. You just can't live like that any more. All you can do is try to reconcile yourself to a world which seems to me to have gone mad. Alan Bennett in this play has a very nostalgic feeling for the Edwardian era, but I know that he would have hated to live in it himself. I'm rather glad we are not taking it to New York because over there people are very sentimental about patriotism, and I think they would hate to see us sending it all up . . . As for me, as I reach sixty-five, life is less a mad adventure, more a matter for careful thought. I have given up reading my own scrapbooks, and I know I have been so lucky with all my Lears and Macbeths and Hamlets. That's why I would really like now to go on acting in new plays by new writers – I feel I've said what I have to say in the old plays, and I am no longer nearly so bossy. I really prefer to be directed, especially in films and television, where I never have the faintest idea what is going on technically. I just sit at the side of the set trying to complete my *Times* crossword and waiting to be told what to do next.

In fact, what prevented *Forty Years On* crossing the Atlantic were not only John's misgivings but also a savage review in the *New York Times* from Clive Barnes on a visit to London. A few years later, Barnes was given a CBE for being the only British critic to have sustained a long New York career. 'Giving Barnes a CBE for services to the British theatre,' muttered Alan Bennett at the time, 'is rather like giving Goering a CBE for services to the RAF.'

In the thirty years since *Forty Years On* first opened at the Apollo,

'I'll break my staff, bury it certain fathoms in the earth':
the second Prospero, Old Vic 1940

With his beloved Peggy Ashcroft as
Titania to his Oberon, Haymarket 1945.
A year later, Raskolnikov (below, kneeling)
in a rather less successful dramatisation of
Dostoievsky's *Crime and Punishment*.

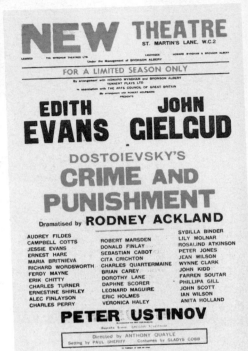

NEW THEATRE
ST. MARTIN'S LANE, W.C.2

LESSEES   THE WYNDHAM THEATRES LTD   LICENSEE   HOWARD WYNDHAM & BRONSON ALBERY

Under the Management of BRONSON ALBERY

FOR A LIMITED SEASON ONLY

By arrangement with HOWARD WYNDHAM and BRONSON ALBERY
TENNENT PLAYS LTD

In association with THE ARTS COUNCIL OF GREAT BRITAIN

by arrangement with ROBERT HELPMANN

PRESENTS

EDITH EVANS   JOHN GIELGUD

DOSTOIEVSKY'S
CRIME AND PUNISHMENT

Dramatised by **RODNEY ACKLAND**

AUDREY FILDES	ROBERT MARSDEN	SYBILLA BINDER
CAMPBELL COTTS	DONALD FINLAY	LILY MOLNAR
JESSIE EVANS	SEBASTIAN CABOT	ROSALIND ATKINSON
ERNEST HARE	CITA CRICHTON	PETER JONES
MARIA BRITNIEVA	CHARLES QUARTERMAINE	JEAN WILSON
RICHARD WORDSWORTH	BRIAN CAREY	WYNNE CLARK
FERDY MAYNE	DOROTHY LANE	JOHN KIDD
ERIK CHITTY	DAPHNE SCORER	FARREN SOUTAR
CHARLES TURNER	LEONARD MAGUIRE	PHILLIPA GILL
ERNESTINE SHIRLEY	ERIC HOLMES	JOHN SCOTT
ALEC FINLAYSON	VERONICA HALEY	IAN WILSON
CHARLES PERRY		ANITA HOLLAND

PETER USTINOV

Rusticka Scene GREGORY SCHERFSKA

Directed by ANTHONY QUAYLE
Setting by PAUL SHERIFF   Costumes by GLADYS COBB

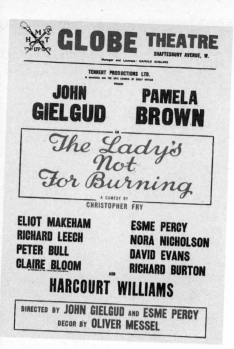

As Thomas Mendip in his own triumphant production of *The Lady's Not for Burning*, one which also established (in a minor role) the career of a young Richard Burton

With Alan Badel as the Fool in a 1950 Stratford *King Lear*, and backstage in the dressing-room which was always his only true home

With Margaret Leighton (left) and Gladys Cooper in his first British television appearance, *A Day By the Sea* (1959); and Laurence Olivier (left) John Mills (centre) and John (right) camping it up as Coward's *Three Juvenile Delinquents* for a midnight charity matinee at the London Palladium in 1953

With Dorothy Tutin as Desdemona in the catastrophic Zeffirelli *Othello* at Stratford-on-Avon in 1961

Orson Welles' Falstaff film, *Chimes at Midnight*, with John as Henry IV, though unsuccessful on its first release, has recently been considered a classic

As the Goose King in a 1984 charity matinee of *Mother Goose* at Drury Lane, in which Gielgud appeared with Elton John

Two knights and a dame on a park bench: John with Sir Ralph Richardson and Dame Peggy Ashcroft, the two most beloved and long-lasting of all his stage partners across half a century from the early 1930s

The Brokers' Men: Gielgud and Richardson in their two late-life triumphs, (above) David Storey's *Home* (1970) and (below) Harold Pinter's *No Man's Land* (1975), both of which they played in London, New York and on television

'We are such stuff as dreams are made on, and our little life is rounded with a sleep': the last Prospero, 1991.

both Paul Eddington and Alan Bennett himself (who were playing junior masters in the original) have taken on from Gielgud the role of the headmaster. Good as both were, on stage (Eddington) and radio (Bennett), neither could remotely recapture the curiously haunting, evanescent quality of the Gielgud original. Here, quite simply, was a man who had lived through almost the entire period of the play, and was looking back at it not so much in anger as in weary, mild amazement at the way the twentieth century had gone. I was lucky enough to see Gielgud in many supposedly greater plays than *Forty Years On*; but I never once saw him so funny, so moving or so totally wrapped up in the material.

As for the play itself, it remains an amazing mixture of postgraduate satire ('When society has to resort to the lavatory for its humour, the writing is on the wall') and insights into a state of the nation that have really never been overtaken or improved. Bennett's final vision, of an England at the crossroads of the world – 'at present on offer to European clients, outlying portions of the estate already disposed of to sitting tenants. Of some historical and period interest. Some alterations and improvements necessary' – remains as topical in the year 2001 as it was in 1968.

It was Benedict Nightingale, for the *New Statesman*, who summed up: 'Gielgud dominates all with an unexpected caricature of a fastidious, maudlin old spinster. He is at his most elegant, attenuated and mellow, like a Stradivarius playing Mozart. From the great Mandarin of the theatre, a delicious comic creation.'

After a year in the role of the headmaster, having revitalised his career and played to capacity houses, John felt the need for a rare holiday, and was briefly replaced by his old friend Emlyn Williams, whereupon the run came to an abrupt halt. John now had something still more exciting in prospect: it was formally announced in October 1969 that he would come together with the director Richard Attenborough (for whom he had recently filmed a cameo in *Oh! What a Lovely War*) and the composer Benjamin Britten for a film of *The Tempest*, which was to be made on the isle of Bali, as John now told a press conference.

Prospero is one of the very few interpretations of mine that I would like to leave behind. *The Tempest* is a romantic, mysterious, religious play about revenge and compassion, and we all think that Bali, with its mysterious terrain, would be very evocative. I want to try to reconstruct the play from my knowledge of the scaffolding, and make it more coherent for the screen. I wouldn't harm the text, but I would put in episodes that the play merely describes. The cinema has, in my opinion, with the possible exception of Larry's *Henry V*, missed out on a great opportunity in Shakespeare. Zeffirelli, whom I much admire, put in a lot of extraneous business and pageantry into his film of *Romeo and Juliet*, and only succeeded in slowing it down by wasting vast amounts of screen time.

Sadly, the Shakespearean film techniques that John began here to advocate really only came good in the very last year or two of his life, by which time he was too fragile to play any major roles in them. As for his long-projected film of *The Tempest*, both Attenborough and Britten fell by the wayside, and although John did finally get to make it for Peter Greenaway, *Prospero's Books* was never really going to be the orthodox *Tempest* that he had always yearned to film.

Forty Years On did however end for John on a note of triumph, as both he and Alan Bennett won Variety Club awards of that year.

Chapter Twenty-three

❧❧

HOME, SWEET HOME
(1970–1973)

To be fired, on the brink of my seventieth birthday, from directing
a Debbie Reynolds musical in Philadelphia did not perhaps
constitute the high point of my theatrical career thus far.

As the 1970s began, John became increasingly inclined to take up any stage or screen project that came his way (in this decade alone he was to make fifteen films), largely because he and Martin now wanted to restore, to all its original architectural and interior finery, the dream house they had found in the country; their South Pavilion of Wotton Underwood just outside Aylesbury was ornate, baroque and in need of considerable refurbishment, but one of its most important assets, as Irene Worth recalled, was the land surrounding it:

> John always had a profound love of architecture and a piercing eye. His taste pervaded his personal life so that wherever he lived had great warmth and allure, as well as immaculate taste. The garden of Wotton Underwood was large, simple, classically drawn and surrounded by smaller charming gardens created by Martin Hensler. On autumn days there you could see John making huge bonfires and surrendering totally to the countryside, which until now he had totally ignored. Away from Shaftesbury Avenue, which as he always said now was no longer the street he knew, he became privately a completely different character – no longer in the heart of the West End, but still fervently eager to keep in touch with all the gossip.

The departure from 16 Cowley Street of John and Martin did not go unnoticed or unmourned by the homosexual showbusiness community, who still regarded it as a safe haven and a good address for discreet parties: Derek Jarman, whom John had first encouraged as an opera designer, and who was always hoping to make *The Tempest* movie which went at the last to his rival Peter Greenaway, wrote in his diary: 'After Gielgud's parties in Cowley Street broke up, I was often propositioned by cab drivers hired to take me home to Islington . . . the queer cabbies stalked out us stately homos, saying as they dropped me off, "Aren't you going to invite me in for a cup of coffee then?"'

The films that John made at the beginning of this decade included the rather nondescript *Eagle in a Cage*, in which he and Ralph Richardson both appeared in a somewhat somnolent account of Napoleon's last years on St Helena, and then an unwise remake of *Julius Caesar*, in which John now played the title role to the Mark Antony of Charlton Heston, the Brutus of Jason Robards and the Cassius of Richard Johnson. As Heston recalled: 'Sir John was the ultimate professional, always on time and word-perfect, though he had of course had rather more experience of the play than the rest of us put together. When I had to do the great speech over his dead body in the Capitol, he volunteered to lie there immobile, if it would be of any help. But I persuaded him to go home. The idea of having to do that speech in the presence of the greatest Shakespearean actor in the world was just too much.'

As *Variety* was to note when the film opened, to some mildly terrible reviews: 'Gielgud in the significant but smallish title role gives the rest of the cast a lesson in making every word and phrase of Shakespeare count. Of all the performances here, this is the one that comes nearest to true.' And as always with Heston, the most moving thing about his performance was his hairpiece.

In a thin time, John also took on the Ghost in an undistinguished BBC Television *Hamlet* and, somewhat more exotically, the Caliph in another television version of the old *Hassan* potboiler. What he was really doing (apart from occasional stints in the garden at Wotton Underwood, frequently consigning to his beloved bonfires there what appeared to him to be weeds, and were only later discovered by

Martin to have been miniature bonsai trees that he had spent several years nurturing) was filling his days while awaiting the arrival of something new, preferably by a living writer. When this eventually came, in the early months of 1970, it proved to be a rather mixed blessing.

The playwright Peter Shaffer, whom Gielgud had of course launched with his production of *Five Finger Exercise*, was very hot indeed, having had triumphs at the National and elsewhere with the *Royal Hunt of the Sun*, and *Black Comedy*. But what he had written now was *The Battle of Shrivings*, an immensely dark and ambitious work about human perfectibility as expressed through the career of an elderly philosopher (not unlike the recently deceased Bertrand Russell), who has adopted the role of figurehead in anti-arms demonstrations and built an entire, miniature, perfectly enclosed world in which he now lives surrounded by acolytes and an embittered wife. Into this idyllic Cotswold setting erupts an old pupil, an earthy poet, back from a lifetime of Mediterranean sun and sin, and now determined to prove his old mentor wrong in every possible way.

These two characters (to put it crudely, the head versus the heart) are of course variants on the central figures of almost all Shaffer's major plays: Pizarro and Atthuallpa in *Royal Hunt of the Sun*, Salieri and Mozart in *Amadeus*, the psychiatrist and the boy who blinds horses in *Equus*. This time, Shaffer had specifically written them for Gielgud and Richardson, but when Richardson turned the play down, the poet who comes back to Shrivings to taunt his tutor was played by Patrick Magee, with Wendy Hiller as the wife trying to hold the ring between them. Despite that starry cast and a production by Peter Hall, *The Battle of Shrivings* was a fair old disaster – generally reckoned to be over-long, portentous and ultimately somewhat pointless. To make matters worse, Hall had chosen to do it rather than another play by Shaffer's twin brother Tony; this one was *Sleuth*, which ran on both sides of the Atlantic for about as many years as *Shrivings* managed weeks.

Despite entreaties by Hall and the producer Binkie Beaumont, Shaffer was unenthusiastic about cutting any of several very long monologues about the loss of faith. The poet, loosely based on Robert Graves or Ezra Pound, and the philosopher took very nearly three hours to slog out a familiar struggle, and in the end the losers were really the audience, despite a couple of strong performances. 'An honourable play,' thought *The Times*, 'but very heavy going.'

One good thing did however emerge from the deadlocked *Battle of Shrivings*. During the last days of a very short run the director Lindsay Anderson, recognising John's new-found eagerness to work in new plays, and his desire to renew his old partnership with Ralph Richardson, came upon a script that was to be the answer to all of those prayers. *Home*, by the novelist and poet David Storey, had begun as a conversation between two increasingly eccentric old men in what seemed to be some kind of a resort hotel. Halfway through writing the first scene, Storey came to realise that they were in fact the inmates of a mental home, though Jocelyn Herbert's minimal set never suggested this, and as no nurses or doctors were ever seen to appear in uniform, the audience only gradually came to realise precisely where they all were.

As the critic Gavin Lambert was to write: 'In a fine example of less as more, a bare stage frames an isolated world containing only one white table and two metalwork chairs. Harry (Gielgud) and Jack (Richardson), the central figures, are not obviously mad or dangerous, and, unusually for Storey, they clearly belong to the upper middle class . . . They may not even be clinically insane, just too estranged from reality to be capable of looking after themselves. Rejected by their families, who don't want to be responsible for them, their only "Home" is an asylum – which makes *Home* a doubly ironic title for a play about the metaphorically homeless.'

In its first production, *Home* seemed to many of us as despairingly funny and human as any of Samuel Beckett's plays, and considerably more accessible. John was, in rehearsal, far more nervous than Richardson, and there was a wonderful exchange of Pinteresque dialogue as recorded by Lindsay Anderson:

GIELGUD: Lindsay, it just is not possible for me to sit here without moving for twenty-five minutes.
ANDERSON: Move, in that case, if you feel like it.
GIELGUD: It's strange, but once sitting here I don't feel I want to move.

ANDERSON: In that case, don't.
GIELGUD: I shan't.

Anderson, in his diary, also came up with a careful distinction between the two men who were now, in Richardson's own phrase, resembling 'the broker's men' as they moved into this autumnal partnership:

> John can produce the most sensitive, apparently deep vibrations with apparently only a minimum of thought. Likewise, he is weak at concretely imagining – creating for us the clouds, the church in the distance, the dust on the table – or rather not weak (since he can do it brilliantly, magnetically) but just negligent. Such is his relationship, I suppose, with the world outside him. Ralph is a brilliantly contrasting talent. He thinks a great deal, but often tortuously, creating and sticking to an idea which is eccentric and quite wrong. Together, their relationship still has an element of distance, friendly and touching, but somehow formal, with Richardson always amused by John's inability to talk about anything that doesn't impinge on acting. 'Sometimes,' Ralph told me, 'I talk about diesel engines, just to see the horrified look in John's eyes.'

In rehearsal, John could still be surprisingly waspish, even about his oldest friends. 'I was disappointed,' he told Anderson now, 'in Peggy's Ranevskaya and her Arkadina. She seems to have lost her way. Of course, she always had a very active sex life, and now that's over I think she rather misses it. She's never been good at getting her hair done, or spending money on dresses.'

Rehearsals for *Home* continued in this gossipy, sometimes tempestuous way, with Richardson walking out one afternoon when Anderson had been more than usually dictatorial. 'I am not,' said Richardson, 'any longer a schoolboy, and I don't like your fucking headmaster act.' Nevertheless, *Home* opened in utter triumph at the Royal Court, soon transferring to a long West End run, and then Broadway.

Although it is frequently revived elsewhere around the world, *Home* has only once returned to the West End, with Richard Briers and Paul Eddington, shortly before the latter's sadly early death from cancer. And even those critics who were less than totally happy with it as drama could not fail to recognise the magic of the original Gielgud-Richardson double act: '*Home* may not be where my heart is,' wrote one of them, 'but there is no greater exponent of mannered eccentricity than Sir Ralph, no more moving actor alive today than Sir John.'

Richardson however already felt that they could be nearing the end of the road: 'Actors like us never retire, they merely get fewer and fewer parts until they are offered none.'

But after the fiasco of their last joint appearance in *The Last Joke*, both warmed and mellowed in this new-found success. David Storey once likened them to a couple of racehorses, hoping they would run out of steam before they reached the edge of the cliff. 'One reason,' John later explained, 'why I so enjoy working with Ralph is that we are old friends and we laugh a lot, and seem to balance each other's style in a very happy way. It is wonderful to play with somebody who is so absolutely opposed to you in temperament. We are a tremendous contrast in personalities.'

Unlike John, who still guarded his privacy and was only ever really willing to talk in public about his work, as if terrified that somebody might still be tactless enough to bring up the events of 1953, Richardson now became a familiar figure on television chat shows, where, somewhere halfway from Merlin to Mephistopheles, he would drive his interviewing hosts mad by the apparent incoherence of his answers. Asked once about his work with John, he replied, 'I once took him pillion on my motor bicycle. I fear he didn't care for it. He's not a car or bike man, really, although the finest speaker of verse in the world today. I always loved him as Richard II and, of course, Richard III.' The interviewer never dared point out that John had never in fact played Richard III, because by that time Richardson was already into a detailed account of the problems of wheel-wobble at high speed.

Because they also televised *Home*, Richardson and John became more famous for these two roles than they had been in anything they had recently done individually. As Keith Dewhurst wrote of the broadcast: 'When we watch Gielgud and Richardson, there is something sad and majestic and frail about them, like the Indian summer of great athletes.' And it was left to Harold Hobson to sum up for the stage version: 'In the enormous roll of their past triumphs I can find nothing more memorable, more controlled or more affecting than Gielgud and Richardson in *Home*. Mr Anderson's direction is soft as silk, durable as steel . . . At the very end, they stand, staring out above the heads of the audience, cheeks wet with tears in memory of some unnamed misery, weeping soundlessly as the lights fade on them. It makes a tragic, unforgettable close.'

John and Richardson were only now making their first crossover to the Royal Court, some twelve years after Arthur Miller had first convinced Olivier to do the same; Peggy Ashcroft, always in the vanguard of theatrical innovation, had also begun to work at the Court years earlier. It would still be wrong, however, to underestimate the courage it took for Gielgud and Richardson, still steeped in the ways of the West End and the traditional Shakespearean life of Stratford and the Old Vic, to put themselves in the hands of writers like David Storey and directors like Lindsay Anderson, who really did seem to them at first like creatures from another theatrical planet. The feeling was probably mutual, as Richardson later reflected: 'At first, neither John nor I trusted ourselves at all with the idea of a play like *Home*, and it wasn't until we actually met Storey and Anderson, both of whom inspired us with some confidence, that we had the courage to take on the play. Even so, during the early rehearsals we were extremely baffled by it, and extremely reluctant to go ahead. We thought we had both made a grave mistake in taking the play on – we couldn't understand it ourselves and we feared, in that case, we would never be able to make anyone else understand it either.'

As for John, this was, all in all, a kind of career rebirth as he later recalled:

When *Look Back in Anger* opened, Olivier was immediately converted to the kitchen-sink school, as it was then christened, and was to be one of the first of the so-called West End stars to undertake a quite new kind of work in his superb performance in *The Entertainer*. There was later some talk of my appearing with him at the Court in Anouilh's *The Rehearsal*, but I was not able to undertake it at the time he suggested it. Much as I admired *Look Back in Anger* myself, rather to my surprise,

I did not imagine that the new writers would want me in any of their plays. I also lost touch with George Devine, as I greatly now regret, since we had worked together a great deal through his early career. When I was asked by William Gaskill, Lindsay Anderson and David Storey to appear in *Home*, Devine was already dead.

The text of *Home* naturally intrigued me but also somewhat mystified me. Construction, situation, dialogue – all were quite unlike anything I had ever been asked to tackle but, as I had greatly enjoyed Storey's earlier play *The Contractor*, I thought I would like to take the chance. I had not liked Lindsay Anderson when I had met him on two previous occasions, once in England and once in New York, and I had the impression that he did not like me either, but David Storey approached us both with much confidence and charm. And once I began to work, the atmosphere of the rehearsals began to become enormously sympathetic and exciting, especially as my old friend Ralph Richardson was in the play, as well as two brilliant actresses, Mona Washbourne and Dandy Nichols.

Lindsay's quiet and subtle method of handling the production appealed to me tremendously, though we were all dismayed by the difficulty of learning the text correctly and convincing ourselves and one another of the essential task of communicating the play's implications. Jocelyn Herbert contributed a set with inimitable charm and purpose. And the theatre seemed to welcome us as friends and colleagues and did not, as we had feared, find us stuck-up West End Establishment figures, hidebound by tradition and a superior attitude towards experiment and innovation. I am intensely grateful for the experience of *Home*. It gave me the greatest pleasure and encouragement to persevere in a new field so late in my career, and I shall always remember the play and all connected with it with the greatest affection and satisfaction.

One of the many things John and Richardson now had to learn was that in this modern theatre a pause was not necessarily (as they had always believed) a sign that one or other of them had forgotten what to say next; John in particular had always dreaded any kind of silence on stage, ever since the night some years earlier when, during a very brief pause in his production of *The Importance of Being Earnest*, he heard a voice from the circle announcing, 'Ooh look now, you've come all over my nice umbrella.'

But in the end it was Lindsay Anderson who, shortly before his death, best summarised the entire experience of the two knights at *Home*:

Nothing in John's wonderful career is more wonderful, it seems to me, or more exemplary than his sanguine acceptance of the passing of time, and his coming to friendly terms with a whole new generation of writers and directors and fellow artists . . . I always thought of him as a remote, distinguished planet circling with a certain hauteur above the contemporary struggle. I think at first he regarded our Royal Court activities with suspicion, and he had never replied when I once invited him to play Caesar there . . . but by the time we reached *Home*, he was by now completely transformed from the careful conservative who had advised Ralph not to do *Waiting For Godot*. In fact it was he who suggested Ralph for the other role, and then, with Dandy Nichols and Mona Washbourne as the women, we began one of those uniquely happy, harmonious and fulfilling theatre experiences that happen, if one is lucky, once in a lifetime – the kind that forge friendships that last the rest of one's life . . . we had a marvellous time exploring the long duologue, apparently so inconsequential but profoundly revealing, comic yet suggestive, with which the play begins . . . It is hard to express the sheer and absolute acting genius of John Gielgud. Not his lyrical voice and perfection of phrasing, which became a trap of which he was very well aware. Not his great, inherited actor's intelligence. Not intellect – John himself was always amused at the thought that he was considered an intellectual actor, as they are almost always bad actors. John Gielgud is an actor of instinct, sensibility, and emotion. His rhetoric is impeccable; but his moments of pure, exposed emotion are inexpressibly touching. In this, for me, lies the unique poetry of his playing.

But, as *The Times* critic Irving Wardle was to note, even rave reviews are not without their problems: 'One reviewer' (in fact Wardle himself) 'likened the partnership of Gielgud and Richardson in *Home* to a violin and cello duet; after which, the partners strove so hard to live up to this comparison, that all verbal sense vanished under the musical phrasing.'

Unusually, but realising that he had now moved into a late and golden summer, John stayed with *Home* (as did Richardson) right through the Royal Court, West End and Broadway runs, only finally letting it go with some reluctance after the television recording in 1971. But in the absence of any other major offer in the immediate future, John fell back into his usual late-life pattern of accepting every odd job that came down the phone. Thus, as 1970 turned into 1971, he did a BBC Television version of *In Good King Charles' Golden Days*, of which the only moment of distinction was the penultimate scene, which John got to play for the only time of his life opposite one of his great idols, Elisabeth Bergner.

He also, in this period, did a considerable amount of radio drama, both ancient and modern, put several Shakespearean plays on to long-playing records, turned up as a guest star in television celebrations of Noël Coward and Carol Channing, guest-starred in two television thrillers, narrated a life of Leonardo Da Vinci, and appeared in *QBVII*, the movie of the Leon Uris courtroom bestseller. None of this did him any actual harm, but it was not exactly what he might have hoped for after the brave new world of *Home*.

It was therefore with a certain relief that, in the summer, he accepted Patrick Garland's invitation to make his debut at the Chichester Festival in a Robin Phillips production of Shaw's *Caesar and Cleopatra*, opposite Anna Calder-Marshall. John had already had the experience of playing Caesar for Charlton Heston, and in earlier times he had played both Shakespeare's Brutus and Cassius. But the Shaw version is something else altogether, and had proved treacherous territory for Vivien Leigh and John's old tutor Claude Rains in the movie of 1945 – the most expensive film ever then made in Britain, the one that effectively ended our chances of ever being a world power in cinema because of its massive failure at the international box-office, and the one for which Gielgud rather than Rains had been the first choice.

For this Chichester revival of the original Shaw script, which had hardly ever been seen on stage since the then Oliviers had doubled it with *Antony and Cleopatra* at the old St James's in 1950, Robin Phillips now decided to set the whole affair in a kind of children's nursery, complete with sandpits and rocking horses. Given that he had worked with Peter Brook on the National *Oedipus*, and Lindsay Anderson on the Royal Court *Home*, nobody could any longer accuse John of being unwilling to experiment with the avant-garde.

Even so, the sight of John's new Caesar bouncing across the stage on a white beach ball was rather more than most critics could stand, and the production opened to some distinctly lacklustre reviews, thereby pre-empting any thought of a West End transfer. John was later to note that his luck was never great when it came to Shaw.

> GBS originally wanted me for the film of *Caesar and Cleopatra*, but I took an instant dislike to the director, and in later years although I have played the Inquisitor in *Saint Joan* several times, most recently in a television version with Janet Suzman, I have never really been happy in Shaw. I played Marchbanks for a week once at Oxford, and took over as Dubedat in a wartime *Doctor's Dilemma*, and once at the Vic I was the Emperor in *Androcles*, but I have never played his really good parts, except Shotover once in a rather bad television of *Heartbreak House*. The truth is, I'm afraid, that I'm not enormously fond of Shaw's plays; I have always enjoyed reading them much more than watching them, and I find it maddening, the way he puts in rather feeble gags and comic nicknames to keep the audience awake in his longer passages. Now that he is dead, of course, one can cut the plays, and they are much better for it. He said *Heartbreak House* was inspired by Chekhov, but it has always seemed to me a curiously bloodless play, quite fun and with a lot of eccentric characters, but none of the subtlety that Chekhov always achieves.

So much for Bernard Shaw.

With John at Chichester that summer was the actor, composer and broadcaster Hubert Gregg:

> Acting with John was a joy, especially as my memories of him went back to my schooldays in the 1920s when I was theatre-mad and haunted the Old Vic. We had dressing-rooms next door to each other and shared *The Times* crossword every night. John as always was obsessed by this and used to go bright red under his make-up when

he couldn't finish it. Years later I would find him at the Garrick, where he always seemed nervous and over-polite. 'Hubert!' he would shout across the table. 'What are you doing? Something terribly exciting, I'm sure I've read about it.' Quite often I wasn't doing anything at all. But on one occasion I had been asked to talk about Shakespeare on a *QE2* cruise. 'Oh, that should be lovely!' said John with a beatific smile. 'Of course they asked me, and I turned it down.'

John's next offer brought him back into the land of living dramatists, and in particular Charles Wood, whose father had by coincidence been the stage-manager of the 1945 Gielgud tour of the Far East, on which John played his farewell Hamlet. He and the younger Wood had first got to know each other on the long Turkish location shooting of *Charge of the Light Brigade*, where Wood had become the last of its several writers. On their return to England, Wood had written a play called *H*, and sent it hopefully to John, who declined but did suggest a suitable alternative title: *Monologues in Front of Burning Cities*. In the event *H* proved something of a disaster, and John was well out of it; undeterred by this, the author now sent him an altogether different script, *Veterans*, a play inspired by the shooting of *Charge of the Light Brigade* and, as Wood wrote, 'that period in Turkey, the long waits in the sun, the weekend picnics, and distinguished old actors waiting about for hours to perform a few lines'.

This one, not entirely surprisingly, John warmed to at once, even though the part he was being asked to play, a gossipy old actor-knight who nearly always gets his own way by using his lethal charm, was effectively a kindly parody of Gielgud himself. But his experience with Alan Bennett in *Forty Years On* had taught him the virtues of self-mockery on stage, and John now took an eager part in casting the rest of the production, only mildly irritating Wood when a particular actress was discussed and Gielgud was heard to murmur, 'No, no, she's doing awfully well now, and wouldn't want to do anything that wasn't absolutely first class.'

Nevertheless, a starry cast was duly assembled for the Royal Court, with John Mills and Bob Hoskins at the head of it. The problem with the play was the usual one of backstage, or rather off-screen, parody. Anybody who had had anything to do with *The Charge of the Light*

Brigade, and that included a good many people who were still around the Royal Court, found *Veterans* utterly hilarious; but audiences who had not been on the location were apt to get a little confused. They weren't the only ones: three weeks into rehearsal, horrified by what they saw, and Gielgud's apparent inability to learn a very long part, the Royal Court management had insisted on delaying the London opening while sending them out on the road for three or four weeks, as John Mills recalled:

I'd known Johnnie for many years, and been directed by him in *Charley's Aunt,* but we had never acted together before. Even during that, we had never exactly been close; after a dress-rehearsal I asked Gielgud as director for some notes on my performance, and all he could come up with was the single word, 'interminable'. The play was concerned with the private lives of the actors and the goings-on around the set, during the shooting of a film on a foreign location. It was obviously *Charge of the Light Brigade,* and Johnnie played Sir Geofrey Kendall (obviously himself), and I played Laurence d'Orsay, who was obviously Trevor Howard. It was full of in-jokes about location filming, of which I too had done a good deal, and there were several scenes containing language that was definitely not for the ears of Auntie Mabel or the grandchildren. It was fine for the Royal Court, but the management insisted that we open first in Edinburgh, where we played it to total silence – they simply didn't laugh at all. Manchester was slightly different. The audience was restless, uneasy, and there was a nasty feeling in the house. The curtain came down to little or no applause. Later I found a note in my dressing-room saying, 'Dear Mr Mills, you must be very hard up, I enclose a pound.' They told us that Brighton would be different. They were wrong; one night there my wife Mary, standing at the back of the dress-circle, saw a large man storming down the aisle shouting, 'I have been coming to this theatre for years, and John Gielgud and John Mills should be ashamed of themselves. There are ladies in this audience, and I have never heard such disgusting, filthy language in my life. If you're not leaving, I am.' As he pushed past Mary, purple with rage, she heard his last, furious line. 'And,' he said, as he charged towards the exit door, 'I paid good money to see them two fuckers!'

Also in the Brighton audience was Alan Bennett:

> The audience left in droves, something audiences in Brighton are very
> prone to do. Indeed, having toured there several times myself, I am
> convinced that one of the chief pleasures of going to the theatre in
> Brighton is leaving it. The sleek Sussex matrons sit poised in the stalls
> like greyhounds in the slips. The first 'fuck' and they're a mile down
> the front, streaking for Hove . . . Actors of Gielgud's generation had
> a strong sense of what an audience expected, and what it should be
> given. In the Fifties and Sixties it was Gielgud's sense of 'my public',
> as much as a shortage of opportunity that kept him trundling out *Ages
> of Man*. In the last ten years he has shed his public and found another;
> so has everybody else, though not as painfully . . . audiences are now
> so polyglot that they no longer constitute an entity . . . the actor is a
> spectacle, and someone from Taiwan goes to see Gielgud in the same
> spirit as he takes in the Changing of the Guard – which he marginally
> prefers, if only because he is allowed to film it . . . Gielgud continues
> to amaze and delight, because at his best nowadays he does not seem
> to be acting at all. The skill lies in letting it seem that there is no skill.
> He has broken his staff, but he has kept his magic.

Once they reached the Royal Court, *Veterans* improved drastically,
as every actor in the business came to see a play very largely about
themselves, but based on the experience of the tour it was decided
not to risk playing it in front of a wider civilian audience, and it duly
closed after only six weeks in Sloane Square. As Jeremy Kingston noted
for *Punch*: 'Mr Wood's previous plays have all been set either among
soldiers or among actors, and now he brings the two together with
Gielgud as a much-loved and respected actor-knight who talks on and
marvellously on, fussing, gossiping, courteously apologetic, pleading
for cigarettes, thinking aloud, an expert in back-handed compliments.
It is a beautifully realised portrait of a man whose mind is almost
totally concentrated on his own self and work, and who can only with
an effort involve himself in the affairs of others.'

For J.C. Trewin: 'This is Gielgud's night, whether he is sitting
bemused on a wooden horse high above some incomprehensible
battle; or just worrying about his own fading memory. At length,

unable to concentrate on what he is supposed to be doing (whatever that may be), he simply removes his toupee and withdraws his labour. It is one of the most eloquently comic scenes on the London stage today . . . never has Gielgud's sense of ironic comedy worked more perfectly.'

This was not, however, an opinion shared by Kenneth Williams as his diary indicates: '*Veterans* is spiritless and depressing. Endless trivia delighting in bad taste, like a man exposing his penis, denigration of queers, laughing at queers, and the terrible, masochistic self-indulgence of Gielgud. One becomes so sick of those half-strangulated, elongated vowels and breathlessness, and he is so dreadfully unattractive . . . I knew all about this kind of rubbish within ten minutes of the first act.'

After *Veterans* closed at the Court, it was to be another two years before John took to the stage again, but in the meantime he was, as usual, seldom idle. His films in this period included two more undistinguished thrillers (*Gold* and *11 Harrowhouse*), but his most memorable appearance at this time was as a wandering priest in a spectacularly and hilariously terrible musical remake of the classic *Lost Horizon*, which became a collector's piece of high Hollywood camp, not least for the moment when John G, attired in a weird kind of tea cosy, greets the lost time-travellers, among them Peter Finch, Liv Ullmann, Michael York and Olivia Hussey, with the news that 'I come from a nearby lamasery'. How this movie was ever made without a cast breakdown into hysterical fits of mirth has never been entirely clear. As the unforgiving Pauline Kael noted in the *New Yorker*: 'It is quite rare to see a 1937 movie remade into one from 1932; I doubt it will ever play again outside Shangri-La itself.'

But Gielgud did here manage to make a new friend of the actor Michael York, who recalled:

John called me 'the Juve', and I basked in his affection . . . his mind and spirit were irrepressibly youthful. Besides his famous ability to complete *The Times* crossword with contemptuous ease, I discovered that he had also read all the latest books, seen all the newly released films and was au fait with all the current gossip. Wreathed in scented smoke from his distinctive oval cigarettes, the eyes set far behind the noble nose would beam with wicked delight when struck by an amusing thought, and the incomparable mechanics of his diction would then smoothly engage to deliver it. He had an instinctive ability to turn a phrase, the elegance of which was doubly enhanced by his own stylish dress and demeanour. Even his laughter was finely wrought.

When they weren't needed on the set, Michael and Patricia York took John on guided tours of the Grand Canyon, over which John gazed 'like an omniscient Prospero, reviewing his wild kingdom'. The two actors also ventured on to see Debbie Reynolds dance in a Las Vegas spectacular, since there was now talk that John might direct her in a Broadway revival of the 1920s musical *Irene*.

As far as the press was concerned, John had developed the useful technique of lending his name and his presence to, but then escaping unscathed from, an amazing number of rubbishy scripts: somehow critics never blamed him for taking the money, and he himself was by now managing to create an almost Zen-like separation between himself and the Hollywood trash with which he was so often to be involved. He had, quite simply, no shame, and nor, by this time, had Olivier or Richardson. They would turn up in movie after movie as if they were working in some foreign country – which often, on location, they were – and as if their performances, such as they were, would have no effect on their real careers in the theatre. In this of course they were, amazingly, absolutely right.

Back in the theatre, the *Irene* experience was to prove deeply unhappy; John had always longed to direct a musical, and formed a happy rehearsal relationship with Debbie Reynolds (rather happier than with the lyricist Ed Kleban, dismissed in rehearsal by John but later to write *A Chorus Line*); but his utter inexperience with the million-dollar genre, and some truly terrible touring reviews, led to his being ignominiously fired in Philadelphia, for the first and last time in his career, weeks before a deeply troubled revival ever reached Broadway. He was replaced by the expert Gower Champion. John's feelings were however at least partly assuaged by a pay-off of £40,000: 'I kept telling them all in rehearsal how very little I knew about musicals, and I suppose that was a mistake because eventually the producers concluded that I was right, and they had better bring in someone who did know a thing or two about how to stage them.'

From this débâcle John progressed, if that is exactly the word, to playing Joan Collins's butler in a television *Tales From the Unexpected*, and the mad vicar of a small Cornish community who locks up his parishioners to keep them from evil in a television horror (in more ways than one) called *Deliver Us From Evil*. There were, however, one or two brief moments of distinction amid these minor cameo roles, not least when he appeared as the Old Cardinal in Joseph Losey's television movie of Brecht's *Galileo*, and then as the faithful manservant of the murder victim in the all-star 1974 *Murder on the Orient Express*, which happily reunited him with such old and new friends as Michael York, Lauren Bacall, Ingrid Bergman and Wendy Hiller.

In this period he also found the time to direct two major West End productions. The first of these should have worked out very much better than it did. His old friend Noël Coward, now only a year or so away from his death, had come back into fashion and favour with the knighthood of 1970, and it seemed high time that there should be a major Shaftesbury Avenue revival of a play that is still considered his signature piece, the 1930 comedy of bad manners, *Private Lives*. And who better to play this now than the couple who were at the height of their post-National Theatre fame and fortune, Maggie Smith and Robert Stephens?

Unbeknownst to Gielgud, however, that marriage had already begun to fall spectacularly apart, leaving neither of them in any condition to play a light comedy which crucially depended on the relationship of its stars. As Stephens later told his biographer Michael Coveney:

Our performance together in *Private Lives* was the last-ditch attempt to salvage something from the marriage, and Binkie was the broker, just as he had been when he tried to help Maggie Leighton after she had been deserted by Laurence Harvey. He had always been very annoyed that Maggie had joined the National so soon after she had established herself as a West End star, but Binkie was now coming towards the end of his life and was feeling magnanimous. Within the year, both he and Noël would be dead, popping off within a few days of each other in 1973. This was to be their last big splash in the old-style West End together; and it was also the end of Maggie and me. She refused a great many directors (Bill Gaskill, Lindsay Anderson, John Dexter, Peter Wood) until finally she agreed to Gielgud, who told us that we didn't need a director for Coward, we needed a conductor. There's no action (apart from the fight in act two), just the music of people talking. And the fight, he said, we had to do ourselves because he was no good at comic business. So we did. And we thought that the show might save the marriage, but of course it didn't . . . We played to capacity business at the Queen's Theatre, but that tragic dilemma in the play, of two people who love each other too much to be able to live together, was horribly appropriate. I learned much later on that Gielgud had misgivings over my performance as Elyot, but that may have been because I dug quite deeply under the surface. There's an awful lot going on in that play, and I must say, having come back from the brink of suicide during the filming of *Sherlock Holmes*, I could appreciate the call for triumphant triviality. There is a quality of savage hedonism about Elyot, which no doubt reflected the last-gasp quality of my life with Maggie.

But backstage their relationship now unravelled entirely; Binkie and the Johns Perry and Gielgud ganged up against Stephens, and persuaded him to leave the cast for a summer season with Jonathan Miller at Chichester. He was replaced by the infinitely safer pair of hands of John Standing, who (with Maggie) took the play on to Broadway and a sold-out North American tour which finished in Toronto. Maggie was now to stay there for several seasons, marrying her very first love, the playwright Beverley Cross, and playing for Robin Phillips a number of major Shakespearean and other roles which she had unaccountably never yet been offered in London.

This troubled revival of *Private Lives* was also effectively the end of John's old life; from now on, although he would occasionally return to the West End as both actor and director, the world that he had known so well, the world of Binkie and John Perry and Terence Rattigan and Emlyn Williams, and the life centred around the neighbouring houses behind Westminster Abbey where he and Binkie had lived for so many years, was now fragmenting and dying almost by the day. John and Martin had begun to establish a whole new life for themselves at Wotton Underwood, a life in which London no longer really played any major part. Most of John's work was now in film and television studios at home and abroad, and it wasn't until close to his death, when they renamed the Globe Theatre the Gielgud, that he said to me, with a mixture of sorrow and satisfaction, 'At last now there is a name I actually recognise in the lights along Shaftesbury Avenue.'

And yet, for at least a short while after Binkie and Noël died in the spring of 1973, John was unable to sever his links with the old-fashioned Shaftesbury Avenue star theatre in which they had all spent so much of their lives. Accordingly, a few months later, he agreed to direct Ingrid Bergman – 'Poor darling Ingrid, speaks five languages and can't act in any of them' – in a minor Somerset Maugham drama, *The Constant Wife*. This was essentially Ibsen's *A Doll's House* turned into boulevard farce; Ingrid Bergman was her usual self – charismatic, uncertain of her lines, but radiant even when reducing her fellow actors to a kind of panic, as night after night she inadvertently cut several key moments and even entire scenes. But now, sadly, it was all too late. Even the combination of Bergman and Gielgud and Maugham was unable to get this creaky 1927 comedy back on its feet, and as for John there was now a strong critical feeling that he really ought to be able to find better things to do on stage and screen in his old age. *The Constant Wife* was seen as at best whimsical, and at worst totally anachronistic to the London theatre of 1973. Nevertheless, Ingrid Bergman still had enough followers to keep the play running through the winter, though as she was robbed of £25,000 of jewellery while at the theatre one night, this may not have been as profitable a venture as she had intended. On stage she was at least constantly entertaining, even when turning a domestic instruction – 'Give cook her head' – into something more frightening, as she told the amazed actor playing her husband, 'Give cook your head!' Tragically, it was also during this run that she found the lump on her breast which alerted her to the cancer of which she was eventually to die in the August of 1982.

Chapter Twenty-four

❧❦❧

BLEAK HOUSE
(1974–1977)

No Man's Land will not change, or grow old, or move –
it remains forever icy.

Early in 1974 John returned to one of his earliest film roles, that of Benjamin Disraeli, for an epic thirteen-episode television drama series, *Edward VII*. It was also now that he would rejoin the National Theatre company, from which his old rival Olivier had just been somewhat unceremoniously ousted, a changeover which meant that several actors who had declined to work under him there were now prepared to go to the South Bank for the first time. The new director, a role hotly contested by Michael Blakemore and Kenneth Tynan and Jonathan Miller, was now to be Peter Hall, who for his first production at the Old Vic (where the company was still lodged while work continued amid myriad delays on the new building) announced that Gielgud would star as Prospero in a radical new *Tempest*.

Apart from *The Ages of Man*, this would be John's first return to Shakespeare since 1958, and it came just in time for the celebrations of his seventieth birthday in April, while he was not only playing for Peter Hall, but also campaigning for the freedom of the Soviet dancer Valery Panov and announcing that he was about to play Shakespeare himself in a new Edward Bond play for the Royal Court. To celebrate this seventieth, a birthday book, signed by countless actors and the likes of Tennessee Williams and Artur Rubinstein, was solemnly presented to him. 'He is,' wrote Alan Bennett, 'a gentleman in the old-fashioned sense of the word. He's an almost Russian character, he's saintly, but it requires no effort. He was just born good, there has been no struggle to get there, and when he speaks Shakespeare it is as though he had also written it. If we don't understand a line, we always know it is our fault rather than his.'

John was not exactly wasting any time during these Prospero rehearsals; he was also filming a new thriller on a boat moored by Tower Bridge, and commuting to Leeds to read extracts from the Bible for Yorkshire Television's hugely popular *Stars on Sunday*, a task for which he was delighted to find there would be a large cheque, having vaguely assumed that as it was to do with God, he would probably be working for nothing.

Now that John had at last become fully accustomed to film and television cameras, Mark Amory asked him if he regretted not having gone into movies rather earlier:

Before the war, they used to send me all the scripts that Leslie Howard had turned down, just as Larry was always getting Ronald Colman cast-offs. Then there was the possibility of my playing Louis XVI in *Marie Antoinette*, but Robert Morley got that, and then one day when Charles Laughton was proving difficult they even suggested I should be the *Hunchback of Notre Dame*. During *Julius Caesar*, Marlon Brando asked me to direct him on film as Hamlet, but nothing came of that either, and I was so awful in *The Barretts of Wimpole Street* that when I eventually went to see it, at the Odeon, Leicester Square, whenever I appeared on screen a lady in the row behind me said to her friend, 'Oh God, here comes old beastly again!'

I suppose that over the years I have tended to rely rather too much on the Terry charm and the Terry tears. But people do seem to like that. Although of course I have had my disasters. When I explained to Emlyn Williams what Noguchi wanted to achieve by way of a stripped-down production, all Emlyn said was, 'I see, you're now going to play Gipsy Rose Lear at last!'

When *Look Back in Anger* opened at the Royal Court, the aims of the company seemed to me to be both alien and ugly. The novelist Peter De Vries said I was just guilty of Noël Cowardice. Since then, I've had my toe in the avant-garde, but just paddling around, not yet up to my knees. I still feel rather guilty about my *Ages of Man* because it's really just all the purple passages stuck together, but people do seem to like it . . . I've always been eager to please an audience in my old-fashioned sort of way. I was terribly unhappy when lots of old fans from *Richard of Bordeaux* came to see me on the road in *Veterans* last year, and I could almost feel their loathing of the language. One woman sent me a postal order for 40p saying, 'If you are really so hard up that you have to do all this filth . . .' but by the end of this summer, I will have appeared over the last five years in the work of five playwrights, each of whom is at least a generation younger than me. So my life now is really not all rhetoric and robes . . . The theatre has given me all that I ever asked for, but perhaps rather too soon. I have never had any outside interests; politics and world affairs leave me totally cold, though I suppose I might have been a better actor if I had been rather more worldly.

The inaugural Peter Hall *Tempest* at the Old Vic should have been rather more enjoyable for John than it was. This, after all, was to be his fourth Prospero (he had played the role in 1930 and 1940 at the Old Vic, and for Peter Brook at Stratford in 1957). This time, Hall was very keen to play it as a masque, with a great deal of flying, as John recalled: 'I found it very hard to know whether to start again from scratch, or throw in all that I had learned about the role in earlier productions. Prospero is really very difficult; he is a very passionate man, but he doesn't have any real contact with the other characters, and he can easily become either priggish, or boring, or didactic. There is not a single grain of humour in him.'

When they opened in March, reviews were rather better for Gielgud than they were for Peter Hall. Milton Shulman for the *Evening Standard* complained of 'too many styles jostling each other for domination, like too many spices in an exotic meat dish', while Irving Wardle for *The Times* added: 'Gielgud stands outside the stylistic framework of the production. The part is peculiarly his own property, in the sense that the character of Prospero resides in its verse rhythms; and no other actor in the world is so well-equipped to handle those huge metrical paragraphs, with their abrupt contractions and extensions of imagery, almost beyond the bounds of syntax.'

Peter Hall himself felt 'this production didn't come off at all well;

I had tried to interpret the play as a masque, using my experiences of Baroque theatre at Glyndebourne, but the play's complexities sank under the heavy effects.' Michael Billington, for the *Guardian*, called it one of the four worst Shakespeare productions he had ever seen; Hall gently replied that he couldn't be sure, as he had never seen the other three. In fact, Gielgud had not been Hall's first choice here; he had originally offered the role to Alec Guinness, and only when Guinness refused did he turn to John, despite the fact that, as he wrote in his diary:

> John is too gentle and too nice, but I hope I know him well enough to push him into a sharper area of reality . . . John runs around in circles, with huge charm and energy. He keeps making self-deprecating remarks, then reminding us that we shouldn't listen to him, and that he is really just a romantic who loves the old-fashioned theatre. I think I have persuaded him not to sing or emote so much, but now he worries about being boring. Larry, who is still hovering around backstage, insisted on coming to some of the early rehearsals, and I think he knows how uneasy he makes John . . . later John talked to me with the kind of modesty and frankness which makes him a great man. He said he knew that in some sense he had become old-fashioned – all actors do . . . the stage, he said, always went to his head. He loved to wander around, swinging his cloak and dominating the audience. It was a romantic style of acting which had served him well all his life, and his public loved it but, added John, I now want to get rid of my easy solutions . . . during the dress-rehearsal, at one o'clock in the morning, we were trying out the trap-door when to my incredulous eyes Sir John fell through it, apparently in slow motion. There ensued a long silence. I ran, and looked down. John was smiling amiably as he picked himself up from the entangled limbs of Miranda and Ferdinand, who were waiting below to come up. Miraculously, nobody was hurt.

Matters were not helped when, on the morning after the first night, Michael Feast, who was playing Ariel, and had collected some of the best reviews, fell into a sudden, brief but bleak depression, which meant that they had to play an unready understudy for a couple of performances, before Feast reappeared as mysteriously as he had vanished. A few days later, Hall had the chance to take John and Ralph Richardson on a tour of the still incomplete new building. 'It was very funny. John, who is about to be seventy, treated Ralph, who is seventy-one, as if he were an extremely aged and endearing relative up from the country, and unused to city ways: "Mind those holes . . . don't trip over those wires." Both wore long coats and large trilbys, Ralph sporting a stick. They could have been nothing but actors. And great ones too. Both sleek with success.'

During the run, Hall organised a surprise seventieth birthday celebration for John: 'I introduced Larry, who introduced Ralph, who said happy birthday to John. Ralph is like an old soldier scenting battle when the audience is there. Suddenly he came to life and stamped round the stage, joking and shouting. John cried, which is appropriate, and was genuinely surprised. We had a short party upstairs in the rehearsal room afterwards. There was a cake, with seventy candles, and the presentation of a Doulton figure of Ellen Terry, which all the company had subscribed to.'

As *The Tempest* ended its Old Vic run, with Hall's National company now beginning to move into their new premises despite the builders, and John rather sadly aware that he would never play at the Vic again, he consoled himself with two more brief movie roles: the headmaster in *Aces High*, an unsatisfactory, airborne adaptation of R.C. Sherriff's *Journey's End*, and then a television version of Wilde's *Picture of Dorian Gray*, in which he played the elderly Lord Wooton. But his attention was really focused now on his return to the Royal Court, where he had scored such a personal success playing a version of himself in Charles Wood's *Veterans* a couple of years earlier.

This time the role was that of Shakespeare himself in Edward Bond's *Bingo*, a stage biography of the playwright which eventually developed into an attack on his double-dealing as a Warwickshire landlord in the last years of his life. Bond's drama was effectively a series of duologues between Shakespeare and his relatives and neighbours, but its high point was a confrontation with Ben Jonson, intriguingly played by Arthur Lowe, who on his way to Scotland stops in at Stratford to tell Will that the Globe has burned down, and to touch him for a loan. It was in this confrontation, between

Gielgud as the ascetic but now retired Shakespeare and Lowe as the Rabelaisian Jonson, in and out of prison four times, but better educated than Shakespeare and determined never to let him forget it, that a somewhat sedentary drama suddenly kicked into life.

John, in a neat beard, had no alternative than to play Bond's Shakespeare low-key and on a note of sustained melancholy; this was a curiously unrewarding part, in that all Shakespeare really gets to do in *Bingo* is sit around listening to other people yell at him. As Milton Shulman summed up for the *Evening Standard:* 'Gielgud measures almost exactly our preconceptions of Shakespearean facial features, and throughout the entire evening he bears a concentrated look of contemplative sorrow. This is not only a gentle bard, but a very woeful one. Was such a gloomy fellow really capable of inventing the glorious clowns and provoking the heavenly laughter that graces so many of his plays? The major weakness of *Bingo* is that it never gives us the whole Shakespeare, only a philosophical argument based on one tiny sliver of his complex, mysterious and diverse character.'

But there was better, much better, to come. During the run of *Bingo*, Peter Hall came back to John with something vastly more intriguing than yet another Shakespearean revival. Harold Pinter, now an associate of Hall's National Theatre, had delivered a new play, as Hall's diary indicates: 'It is called *No Man's Land*. I was amazed by it. It is not at all what I was expecting. There is an icy preoccupation with time; and the long, sustained speeches have a poetic validity which would have seemed incredible in the days of the brisk, hostile repartee of *The Birthday Party* . . . it is extremely funny, and also extremely bleak. A play about the nature of the artist: the real artist harassed by the phony artist.'

The 1975 season was, after a distinctly rocky start, the one in which Peter Hall finally hit his form, having seen off the last of the dissenters from the previous Olivier regime. This was the season of Bill Bryden's *Spring Awakening*, John Schlesinger's *Heartbreak House*, the Peggy Ashcroft *Happy Days*, and the Ashcroft/Richardson (and Wendy Hiller) *John Gabriel Borkman*. But even in an unusually good time, *No Man's Land* was still the crowning achievement.

Hall and Pinter had given the script to John, thinking he would want to play the grander role of Hirst. In fact, John recommended

Ralph for that part, seeing immediately the potential for himself as Spooner: 'It was very exciting to find a part like nothing I had ever played before, and I quickly found a way that he should look and dress. I remember saying to Harold Pinter, "I think Auden, don't you? Do you think sandals and socks?" And Harold jumped at the idea. Then I said, "What about spectacles?" And he liked that, too. After the first week's rehearsals I came on stage with the wig, the suit and the spectacles, and everybody said, "It's exactly right, perfect," and I said, "Yes, all I have to do now is find the performance to go with it."'

He did, largely because, as Hall noted:

in rehearsal John is as quick as a thoroughbred horse, speeding this way, then suddenly changing direction and speeding the other. He improvises, takes risks, lives dangerously and is perfectly prepared to play a seedy, unsympathetic character like Spooner. He has the quality of mercury, and his instincts and his diction are so incredibly swift that I am sure it is this, together with his timing, wit and infallible sense of rhythm, that breeds such excitement in an audience. He seems to live several points faster than ordinary human beings. He is also very easy to direct. He demands help, demands stimulation, and he leaves you exhausted. But he also leaves you feeling slightly cleverer than you know you are.

Pinter's pauses in *No Man's Land* induced terror in both John and Ralph; it was terribly difficult to get them to understand what a Pinter pause was about – that you went on acting through it, and it wasn't just a great big hole.

Pinter himself recalls the first dress-rehearsal, when suddenly John changed one of the moves:

Ralph stopped the play as if paralysed, and turned very slowly to stare at him. 'Are you going to do that, Johnny?' John leaped up as if stung by a wasp and immediately began to apologise, retreating from Ralph as he did so, until he had almost entirely left the set. I suddenly realised that Ralph had absolute authority on stage over John, although he very seldom had to use it.

This was the first time that I had actually worked with John, though of course I had watched him on stage since his Raskolnikov in *Crime and Punishment* just after the war, when I was still a young actor myself. I was in Wolfit's company for a while, and I think if there was anyone Donald hated more than John G it was probably me, because he had so little faith in my acting. Perhaps rightly.

As I watched John over the years, he never failed to impress me – although he always seemed terribly gaunt, his nervous energy on stage was electrifying. I never agreed with those who said that all he had was the golden voice; John always seemed to me to be acting with every fibre of his presence. His precision and grace and intelligence, in such roles as Benedick, is something I shall never forget. In the 1980s, I was responsible for organising a benefit at the Royal Court to raise funds for imprisoned writers overseas. Ralph disapproved thoroughly, and refused to take any part; indeed, he sent me a sharp note, reading, 'Got to have a bit of law and order, old boy.' John, on the other hand, always the more liberal of the two, agreed to do a speech from *Richard II*; and my greatest recollection of that night is of every great actor in the business crowding into the wings to watch John doing a very brief reading from Shakespeare. It was as though they all knew that he was their master.

As soon as I had shown *No Man's Land* to Peter, and John had asked to play Spooner, I think we both knew that although he had never played a character in any way at all like that, he knew something more than we did of the Bohemian world from which Spooner came. I'm not suggesting, of course, that John also used to hang around Hampstead Heath at night, but he had certainly known people who did, and he had an instinctive understanding of Spooner which was simply wonderful to watch. The whole Auden connection came from John and I thought it was absolutely right for the character. He used elements of Auden and indeed of himself, but to build up a totally new character in a way that I certainly had almost never seen him do before; it was an act of creation rather than interpretation.

Early on, Peter and I had lunch with John to discuss who should be playing Hirst; we went through a long list of actors without mentioning Ralph, because we somehow thought that he might not now be up to learning it. John disagreed at once. 'I think you should approach him;

it's very important for the play that the actor playing Hirst should not have a weaker stage presence than me. And with Ralph, of course, you'd be getting a stronger one!'

They had of course already worked together in David Storey's *Home*, but I knew from the beginning that there was no danger of them repeating themselves, because the roles in *No Man's Land* are so totally different. I saw less of them in rehearsal than I would like to have done, because my home life was in total chaos – it was the time that I was leaving home and my wife Vivien Merchant to live with Antonia Fraser. Whenever I did look in, they seemed to be having a really good time, and I was just so pleased and honoured with what they were doing in my play.

They were both of course great worldwide stars with tremendous individual followings, and I'm sure that some of their fans couldn't make any sense at all of *No Man's Land*; but I'm used to that, and most of the audiences always seemed to be having a really good time as well. During the run in London and later on Broadway, Antonia and I used to take John and Ralph out to lunch sometimes, but they would hardly ever talk about themselves or their work. Instead, they both seemed fascinated by Antonia's history books, and by other times and other places. Between them, they really did have an extraordinary range of knowledge and interests. And they both read widely, all the time. They both had wonderful theatre stories, but I always knew not to go into politics, not because I thought they would necessarily disagree with me, but because they both seemed so bleakly uninterested in that whole territory.

Ralph was somehow always more suspicious than John, who had an extraordinary kind of innocence. And although they had been friends and colleagues for almost half a century, they seemed to lead very separate daytime lives, only coming together on the stage at night, or at matinées. 'When we do meet,' Ralph once said to me, 'it is always as other people.'

What was remarkable about John, quite apart from his extraordinary intelligence, was that although he may not have been any greater as an actor than Olivier, Gielgud alone was at the centre of every development of the British theatre in the twentieth century. As an actor and a director he was just somehow always there.

'No Man's Land will not change, or grow old, or move – it remains forever icy,' as Spooner says to Hirst, a line that is repeated at the end of the play, and will also serve as its epitaph. As the play begins, an ageing alcoholic man of letters, much prone to sudden physical collapse (Richardson), is being visited by a distinctly crumpled poet (Gielgud) whom he has encountered on Hampstead Heath, where the latter is wont to indulge in a little light voyeurism when not washing up the glasses at Jack Straw's Castle nearby. It later transpires that this is no mere chance encounter; the two men are known to each other, inextricably linked by an unseen wife whom one married and the other lived with, and their relationship is as ambiguous as that of the two sinister servants with whom the Richardson character shares his house – a house in which the conversation is apt to roam from high comedy ('Lord Lancer? One of the Bengal Lancers, is he?') to lengthy discussions of the utter impossibility of reaching Bolsover Street by any form of human transport except legs.

What we have here are four characters in search of several answers ('Tell me about your wife – did she google?'), none of which is forthcoming; but along the way the sight and sound of Sir John and Sir Ralph in Pinter's spare, ritualistic drama was a sustained joy – the last high-water mark of both their careers.

As Pinter's biographer Michael Billington has noted: 'I took Hirst and Spooner to be projections of Pinter's own darkest fears. Hirst – wealthy, immured, isolated and increasingly cut off from the source of his original inspiration – seemed to me Pinter's nightmare vision of the kind of artist he might, unless he were careful, become. Spooner, the pub poetaster, haunted by memories of other men's lines – was a distant memory of the marginalised versifier Pinter might once have been . . . Like all his best plays, No Man's Land addresses universal issues while stemming from some deeply personal core of anxiety – Pinter's nightmares and fears become ours.'

It was Antonia Fraser who pointed out that the play also stems from a very unhappy period in Pinter's personal life, when his first marriage was in terminal decline and when many of his natural political instincts were repressed: 'No Man's Land is a very bleak play, which I only understood when I visited his house in Hanover Terrace, immaculate with terrible silence. This is not the work of someone who was going to take a banner and protest about the state of the world.'

When reviews of the National Theatre production first appeared, they were ecstatic, strong enough to ensure a long West End and Broadway transfer. But in the last few rehearsals Hall had suddenly started to worry about what John was doing as Spooner: 'At the moment, John is inclined to play what the audience should conclude about the character, rather than the character himself . . . He is over-experimenting: playing it humble, playing it conceited, playing it creepy, playing it arrogant. He is searching for a simple key, whereas the truth is that Spooner is many things and changes his posture from second to second, so there is no simple key.'

But Gielgud had solved this problem by opening night, and came through so strongly in the reviews that Peter Hall felt constrained to reflect, 'Richardson is being undervalued. John's performance is magnificent but there are other actors who could do it, whereas I do not think any other actor could fill Hirst with such a sense of loneliness and creativity as Ralph does.'

Once again, as had happened on Broadway with Richard Burton and Elizabeth Taylor, John now found himself at the centre of a publicity storm which had nothing at all to do with the work in hand. By the time of the opening of *No Man's Land*, the press had suddenly begun to pick up on the end of the Pinter marriage to Vivien Merchant, and Pinter had to insist that Hall stay close to him all through the first performance, to fend off unwelcome enquiries. As Hall had predicted, 'When Harold tells Vivien about Antonia, the explosion will be heard the other side of Regent's Park.'

Critics, ecstatic about the reunion of John and Ralph Richardson, had also begun to notice that they were now the best double act since Laurel and Hardy; as Billington wrote for the *Guardian*: 'Richardson's Hirst, contrasting a peppery, ramrod-backed power with chilling geriatric collapses and exits on all fours, has precisely that other-worldliness which makes this actor such a magician; and Gielgud's Spooner, based on a mixture of Auden, his brother Lewis, and the Bohemian semi-failures who run ballet bookshops off the Charing Cross Road, comes as a shock; the baggy, grey pinstriped demob suit, the untidy, sandy hair, the beer belly, the sandals implying slightly odorous socks, the creased, tobacco-breathed quality of the kind of ageing 1940s relic that you still meet in BBC pubs like The George, superbly sly, mellifluous and ingratiating.'

As Irving Wardle wrote in *The Times*: 'No Man's Land remains palpably the work of our best living playwright in its command of language and its power to erect a coherent structure in a twilight zone of confusion and dismay.'

Final evidence that Gielgud and Richardson had now become the most distinguished classical double act in all theatre history was confirmed by a two-page conversation in the *Observer* as transcribed by the critic John Heilpern:

SIR JOHN: Come on the motorbike?

SIR RALPH: Best way.

JG: The last time you took me pillion, I practically had a fit. I was a stretcher case.

RR: I have been killed several times myself . . . Would you say we look alike, Johnny? I have several times been mistaken for you.

JG: I've been stopped twice in London for Kenneth Clark.

RR: I should be most flattered to be mistaken for him.

JG: I was so angry with myself at the Garrick the other day. I just couldn't remember the name of an actor I knew, and even now I can't think of it. Someone like Sybil Thorndike never forgets anybody.

RR: Never.

JG: She even remembers people she met in Australia.

RR: She remembers everyone.

JG: I have to look up names in *Spotlight* [the actors' casting directory]. Emlyn Williams used always to turn the pages, and whenever he saw a photograph of an actor wearing a hat, he would shout 'Bald!' Emlyn could always spot that.

RR: What was that terrible production you did for Peter Brook?

JG: *Oedipus*?

RR: That's it. Awful.

JG: Oh, I thought it was extraordinary. I'll never regret doing it. I wasn't very good, I didn't know how to do what he wanted. But you know, there were some terrible rows between Brook and Olivier. When Olivier saw that great phallus on the stage, he thought the

Old Vic would be closed down by the police. Brook wouldn't give in, though, and they were arguing in my dressing-room. So I left them to fight it out between them. When I came back half an hour later, there was a huge mirror with a crack going right through it, just like *The Lady of Shalott*. I never did find out which of them did it.

RR: Here comes our photographer. It must be so difficult. Whenever I try to photograph anyone, they always look as if they've been hit over the head with a meat axe.

JG: I'd still rather be photographed than drawn. David Hockney did a drawing of me at seventy, and I thought if I really look like that, I must kill myself tomorrow. Richard Avedon once made me cry for two hours to get an unusual angle, so I thought of everyone I knew who had died, and the tears fairly flowed like mad, but he never used the shot. So that was a terrible waste of an afternoon.

From the Old Vic, *No Man's Land* moved to Wyndham's through the winter of 1975, and then back to the finally completed Lyttelton auditorium of the National Theatre on the South Bank; during this effectively year-long run, John took part in a moving farewell to the Old Vic, and also found the time to direct Judi Dench and Daniel Massey in a disappointing West End revival of Pinero's *The Gay Lord Quex*. This, as Judi Dench's biographer John Miller notes, was a play that Gielgud had yearned to direct for years; it had been a favourite of his mother's, and she had passed on her enthusiasm for a drawing-room drama that had not been seen in London for more than half a century. 'Stupidly,' said John, 'I became obsessed with the idea that I must do it exactly as it was written in the 1890s. So we did it very elaborately, spent an awful lot of money, and I miscast several parts in it.'

As Miller also relates, 'The rehearsals had some memorable moments for Judi: "We were rehearsing in the crypt at St James's Piccadilly one morning, when suddenly, out of the men's loo, ran a man carrying a pair of trousers, followed by another without any, and John laughed so much that he had to give us the day off, he simply couldn't go on rehearsing."'

There was also a memorable moment at the costume parade, when Judi Dench came on in her nightgown, only to be greeted by an anguished Gielgud voice from the stalls: 'Oh, no, no, no, Judi! You look just like Richard III!' Things were not much better when Siân Phillips arrived in her long evening gown. 'It's dreadful!' came the voice from the stalls. 'The trouble is, Siân, when you're standing up, you are so terribly tall!'

Reviews for this hopelessly dated theatrical folly were generally terrible, and John was unable to find any real escape from the disaster, because *The Gay Lord Quex* was playing at the Albery, whose stage door backed on to that of Wyndham's, where he and Ralph were still playing *No Man's Land*. Judi Dench's last memory is of going into the Albery stage door one night with Massey, and hearing John call out 'Hello, Dan. I hear your show is coming off. No good? Oh, my God, I directed it!'

It was therefore with some relief that John took *No Man's Land* back to the National, and then on to Washington and New York where, late in 1976, he and Richardson, appearing on Broadway for the first and last time together, scored the greatest hit of their late lives. In Washington, however, they did not get off to the best of starts, when Peter Hall was introduced on a local chat show. 'And now,' said the host, 'we are very honoured to have on the programme, the famous international actor, I mean director, who founded the Royal Shakespeare Company and is now running the National Theatre. Ladies and gentlemen, it is a pleasure to welcome on to the show Mr Peter – I'm terribly sorry, I can't remember your name!'

Gielgud and Richardson basked in the autumnal glow of a huge Broadway success; they were beyond doubt the snob hit of the season, and it was now that Kenneth Tynan wrote, for the *New Yorker*, his epic profile of Ralph Richardson, in which of course John inevitably co-starred:

Since the two knights appeared together in *Home* seven years ago, they have been endlessly interviewed and photographed together, and are frequently mistaken for one another on the street. 'We are just like the broker's men in *Cinderella*,' said John. And for interview purposes he and Sir Ralph have evolved what amounts to a double act in which certain routines and catch-phrases, including the one about the broker's men, ritually recur:

> SIR RALPH: You're looking very well, today, Johnny.
> SIR JOHN: Thank you.
> SIR RALPH: I haven't seen much of you lately.
> SIR JOHN: We only seem to meet in costume.

As Tynan somehow fails to note, neither Pinter nor Beckett could have written that impromptu exchange better. In fact, their enduring friendship and stage partnership was based on an absolute under-standing that they would separate their private from their public lives, only really meeting in rehearsal or performance, except on very special celebratory occasions. Richardson still took a wary view of John's now rather tranquil homosexuality, which consisted of little more than the occasional visit to gay movies, and Richardson had also been involved in a celebrated contretemps during the Peter Brook *Oedipus*, when he insisted on trying to purchase a programme from one of the actors whom Brook had lashed to the pillars in the dress-circle. In Richardson's view, John was rather over-eager to go with the prevailing theatrical fashions of the time, whatever time it happened to be.

While they were in New York, Gielgud noted rather sadly, 'Ralph always insists on the best restaurants, whereas I seem to eat out of tins. He loves the craftsmanship of his art – he prepares his work and then exhibits it with utmost finesse, rather like Edith Evans, who would open a window to her heart and then slam it shut again, so that the audience would come back the next night to see more. My own tendency is always to show too much, too soon, whereas Ralph has acquired such control of movement, such majesty. Of course, he does have a violent side to his nature – a powerful sadistic streak, sudden outbursts of temper.'

Profiling Gielgud some years earlier, Tynan had written:

His uniqueness lies in the fact that he is greater than the sum of his parts. But his style lacks heart and stomach. When Olivier enters, lions pounce into the ring and the stage becomes an arena. Gielgud, on the other hand, just appears. He does not make an entrance, and he looks like one who has an appointment with the brush of Gainsborough or Reynolds . . . Gielgud's sheer technocratic art is transparent, and shows through his skin . . . like Irving, he is not really a tragedian, but a romantic – ductile and aloof. His inherited task is to preserve tradition, which has seldom had a more jealous custodian. Both as director and as actor he takes few risks and becomes in time predictable, as only the dedicated and single-minded can be . . . He is still about the only English actor of any eminence who has consistently disregarded films – he believes that acting should always be an ephemeral business, passed on by word of mouth . . . His energy is unwaning, and his hold on the reins of rhetorical acting is unchallenged in all the world . . . In modern terms, John Gielgud is Kemble to Olivier's Kean – the aesthete as opposed to the animal. John is claret and Larry is burgundy.

Tynan later extended this comparison to make two lists. 'Gielgud: Air. Poet. Mind. Spiritual. Feminine. Introvert. Jewel. Olivier: Earth. Peasant. Heart. Animal. Masculine. Extrovert. Metal.'

While he was in New York, John also gave a long interview to the historian Toby Cole about his life as an actor.

I still have extremely good eyesight, and I am very observant. From the stage, if I am not careful, I can recognise people I know, eight or ten rows back in the stalls. Even on a first night, when I am shaking with nervousness. Latecomers, people who whisper or rustle chocolates, or fall asleep, I have an eye for every one of them, and my performance suffers accordingly . . . to play the same part eight times a week for more than a year, as I have in *No Man's Land*, is a severe test for any actor. The routine is nerve-racking, and it is agonising work trying to keep one's performance fresh, without either slackening or over-acting. I am usually guilty of the latter fault, and my tendency to exaggerate every effect becomes more and more marked as the weeks go by . . . I have frequently envied painters, writers and critics. I have thought how happy they must be to do their work in private, at home, unkempt and unobserved, able to destroy or renew or improve their creations at will, to judge them in their unfinished state, to watch their gradual development and to admire the final achievements ranged round them on their bookshelves, or hung upon their walls. I have often wondered how these artists would face the routine of the actor, which demands not only that he shall create a fine piece of work, but that he shall repeat it with unfaltering love and care for perhaps three hundred performances on end. In my envy, I have often wished that I were able to rise in the middle of the night, switch on the light, and examine some performance of mine, calmly and dispassionately, as I looked at it standing on the mantelpiece.

An actor is really no good to anything except the theatre. Actors are the most selfish people, especially in domestic life. We can be such bores. We are tediously self-examining. An actor has nobody but himself to take counsel with, because nobody really cares what is going on inside him. Communal work troubled me as a young actor. I didn't want to rub shoulders with other people. In real life, I'm not very communal; I have a tendency to cut others off and be by myself. Now I find that in the theatre I can work communally and at the same time be private. I can give a stage performance when I'm ill and not feel it. I never notice when I'm hurt on the stage until the play is over. Onstage, it's not terribly difficult for an actor to put troubles or worries out of his mind. Even outside the theatre, if there's unhappiness around you, you're likely to be observing it rather than feeling it directly. You constantly catch yourself trying to study how people really feel emotion. You store it up for further use; you reproduce it later in other forms. If I see a bad accident I watch the expressions on the faces of the people. The dramatic side of every emotional experience seems to be always first with the actor. You jot it down. When you see somebody dead for the first time, you can't resist making notes of the way you yourself feel. It's one of the poignant things you remember when poignancy is called for. Almost as soon as you get a feeling, you begin to observe it. It makes you rather a monster, I think.

In the theatre I have quite good taste: in my real life I'm absolutely tasteless. Outside the theatre, I'm clumsy with my hands. I'm a very bad judge of character, I'm not learned. I'm always so terribly aware of how little I know. I'm sure that Laurence Olivier and Michael Redgrave are so much more learned than I am. I'm sure that Picasso must know so much and must have all the wisdom I lack. I know that I am terribly adolescent, romantic and naive. It's alarming when an actor becomes a success. Immediately, he's quoted on things, and you find actors going into political areas and places they have no business being in. I don't need any other places myself. I find everything I love in the theatre. When I go into a theatre and get into a dressing room, it's like going into a safe place that I know, without thinking, is mine. It's like going home.

When *No Man's Land* eventually closed on Broadway, at the end of the 1976–7 season, John G returned to London to the welcome news that he had been awarded not only the Companion of Honour, one of the highest orders in the Queen's gift, but also had been made a Companion of the French Légion d'Honneur, both of which he now added to honorary degrees from the universities of Oxford, London and St Andrews. Olivier may have beaten him to the peerage, but John now seemed to be collecting every other honour in reach.

In the absence of any stage offers, he soon made three more screen appearances: Captain Shotover in a rather unsatisfactory BBC Television adaptation of Bernard Shaw's *Heartbreak House*, and the brief role of the preacher in Joseph Strick's art-house movie of *A Portrait of the Artist as a Young Man*; he also turned up for BBC Schools Television in the title role of Dostoyevsky's *The Grand Inquisitor*.

But then, in the summer of 1977, something very much more intriguing came along. The film director Alain Resnais (who had made his name with *Last Year In Marienbad*) had decided to make his first English-speaking picture. *Providence* would have a complex, multi-layered screenplay by David Mercer which, like Pinter's *No Man's Land*, was to take John into areas of acting altogether new to him. His role in the film was to be that of a roaring, drunken, foul-mouthed, randy seventy-eight-year-old novelist, determined not to go gently into any kind of night: 'You won't get me, you fucking bastards.'

The sight of John drinking bottle after bottle of Chablis, while sticking pessaries up his backside, came as something of a shock to the more faithful of his audience, but then again, as Robert Tanitch has noted, 'Gielgud seemed to relish all the scatological abuse, self-disgust and even the pain of one of his most challenging screen roles.' Tom Hutchinson, for the *Sunday Telegraph*, reckoned: 'This must be Gielgud's finest and most sustained film performance – an elegantly ferocious gauge against which others must be compared in the future. We have heard his rapier-swish before, but never his sledgehammer-smash – this is acting with the guts, as well as the mind.'

The premise of *Providence* was that John, as the dying author, would be spending his last night on earth casting his own family as the characters in his latest novel. But a highly extravagant structure (the narrative is constantly interrupted by flashbacks and memories and nightmares) meant that the audience had a hard time working out what was real and what was merely fantasy. John said this was 'by far the most exciting film I have ever made', and apart from him and Dirk Bogarde, there were only three other actors involved: Ellen Burstyn, David Warner and Elaine Stritch.

'Here we all are together,' as Dirk Bogarde said one morning to John on the set, 'in some extraordinary part of France. After all the time we have both spent on our various careers, we are now ageing gentlemen [John was seventy-three, Dirk a mere fifty-six], both in a new script written specifically for us by David Mercer, both in a new form of an old craft. We are both going ahead, that's what's exciting. At least we are not doing a revival of *No, No, Nanette*.'

When the reviews appeared, virtually all came out in favour of John (how often after all do you get to see the greatest actor of his time stuffing pessaries up his backside?), but proved much less enthusiastic for Bogarde and Resnais. The film never really came into its own, despite yet another of Gielgud's remarkable valedictories: 'Just leave . . . now please . . . neither kiss nor touch . . . go with my blessing.' As Anthony Lane wrote for the *Independent*, John's was 'a camp and succulent portrait of decaying daydreams'.

Originally, Dirk Bogarde himself had rather hoped to play the old man:

It was a brilliantly placed role, and I knew that with John Gielgud playing it, none of the rest of us would stand a chance. He'd pinch the picture. Which he did . . . shortly before we started work, Resnais suggested that I might like to give a little supper party for him in the small hotel where I was staying on location . . . Resnais really just wanted the chance to observe John closely; he talked and talked, happily aware that he was holding the table and that nobody would interrupt him. I don't know what Resnais knew before about Ellen

Terry, Marie Tempest, Peggy Ashcroft, Edith Evans, Eleanora Duse or the third act of *King Lear*, but by the end of that supper he should have known all that he ever needed to know. John's fund of stories, funny and often gloriously irreverent, was limitless, and he was enjoying himself tremendously.

Later in the shooting, Bogarde had to persuade John to tape-record a birthday greeting to Resnais. As John demurred, Bogarde said desperately, 'Please do this, you probably have one of the most beautiful English-speaking voices in the world.' John looked up over the top of his glasses. 'THE,' he said sharply. Curiously, that was almost the beginning and the end of Bogarde's relationship with John. On the face of it, the two actors, though from very different generations and backgrounds, had a great deal in common. Both had remained closeted homosexuals throughout most of their careers; both had an aquiline, poetic quality which made their performances even in minor screenplays unmissable. Both read and wrote far more widely than most actors, and were blessed with considerable native intelligence. Both had partners (Martin Hensler and Anthony Forwood) who managed their lives with remarkable efficiency and discretion, and exhibited a passion for gardening. Unlike Bogarde, John never exiled himself from the heartland of his trade; but precisely because they had so much else in common, the two men, while maintaining a warily distant respect for each other's work, never became close friends. They were perhaps just too alike.

There was, though, one great difference between them: while Dirk Bogarde, like Alec Guinness and James Mason but precious few other British actors of John's time, took filming very seriously indeed, and turned down many screen roles for which he felt himself in some way unsuited, John, like Olivier and Richardson and Redgrave, spent the last years of his long career effectively grabbing every offer that came down the phone. John's decision about whether or not to make a film depended almost entirely on if the money was good, and if the diary was clear that week. He made almost no real distinction between prestigious projects like *Providence* and another episode of a minor Hollywood mini-series. Filming, to him, was now a convenient way of living well, keeping in touch with old friends in the acting business, and going on location at the expense of others to see the comparatively few countries he had never yet visited. The idea, central to Bogarde's way of thinking, that cinema was somehow an art form, to be taken as seriously as theatre, simply never crossed John's mind.

Chapter Twenty-five

🙢🙢🙢

GORED BY VIDAL

(1977–1984)

*Half my new cinema audience comes to see if I really am still
alive; the other half think they had better catch me before I die.*

Back in England, after the shooting of *Providence*, John now re-
joined Peter Hall's National Theatre for three farewell
performances. In the first of these, he was yet again to play
the title role in *Julius Caesar*, this time in a production by the film
director John Schlesinger which, as Peter Hall recalled, was in trouble
from the very first preview: 'I don't think it's going to work. I
believe we shall be slaughtered for the weaknesses in the young and
inexperienced cast (among them Brian Cox and Gawn Grainger), for
all the clarity of Schlesinger's direction. A great, great pity, just when
we've turned the corner. But there's little I can do.' Of the first night,
Hall simply added: 'The audience were way ahead of the play, and
that always spells death. I went backstage to find a great number of
dispirited actors, all in shock.' For the *Guardian*, Michael Billington
merely noted of Gielgud: 'a gratuitous attempt to kill off the best
verse speaker on the English stage'.

From that, Gielgud went on to work for Peter Hall himself in a
reunion with Paul Scofield for *Volpone*, although despite a very strong
supporting cast (Ben Kingsley, Paul Rogers, Elizabeth Spriggs) this
too proved a disappointment, with Gielgud uneasily cast as Sir Politic
Wouldbe. Both these productions were withdrawn from the National
repertoire as early as could be arranged.

Luckily, however, John's third – and in fact farewell – appearance
for Hall's National company, the last he would make in any classical

395

surroundings, worked out considerably better. Opening next at the Cottesloe was Julian Mitchell's *Half-Life*, in which Gielgud played Sir Noel Cunliffe, a professor of archaeology who, discovering that his whole life has been built on a lie, determines to avenge himself by making sure that neither his university nor his so-called friends will profit in any way by his death.

As Milton Shulman for the *Evening Standard* noted: 'Gielgud spits and hisses insults like a self-satisfied snake, enchanted with the sound of its own rattle. When, for a moment, his past looms up like an awful lie, his temporary loss of composure is deeply moving.'

Early in 1978 John moved *Half-Life* from the Cottesloe into the Duke of York's, but somehow this was to prove a mistake; anybody who had wished to see Gielgud as the acid old archaeology don had probably done so at the National, and John, unusually, began to find himself playing to distinctly empty houses. The commercial run soon closed in the West End, and he threw himself back into the usual range of movies, good, bad and indifferent. He played Gillenormand in an American television *Les Misérables*, sadly without the songs that have now made Hugo's novel such a musical triumph all around the world.

From that, John progressed to a BBC Television version of *Romeo and Juliet*, for which he spoke the chorus, dressed like a Doge of Venice, and another BBC classic Shakespeare, this one the Derek Jacobi *Richard II* in which he played John of Gaunt, looking – said the *Daily Telegraph* – 'like a burst horse-hair sofa'.

From those unexceptional but perfectly respectable appearances, Gielgud now moved on to what was quite clearly the single most embarrassing chapter of his entire film or stage career. The publisher of *Playboy*, Bob Guccione, had developed, with his employer Hugh Hefner, a surprising taste for making movies. Undeterred by the fiasco of their Roman Polanski/Kenneth Tynan *Macbeth*, they now moved on to a Gore Vidal version of *Caligula*, for which John was originally offered the title role. Even he, seldom able to reject a few weeks on a rich movie, sensed troubled here, especially when he began to read a script that was clearly pornographic. He therefore politely had his agent reject the offer to play Emperor Tiberius, only to receive an outraged letter from Gore Vidal himself, saying how impertinent it was of John to refuse the role, and that if he only knew what Tennessee Williams and Edward Albee were saying about him behind his back, he would not be so grand. Somewhat chastened, John finally agreed to play the smaller, and at least theoretically more innocent, role of the old tutor to Tiberius, now being played by Peter O'Toole, with Malcolm McDowell in the title role.

Unfortunately, once a *Playboy* film, always a *Playboy* film: although John's sequences had been shot in relative isolation, the finished print shows him in a pool full of very small boys and buxom blondes: 'I played my whole scene in a bath of tepid water. It took three days to shoot, and every two hours some terrible hags dragged me out, rubbed me down, and put me back into the water again. It was all most extraordinary.'

It was also a considerable tribute to John's now apparently impregnable critical standing that although the film eventually opened on a budget of $17 million to some of the worst reviews since Pearl Harbor, nobody actually blamed John at all; critics seemed to assume that in some vague way the film had been shot without his knowledge, and that his presence in the midst of these appallingly seedy, soft-porn surroundings must just have been some kind of mistake. It was now almost as though there were two Gielguds: the real one who would appear in scripts of some merit, and then a kind of virtual John, almost a hologram, who would be seen in rubbish for which he was somehow never taken to task. Movie-makers specialising in the latter were somehow assumed to have borrowed his image, much after the fashion of Madame Tussaud, without ever directly involving the actor himself.

Fully ten years were to elapse between *Half-Life* in the West End and John's next – and last – stage appearance there or anywhere, in 1988; in these ten years he made an astounding total of twenty-two films, not counting several television appearances. Of this collection, perhaps only six films (*The Elephant Man*, *Chariots of Fire*, *Gandhi*, *Arthur*, *The Shooting Party* and *Plenty*) could be considered in any way notable, and in most of these he was to play relatively minor roles. Nevertheless, for a man now in his seventies and eighties, the output was prodigious, and even of the really bad movies it could safely be said that John did not make any of them actually worse, sometimes even lending moments of grace and charm and distinction to screenplays that little deserved them. All the same, this was the late-life movie career of a Redgrave or a Richardson or an Olivier; there was still no sign that he was going into the twilight, as was Alec Guinness, making only those films about which he truly cared.

After *Caligula*, his first guest-starring role was as Lord Salisbury, the Prime Minister, in *Murder By Decree*, in which Christopher Plummer and James Mason played Sherlock Holmes and Dr Watson, hot on the trail of Jack the Ripper. Next came *The Human Factor*, another of those movies that started with distinction and ended in chaos. Graham Greene's novel, about an innocent man mistakenly believed to be a Foreign Office spy, had been adapted for the screen by Tom Stoppard, and the director Otto Preminger duly assembled a stunning cast, led by Nicol Williamson, Richard Attenborough, Derek Jacobi, Robert Morley and John himself. Unfortunately, and this was truly a sign of the new Hollywood times, Preminger's money ran out halfway through the shooting, thereby resulting in a botched ending to the story, and lawsuits which dragged on for several years, as the actors desperately tried to get their money.

John was, however, to have rather better luck with his next movie, *The Elephant Man*. David Lynch, the leading avant-garde director of his generation, had decided to film the real-life story of the 'Elephant Man', a destitute vagrant in 1884 London, deformed by a rare illness, and finally turned by a pioneering doctor from a fairground freak to someone much pitied and visited by fashionable society. With Anthony Hopkins as the doctor, Gielgud played a pillar of the Victorian medical establishment who is won over to the Elephant Man's case when he hears him reciting, by heart, one of the psalms. John's performance, more central to the picture than was now usually the case, won him another batch of enthusiastic notices and the rare friendship of Anthony Hopkins, who from now on became one of his most devastatingly accurate mimics.

That year, 1979, was also that of John's seventy-fifth birthday, an anniversary marked on a wide selection of fronts. He himself, determined not to be thought of as in any way retired, announced that he still had a Prospero and a King Lear to play, quite possibly for Hall's National Theatre if the right casts and directors could be assembled. Sadly, they never were, but in the meantime John published revisions of two of his earliest books, *Early Stages* and a collection of essays about the great stars of his childhood. He also took part in a fascinating project for which the Radio 4 producer John Powell and the interviewer John Miller recorded more than twenty hours of Gielgud talking about every facet of his career, resulting in a memorable radio series and subsequently a book which stands as the best hardback documentary of his working life, though John was as ever determined to keep his private life well out of the public gaze.

This was also the time when most theatre critics and historians began to consider Gielgud in a rather new light, as the grand old man of the British classical theatre. As Michael Billington noted: 'Gielgud has made the difficult transition from the world of Beerbohm Tree and Du Maurier to that of Harold Pinter and Peter Brook, partly because he is a restless workaholic, partly because he is totally without false pride, and partly because, for him, the theatre at its best is life raised to the pitch of ecstasy.'

John himself, perhaps unaware that his working life had twenty more years to run, also began now to sum up:

Like all professions, acting has terrible drawbacks. It can be fearfully boring and fearfully unglamorous. But what is such fun about our profession is that we do get our prizes while we are still alive to enjoy them. We have the pleasure of audience reaction, we have the applause, we have the publicity, we have the tributes and the honours, many more than probably we really deserve.

I must admit that now, though, I have given up on London. All those hideous new buildings, you can't find a taxi, the buses and the underground are filthy, and even walking is painful – they don't let you cross the street, so you have to go down some smelly passageway. My life is now that of the Buckinghamshire countryside, and of course anywhere that a film is being made. For years, people only thought of me in costume parts, and then my older fans were rather disappointed when I started having to say four-letter words on stage and screen. But the truth is that they don't come to the theatre much any more, and I have found an entirely new public, which you need to strip your work of its affectations. We live in a much more realistic world now, and

I hope I have managed to get rid of the romantic mannerisms of my youth – lately, three directors have been the making of me: Lindsay Anderson, Peter Brook and Peter Hall.

Another cause for anniversary celebration was the television screening of *No Man's Land*, which worked very much better than any of John's other attempts to transfer stage hits to the small screen. And it wasn't as though he was totally detached even now from the realities of Britain in the late 1970s. He, Olivier and Richardson all campaigned for Peter Hall in his struggles against the backstage unions who were at this time frequently closing down the National Theatre in a series of sudden stoppages. John was now and always a fervent petition-signatory, ranging over a wide area – he signed everything, from demands that the BBC World Service be allowed to retain autonomy to the campaign for preserving wild minks from being turned into fur coats. He also crusaded for the right of Russian artists to defect from the totalitarian USSR, and joined yet another campaign, this one rather more successful than most, to prevent the threatened demolition of the Old Vic.

For those few who wondered, at this golden time in his career, why he still picked up every unconsidered trifle that came his way on screen, the answer was very simple, albeit one that he never gave in public. First, the current rates of taxation under a socialist government were so prohibitive that he was actually keeping very little of the money he made; second, the close community of actors on a film set still provided a welcome and gossipy change from the seclusion of life with Martin at Wotton Underwood, which tended to seem desirable when he was actually working elsewhere, but to pall quite rapidly when he actually got home. John also now began to contribute an amazing number of book reviews and nostalgic articles to publications at home and abroad. He had always been a writer and a historian, but now the fact that almost alone he had total recall of the West End during and just after the First World War made him much in demand for all kinds of historical, scholarly and archival projects. John had suddenly become, faintly to his own surprise, the living history of the British theatre in his century.

Despite all this late-life acclaim, John G amazingly had still not resolved his financial headaches:

> After thirty years living in Westminster, I have quite taken to life in the country, but it is costing me a fortune. I live in quite an old house, and the other day one of the walls just fell down, but they said it was an Act of God, and so I couldn't claim any insurance. I would rather like to keep a flat in London for when I am working there, but I simply can't afford two addresses. I have never really had such financial difficulties. The more you earn nowadays, the more they tax you, and my accountant has told me I will never be solvent again until the day I die.
>
> Sometimes I think of moving to America because you really can live better there, and the money is wonderful. I have just been over to introduce twenty-two episodes of *The Pallisers* on American television and to do some documentary voice-overs, and they really pay you a very handsome sum. But I love England, and I could never really live anywhere else, although I am having to sell some family treasures to make ends meet. The expense of a chauffeur is the most awful drain, but I was such a menace on the roads that I gave up driving at the age of twenty. I find I depend more and more on the kindness of strangers, and usually they come from wealthy American television companies. It really worries me that I may be taken ill or lose my memory. What on earth would I live on? Savings are worth so much less now, and food has gone up fivefold, even though I am paid better now than I ever dreamed I would be.

So saying, John went back into make-up, to get his face covered in warts for an unsatisfactory Tony Richardson film of *Joseph Andrews*. 'Just my luck,' said John later, 'to have Tony offer me that one and not *Tom Jones*.'

'I am terrified,' John told another interviewer at this time, 'of becoming ridiculous in my old age. What I've always had is an athletic quality of voice and attitude, but I have only just begun to learn how to control it. One of the great things about growing old is that you suddenly dare to stand on stage and do nothing, and people start to listen and to understand.'

One of John's more mournful duties now was to start writing lengthy obituaries for stars such as Edith Evans and Sybil Thorndike, with whom virtually his entire stage career had been spent. His own strength of survival continued to stand him in good stead; although he had seemed in so many ways to be the leanest and weakest of the great Olivier-Richardson-Redgrave generation, he was in fact to outlive all of them, and sometimes by almost twenty years.

John also began ceaselessly to reflect on the changing times: 'I've never forgotten my grandmother telling me when I started out as an actor – "Be on good terms with your colleagues, but be intimate with none of them" – and I suppose I have rather kept to her advice, although I have come to love walking around a film set chatting to everyone. When I started, stars never even spoke to minor players, but all that has changed, and I think acting is a lot more fun today. I have finally learned not to be frightened of the camera, and I really can relax on a film and start to enjoy it, especially as time goes on. Nowadays the whole thing does not really depend on me. I am just hired to lend a bit of elderly grandeur.'

His private life was still just that, though there was an unwelcome burst of sudden publicity when John's cousin, the actress Hazel Terry, took her own life and John had to explain to the coroner's court about her depression and alcoholism. Although he did now begin to take an interest in his niece Maina, who, in her career as a ballet dancer and choreographer, was the only one of his relatives to continue the Gielgud artistic line, he and Martin always took care to distance themselves from the rest of an extended family, as if terrified that some child or grandchild of Lewis or Val would invade the privacy of Wotton Underwood. The relatives, however distant, were still kept on the Christmas card list, but closer communication was never sought, and sometimes actively discouraged by Martin, who took the view that when John was home between movies he should only be disturbed by a very small group of approved friends. One cousin hit the headlines around this time on a drugs bust, while John, despite the pleading of Val's daughter-in-law Irene Gielgud, would not take more than a polite, rather distant interest in her son Piers; and even this eventually trailed off. She had written to him explaining the troubled background to her marriage to Val's son, Adam, in response to which John agreed to meet the boy, but he clearly didn't want to go any further than this so gradually eased himself out of any contact with him. This was precisely the sort of potential upset, or at least distraction, that Martin was most determined to protect John from, so when one day Piers decided just to turn up unannounced at Wotton Underwood, it was Martin who ensured that he was forbidden entrance to the house.

John's next three films were again somewhat patchy, although one by the great Polish director Andrzej Wajda (*The Conductor*) did achieve a brief art-house life. John's diary of this filming noted: 'The Poles are infinitely courteous and considerate, and work with a dedicated enthusiasm. But the technical problems are considerable; I speak no Polish, they speak no English, there are no stand-ins, and because film stock is terribly expensive we only ever get to do a scene once. Wajda is a dynamic personality, utterly concentrated and direct, though once or twice when he is very tired I find him curled up on the floor, where he sleeps soundly between scenes. I have to appear to listen intelligently to Polish speeches spoken by the other actors and devise a way to warn them when it is my turn to speak.'

It was on the location for *The Conductor* that John formed the last crucial partnership of his life. Mavis Walker had started her career as an actress, and first worked with John as the understudy to Peggy Ashcroft during the London run of *The Chalk Garden* back in 1956. From there, she went on to become a director at RADA and to accompany Michael Redgrave on his American tour of *The Hollow Crown*. Mavis was thus immediate and logical casting when John decided that, with more and more of his life now being taken up by foreign location shooting and Martin unwilling to leave Wotton Underwood empty, the time had come to hire a secretary and travelling companion. Mavis Walker herself explained the precise division of labour:

I was to take care of John while abroad, everything from unwrapping his plastic lunches on aeroplanes to making sure that his bedroom was roughly the right temperature at night. Martin meanwhile stays at home in Buckinghamshire where he cooks, shops, gardens and deals with John's fan mail and Christmas cards. He also redesigns, repairs and repaints bargains he picks up in salerooms, feeds the peacocks and cockatoos, walks the dog and talks to the tortoise. He is never seen eating in public, and apart from John of course, I think he far prefers animals to people. Wherever we go in the world from now on, he rings John every night to keep him in touch with the real world – floods, earthquakes, obituary notices and other interesting topics; John greatly looks forward to this.

In fact, as I discovered in Poland, in spite of his elegant home life, John is wonderfully adaptable, and perfectly happy with a small hotel bedroom and bath. When he is not working he sleeps a lot, reads other scripts and tries to work out how to communicate with Wajda. While we were in Warsaw the great event was the visit of Pope John Paul. We saw him on television kissing the ground of his native land, and John managed to get a window overlooking the motorcade: 'Funny,' he said, 'His Holiness looks just like Harry Andrews!'

One night we went to see a production of *The Seagull* in Polish, and at the end John with extraordinary serenity listened while all the cast made incomprehensible speeches. The only time in filming that he ever seems unhappy is when they put him on a horse, whereupon he always says nervously, 'When does it start?'

One night we were taken to a terribly depressed area of the city, where nothing happened for hours until John, boredom getting the better of him at last, suddenly rose to his feet, and in the stentorian tones of his uncle Fred Terry called out, 'I am Sir Percy Blakeney. Lady Blakeney is my wife. And I am the Scarlet Pimpernel!' The Poles took all this in their polite but incomprehending stride.

When we finally got the plane back to Heathrow, there were two Poles sitting across the gangway. 'Gielgud?' said one. 'Yes,' replied John. Then the other Pole pointed at me. 'And wife?' he asked. 'No, no!' replied John. 'Only on film!' This seemed to confuse them so much that we spent the rest of the flight in total silence. When we landed, John's faithful driver Peter met us with a parcel 'from Mr Martin'. It consisted of two large smoked salmon sandwiches, a reward for all our travails.

The other two films he was making now, *Lion of the Desert* and *Sphinx*, were both deeply embarrassing. For *Sphinx*, John was cast as a Cairo black-market antique dealer, who mercifully gets murdered early on, leaving only Margaret Hinxman in the *Daily Mail* to note that he looked 'like an Egyptian Old Mother Riley'.

On the Cairo location for *Sphinx*, talking to the *Evening Standard*'s arts editor Michael Owen, John gave a brisk insight into the kind of breathless life he was now leading as a film actor: 'I worked here in Cairo once before, you know, in 1945 when I played my very last Hamlet. It was a riot; Horatio had an epileptic fit halfway through the last matinée, and fell into my arms. We had to carry on with the understudy. He was Egyptian of course, but nobody seemed to notice.

I keep myself busy in old age doing nice, small parts. I've been to three countries and now I'm off to do one scene with George C. Scott in a Marlon Brando film, though I don't think I ever get to meet him. I've also been to Poland for Wajda, to play a conductor, and they had to give me a crash course in how to conduct Beethoven's Fifth, which was all very strange as nobody but me seemed to speak any English. Next I go back home to do *Brideshead Revisited*, and then of course *The Elephant Man*, and I got my little part in *The Human Factor* all done in one day, which was lovely, though I'm still trying to get the money. It is so nice now being asked to do so many little things, only I have real difficulty in remembering the names of all the directors, but they are terribly patient with me and I find I can turn it on very quickly. I just try to be agreeable and never get temperamental or cross.

Everybody keeps asking me about another *King Lear*, but Peter Hall can never decide if it should be in the Olivier or the Cottesloe Theatre, and whether he or John Dexter or Peter Gill should direct, so I think I'm going to cancel the whole thing before people think I am just getting ga-ga or too nervous to do it at my advanced age.

Unlike poor Larry and Michael Redgrave, who have had to fight the most terrible illnesses in their old age, I have really been very lucky with my health, and there's not a lot I really want to do. The trouble with the National and the Royal Shakespeare nowadays is that they are so huge, and they keep doing far too many plays. People like Alan Howard and Judi Dench must be absolutely worn out, poor things.

Filming, for me, has come as a surprising extension of my stage career. A new film is like a visit to another planet, with unknown territory to explore. It's also like being on tour, seeing new towns and lands and meeting a variety of people . . . working with young directors is always instructive. It gives one a glimpse of tomorrow.

When I'm not working, I'm amazed to find how little I miss the bright lights. You make a new life for yourself when you're old. I sleep in the afternoon, I play my records, do my crosswords, watch television for an hour after dinner and then go to bed early with a really trashy American novel. I find Harold Robbins is a great read, as is Judith Krantz, and I always wonder how many pages their publishers demand between sex scenes. Somehow I have never managed Barbara Cartland; she is altogether too pure, whereas I love all the filthy details.

For *Lion of the Desert* he was cast as the treacherous Sheikh Gariani, a performance that John presumably gave in the comforting knowledge that he couldn't have been any worse than Olivier had been as the Mahdi in *Khartoum*.

This film finished up with a week in Rome, at a time when Alec Guinness was also working there. 'Hello, Alec!' said John, meeting him in the street. 'What are you doing here?' 'Lying in state,' replied Alec. 'Ah,' said John, 'I've done that twice this year, usually as the Pope. How long have you been lying in state? Isn't this getting all rather sinister?'

To complete this mediocre run, John also turned up in two Agatha Christie whodunnits for LWT: one was *The Mystery of Seven Dials* and the other was *Why Didn't They Ask Evans?* He also, reflecting his – or at any rate Martin's – obsession with flower-beds, agreed to host and narrate a seven-part Thames Television series called *The English Garden*, and to make another *Tales From the Unexpected*, this one based on a Roald Dahl story about a crooked antique dealer, masquerading as a clergyman.

Mercifully, 1981 was to find him in two crucial new movies, one of which was to prove the key to his late-life fortune. In the first of these he played the Provost of Trinity College Cambridge, in Hugh Hudson's *Chariots of Fire*, the film about the 1924 Olympic running champions Harold Abrahams and Eric Liddell. This was the film that, more than any other, put the British cinema back on the Hollywood map; it won Oscars for Best Picture, Soundtrack, Costume and the scripting of Colin Welland, and in it, John and his old *Home* director Lindsay Anderson were cast as the two reactionary Masters of Cambridge colleges, both racially and socially bigoted, who do their best to hinder Abrahams right down to the winning stretch.

The other film was to involve John in his longest Hollywood stay since the making of *Julius Caesar*, almost thirty years earlier, and this again was to be an unexpected but total triumph.

Dudley Moore, the actor and pianist whom John had solemnly introduced to America as Stanley Moon, was now at the height of his Hollywood fame, and about to embark on *Arthur*, the story of a playboy millionaire who refuses to grow up, despite the attempts of his butler, a Jeeves figure but with a much more vicious and scatological vocabulary. This was where John won his only Oscar, not least for the scene where Arthur announces that he is going to take a bath and John replies, 'I'll alert the media,' followed by, 'And I suppose you want me to wash your dick for you, you little shit!'

But, as so often where John and movies were concerned, he had totally failed to see the potential of this one, and indeed twice turned down the role because of its foul language. Eventually, however, he was persuaded by his agent, Laurie Evans, that this could well be something more than just another Jeeves, and for Dudley the experience was to prove one of the happiest of his California career:

I had seen John in Alan's *Forty Years On*, and I thought his aptitude for comedy was delicious . . . He brought to comic situations the same kind of passion that he had for the classics, and I loved his no-nonsense approach during the filming. Neither of us believed in too much discussion, so we just did it, and he brought a sense of humanity to the part of Hobson which, coupled with his wonderful sense of the acerbic and the priggish in that character, made for a marvellously rounded performance. Above all, I love the scene when I am looking after him in hospital and he says, 'Arthur, you're a good son.' That moment expresses all the longings we all have for approval from a gentle father . . . the poetry in John always sustains him and nurtures his spirit . . . we all need to find what John has.

Liza Minnelli, who had also turned the film down twice, came (like

Dud) to realise the joy of having John on the set. 'He hated being called Sir John, so I called him Uncle Johnny, and he seemed to like that, but he never quite knew just how funny he was: some of his lines were very raunchy, and to hear them spoken in his brilliant accent was magic. We used to improvise a lot, throwing in jokes and gags, and John was never at a loss. He just caught everything we threw at him.'

For once, John was actually sorry when the filming came to an end. 'Both Dudley and Liza were very sweet to me, and enormously professional and proficient. It was really their film, but they must have seen what a good part I had, and yet they made me feel totally at ease. I am only sorry that I didn't see more of them off the set, but we were all working very hard and somehow there didn't seem time for anything else.' The following year he collected the Oscar for his role, and the statuette was to remain on his bathroom shelf for the rest of his life. It was not exactly lonely there: *Arthur*, John's most honoured film performance ever, also won him a Golden Globe and awards from both the New York and the Los Angeles Film Critics' Circles.

Yet he was still not getting much more than $100,000, for a movie which paid Moore and Minnelli in millions; but just as he was winding up his role, he got an offer which really would make him, for the first time, very rich indeed. He was invited to repeat his new butler role in a series of television commercials for Paul Masson California Wines, and over the next few months, entirely because of these, he was finally able to pay off all the costs of Wotton Underwood, and put money in the bank. Ironically, the previous star of these commercials had been John's old nemesis, Orson Welles, now considered rather too chubby to sell a light Californian wine. 'I'm very fond of Orson,' said John at this time, 'and I don't like doing him out of a job.' All the same, he did so with remarkable alacrity.

Back home, in England, the best was yet to come. Charles Sturridge now approached him with the offer of Edward Ryder in the Granada Television series of *Brideshead Revisited*. In fact, it had been Olivier whom Sturridge first approached with the offer of either this role, or that of the old, dying Lord Marchmain. Larry, never one to refuse a good death scene, plumped for Marchmain, only later to realise that the senior, cranky, irritable Ryder was far and away the better part. In this whole series, the scenes between Jeremy Irons as Charles and John as his craggy, unrelenting, petulant, malicious father are as good as it gets. As Peter Ackroyd wrote in *The Times*, 'Gielgud plays Mr Ryder as if he has been doing it all his life, and perhaps he has – aloof and yet alert, calculating but dismissive, he seems to have sprung on to the screen from the pages of Evelyn Waugh without pausing to alter that wry, malevolent expression.'

In *Brideshead*, as in *Chariots of Fire*, John had now somehow managed to plug himself into the heart of the whole new 'heritage' industry of Britain in the early 1980s. Although he was never actually to appear in one of the Merchant/Ivory carpets-and-curtains extravaganzas, they were to some extent made possible by the success of *Brideshead* and *Chariots of Fire*, which opened up for cinema and television audiences alike a whole new world of nostalgia and snobbery with violence.

But sadly, that was also where, for John, it almost came to an end. Of the thirty more movies he still had to make, only *The Shooting Party* and *Plenty* and *Prospero's Books* could really be considered distinguished additions to his long career, though he was also able to make very fleeting appearances in three other hits: *Gandhi*, *Elizabeth* and *Shine*. But these were the exceptions to the rule under which John still lived his film career, that rule being to accept everything on offer, so long as the money and the dates were roughly suitable.

In this mood he went straight from *Arthur* to play Albert Speer, Hitler's architect, in a Third Reich movie, and followed that with a deeply embarrassing black comedy called *Scandalous*, which required him to dress as a Hell's Angel, complete with ear studs and studded leather jacket. As if hoping to be forgiven, he then hastened on to Rome to play another Pope, this one Pius XII, who failed so conspicuously to speak out against the wartime persecution of the Jews. By now, there was virtually nothing that he would not do on camera, and to prove it he went into a Michael Winner remake of *The Wicked Lady*, with Faye Dunaway now in the role made infamous by Margaret Lockwood forty years earlier. Asked to explain what on earth he thought he had been doing in this, John merely noted that it reminded him of the kind of silent-movie rubbish that he had been taken to see as a child.

After that came an extraordinary reunion. For the first and last time, Gielgud, Olivier and Richardson all came together on screen as three ministers at the court of the mad Ludwig II for Tony Palmer's epic (ten-hour) television series, *Wagner*, shot on location in Vienna. It was however not an entirely happy experience. Burton – playing Wagner – was still drinking heavily, Olivier was in the midst of the television *King Lear* which John had always wanted to do himself, and Richardson was as usual by now appearing to be several slices short of a Sacher torte.

The three surviving knights had of course all been in Olivier's *Richard III* thirty years earlier, but not in the same scene, and the only saving grace now was to watch them discreetly and sometimes not so discreetly trying to upstage each other. The rivalry continued off-screen as well; each of them decided to give a celebration Viennese dinner for the other two, plus Burton. Richardson's party was ruined by waiters, John's by an ugly scene with the chef, and Olivier gave his guests the wrong arrival time and spent an hour or two sitting at an otherwise totally empty table. On the set, Burton found Olivier 'a grotesque exaggeration of an actor – all technique and no emotion', while Richardson had to have his lines written out on idiot boards. John, as usual, just did the work and left as soon as possible, once his scene was safely in the can.

This was to be yet another of those end-of-an-era moments; Richardson now only had a few more months to live, and John kept in close touch, though his relationship with Olivier had grown distinctly chilly. They had really only been kept together in private by John's devotion to Vivien Leigh, and so, following her divorce and death, they had once again gone their separate ways, with John later never able quite to forgive Olivier for publishing in his own memoirs so much of the truth (at least as he saw it) about her.

Professionally, in film and television, John simply went on doing what he had always done best – in Hazlitt's definition of a great actor, 'showing us all that we are, all that we wish to be, and all that we dread to be'.

John's sheer survival now seemed to give him an extraordinary kind of late-life courage. When he wasn't working he would stay quietly in the country, often writing learned theatre articles for specialist magazines, reviewing biographies for the Sunday papers (among actors, only Dirk Bogarde now seemed to do even more of this) and re-editing yet another series of reprints of his early autobiographies and collections of theatrical essays. At the other end of the spectrum, he was perfectly prepared to turn up as the Goose King in a one-night charity pantomime also starring Elton John and, more sadly, to read the lesson at countless memorial services for actors and actresses who had often led far briefer lives than John himself.

Something better did now come along: the minor role of an eccentric animal-rights campaigner sharing one rather good scene with James Mason in the film version of Isabel Colegate's *The Shooting Party*. This, like *Brideshead Revisited* and *Chariots of Fire*, was another of the heritage movies at which John now excelled; as the title suggests, it told the story of an aristocratic house party on the very verge of the First World War, and in his last film Mason gave one of his very best performances, reunited for the only time since *Julius Caesar* with Gielgud himself. In fact, this might have been a still more intriguing reunion; Paul Scofield was to have played the Mason role, and only lost it by being severely injured in a carriage accident on the first day of shooting, whereupon he had to be replaced by Mason. But in this account of an aristocratic, Edwardian pre-war society on the verge of being as surely blasted away as the birds they have gathered to shoot, John was cast for once totally against type as an impoverished outsider, yet again reminding audiences of his new-found versatility on camera.

As John approached his eightieth birthday in April 1984, his work-load continued to be prodigious. When he wasn't actually filming, he would spend long hours still reading the Bible for Yorkshire Television, or taking part in a marathon sixteen-part series called *The Centuries of Verse*, in which he read everything from Chaucer to Ted Hughes, sharing the readings with his old friend Peggy Ashcroft. Asked why it had now been five years since he last worked on stage, John replied, 'I suppose I have failed to find the right part. I'm very lucky in that, at eighty, I have hardly ever had a day of illness in my life, but I am still not sure that I want to go back to touring, or playing eight shows a week.'

His actual eightieth was celebrated at a press conference on the stage of his beloved Old Vic, where he had first appeared at the age of eighteen. The celebration ended with Christopher Reeve producing a birthday cake, but John was always deeply uneasy about parties like this. Quite simply, he believed that if he went around advertising his age he would lose work. And as, apart from Martin, work was really all he had to live for, he remained determined to do nothing that could in any way endanger his employability. It was also in this mood, and at this time, that he (like Emlyn Williams and Alec Guinness) wrote the will that came as such a surprise to many on his death in 2000, ordaining a totally private funeral and that there should be no memorial service of any kind. They had perhaps attended all too many of these already, and feared for the casting and audience make-up of a production over which they would, inevitably, have no control at all.

There was also another birthday book, this one called *The Ages of Gielgud*, edited by Ronald Harwood, in which Derek Granger attempted, as had Tynan so many years earlier, to work out what separated the great actor-knights. 'If Olivier is fire, thunder, animal magnetism and danger, and Richardson is bemused wonder, slyness and compassion, then John is poetic sensibility, philosophical intro-spection, detachment, reason, quicksilver wit, and everything that is expressive of an intense inner life.'

John himself had now taken very occasionally to commenting on Olivier. He never said in public how sad he felt that Olivier's intense, neurotic jealousy had always made him unable to be his friend, or how Olivier had on several occasions done his best to keep John well away from whatever theatre or movie he was currently organising. But John did allow himself to note: 'Larry seems to spend ages preparing for parts, doing gymnastics and things. I fear I am too lazy for all that. I just turn up on the set nowadays, and hope that inspiration will strike.'

In the old days, John had often joked that when his friends tired of his intense round-the-clock theatricality, they would simply stick a crown on his head and send him onstage. Now, even that option seemed closed to him. Awards were still coming his way from all over the world, and *Time* magazine jokingly described him now as the hot-test young actor around, one without whom it was all but impossible to make an English film. Several of his surviving colleagues and critics contributed essays to Ronald Harwood's birthday celebration volume, though John himself remained oddly uneasy:

I fear I no longer really enjoy my birthdays; in fact I no longer like public occasions of any kind. They tend to remind me how quickly time is passing, and regular events like Ascot or the Trooping of the Colour all seem to come around again much too fast. Also, I worry more and more about illness, and the death of so many of my friends. In my early days I used to have great ambitions, but I think I am much less impatient, and more philosophical now.

Away from the theatre, I have always been a very timid, shy, cowardly man, and I was only ever able to show my emotions through acting. I still find that true, but although I sometimes miss the rehearsals and the planning of productions nowadays, if I were to come back to the theatre I would also have to move back to London, and I really don't want that . . .

I am really in two minds about doing all the cameo roles I now get offered. Financially, they have been a godsend, because when my accountant died last year, I suddenly found I owed £70,000 in back tax, and I could never have paid that off had it not been for the films and the Californian wine commercials. On the other hand, I've only really been proud of two things I've done in the last ten years or so – the Alan Resnais *Providence*, and the television of *Brideshead*. I rather like being paid to go and perform on wonderful locations all over the world, and it means I never have to pay for a holiday, but I think there is a danger that if one keeps turning up in everything, the audience will get tired of me. I seem to have an enormous range of acquaintances, but maybe only a dozen real friends. I shun parties, gatherings, public dinners – all the stuff I used to enjoy so much. I can't drive a car. I can't shoot, or fish, or play cards. I have no inclination to go riding. I am not remotely capable of doing anything really, except acting, and I rather thank God I never had a family, as I don't think I would be very good, even with grandchildren.

Perhaps the most surprising of the essays was one by the drama critic Harold Hobson who, amazingly unaware, it would seem, of John's homosexuality, wrote:

I remember on one occasion asking him if he had ever thought of marriage . . . he said no, because he could not bear taking the

responsibility for someone else's life, or of children . . . In all the sixty
years that I have known Gielgud, I have never seen him otherwise than
poised and happy, buoyed up by his irrepressible enthusiasm . . . and
yet I have always felt that there is something in him which life has
not satisfied, and for which he is still constantly searching. Of all the
people I have known in the theatre, he is the man who goes about
most constantly questioning. He gives me the impression of someone
who, deep down in himself, knows that there are fundamental things
which he does not comprehend, and who is determined to find them
out . . . Gielgud has a capacity to suggest ice which even at its thickest
yearns for the sun.

Invited, around this time, to a local dinner party, he was amazed
to find John Mortimer and his second wife Penny bringing their
new-born baby with them. Peering nervously into the carrycot, John
enquired, 'Why on earth would you bring it with you? Are you afraid
of burglars at home?'

When he wasn't actually working, or following Martin around the
garden with a wheelbarrow, John found himself becoming passionately attached to such American television series as *Dynasty* and
Dallas. Ever since his earliest silent film-going days he had acquired
a devotion to serials, one that only the small screen could now satisfy.
When he did come to London, it was only for the occasional meeting
with his agent, or lunch at the Garrick. 'I walk down Shaftesbury
Avenue, so close to where I spent most of my early life, and find I
can no longer recognise any of the names in lights.'

Although *Arthur* had brought John to a whole new and younger
audience around the world, his movie career could still be subject to
strange humiliations. He was, for instance, at this time paid very well
by Woody Allen to record the commentary for *Zelig*, only to be cut out
later because the director had found his voice 'altogether too grand'.
But there were also moments of such rare delight as a reunion after
more than forty years with the veteran Lillian Gish, who brought, for
his birthday, a pocket watch which had once belonged to the pioneer
silent film director D.W. Griffith. It was still in working order, and
John was to carry it for many more years.

His affection for radio drama, one that dated back to his relationship with his brother Val, who had only recently died, meant that he continued to be a familiar figure around the corridors of Broadcasting House, where he had by now recorded virtually all the major plays in the Shakespeare canon, but was also perfectly happy to turn up in such brand-new work as (in 1984) Rhys Adrian's wonderfully aptly titled *Passing Time*.

He also continued to write articles and essays about his now all-too-rapidly vanishing generation: 'How sadly I now miss Ralph's cheerful voice on the telephone, telling me of a new book he had just finished reading (a copy would arrive by the next post), and his patience with my chattering tongue – I have lost a most dear friend, and that loss is only equalled by the loss of one of the greatest men of the English theatre.' Apart from Peggy Ashcroft, there were really only two actors now who could be said to share Gielgud's greatness and many of his more reclusive characteristics, but precisely because both Alec Guinness and Paul Scofield shared John's distaste for any kind of social life, they too were now somewhat distanced by geography and inclination from John's daily life.

His eightieth birthday had prompted the *Evening Standard* to give him a Life Achievement Award for sixty years in the theatre; only Olivier, Ashcroft and Richardson had ever been so honoured.

A few weeks later, John went back to work as a Texan missionary in *Invitation to a Wedding*, all the while campaigning for a Theatre Museum in Covent Garden, and preparing for his next important role, as Major Sir Louis Cavagnari in M.M. Kaye's *The Far Pavilions*. This was a six-hour television mini-series, in which John was seen in shirt sleeves with a pistol defending the British Mission at Kabul against the Afghan rebels.

Occasionally now, as much out of boredom as anything else, John would invite the kind of journalist who could be trusted not to rake up his past, or make any mention of his life with Martin, to Wotton Underwood; one wrote in open-mouthed amazement of 'a vast drawing-room which might have been part of a palace, with its blue silk sofa, priceless vases and chandeliers, and the floor hand-painted with an intricate gold-feather design . . . three gardeners are required to toil outside on half-completed gazebos, flower-beds and patios.' Waving at the thirty-foot-high ceiling and the ornate carved gilt mouldings, John said, 'There's a certain kind of cosiness here, don't you think?' apparently wonderfully oblivious to the way that a bronze bust of himself, and candelabras in the downstairs lavatory, might strike less theatrical mortals.

He also, at this time, gave a long and thoughtful interview to Michiko Kakutani of the *New York Times*.

I have just begun to realise how very hermetic my life has been. What first attracted me to a life in the theatre were the gilt boxes and big curtains of the old London playhouses, their sentimental melodramas with noble heroes and evil villains, and the old-time stars with their fur coats and their grand gestures; but now I find there is not much in the West End that I want to see any more, so I stay in the country, keeping up with all the new actors and actresses by watching television, which spares me the embarrassment of having to go backstage and tell them what I thought of the play. The only thing I'm ashamed of is that the whole drama of life has totally passed me by. It wasn't until quite lately, when I started watching television, that I suddenly became aware of all the troubles and horrors of the world. I honestly had never noticed them before . . . I'm very helpless as a person. I've never understood politics, and I was never any good at games or sports . . . I love to have everything done for me, except of course in the theatre, where I do everything myself . . . except for reading and doing puzzles and going to art galleries, I have never had any hobbies at all . . . I still have a sort of dream of playing King Lear again, but now that Larry has done it on television, I think perhaps I won't. Acting is half shame and half glory. The shame of exhibiting yourself, the glory of forgetting yourself, but there is something about being eighty that seems to appeal to the public. Survival fascinates them – half the audience is amazed that I have lasted so long, and the other half think I am some sort of sacred monster and that they had better catch a final look at me before, as Noël once said, my death places that somewhat macabre pleasure beyond their reach.

And there was yet another birthday honour still to come, this, perhaps, the least likely of all: his recording of *The Ages of Man* won him the Grammy for best spoken-word disc of the year, the first non-American ever to receive this award.

Chapter Twenty-six

❦❦❦

THE BEST OF FRIENDS
(1984–1994)

The angel of death seems quite to have passed me by.

John continued making films almost as if they were going out of fashion. A minor role in *Gandhi* for Richard Attenborough was followed by a television appearance as Lord Durrisdeer in Robert Louis Stevenson's *The Master of Ballantrae*, this one provoking Daniel Farson in the *Daily Mail* to comment: 'If Gielgud is going to prostitute his talent by accepting such absurd parts as this one, he really should not give the impression that he is slumming in a smelly neighbourhood, or has just swallowed the juice of eleven lemons.' But there was better to come.

Early in the following year, he turned up in the film of David Hare's *Plenty* as the old-school diplomat who resigns at the time of Suez, putting honour before patriotism, a performance that drew a rave from Pauline Kael in the *New Yorker:* 'Gielgud can make you laugh by an almost imperceptible straightening of his hand or neck; there was an audibly happy stir from the audience each time he appeared, and when he makes an exit speech, you pity the poor actors who are left behind, because he invariably takes all the energy of the scene out the door with him.'

After *Plenty*, came *Romance on the Orient Express*, an American television drama starring Cheryl Ladd, in which John played an ageing executive and, also for television, a nostalgic appearance as the patriarch of an eccentric Anglo-Irish family living in a derelict house in County Wicklow. John's reason for doing this was simply that it derived from a novel, *Time After Time*, by his old friend Molly Keane, now enjoying an autumnal kind of fame, and a supporting cast included Trevor Howard, Googie Withers, Helen Cherry, Ursula Howells, Brenda Bruce and Freddie Jones. The filming, for BBC2, brought back charmed memories of a world that John and Molly had once shared, when indeed he had become godfather to her daughter Sally: 'All of us who were brought up in the Edwardian era can't help but regret the passing of the big house. We were all at ease there, servant and master. We were fearfully arrogant, but I do miss that mixture of privacy and ostentation. I miss the extravagance of those times.' Asked by Googie why he had never given her a job, John replied brutally, 'Because you have such a stupid name'.

From Ireland, John and the faithful Mavis Walker went straight to Paris, where John had now located some useful European employers who specialised in what he memorably called 'potted classics'. The first of these had been *The Hunchback of Notre Dame*, and now came *Camille* in which John once again had just a couple of scenes as the Duc de Charles, protector of Marguerite Gautier as played by the young Greta Scacchi. As so often, the fun here was entirely the chance for John to catch up with such old friends as Denholm Elliot, Billie Whitelaw and Rachel Kempson.

Next came an appearance as the writer John Middleton Murry, in a film about his life with Katherine Mansfield (*Leave All Fair*), and then, for BBC schools television, a classical double, playing Tiresias in Sophocles' *Antigone* and *Oedipus the King*.

John also found the time, now, to round up three surviving members of the *Hamlet* company which forty-six years earlier had closed the Lyceum Theatre. He, Harry Andrews, Andrew Cruickshank and Marius Goring wrote to *The Times*:

We members of that *Hamlet* company bade a sad farewell to the Lyceum; however the threatened demolition and translation into a traffic roundabout were mercifully averted by the outbreak of war. But today, the same owner, now the GLC, is deliberating whether to perpetuate the 200-year-old Lyceum's temporary post-war service as a ballroom, or rather to encourage its restoration to full theatrical use . . . We now welcome another generation's rediscovery of this great theatre, and we echo the last words spoken from that stage in 1939: 'Long live the Lyceum! Long live Henry Irving! Long live Ellen Terry!' A theatre with such resonance of the past and such promise for the future cannot be allowed to perish.

And, amazingly, it wasn't; unlike so many other campaigns for doomed theatres, such as Vivien Leigh's memorably manic crusade for the St James's, this one actually worked, and after another few years of uncertainty the Lyceum was handsomely refurbished and restored to become the home for such major musicals as a revival of *Jesus Christ Superstar*, and *The Lion King*.

John also now took on a long and punishing role in *War and Remembrance*, an epic twelve-hour American television series for which he played a victim of the Nazis in concentration-camp sequences that were truly horrific, both to shoot and to watch. This entire series was in fact a sequel to *The Winds of War*, also by Herman Wouk. In that, Gielgud's character had first been played by the John Houseman who had produced him in *Julius Caesar*. 'The sequel,' he said, 'takes place all over Europe, in gas chambers and crematoria. I think Gielgud's figure will be more convincing in a state of emaciation than mine could ever be.'

As Mavis Walker recalled,

War and Remembrance was incredibly punishing for Gielgud. One week they filmed in three different countries, and although John felt enormous sympathy for the character, he was keen not to make it sentimental.

I rather see him as a kind of Bernard Berenson, a self-centred and bookish kind of man, who doesn't mix with the ordinary world very much. We finished up in Yugoslavia where John had to be filmed being thrown naked on to a pit of dead bodies. He never admitted to being tired, although he did once say how awkward it would be if he were to die in real life. The six-month shooting schedule was really punishing; long tramps through the snow, or through the blazing heat, according to the season. Standing about in the rain, real and artificial, waiting to board the death trains to Auschwitz. An interminable walk at night to the gas chamber. Sitting there stark naked, and enduring the overheated atmosphere and the smell of humanity. Finally, lying on a stretcher and pretending to be put into a red-hot burning furnace. At the end of it all, I told John how terribly moving I had found it. 'Yes,' he said. 'And what's more, I even managed to finish the crossword.'

John's attitude to these tragic scenes is always professional. As he says, 'I try not to be too aware of the horror of it all. I don't allow the setting to interfere any more than in the theatre I ever allow the scenery to overwhelm me. I suppose I am slightly dismayed to be making money out of the sort of horrors that people suffered – still, it's all a part of acting.'

During the shooting in Cracow several weeks later, John was able to introduce Herman Wouk to some young and distant cousins whom he had managed to track down – almost the only occasion when John was to have any contact at all with his father's side of the family.

When, several year earlier, John had taken his *Ages of Man* to Warsaw, he had become fascinated with the young Soviet actors and playwrights, as the then cultural attaché at the British Embassy, Alan Brooks Turner, recalls:

'We gave a dinner for Sir John, so that he could meet some of the more interesting theatre people, at which he explained almost apologetically how hard it was for him to find work in new plays. Years later the dinner party became the basis for a rather Chekhovian short story by Yuri Kazakov, but I think my lasting memory of John in Moscow was taking him to a Russian church where we found six babies in cots awaiting baptism and one old man in an open coffin awaiting burial. "Now," said Sir John, "I really have seen everything – the Ages of Man indeed."'

With some relief, through the end of 1985 and well into 1986, he then took on three infinitely easier roles: as the headmaster of the language school in a television version of Simon Gray's *Quartermaine's Terms* (a role he had rejected on stage); also for television, he turned up in a ludicrous updating of Oscar Wilde's *The Canterville Ghost*; and then on the wide screen as a KGB mole in Michael Caine's *The Whistle Blower*. He also, on a brief but luxurious location in Venice, celebrated his eighty-third birthday while making a real curiosity, a film called *Barbalu, Barbalu*, in which he played an aged Bluebeard, on to his third marriage. John, the only English speaker in the film, was dubbed into Italian, from a soundtrack that never reverted to English.

The four other films that John completed in these still workaholic 1980s were of little merit. One was yet another glossy but soft-centred Agatha Christie thriller (*Appointment with Death*), with Peter Ustinov now replacing Albert Finney as Hercule Poirot, and another was a catastrophic sequel to *Arthur* (*Arthur II*) which started Dudley Moore's precipitate Hollywood decline. For John, this merely involved a few lovely days just before Christmas, filming in New York, and organising reunion dinners with Irene Worth and Lillian Gish whom, he told a rather surprised Mavis Walker, was the only woman he might ever have married, if only he could have found the courage to ask her. The day after the filming finished, Mavis with some difficulty obtained two tickets for Peter Brook's sold-out, nine-hour *Mahabarata*. John considered the prospect for a moment. Then, he told Mavis, 'I think you had better go, and tell me all about it. I shall be at the matinée of *Anything Goes*.'

The other two films he made at this time were a dire comedy loosely based on a novel by Elizabeth Jane Howard about a hairdresser in the London of the Swinging Sixties (*Getting It Right*), and a pointless remake of Graham Greene's *Loser Takes All* with John in the role of the sinister millionaire (one that had been turned down by both Alec Guinness and Max Wall), based on Alexander Korda and played in the 1956 original by Robert Morley. This new version, starring Robert Lindsay and Molly Ringwald, proved uneventful for John, except for one sequence on a yacht, when a sudden swell threw the ship broadside, landing him in a heap of lighting apparatus with very sharp edges. To the relief of the crew, he picked himself up unhurt, and sat down to light a cigarette. From his earliest days in pictures with Alfred Hitchcock, he said, he had always been taught how to fall.

At the end of these few days' filming in Nice and Cannes, John drove up into the hills above Eze to meet his former sister-in-law, Zita Gordon, once married to Lewis but now living in considerable luxury and eager to tell John about her daughter Maina, who was already making a name for herself in the Australian Ballet.

As these 1980s came to an end, John had the chance to make a farewell appearance in the West End, as well as the film he had always yearned for: Shakespeare's *The Tempest*, as now drastically revised by Peter Greenaway.

Coming in to the Apollo, Hugh Whitemore's *The Best of Friends* was an epistolary play in the tradition of *Dear Liar* and *84 Charing Cross Road*, but built this time around three people (the playwright Bernard Shaw, the Fitzwilliam Museum director Sydney Cockerell and the Stanbrook abbess Laurentia McLochlan), who for most of their long lives wrote a marathon series of letters to each other. Those letters made up the whole of this evening. Whitemore wisely did not attempt to dramatise anything that was not already in the correspondence, and so what we got is what they wrote about: distant memories of Cockerell's lunch with Tolstoy, Shaw's thoughts on being offered the Nobel Prize ('I can forgive that man for inventing dynamite, but only a fiend incarnate could have invented the prize'), ideas about travel, sex, friendship, careers, and of course religion – in which last area the formidable abbess was dominant, never more so than when banishing Shaw from her friendship for several years for having dared to write *The Black Girl in Search of God*.

The Best of Friends was admittedly the kind of play you expect to hear in the middle of a Radio 4 afternoon, but its overriding importance was that it brought John back to the London theatre after an absence of ten years, for what he well knew would be his farewell stage performance, not least because, despite an almost sold-out run of four months, he never entirely managed to learn it. Though he never announced this as a farewell performance, audiences seemed somehow to sense that they were never going to see him again in the flesh, except possibly at an increasing number of other actors' memorial services for which he was still much in demand.

But as farewell characters go, Cockerell was a little gem; by his own admission, he was a collector of the famous, a man so cautious that he had bought his engagement ring on sale or return, and eventually a museum curator ageing happily in the knowledge that he could still afford an egg with his tea. While Ray McAnally as a jovial Shaw and Rosemary Harris as the abbess were allowed occasional bursts of irritation and anger, John's Cockerell moved sublimely and gracefully, if forgetfully, through their triangular friendship, the orchestrator of a rich and rare conversation piece which concluded with him alone in the spotlight, the sole survivor of the trio, noticing that the angel of death seemed quite to have passed him by. It was a solo moment of breathtaking theatrical poetry at the end of an evening of whimsical and wayward charm, and few of us who saw it could have failed to realise that here, too, was John's very own farewell to the West End where he had now been working for all of sixty-six years.

During the run at the Apollo, the new British Theatre Museum in Covent Garden was finally opened, after much political and financial wrangling, and several campaigns in which John had always played his part; now he was delighted to find that the museum contained its very own Gielgud Gallery, and walking around the exhibits he was able to find memories of Ellen Terry, Lilian Baylis and all the theatrical figures of his own past. He also found, somewhat to his surprise, a portrait of himself as Hamlet: 'Amazing, I can't ever remember selling that to anyone, but I suppose I might have given it away. The artist was Nigel Newton, brother of the actor Bobbie who was a legendary drunk. Did you know that when he died they found two hundred empty bottles of whisky at the bottom of a lake in his garden? I love seeing all this, but I really don't think I want to be immortalised any more. I really must stop living in the past, although I do find it absolutely fascinating.'

While he was playing in the West End, several magazines took the opportunity for what were effectively to be the last profiles of John as a working West End star.

Here he comes [wrote Nicholas de Jongh for the *Illustrated London News*] striding with that quick, young man's walk into his eighty-fourth autumn; broad-shouldered, back as straight as a schoolboy's ruler, memory clear as a bell, eyes a little hooded, but not missing a trick. He looks like a Harley Street physician in his early sixties, or a recently retired Permanent Under-Secretary. For Gielgud is still in a lucky and long Indian summer, at a time when the best of his acting generation have mostly shuffled from the limelight or been laid to rest. He has dodged the sly, persistent ambushes of old age – apart from twinges of lumbago – as if to ensure that he could go on working at full stretch; the need to act still courses through his blood. It is his adrenalin and his addiction, and he could never voluntarily retire.

And yet, although he has been all his life the most extrovert of performers, tearing passions to a tatter of tears and grief, he is himself a natural introvert. There are in him traces of unease, and that air of studied aloofness, a sense of mountain-high remoteness. But such *froideurs* are compensated for by the fantastic fizz, dazzle and exhilarating comedy of Gielgud caught in conversation. His mind is like a butterfly. It skims, darts and settles in a helter-skelter of insight, opinion, revelation and analysis, not to mention gossip.

Honours were now raining down on him from all sides. The Theatre Museum staged its largest-ever celebration of his career, and RADA, of which he had so long been president, made him its first-ever Honorary Fellow, thereby allowing the new Princess of Wales to succeed him as president.

John was now beginning to allow himself, in occasional interviews, to speak his mind in a way that he never had before. Talking to me during the run of *The Best of Friends*, he said:

I really hate the new National Theatre. It looks like an aircraft hangar, and the dressing-rooms are all so uncomfortable. The only decent theatre is the Cottesloe, and even that is like a coffin. I tried to persuade them to put a nice big sign on the roof to brighten it up, but they said the architect would never allow it. As for the Barbican, it looks like a hospital, and there really is no point any longer in coming up to London. Most of my friends now seem to be either dead, extremely deaf, or living in the wrong part of Kent, and when I go backstage after a play, the cast all regard me as some terrible old Dalai Lama come to give them advice. Which I never do, as it always leads to trouble.

The truth is that I also hate a lot of what is happening in the modern theatre, especially the idea some directors have that they must impose their own ideas on a classic text. In my time we knew the audience had enough trouble just dealing with the verse, let alone a lot of 'relevance' rubbish as well. I find I still yearn, though, for a theatrical routine, the night after night of improving or changing a performance rather than sitting around in some caravan abroad, waiting for a film crew to get themselves organisée. I fill up the time, when I can't find a crossword, by listing to myself the names of all my schoolfriends at Westminster three-quarters of a century ago, or the names of all the assistant stage-managers when I started at the Old Vic in the 1920s. Rather embarrassingly, I find I can recall all of those accurately, but almost never the name of the film director I am currently working for.

I'm not altogether sure I like this sudden burst of interest in me. It's probably because journalists and producers all think I'm about to die. Most of the scripts I get sent nowadays are about men at death's door, and the television people keep saying they want to film a celebration of my life, when I know very well that what they really want is to have the obituary ready in the can in case I suddenly pop off.

I've reached an age now where I really dread talking to people unless they are very old friends . . . I do miss Ralph terribly, although I was never really nearly as close to Larry. We had a kind of love-hate thing, and I think he thought me basically rather frivolous. Whenever I went to stay for the weekend it was always at Vivien's invitation, and Larry seemed to be disguising himself for the next role, always keeping a beady eye on what I was doing. A few years ago he suddenly said, 'Not thinking of another *Lear* by any chance are you, old boy?' and I knew that he had probably got one in mind . . . As for Ralph, he always said that it was disgraceful of me to appear in those California wine commercials and that a classical actor should never dirty his hands with work like that. Months later I discovered that he had slyly gone off and done one himself for Concorde. My real ambition was to do one for underwear which would start with me saying, 'At my time of life, all is quiet on the Y-front.'

The director James Roose-Evans recalled:

After the last matinée of *Best of Friends*, and before the final perfor-mance at the Apollo, John said to Ray McAnally, 'Tonight is the last night,' meaning that he would not return to the stage again . . . he had returned in triumph, and that was enough. The audience that night must have sensed this, even though they did not know it, for at the curtain call, as Rosemary Harris and Ray McAnally deliberately stepped away from Gielgud, leaving him alone at the centre of the stage (something they had never done before because, in the nature of the play, they had always shared the curtain call) the entire audience rose to its feet, stalls to circle, circle to upper circle and gallery, cheering, pouring out its gratitude for the greatness and gentleness and wit . . . and for his lifetime of work in the theatre.

At the time of this interview, John and Larry had been regularly appearing together for some years in front of a television audience on the satirical programme *Spitting Image*, whose caricature puppets were matched by some remarkable vocal impressions. They were portrayed as a couple of old luvvies constantly mourning the passing of colleagues or commenting on current ones, always using the preface 'Dear, dear' before the name of the thespian in question. Olivier's puppet was given an expression of pinched malice, which matched his usually caustic comments, while Gielgud's was a gentle, other-worldly creature with an elegiac approach to life.

That life was now increasingly spent in retrospection; John Miller, the producer for whom he had recorded his epic series of radio interviews, put together a television programme in which John was again able to reflect on the changes in the British theatre through which he had lived, from Pinter all the way back to Pinero. At the same time Gielgud published yet another slender volume of memoirs, this one largely made up of the reprinted *Distinguished Company*, and a further selection of profiles of the leading characters of his past.

As another actor, Paul Daneman, who was with Gielgud at the Old Vic in *Richard II* and on a television *Antigone*, noted in his review: 'Gielgud's gossip should never be mistaken for mere actor's tattle . . . he illuminates a whole lost world of theatre in the first half of this century, a theatre dominated by commercial interests and imperious personalities and still undisturbed by the inroads of cinema and radio and television. When he describes walking down Shaftesbury Avenue, seeing an open taxi slowly driving along, and Elisabeth Bergner sitting on the hood with flowers in her lap, waving to a mass of shouting fans, it seems hard to believe that it's the same sleazy old traffic jam we struggle through today . . . Gielgud recaptures the excitement of going to the theatre, as opposed to just being there.'

John G's next assignment was to rejoin Charlton Heston, for

whom he had played Julius Caesar, in yet another pointless television remake, this one of Robert Bolt's *A Man For All Seasons*, which had already been definitively filmed by Paul Scofield for Fred Zinnemann. But Heston had long been giving stage appearances as Sir Thomas More, and now he was determined to commit it to film, with Vanessa Redgrave as his wife, and John Gielgud as a rather thinner Cardinal Wolsey than the original Orson Welles. Heston and Redgrave had already played *Macbeth* on stage in Los Angeles, a production mainly notable for the efforts of the redoubtable Australian actress Coral Browne to get tickets for the first night. Having tried with no success in both her own name and that of her husband Vincent Price, she decided to dial the box-office one more time: 'Hello,' she said, to a surprised box-office manager. 'I'd like two tickets for just after the interval of the first night of the Charlton Heston *Macbeth*.' By that time of the evening, she could have had several dozen.

Back on the set of *A Man For All Seasons*, John now reflected that what you really got paid for as a screen actor was the hours you sat around waiting for something to happen. The acting he did for nothing; it was the waiting he charged for, and he was no longer sure that he approved of all the attention he was getting in an old age now sustained by a nourishing diet of wine and cigarettes and no exercise of any kind: 'Now I have people calling me Sir John, and opening doors for me, but I've never demanded, or even wanted, all this red-carpet treatment. I like it when the technicians just shove past me, calling me John. The one thing about being eighty-four is that you must never risk being ill, because everyone then thinks you are done for, and I am really terrified of that.'

John was therefore still determined to keep his screen career in overdrive. Pausing only to appear as Virgil in several episodes of a quirky television version of Dante's *Inferno* for Peter Greenaway, John now went to work in Italy on what was to be his last sustained television serial.

John Mortimer, who had already given John one of his best television roles in *Brideshead Revisited*, had now adapted his own bestselling *Summer's Lease* for the small screen. This was essentially an elegantly comic look at the British in Tuscany, and for it Mortimer had created one of his best comic roles, that of Haverford Downs, a spry, elderly, would-be roué living on memories both real and imagined, and the precarious proceeds of his weekly column 'Jottings from Chiantishire'.

In the novel Downs was a rather subsidiary character, but by the time John had taken him over for the screen, there was no doubt about who was going to run away with the series, much as he had with *Brideshead*.

It was not to be an easy shoot. The plan was to spend two months living outside Siena, but halfway through the filming John was shocked to hear over the phone of the death of his lifelong opposite number, Laurence Olivier. The two men had never exactly been best friends, yet John now found himself feeling suddenly bereft:

> Now that Larry is gone, I cannot help feeling sad, and somewhat ashamed too, that I did not strive to know him better, as our careers and ambition spanned so many of the same years. Of course, we acted many of the same classical parts, and the press hinted of rivalry between us, which was not the truth . . . to me, he seemed personally rather secretive, and knowing my frivolous and often indiscreet nature, he never confided to me his fears or deepest thoughts. I was happy to feel sure that in his last marriage to Joan Plowright he achieved so much private joy, and lived to delight in the children he had always longed for. He was certainly the proud successor to the very great ones – Kean and Irving – and he respected tradition, while delighting in breaking it . . . I shall always think of him as one of the most brilliant, gifted, indefatigable and controversial figures of our time, and I am very proud to have been lucky enough to be his contemporary and colleague over these long, eventful years.

He did not use the word 'friend'. A few months later, John was to read Donne's sonnet 'Death Be Not Proud' at Olivier's epic, majestic, wildly over-the-top memorial service in Westminster Abbey. John, Peggy Ashcroft, Alec Guinness and John Mills were now the surviving quartet of the greatest generation of actors the world had ever known, but for John G at least, the Olivier memorial was a bridge too far. He found it inexpressibly vulgar and curiously impertinent to the memory of the statesmen and monarchs who were also buried, in his view rather more rightfully, within the Abbey. As for Kean's sword, which John had handed over to Olivier as part of an ongoing custom in the British theatre whereby one great Hamlet saluted the next, it all stopped with Olivier, who let it be known to general amazement that he now regarded the sword as his in perpetuity, whatever the historical precedent. It thus went with Olivier even unto the grave.

Back in Siena, on the *Summer's Lease* location, there was worse to come. A few weeks after hearing of Olivier's death, John himself collapsed with a blood clot in his leg and had to be flown home to hospital near Aylesbury. Determined not to acquire a reputation for being ill and therefore uninsurable and so unemployable, John struggled back to the location and completed the filming only a week behind schedule, later collecting yet another clean sweep of glowing reviews.

Back home at Wotton Underwood, John's health continued to be fragile; he'd been forced to miss a gala lunch for his eighty-fifth birthday earlier in 1989, and a good deal of his time was now taken up with writing obituaries or regretful letters to the papers about the death of yet another friend – Anthony Quayle was one who died towards the end of this year.

To keep working now became a kind of urgency; no longer was the money really essential, although Martin was still perfectly capable of going through it at more than reasonable speed, but for John the next assignment was really the only indication that he was still desirable. Having taken on a new agent, Paul Lyon Maris, he could now command £50,000 for a day's work on film or television, though for this rate he would usually throw in the second or third day for free. His time was also now taken up increasingly in paying tribute to deceased contemporaries in a vast range of television documentaries. In one week of 1989 alone, he paid eloquent and elegant tributes to Vivien Leigh, Coral Browne and Michael Redgrave. For all of these, he was filmed sitting on one of the magnificent sofas in Wotton Underwood, telling stories both touching and irreverent, as he delved back into his own shared heritage with the dramatic deceased.

He also at this time did a long interview on the stage of the Playhouse with David Frost for American television, and began to work on a massive two-part *Omnibus* which was to go out a year later, as well as to narrate a *South Bank Show* on the composer Hindemith.

It was not, however, until the beginning of 1991, by which time he had also published a new collection of Shakespearean essays, that he finally got the offer to make what was not only to be his last major film appearance, but also the one that he had most desired. A film of *The Tempest* had been on his wish list since he had first played Prospero more than half a century earlier. Many previous attempts had failed for lack of financing, and at eighty-seven he was now being at last offered it by Peter Greenaway who (with *The Draughtsman's Contract* and the television Dante in which John had appeared as Virgil) was making his name as an eccentrically individualist film director. As John recalled:

> I had always wanted to make this film, more than any other. Prospero has always been a favourite part, and I felt that the magical aspects of the play would work very well on screen. The problem has always been to find the right director. I wrote a synopsis myself years ago, which I passed around a few friends, and I remember having long conversations with Benjamin Britten about the soundtrack – he wanted to use real sounds like crashing seas, cries, shouts and footsteps on flagstones for the early part of the film.
>
> I then had wild ideas about Kurosawa and setting it as a Japanese fairy tale, but I could never find anyone who knew where he lived. I wrote to Ingmar Bergman, who sent me a telegram explaining that his English wasn't up to it, and eventually I talked to Alain Resnais and Giorgio Strehler, and Derek Jarman asked me to be in his television version, as did the BBC, but I turned them both down – somehow I must have had a feeling that this film was just around the corner, and quite soon Peter Greenaway rang me with the offer not only of Prospero, but of reading the whole of the rest of the text on the soundtrack.
>
> We filmed for four months in Amsterdam, and I had to wear the most extraordinarily heavy cloak, which took four people to put it on me. Back in 1934 I said that Shakespeare was not a good idea for the screen, but since then we have had Larry's *Henry V* and Orson Welles's *Chimes at Midnight*, and I have had to reconsider my opinion.

When *Prospero's Books* first opened at the New York Film Festival in

November 1991, Vincent Canby reviewed 'a movie which is a kind of obsessed collector's inventory of the Renaissance – its thought, art, architecture, religion, superstition, music and painting . . . this tumultuously over-packed movie is less a screen adaptation of Shakespeare's haunting and elegiac last play than a grand jumping-off spot for a work that will make some people run for the exits, and others more than angry at the liberties taken . . . Gielgud holds his own against all of the magnificent technical effects, but only just.'

Inevitably, however, this was to be Greenaway's rather than Gielgud's vision of *The Tempest*. It had such brilliant conceits as the opening storm sequence beginning with a single drop of water in immense close-up, splashing into Prospero's outstretched palm. But as the film went on, the decision by Greenaway to load whole layers of other meanings on to the Shakespearean original meant that John was somehow out of his depth. Greenaway himself agreed with Donald Sinden that Gielgud alone could speak Shakespeare as though he had written it: 'We got on very well, though as usual the studio in Amsterdam meant ninety per cent waiting and ten per cent frenetic activity. John never seemed to tire and eventually I thought of him as Prospero/Gielgud, the puppetmaster who writes and speaks the words so that he in his double role and Shakespeare are really all one and the same. We also had a great choreographer, Michael Clark, and although as usual the English critical reaction was rearguard and shocked, around the rest of the world the film has done a great deal better and I think that Gielgud really trusted me. Our Ariel, by the way, was a grandson of Charlie Chaplin.'

As for John: 'I wanted to leave something behind as a record of my Shakespearean work, and it's the only part that I was the right age for. I do hope that it's all right. I was so frightened that I would come out very hammy and old-fashioned and declamatory, having played it so often on stage. It was an extraordinary appearance; one morning Peter told me to take off all my clothes and be naked in the bath, and there were all these girls and fat women in the nude, but after a day or two one had completely forgotten. I don't think it offends in the least, except in Japan, where they have had to cut out all the genitals.'

Greenaway was to recall John 'thoroughly amused by the entourage, naked except for their body paint; he made a lot of unrepeatable jokes'. For *Prospero's Books*, as for *Caligula*, John seemed to be giving over a surprising amount of his late-life screen time to frolicking in pools surrounded by naked men and girls.

While John was in Amsterdam, news came of the deaths of both Peggy Ashcroft and Ralph Richardson, and he was somewhat unnerved to hear a reporter murmuring audibly, 'I suppose this one will be the next to go.'

Prospero's Books duly opened a few months later, to surprisingly mixed reviews. Greenaway himself wrote of John as 'the still, calm figure in the midst of all my pyrotechnical extravagance – whatever else is going on in the film, it is always Gielgud you watch.' John himself, however, was sharply aware of the problems here:

I think the film is original and fascinating, but very over-elaborate. I liked Greenaway very much; he assembled a strong cast, with Mark Rylance (soon to direct Shakespeare's Globe) as Ferdinand, and because Greenaway is a painter himself, strongly influenced by Tintoretto and Titian, he organises and choreographs all his scenes with remarkable taste and feeling for depth and colour. With him, I had the same feeling I'd had with Peter Brook and Granville-Barker, and Lindsay Anderson and Peter Hall and Alain Resnais, but no other directors in my entire career, that I could really trust his judgement and criticism, and put myself entirely in his hands . . . Above all, I was greatly impressed by Greenaway's control. A very quiet man who never raises his voice, he walked about the studio all day long, never sat down, and seemed to work equally easily with the sound man who was British, the lighting man who was French, and a mixed crew, many of whom were Dutch . . . there was no hammering or tantrums or bad behaviour, and for once the whole thing was wonderfully organised.

True, there did seem to be an awful lot of people sitting around without clothes, and I wasn't always quite sure what Greenaway really wanted, but I did my best to go along with it.

For the *Independent*, Anthony Lane had severe reservations:

It is all very well asking us to imagine the whole of *The Tempest* being played out on the stage of Prospero's capacious brain . . .

he can wheedle his enemies into the storm as he splashes about in his bath, or freeze them as if they were celluloid and he the divine projectionist. Gielgud's Prospero is sadist, conjuror and scribe . . . he bosses everyone else around and speaks almost all the lines, rolling the pentameters around like an archbishop tasting burgundy . . . the trouble is that Greenaway, unlike Shakespeare, never bothers to make it clear who anybody is – the men all wear ruffs the size of dustbin lids and the kind of platform clogs that you would hire from Elton John . . . Oh, wow, you think, isn't that Tom Bell, imagine him dressed up like that, what a plonker he must feel . . . and isn't that the baldie from *Monsieur Hire*? And look, that's the guy from all the Bergman films. Hang on, you must be Gonzalo, so which is Antonio, and where the hell is Sebastian? Michael Nyman's music still parps on in its dreary Rolf Harris stylophone way, and finally the players break off and sidle past the camera, looking really embarrassed. Our revels now are ended, and thank God.

And, as Douglas Brode added: 'whereas Shakespeare, in his own theatrical endgame, provides answers in *The Tempest* that more or less explain the meaning of life (which is that the secret to happiness is maintaining a perpetual, if guarded sense of optimism despite endless disappointments) Greenaway only wants to transform the play into another of his cinematic conundrums, which are puzzles without any answers, less truly complex than simply confusing.'

On his return to England, John went to work, suitably enough, as God, in a BBC Radio dramatisation of the Book of Genesis, and then put together, with his faithful chronicler John Miller, a collection of his thoughts on the acting of Shakespeare. He also began to get his own back on those who he thought had treated him harshly, notably the recently deceased Kenneth Tynan: 'He said I only had two gestures, the left hand up, or the right hand up. What did he want me to do, get out my prick?' Looking back at his 1950s *King Lear*, he also noted:

I should have remembered that you have to have a light Cordelia. Peggy Ashcroft was wonderful, but lifting her in the last act every night made me wish I had never taken up the bloody classics . . . I suppose the irony is that now I feel just about ready to play anything,

I am either too old or I simply don't feel like doing it. I also don't approve of all the modern invasions into people's privacy – it must be so embarrassing for the family. One of the great difficulties of the modern world is that people want to intrude now into the private life of celebrities. After *Arthur* they set up five separate fan clubs for me in Germany, and when I was filming in Berlin people laid in wait for me outside my hotel. It was all most extraordinary.

Nor am I really any good at television chat shows – I am sick of becoming a club bore, and trotting out all the old stories. We know that Nell Gwyn sold oranges outside the Drury Lane Theatre, but once she became the mistress of the King, she no longer had to go on selling. But look at me . . . I'm also now getting very embarrassed by Ian McKellen, who keeps on asking me to join him in all sorts of gay demonstrations. I always refuse – they exploit the exhibitionist side of one's nature, which should be kept for one's acting. If I have any regrets, it is that I have led a very narrow life. Looking back, I wish I had been called up into the war, because however bad a soldier I would have been, I would at least have met all kinds of different people.

Peter Conrad, writing of John for the *New York Times*, observed that:

he is now undergoing something perilously like an apotheosis . . . his Prospero is also a revelation of Sir John himself – simultaneously noble and naughty, a high priest and a joker, contemplating at the end of a long life the value of the art he practises . . . what other voice can be an orchestra of special effects – as mellifluous as a violin, as plaintive as a clarinet, and occasionally as ominous as a kettle drum.

In private, he seems to have no Prospero-like regrets, although he does consider Greenaway's film to be both a summary of his career, and a formal farewell to it . . . he now resembles a cross between a rural colonel, with his thin white moustache and a corduroy smoking jacket, and an impish, worldly, ruddy Abbot . . . Sir John's character remains complex and contradictory: his English gentility always vies with his Slavic melancholy.

In another interview around this time, John was as usual asked to explain the longevity of his stage career:

Perhaps it is that I never think about a part too much in advance. I always go into it like a game of charades, I always have, and that seems to keep it reasonably fresh. But years ago I watched the actress Ethel Barrymore doing a death scene three times in three different plays during one year, and I thought how awful it must be, having dress-rehearsals for your own death; but now I, too, seem to be dying rather too much. I always used to think that when I got very old, I would end up in Hollywood as a grand old character man, rather like Sir C. Aubrey Smith, playing ambassadors. But it hasn't happened like that and I am glad, I really should prefer to die in England. The graveyards seem so much friendlier over here.

Even now, John's publicity was not always favourable; there was an embarrassing row when he failed to turn up at Cambridge to receive an honorary doctorate from the university, and there was worse to come when a new history of the Second World War revealed that in March 1940 John had joined Sybil Thorndike and George Bernard Shaw in signing a secret letter to the then Prime Minister Neville Chamberlain, urging him to make peace with Hitler. But John, still bleakly uninterested in politics, was doubtless merely trying to get the lights back on in the West End, and it was reckoned unlikely that Chamberlain had even received the letter. Certainly, it was never answered.

John's visits to London were becoming increasingly rare, and nearly always only in order to speak at the memorial service of yet another beloved theatrical friend. His routine was now very simple. He and Martin had taken on an assistant gardener, Vincent, and a driver, Peter, both of whom were to stay with John until the end of his life. In the meantime, with Peter driving, John would belt down the M40 to the actors' church, St Paul's in Covent Garden, where, usually late because of the traffic, he would simply walk firmly up into the pulpit and deliver 'Fear No More the Heat of the Sun' from *Cymbeline*. This was always fine, and often followed by lunch at the Garrick Club across the road, unless of course the funeral happened to be taking place in some altogether other church. On those occasions, while Donald Sinden or Michael Denison were having to fill in for the absent Gielgud, a totally strange family who happened to be using the Covent Garden church for their funeral would stand around afterwards in some amazement wondering how it was that their own dear deceased had known Sir John so well, without ever telling them.

And now, another of the classical players with whom he started was to leave the stage; in January 1992 Gwen Ffrangcon-Davies died at 101, and a few months later Lillian Gish, his Broadway Ophelia, was also to go, in her middle nineties.

For John, however, it was work as usual. Soon after *Prospero's Books*, he returned to BBC Radio to play a more traditional *Tempest* for the World Service, and then to television for the filming of his last stage role in *The Best of Friends*. Once that was completed, he went to Germany to play the role of a resistance worker in a dire Michael Douglas/Melanie Griffith wartime thriller called *Shining Through*.

In 1992 he also played briefly in a French movie (*Puissance de L'Ange*) and, with Richard Briers (and Kenneth Branagh as director), made a heart-breaking appearance in *Swan Song*, the brief Chekhov script about an old actor, Svet Lovidov, trying to recall his days of glory, one which he had first played in troop concerts in the war. But now the major movies no longer seemed to need him, even as a character player. Undeterred and still determined to get out of the house whenever possible, he began to make frequent appearances in such television dramas or mini-series as could still afford him. Accordingly, between 1993 and 1999, he was to be found to greater or lesser advantage in episodes of *Inspector Morse*, *Under the Hammer*, *Summer's Daydream*, *Scarlett*, *Lovejoy*, *Inspector Alleyn*, *Gulliver's Travels*, *Dance to the Music of Time* and *Merlin*. Additionally he also made a fleeting appearance in Al Pacino's documentary, *Looking For Richard*, in which he somewhat patronisingly explained that Europeans were usually better than Americans at Shakespeare because they read more widely, and had often been rather better educated.

In this same period, effectively the last five years of his working life, he also appeared briefly on the wide screen in *First Knight*, *Haunted*, *Portrait of a Lady*, *Shine*, the Kenneth Branagh *Hamlet*, *Dragonheart*, *Elizabeth* and *The Tichborne Claimant*, not to mention further documentary appearances in programmes about Noël Coward, Edmund Kean and Sergei Rachmaninov.

For an actor now in his nineties this was a remarkable achievement.

Even allowing for the fact that he would not usually put in more than two or three days on any one production, and that in one or two of his last appearances he can clearly be seen reading lines off a prompter, it would still be impossible to find any other actor of his age working at anything like John's rate, and in some of these performances, notably the doctrinaire piano teacher in *Shine*, and the wily Pope in *Elizabeth*, there were still strong traces of the Gielgud magic.

By happy chance, two of these late-life projects, the episode of *Inspector Morse* and the film of *The Tichborne Claimant*, reunited John for the first time in almost half a century with one of the actors he most liked and admired, Robert Hardy:

> John was in a way the great good fortune of my working life. I remember exactly when and where I first saw him: in Oxford, just at the end of the war. It was a time when we were all half in uniform and half in student gowns, and I suddenly saw John on the pavement talking to Nevill Coghill. Then, in my first Stratford season, 1949, when he was directing *Much Ado* for the first time, I was in a group of young actors auditioning for very minor roles. Gossip had it that I was about to meet a monster of homosexual vice who would only cast us if he fancied us; instead, here was this immensely swift, gentle, courteous man already giving us master-classes in verse-speaking, even if we were only about to speak two lines.
>
> A year or two later, he gave me my first West End role, Claudio in the West End *Much Ado* which I believe still holds the record for the longest nightly run of any non-*Hamlet* Shakespearean play in the commercial London theatre. Then again, I was a sort of composite of the Knights in his 1950 *Lear*: I'd started out as an Olivier man, all for realism and slightly doubtful of John's poetic qualities, so I decided to give the Knight a stammer and John never once pointed out what a daft idea that was. His patience with all of us was remarkable; well, nearly all of us. Alan Badel, whom he later came to love, was driving him mad telling him how Lear should be directed. One night I came offstage, and to my horror John wasn't in his usual place in the wings. I thought, unbelievably, he was going to be off, but then through the darkness I heard that unmistakeable voice from further upstage: 'It's all right, I'm over here, just hiding from Alan Badel.'

John was always subtle, always gentle, and just when I had decided that being gay he couldn't play love scenes with women, he would break your heart in one. There's a moment in *Much Ado* when Claudio has to pretend to be Benedick in a mask, and some nights I used to do a real Gielgud imitation to amuse myself and the cast, and any friends out front. One night I had just done, I thought, a really expert bit of mimicry, and we were lining up for the next scene when I heard John say to one of the other actors, 'It's a funny thing, but I have always found that very good mimics are seldom any good at anything else.' That was the last time I tried that.

The filming of *Inspector Morse* led to a wonderful reunion, as we had several days on location in Oxford, where of course we had first met; his energy and his memory were still remarkable, and he would recall in fantastic detail anecdotes and characters from his own student days. He even began talking to me about Larry, who had only recently died. He wondered why I had always been so keen to play Henry V and other Shakespearean Kings in plays that seem to me to teach us the history of our nation: 'I never cared for any of that, crashing and clanking about in armour. They always seemed to me rough and rather boring plays, compared to the romantic comedies of Shakespeare, but then of course Larry too was frightfully keen on all of that. Not my scene, I fear.'

By the time we got to *The Tichborne Claimant*, age did seem at last to be catching up with him; the studio was fearfully hot, and his wig and robes as the Lord Chief Justice must have been agony, though he never complained. I was still struck by the speed of his thought; he was older, calmer, but there was still that certain waspishness, not to be confused with malice. John was never malicious, and if in rehearsal he was sharp, you weren't supposed to bleed. He never bore a grudge, though his tact was questionable. Once he told me that the world was too much with me, that I should appear on stage, 'looking better bred, like me. Oh but I forgot, you are quite well bred, aren't you?' I loved him very much, and my life as an actor was always made better when he was there.

Kenneth Branagh now became one of John's last great heroes, not surprisingly considering that Branagh too had formed his own company at a very early age and was gradually working through the Shakespearean canon. For him, Gielgud played the Ghost in a radio *Hamlet*, Priam in the film, the Chorus in *Romeo and Juliet*, and, to celebrate his ninetieth birthday in 1994, his very last *King Lear* in a BBC Radio 3 production which was also issued on tape and disc, and for which Branagh assembled an amazing cast, all eager to work with John on this quietly festive occasion: Judi Dench (Goneril), Eileen Atkins (Regan), Emma Thompson (Cordelia), Michael Williams (Fool) and Richard Briers (Gloucester). In smaller roles could also be heard Bob Hoskins, Derek Jacobi and Simon Russell Beale, who found himself so paralysed with nerves at meeting the great man that when John asked him for the way to the exit, Simon could only stand aghast and silent.

It was Michael Billington who made the point of this broadcast, that 'it is not something wistful, embalmed or elegiac, but a compelling and urgent study of an imperious tyrant splintering into madness.'

John was still determined, wherever possible, to avoid advertising his age, lest it cause prospective producers to think he was now really past it; accordingly, he spent his ninetieth birthday at home with Martin, and firmly vetoed plans mooted by the impresario Duncan Weldon for some kind of stage gala: it would, he wrote to Weldon, 'look just like my obituary, and I would so much rather just stay in work, proving I can still do a bit, than standing around receiving congratulations on my longevity'. He did, however, consent to be given lunch at the House of Commons by the MPs Glenda Jackson and Gyles Brandreth: 'I should be delighted to join you both, especially as, you see, all my real friends are dead.'

John was also still publishing with amazing regularity: not only the inevitable obituaries and tributes (which he also had to broadcast regularly for radio and television), but also a magical little volume called *Notes From the Gods*, which consisted merely of his own 1920s collection of West End theatre programmes, complete with the notes he had made on them at the time.

And there were still certain ceremonies for which he had to make an appearance. In 1993 he was given the first annual Shakespeare's Globe Trust Award, and a year later the Gielgud Award for Excellence in Dramatic Arts was established in New York. He also, in 1994, won the Imperial Prize of the Japan Arts Association, one to be taken very seriously in that it came with a cash sum of $100,000. There was, however, just one slight drawback: the rules stated that in order to collect this the recipient actually had to fly to Tokyo, a journey that John's doctor utterly forbade him to take. As I had recently taken on the role of John's biographer, he summoned me to sort this out, demanding only that I ensured he would not lose the money. After several difficult conversations with the Japanese ambassador in London, and the production of several medical certificates, it was agreed that the Crown Prince of Japan would himself fly to London to present John with this notable honour, one that had previously gone only to Edward Heath. I sat next to John during a long and sometimes incomprehensible ceremony at the Japanese Embassy, during which he kept audibly hissing at me, 'When do we get the cheque?' Luckily, and to my great relief, it arrived a couple of days later.

John was much in demand also for the new medium of audio books, and happily lent his still unmatched tones to recording work by Dickens, Oscar Wilde, Alan Bennett and Evelyn Waugh. In 1998 he made his last major radio broadcast in a characteristically courageous choice of role – one of the very few he had never previously played, Gower in *Pericles*. He also made a video for Brigitte Bardot expressing his horror of the force-feeding of ducks for pâté and was amused to find, on reaching ninety-five, that reports of his death were now being widely circulated: 'I think people now see death as an indecent race between myself, the Pope, and Boris Yeltsin.'

Inevitably, such conversations as could still be had with his few surviving old friends were almost always conducted on the telephone. A kind of sadness and even loneliness was now creeping into life at Wotton Underwood. John Perry had finally been forgiven by Martin for telling him all those years earlier to stay out of John's theatrical business, but even he found a weekend at South Pavilion almost impossible to endure:

I had no way of knowing that Martin had already been diagnosed with cancer, simply because he never told anyone, not even John. Martin would get up at some ungodly hour like five in the morning to deal with all the birds and peacocks and other weird animals which he had collected into a sort of menagerie, and would not come back indoors until lunch-time. I even thought of offering to help with the gardening, but I realised that while I was into simply digging and weeding, Martin's flower-beds required far more delicate expertise. John would not come downstairs until almost lunch-time, which we ate alone, with Martin hovering somewhere in the kitchen chewing an apple. Then he would disappear outside again. John would fall asleep by the fire, and there was nothing to do until dinner, which again Martin would ignore, having apparently eaten by himself at about six. Then, at about nine, he would start looking at his watch and saying 'bedtime' to John, and that was it for another day.

Another account of John around the time of his ninety-fifth birthday comes from the writer Julie Kavanagh, who was living nearby and had become a late-life friend of John's while she was working on a biography of Frederick Ashton. From this it became clear that the great ballet master and John had once been very close, as Ashton had collaborated on the Nevill Coghill *Midsummer Night's Dream* of 1945 starring, as Ashton wrote, 'Old Ma Gielgud'. Ashton was also among those appalled by John's arrest in 1953, noting at the time: 'He's ruined it for all of us.'

As Kavanagh wrote of an invitation to lunch at Wotton Underwood in 1998:

We sit at a long Regency table laden with crystal and silver. Martin Hensler, John's partner of thirty years, sits at a slight distance in his usual place, his chair against the wall. He does not eat or drink – he cannot stomach much besides bread and black coffee, a legacy he says of his impoverished Hungarian past, but he talks animatedly in a guttural accent, his long Rothman's Royal spilling ash on to his knees . . . Looking like a retired accountant, with heavy spectacles and thick, toupee-textured black hair, Martin was tolerated rather than liked by Gielgud's friends, most of whom resented his emphatic opinions, unremitting nagging or worse . . . Martin was a mystery to everyone, Gielgud included.

He won't speak about his early life at all. I do know that he had a terrible time in Hungary. Obviously they had great estates and palaces and parks and things. I'm fascinated, but I know he hates talking about it, so I never urge him to do so. If people speak Hungarian to him he won't answer.

In fact, there was a very good reason for Martin to be reticent about his Hungarian past, although John remained too innocent, too much in love, or simply too nervous of him ever to work it out. The evidence now suggests that although Martin may well have been Hungarian, the rest of it – the palaces and parks, perhaps even the wife and children – were all total inventions. When in the 1980s it became easily possible to revisit Hungary and track down relatives there, Martin made no effort of any kind to do so; nor, since his death, has anyone emerged to claim his estate, or establish any connection with him.

In these middle 1990s there were still two great tributes to be paid to John. In 1996 the Queen gave him the Order of Merit, the highest honour in her personal gift, and one that (apart from Olivier) had very seldom ever been awarded to an actor. John may have failed to joined Olivier and Bernard Miles in the ranks of the peerage, but in holding both the OM and the CH he established perhaps an even greater distinction.

The other honour came with the strong feeling that his name should now be given to a major Shaftesbury Avenue theatre, just as Olivier's was to be found at the National. At first, the obvious choice seemed to be the Queen's, which he had so memorably reopened with his *Ages of Man* forty years earlier. It was the Australian owner (at that time) of the Stoll Moss chain, the redoubtable Janet Holmes à Court, who remarked in her no-nonsense way that having a theatre known as the old Queen's was not perhaps the most tactful of tributes to Sir John. Besides, she had a still better idea. Shakespeare's Globe had recently been opened, thanks to the tireless work of the late Sam Wanamaker, and London theatre listings could clearly not support two Globes, so it was the one on Shaftesbury Avenue that duly became the Gielgud.

Robert Hardy talked of the great Gielgud paradox, 'his beguiling humility, mixed with his marvellous arrogance'. And talking to yet another admiring interviewer at this time, John was still full of plans for the future:

> For years I've been looking for the financial backing to make a television series about the father of Osbert and Edith Sitwell, old Sir George, an eccentric millionaire who allowed his wife to go to prison for minor debts, but nobody seems interested in that world any more. Bryan Forbes wants to direct, and Maggie Smith has agreed to play the wife, and two or three times in the past year it has almost come to the boil, but then the money falls through, usually because the television people say the public is no longer interested in aristocratic families, which I think is absolute rubbish. So many things now infuriate me – people taking their jackets off in restaurants, or not dressing properly for the theatre. All the pleasant rituals of life have gone, and people now speak so badly; I often can't understand a word they say on television. And Vanessa Redgrave actually went cockney for a period, although I could never understand why. I don't even turn out my old stories any more because nowadays all I can see is my mother's face when Father started up a story she had heard a thousand times before.
>
> I used to adore parties – showing off, giving a performance, being thought very funny and tactless, but I rarely go out nowadays. I dread going back to London where the streets are so full for me of people who are no longer there.

He did, however, turn up for the unveiling of a plaque to Oscar Wilde in Westminster Abbey, in 1995, on the centenary of Wilde's imprisonment. Benedict Nightingale, saluting another rare appearance by John in the great ballroom at Buckingham Palace to celebrate Prince Charles's patronage of the Royal Shakespeare Company, remembered what Lee Strasberg, the American director of the Method School, had once said: 'When Gielgud speaks a line, you can hear Shakespeare thinking.'

At this time, Clive Francis, the actor and caricaturist, published a collection of drawings with, inevitably, some more of his sayings. Ralph Michael recalled asking John during the Second World War whether he thought that Turkey should join the hostilities: 'John put down his crossword for a moment. "Well," he enquired, "are they very keen?"' On another occasion, he was directing the chorus in his celebrated Covent Garden *Trojans*, and was trying to persuade them to show feelings of violent passion, curiosity and fear. After they tried this a few times without notable success, John ran down the aisle screaming, 'This won't do at all! Not at all! You all look as if you are seeing not very good friends off from Waterloo!'

Chapter Twenty-seven

❦❦❦

GOODNIGHT, SWEET PRINCE

(1995–2000)

We are such stuff as dreams are made on;
and our little life is rounded with a sleep.

As if aware that, as he had so often said, his life had been altogether too bound up in acting at the expense of everything else, John now became a fervent campaigner, crusading for the survival of the old Home Service values on Radio 4 – something still especially close to his heart because of his brother Val – and also that of the Theatre Museum and theatrical subsidy. He even, at this late stage, edged on to the political arena, signing with the novelist William Golding and the film-maker David Puttnam an appeal on behalf of the Cambodia Trust, a charity established to alleviate the suffering of Cambodians by providing artificial limbs.

Politics were however still not his strongest suit; he had explained several years earlier that he seldom voted on account of being unable to distinguish between the parties, and at a meeting with Mrs Thatcher during her premiership he solemnly enquired where she was now living.

He was also playing a favourite game on the telephone, of casting unlikely projects: when, in all seriousness, they announced a stage musical based on the life of Sarah Bernhardt, John could hardly contain himself. 'It'll be Barbra Streisand for the first two acts, and then for the third Dame Judith Anderson will take over with a wooden leg.' A caustic sense of backstage humour had clearly been with him since the very earliest days; his recent collection of programme notes from the early 1920s included some vitriolic comments on Barrymore's 1925 *Hamlet* ('Romantic in appearance and good in period clothes, but fails terribly in the graveyard scenes') and of Somerset Maugham's *East of Suez* ('Badly written, scenes loosely strung together and much too long'), and of the robot play *RUR* ('Edith Evans gives her usual brilliant performance but looks even uglier than usual, and the rest of the cast is abominable').

He also now recalled an occasion several years earlier, when on one of the many *Ages of Man* tours which had developed into quasi-ambassadorial progress through distant lands, he had at the invitation of some local British consul had to sit through an entire circus night consisting very largely of men throwing other men around the stage or else forming themselves into endless human pyramids. 'I suppose, Gielgud,' said the consul by way of making interval conversation, 'you had to start like that, too?'

Some indication of the way in which various strands in John's long life were now coming together occurred when the newly refurbished Criterion Theatre on Piccadilly Circus reopened with a screening of his latest film, the Chekhov *Swan Song*, the story of the backstage encounter between a drunken old actor and his admiring prompter, played by Richard Briers. This gave John the chance, on screen, to look back on his performances as Lear, Romeo and Othello. The gala première was held in a theatre Gielgud had first played sixty years earlier (in Ronald Mackenzie's *Musical Chairs*), and all proceeds were going to Sir Ian McKellen's Stonewall group. But John himself was still curiously traumatised by the idea of giving any public support to gay campaigns; only after his death did it emerge that he had frequently sent gay charity cheques to McKellen, with the absolute proviso that there should be no publicity of any kind. The shadows of 1953 still hung over him, almost half a century later.

Privately, however, John had now found a new fan. The Queen Mother, four years older than him, would now regularly send a car to Wotton Underwood to have John driven over to Royal Lodge at Windsor, where he would entertain Her Majesty and a few select guests (often including Hugh Casson) with readings of favourite Shakespearean and other verse. By now, actors were using his tapes of *The Ages of Man* as a master-class, as Ian McKellen explained: 'I play that recording every time I'm about to do Shakespeare, because there is still so much to learn from it. The rapidity with which he delivers the lines, and the agility with which the poet's mind and the character's mind are both revealed. There is no need for pauses while John gets himself into the emotion, which, in turn, is absolutely in accord with the words. Those words are the cello, and John just plays it better than any actor alive or dead.'

Although John went on through 1998 doing two or three days' work on such major movies as *Elizabeth* and *Shine*, he was now often on automatic pilot, as if he had somehow realised that his Prospero for Peter Greenaway really was the farewell to all his magic. But there were still television commercials to make; although the Paul Masson campaign had now died a natural death, John was gainfully employed, along with Alan Bates and Ben Kingsley, to read poems for a very classy series of ads made for the Union Bank of Switzerland, though these were not shown in Britain, where the bank did not have a sufficiently high profile. And then, around Christmas of that year, there was a double disaster in his private life at Wotton Underwood. Martin, although characteristically he never admitted it even to John (who must have known, but also refused to face the truth), was now suffering terminally from cancer, and was reluctantly taken into the local hospital at Aylesbury. Almost immediately afterwards, alone in the house, John fell down some stairs, injuring his foot, and having then to be taken into the same local hospital.

As Keith Baxter recalls: 'There was a kind of Gothic horror about what happened next. Martin was refusing to be seen by any visitors at all, but just down the corridor John could hear him screaming in pain, but was himself unable even to get out of bed.' Eventually his foot was well enough to allow him home, and Martin also insisted on going home to die, so over that Christmas the two men were in their own bedrooms, well looked after, of course, by the faithful staff of Peter and Vincent but still in a kind of agony. One night John shuffled down to the doorway of Martin's room and just stood there, tears pouring down his face, watching his partner. A few hours later, Martin was dead.'

Hensler had insisted on a virtually anonymous cremation and left a will of considerable horror, demanding that all his beloved animals be killed. This was not, of course, what happened. But now, increasingly, it was Peter and Vincent who had to take all kinds of difficult decisions, since John had not even been well enough to attend Martin's cremation.

He himself now had fifteen months to live, and they were months of sad decline; Dulcie Gray, living nearby and herself now mourning the recent death of her husband Michael Denison, became John's most regular visitor, as she explained to Gyles Brandreth: 'Johnny was heart-broken when Martin died. They had, after all, been together for all of thirty years and he missed him dreadfully. Some people had reservations about Martin but I always liked him, and John was never the same after his death. He suddenly became terribly frail, walking on sticks, which he hated. He had always been so erect, so proud of his wonderful posture, so full of style. And when he came to see me for the last time, he was on crutches, and his driver had to help move him from chair to chair. It was sad to see him like that, and he hated it, but the real blow had been losing Martin – his death broke John's spirit, broke John's heart.'

His niece, the ballerina and now choreographer Maina, also noticed a terrible change in John: 'He had always been so cheerful, but now, whenever we spoke on the telephone, he would say to me, "I just wish there could be some work. They have all forgotten me. All I do is wait for the phone to ring, and it never does . . . I can't get over Martin's death; I never thought he would die before me."'

But this, too, was of course a somewhat theatrical exaggeration. Mary Evans and Dulcie Gray would ring him virtually every day, and such old friends as Keith Baxter drove down to Wotton Underwood as often as they could. As Keith recalls:

I had been working abroad for a few months, but I was very touched to hear that when Martin died John kept asking people to find me, and have me come see him as soon as I could. So I drove down as soon as I was back in England. By now, I was one of the very few male friends still around who went back a long way with John. He had never had many close women friends, and it was interesting that now, with Mary and Dulcie, he suddenly seemed to realise, at the end of his life, all that he had been missing with them. Before that, only really Peggy Ashcroft and Molly Keane had been close to him. And I think just as he regretted not spending more time in the real world, he also somehow sensed that he had missed out on the company of women.

And now, there was another one, a splendid New Zealand nurse called Alex, who moved in to take care of Gielgud in these last few months. He seemed for a while to rally, and by the summer of 1999, at least on the telephone, was sounding almost like his old self, always enquiring after the latest theatrical gossip. But the very few people he would allow to visit him were now tremendously aware of his mortality; he was moving very badly and beginning to lose the drift of conversation, seeming suddenly to Dulcie as though he were no longer entirely sure where, or even perhaps who, he was.

On the other hand, Keith found him still sometimes incredibly alert, at least about the past. 'One afternoon he described to me in perfect detail a *Hamlet* he had seen Ernest Milton play more than seventy years earlier. He never talked about death, never talked about Martin, seemed to be living in a kind of theatrical museum, constantly re-examining all the people he found there, as if determined to keep his own memories intact, because they were now really all that he had left.'

In the autumn of 1999, unadvertised and unannounced in advance, John turned up in one last television studio, being interviewed by Jeremy Paxman for BBC2's *Newsnight* on the stage of the Old Vic. Despite his age and his infirmities, John was superbly well-groomed – nothing of the wispiness or untidiness of extreme old age – in a beautifully cut suit, and his voice was clear, if subdued. Yet Paxman chose to focus this brief encounter not on John's remarkable career, or even on his memories, but largely on his feelings about old age and even death. John's strength of feeling on the subject was apparent: 'I hate being old, and I find it humiliating now to have to rely on help from other people . . . I never thought I should be at a loss for someone to phone and say I'm coming to see you . . .' Picking up this theme, Paxman asked whether he feared death himself, to which John replied that he was more concerned with being in pain (Martin's experience had shown him how unpleasant the approach to death can be) and added that he also disliked not being able to enjoy food or parties any more.

'I've had a wonderful innings, I knew all the great people of my time, and I do resent that I can't have some of them back.' Paxman then asked him about the nature of fame, and John pointed out the dangers that it had caused to a career like that of Richard Burton. He also regretted, he said, that his life had been so very cut off from the realities of the world. Clearly he had been too young to fight in the First World War, but he had only recently discovered, to his horror, that Binkie Beaumont had quite untruthfully told the authorities that he was totally unfit to fight in the Second World War, merely so as to keep him on or near Shaftesbury Avenue. Finally, Paxman asked him if he had any regrets: 'Only perhaps that in radio and television now there is never the same companionship that I so loved in the theatre . . . Would I have done anything differently? No, I don't think so.'

John's last Christmas treat, in December 1999, was being taken by Mary Evans to a matinée of *The Lion King*, which predictably he loved, recognising – as always – something new and vital in theatrical fashion. Amazingly, he was still writing, albeit in a very fragile hand; for the biographer Gordon McVay he penned a tribute to Peggy Ashcroft, listing her virtues in precisely those terms that could have been applied to him:

Generous, eager, forthright

No taste for luxury

Extraordinary range of enthusiasm for playwrights – Shakespeare, Ibsen, Chekhov, Brecht, Rattigan, Pinter

Exquisite reader of poetry

Champion of team companies and good causes, but never pressing them on others

No spite or jealousy

Unfailing professional attitude to directors and colleagues – punctual, diligent, humorous, cheerful

Never pompous or unapproachable

Unaffected, wonderful company; warm-hearted

Great control of emotion, and brilliantly selective reserves of power

Unselfish, loyal, affectionate appreciation of fellow artists

Around this time the critic Michael Billington made Gielgud the subject of a *Guardian* lecture:

> I was recently invited by Sir John to have lunch at his club where I sense, not for the first time, how cruelly inaccurate is the *Spitting Image* caricature of Gielgud as a nostalgic old party forever dwelling on the past. He lives very much in the present, works incessantly, and talks as enthusiastically about a new role as an actor just out of drama school . . . he is very much more than the Establishment figurehead and violincello melodist he is often assumed to be. It is true that he has done more than anyone living to keep the classic tradition alive in the British theatre, but he is also a pioneer . . . at a time when the West End was full of fluff and trivia (when was it not?) he swam against the tide by setting up at the New Theatre from 1934 to 1936 and at the Queen's in 1937-38 seasons of classics for which he engaged progressive directors and surrounded himself with the best actors of his day. Gielgud, long before subsidy became part of our common vocabulary, proved that the best results in theatre only come from permanence . . . under the stylish, patrician-seeming surface there lurks a man and an actor fascinated by new currents in the arts . . . Of all the tributes to Sir John, one in particular has stuck in my mind. It came from the playwright, David Hare, who said, 'Acting is a judgement of character,' and that as actors grow older it is who and what they were as human beings that sustains their art. Gielgud's innate dignity, nobility and generosity of temper shine through all his recent work, and today we love and admire Gielgud for what he has achieved, but even more for what he is – an uncommon man who brings to acting a life-enhancing zest, energy and elan.

And this was still a time for introspection; as John had written in an epilogue to his collection of Shakespearean essays (*Shakespeare Hit or Miss?*):

> I was always as absorbed throughout my years in the theatre as a director as well as an actor, though when I combined the two occupations, as I did many times, I sometimes became too divided

to maintain the necessary concentration required. When I was directed by others, I learned a great deal from them. I did not make many enemies, though I was fairly autocratic in the theatre. I never had to be concerned with money matters, always worked for sympathetic managers, was given a free hand in casting and choice of colleagues and designers, and very seldom had to work in plays I did not like. I always found rehearsals fascinatingly lively, matinée days extremely arduous, and long runs as difficult to sustain as they were valuable for practice and selectivity. Often I failed to intimidate, and was apt to listen to too many people, to appear unduly impulsive towards my colleagues, and to change my mind too often. I have always been too fond of popularity, and wanted everyone to like me. I have often been too timid and cowardly in my behaviour, dreading crises and quarrels, because I was always so happy in the theatre. I should perhaps have been a better mixer, and also a more formidable character. Olivier was not always an easy man; like Irving, he was feared as well as deeply respected, but both men inspired enormous devotion and enthusiasm in their companies, and I have always hoped to do the same – 'and thus the whirligig of time brings in his revenges'.

Introspection was mingled with an irritation at what he felt was a falling-away of the offers of work: Brian Bedford, on a brief return to England at this time, remembers a somewhat despairing John complaining about how terrible it was to be out of work. 'And how long has this been going on?' asked Bedford. 'Oh,' replied John, 'since Friday.'

And, for John, almost unbelievably, there was still one more role to play; he spent his ninety-sixth birthday, 14 April 2000, filming for the playwright and director David Mamet a very brief Samuel Beckett play entitled *Catastrophe*, in which the only other player was another world-class playwright, Harold Pinter. That night I rang John to wish him a happy birthday, see if he had received my ritual bottle of champagne, and ask him how it felt to be back in front of a camera. 'Very surprising, but I wish they had told me that it was a non-speaking role. I really am rather too old to appear as an extra!'

And there was yet one more television interview still to record: Richard Eyre, formerly director of the National Theatre, was now filming a six-part BBC series called *Changing Stages* and it was for the opening Shakespearean survey that, for the very last time, Gielgud recalled his tales of Lilian Baylis and Harley Granville-Barker, of Olivier and their perceived enmity over Romeo and Mercutio more than sixty years earlier.

John then made his last public appearance on 18 April, four days after his birthday, at the funeral of one of his last surviving intimates, Ralph Richardson's widow Meriel Forbes, at the church of Our Lady of the Assumption, just off Regent Street. On Sunday, 21 May, he had finished lunch and his driver, Peter, helped him through to the drawing-room at Wotton Underwood to enjoy the thin spring sunshine. As he reached his chair, John collapsed on to it. His death, unlike his life, was achieved with a minimum of theatricality.

The following day, in newspapers and radio and television broadcasts all over the world, the passing of the greatest classical actor in the whole of the twentieth century was marked with due observance; that night lights were dimmed all over the West End, and many leading players paid tribute in their curtain speeches to the actor who was now generally recognised as the head of their profession. Corin Redgrave, recalling how much Gielgud had influenced his father, said, 'The odds is gone, and there is nothing left remarkable beneath the visiting moon', while John's agent Laurie Evans, who had also represented Olivier and Richardson, noted, 'Of the three, Gielgud was by far the greatest actor.'

In contrast to this public praise, however, John had left strict instructions that his funeral was to be intensely private, and so on 1 June, at the little parish church of Wotton Underwood, a very few friends gathered. Alec Guinness, himself to die barely three months later, was there, as were John Mills, Donald Sinden, Paul Scofield, Maggie Smith and Irene Worth.

Donald Sinden read 'No Man Is An Island' by John Donne; John Mills recited the poem 'Do Not Despair For Johnny Head In Air', which he had first spoken in the film *The Way to the Stars*, and Paul Scofield read Shakespeare's Sonnet 71, the one starting 'No longer mourn for me when I am dead'.

Of the multitude of tributes, it is perhaps worth recalling just two, from either end of the journalistic spectrum. For the *Sunday Times*, his only surviving heir Paul Scofield wrote:

> For the vast majority of actors and actresses since the late 1930s, John has been the consummate epitome of style in the theatre . . . his sense of style, together with the extreme beauty and musicality of his speaking (notably of verse) has been the most dominant component of his art, but he was also a deeply emotional actor, and if there could be said to be any conflict in his work, it was to be found in the confrontation of style and feeling . . . his criticism of himself, often shot through with humour, would have been annihilating had it been directed at others; his discipline came from within and was compounded of self-appraisal and care for others, perhaps a rare combination of trust and mistrust . . . he directed other actors with both autocratic authority and a nervous awareness of points of views other than his own, which created an atmosphere sometime uncomfortable, and always stimulating . . . sometimes he seemed too vulnerable to random suggestions, often to the despair of actors who felt their performances threatened by apparently arbitrary changes in physical staging or relationships, but which might in hindsight be seen as anticipation of present improvisational techniques . . . it is a curious fact that the actor most renowned for poetic and aesthetic sensibility should also have been the toughest; that his fastidiousness should have been fortified by nerves and muscles of steel.

At the lower end of the scale of journalism, I think even John himself might have been delighted by a headline in the *Daily Sport* which read, simply but in bold capital letters: 'Butler in Dudley Moore film dies'.

In a curious and oblique way, one he would never of course himself have acknowledged in public, perhaps one of the greatest tributes to John came just two months after his death, with a Home Office report proposing, at last, a change in the sex laws which would finally abolish the crimes for which both Oscar Wilde and Gielgud were prosecuted, those of buggery and gross indecency involving consenting adults. The review finally advocated that public homosexual activity should be dealt with in precisely the same way as public heterosexual sex.

John's will was published some six months after his death. It listed specific cash legacies to friends and organisations such as RADA, the Actors' Charitable Trust, and the King George V Fund for Actors and Actresses. He also left the Theatre Museum in London a number of personal items, including a snuff box which had once belonged to Charles Kean. To the National Portrait Gallery he left a painting of his great-aunt, Ellen Terry. Beyond that, the bulk of his fortune was to be given over to charitable causes chosen at the discretion of his executors, who were also charged with disposing of his papers and archives.

John's name lives on, not only in the theatre that bears his name, but also in countless awards at drama schools around the world: in September 2000, four months after his death, it was announced that a Gielgud foundation for theatre and dance would be set up in his memory, and this was launched by a gala evening of twenty-first-century ballet which was held at the Wimbledon Theatre.

John's estate was eventually valued at £1,468,451, though this did not include his last car, a Volvo which he had cannily sold to his own driver for £2000 a few weeks before his death; the man who had once described himself as 'a silly emotional gubbins' had at the last learnt the value of his possessions.

These were duly auctioned at Sotheby's in March 2001; 'don't open a drawer,' someone had warned the valuers, 'or Ellen Terry's teeth are sure to fall out'. The auction (followed a few weeks later by that of Sir Ralph Richardson) featured such treasures as twenty of John's own pencil-drawings of actors and actresses, his Panama hat, gloves and a brown leather Dunhill cigarette case. Then there were playbills, scrapbooks, a writing table, ornate Venetian mirrors, classical busts. It was the showbiz garage sale of all time, and a day of countless memories for all of us lucky enough to have known John at home.

That was, however, as he recalled in his 2000 Diary for the *London Review of Books*, an experience narrowly missed by Alan Bennett:

21 *May*. Gielgud dies. Asked to appear on various programmes, including the Nine O'Clock News but say no. Reluctant to jump on the bandwagon, particularly when the bandwagon is a hearse. Some notes:

Despite the umpteen programmes of reminiscence Gielgud did both on radio and television there was always more and I never felt he had been sufficiently debriefed. Anyone of any distinction at all should, on reaching a certain age, be taken away for a weekend at the state's expense, formally interviewed and stripped of all their recollections.

It was hard to tell if he liked someone, only that he didn't dislike them. I think I came in the latter category. I went round to see him after *Home* and he said how much he liked David Storey. 'He's the ideal author . . . never says a word!'

In *Chariots of Fire* he shared a scene with Lindsay Anderson, both of them playing Cambridge dons. Lindsay was uncharacteristically nervous but having directed John G. in *Home* felt able to ask his help, saying that if he felt Lindsay was doing too much or had any other tips he was to tell him. Gielgud was appalled: 'Oh no, no. I can't do that, I shall be far too busy thinking about myself!'

The last time I saw him was when we were filming an episode of the TV adaptation of *A Dance to the Music of Time*. We were supposedly talking to one another but the speeches were separately recorded and intercut. His speech was haltingly delivered (but then so had mine been) and we did several takes. At the end he was given a round of applause by cast and crew, which I felt had not much to do with the quality of the speech itself so much as his having stayed alive long enough to deliver it. I imagine this kind of thing happened on most of the jobs he did (and he did a good many) in his nineties, and it was probably one of the things he hated about being old as there was inevitably some condescension to the applause. But he would just smile, do his funny snuffle and say that people were awfully kind.

23 May. Watch the *Omnibus* tribute to John G. in which *Oedipus* and *Forty Years On*, which came after it, both go unmentioned, though much is made of *Prospero's Books* largely because he took his clothes off in it (not, incidentally, for the first time, as he did so in Bob Guccione's *Caligula*; this too goes unmentioned, though more out of kindness, I would have thought). To some extent the omissions simply reflect the material that is available – the programme is archive-led. The BBC did have film of *Forty Years On* but lost it or wiped it or certainly made no effort to preserve it, though I would have thought that even in 1968 it was plain that any film or tape of Gielgud needed to be set aside. Thirty years and more later, I doubt the situation has improved much and it remains a scandal that a public corporation should still have no foolproof archive system.

Letters from Gielgud were always unmistakable because of the one-in-five slope of his handwriting, the text sliding off the page. I always felt it was slightly unfriendly that I'd never been invited down to Buckinghamshire but then I reread a letter he wrote me after I'd reviewed one of his books and in it I find an open invitation to lunch any time, with telephone number, directions, and how to get from the station. So now, of course, I feel mortified.

It would be tempting to end this authorised biography with the obvious Shakespearean farewells of either Hamlet or Prospero, both of which Gielgud had spoken so many times, on stage and in the pulpit, with an unrivalled sense of the verse and the valedictory emotion; but I am inclined instead to go back to the Chekhov *Swan Song*, which John had first played in the war and latterly filmed for Kenneth Branagh only a few years before his death:

Old age? No such thing. Stuff and nonsense . . . Where you've got art, where you've got talent, there's no room for old age, no room for loneliness or being ill. Even death is only half itself . . . Our song is sung, our race is run. What talent do I have? I'm a squeezed lemon, a melting icicle, a rusty nail . . . an old theatre rat . . . off we go, then.

John Gielgud, actor and director, 1904–2000

CHRONOLOGY

In the following list, 'director' is indicated as '(d)'.

Theatre

Year	Theatre	Production	Role
1915			
Dec	Mathilde Verne Pianoforte School	HMS Pinafore	Sailor
1920			
Jul	Battle Abbey	As You Like It	Orlando
1921			
Jan	Old Court Studio	Romeo and Juliet	Mercutio
	Old Court Studio	Belinda	German Officer
Nov	Old Vic	Henry V	Walk on
1922			
Jan	YMCA Hall, Tottenham Ct Rd	The Importance of Being Earnest	John Worthing (d)
Feb	Church Hall, Barnet	I'll Leave It To You	Bobbie
	Training Ship Stork	I'll Leave It To You	Bobbie
Mar	Old Vic	Peer Gynt	Walk on
	Old Vic	King Lear	Walk on
Apr	Old Vic	Peer Gynt	Walk on
	Old Vic	As You Like It	Walk on
	Old Vic	Wat Tyler	Walk on
Apr	Old Vic	Love Is the Best Doctor	Walk on

	Old Vic	The Comedy of Errors	Walk on
Sept	New, Oxford and touring	The Wheel	Lt Manners
Dec	Eton College	The Masque of Comus	Younger Brother

1923

Jan	Apollo	A Roof and Four Walls	Designer
Mar	Inner Temple	The Masque of Comus	Younger Brother
	RADA	The School For Scandal	Peter Teazle
May	Regent	The Insect Play	Poet Butterfly
Jun	RADA	Twelfth Night	Sir Toby
	RADA	The Young Person in Pink	Lord Stevenage
	Regent	Robert E. Lee	Aide-de-camp
Jul	RADA	Hamlet (scenes from)	Hamlet
Aug	Regent	Robert E.Lee	David Peel
Dec	RADA	Les Caprices de Marianne	Celio
	RADA	L'Aiglon	Hartmann
	RADA	Arms and the Man	Sergius
	RADA	Reparation (scenes)	Fedya
	RADA	Joan of Arc	Paul
	Comedy	Charley's Aunt	Charles

1924

Jan	Oxford Playhouse	Captain Brassbound's Conversion	Johnson
Feb	Oxford Playhouse	Mr Pim Passes By	Brian Strange
Feb	Oxford Playhouse	Love For Love	Valentine
Feb	Oxford Playhouse	She Stoops to Conquer	Young Marlowe
Feb	Oxford Playhouse	Monna Vanna	Prinzevalle
Apr	RADA	Romeo and Juliet	Paris
May	Regent	Romeo and Juliet	Romeo
Oct	RADA Players	The Return Half	John Sherry
Oct	Oxford Playhouse	Candida	Marchbanks
Oct	Oxford Playhouse	Deirdre of the Sorrows	Naisi
Nov	Oxford Playhouse	A Collection Will Be Made	Paul Roget
Nov	Oxford Playhouse	Everybody's Husband	A Domino

Nov	Oxford Playhouse	The Cradle Song	Antonio
Nov	Oxford Playhouse	John Gabriel Borkman	Erhart
Nov	Oxford Playhouse	His Widow's Husband	Zurita
Dec	Oxford Playhouse	Madame Pepita	Augusto
Dec	Charterhouse	French Leave	Lt George Graham

1925

Jan	Oxford Playhouse	A Collection Will Be Made	Paul Roget
Jan	Oxford Playhouse	Smith	Algernon
Jan	Oxford Playhouse	The Cherry Orchard	Trofimov
Feb	Royalty	The Vortex	Understudy
Mar	Comedy	The Vortex	Understudy & Nicky
Apr	RADA Players	The Nature of the Evidence	Ted Hewitt
May	Aldwych	The Orphan	Castalio
May	Little	The Vortex	Understudy & Nicky
May	Lyric, Hammersmith	The Cherry Orchard	Trofimov
Jun	Garden	The High Constable's Wife	J. de Boys-Bourredon
Jun	Royalty	The Cherry Orchard	Trofimov
Aug	Oxford Playhouse	The Lady From the Sea	A Stranger
Aug	Oxford Playhouse	The Man With a Flower in his Mouth	Title Role
Sept	Apollo	Two Gentlemen of Verona	Valentine
Oct	Little	The Seagull	Konstantin
Oct	New Oxford	Dr Faustus	Good Angel
Dec	Little	Gloriana	Sir John Harringdon
Dec	Prince's	L'Ecole des Cocottes	Robert
Dec	Daly's	Nativity Play	Second Shepherd

1926

Jan	Savoy (matinée)	The Tempest	Ferdinand
Jan	RADA Players	Sons and Fathers	Richard Southern

Feb	Barnes	Three Sisters	Tusenbach
Mar	Barnes	Katerina	Georg
May	Royal Court	Hamlet	Rosencrantz
Jun	Coliseum	Romeo and Juliet (excerpt)	Romeo
Jun	Lyric, Hammersmith	Henry VI (dramatised reading)	Richard
Jul	Garrick	The Lady of the Camelias	Armand
Jul	Court (300 Club)	Confession	Wilfred Marley
Oct	New	The Constant Nymph	Lewis Dodd

1927

Apr	Apollo	Othello	Cassio
Apr	New	The Good Old Days	Boulter
Apr	New	The Hectic Present	Guest
Jun	Strand	The Great God Brown	Dion Anthony
Nov	King's, Hammersmith	The Constant Nymph	Lewis Dodd

1928

Jan	Majestic, New York	The Patriot	Tsarevitch
Mar	Wyndham's (matinées)	Ghosts	Oswald
Apr	Arts	Ghosts	Oswald
Jun	Globe	Holding Out the Apple	Gerald Marlowe
Jun	Arts	Prejudice	Jacob Slovak
Aug	Shaftesbury	The Skull	Capt. Allenby
Oct	Court	The Lady From Alfaqueque	Felipe Rivas
Oct	Court	Fortunato	Alberto
Nov	Strand	Out of the Sea	John Martin

1929

Jan	Arts	The Seagull	Constantin
Feb	Little	Red Rust	Fedor
Mar	Prince of Wales	Hunters Moon	De Tressailles
Apr	Garrick	The Lady With a Lamp	Tremayne
Apr	Palace (matinée)	Shall We Join the Ladies?	Capt. Jennings
Jun	Arts	Red Sunday	Bronstein
Sept	Old Vic	Romeo and Juliet	Romeo
Oct	Old Vic	The Merchant of Venice	Antonio
Oct	Old Vic	The Imaginary Invalid	Cleante

Oct	Old Vic (special perf.)	Romeo and Juliet	Romeo
Nov	Old Vic	Richard II	Richard II
Dec	Prince of Wales	Douaumont	The Prologue
Dec	Old Vic	A Midsummer Night's Dream	Oberon

1930

Jan	Old Vic	Julius Caesar	Mark Antony
Jan	Haymarket (matinée)	Romeo and Juliet	Romeo
Feb	Old Vic	As You Like It	Orlando
Feb	Old Vic	Androcles and the Lion	Emperor
Mar	Old Vic	Macbeth	Macbeth
Apr	Old Vic	The Man With a Flower in his Mouth	Title Role
Apr	Old Vic	Hamlet	Hamlet
Jun	Queen's	Hamlet	Hamlet
Jul	Lyric, Hammersmith	The Importance of Being Earnest	John Worthing
Jul	Smallhythe	Hamlet (scene)	Hamlet
Sept	Old Vic	Henry IV Part I	Hotspur
Oct	Old Vic	The Tempest	Prospero
Oct	Old Vic	The Jealous Wife	Lord Trinket
Nov	Old Vic	Richard II	Richard II
Nov	Old Vic	Antony and Cleopatra	Antony

1931

Jan	Sadler's Wells	Twelfth Night	Malvolio
Feb	Sadler's Wells	The Tempest	Prospero
Feb	Old Vic	Arms and the Man	Sergius
Mar	Old Vic	Much Ado About Nothing	Benedick
Apr	Old Vic	King Lear	Lear
Apr	Old Vic	Shakespeare Birthday Festival (scenes)	Hamlet
May	His Majesty's	The Good Companions	Jollifant
Jul	Smallhythe	Much Ado About Nothing (scenes)	Benedick
Nov	Arts	Musical Chairs	Schindler
Nov	Tour	The Good Companions	Jollifant

1932

Feb	New, Oxford	Romeo and Juliet	Director
Mar	New	Romeo and Juliet	Director
Apr	Criterion	Musical Chairs	Schindler
Apr	Old Vic	Shakespeare Birthday Festival (scenes)	Richard II
Jun	New	Richard of Bordeaux	Richard II (co-d)
Jul	Smallhythe	Twelfth Night (scenes)	Orsino
Sept	St Martin's	Strange Orchestra	Director
Dec	Old Vic	The Merchant of Venice	Director
Dec	Golders Green	Musical Chairs	Schindler

1933

Feb	New	Richard of Bordeaux	Richard
Feb	Sadler's Wells (matinée)	The Merchant of Venice	Director /Designer
Jul	New	Richard II (scenes)	Richard II
Jul	Ambassadors	La Voix Humaine	Director
Aug	King's, Hammersmith	Musical Chairs	Director
Sept	Wyndham's	Sheppey	Director
Dec	New (matinée)	A Kiss For Cinderella	The Censor

1934

Jan	Shaftesbury	Spring 1600	Director
Apr	Tour	Richard of Bordeaux	Richard II
Jun	New	Queen of Scots	Director
Jul	Wyndham's	The Maitlands	Roger Maitland
Jul	Smallhythe	Shakespeare Sonnets	Speaker
Nov	New	Hamlet	Hamlet (d)

1935

Apr	New	The Old Ladies	Director
Apr	Tour	Richard of Bordeaux	Richard II
May	Drury Lane (jubilee perf.)	The Player's Masque	Mercury
Jul	New	Noah	Noah
Jul	Smallhythe	Hamlet (scenes)	Hamlet

Oct	New	Romeo and Juliet	Mercutio/ Romeo (d)
Nov	His Majesty's	Punch Cartoons	Director

1936

Feb	OUDS	Richard II	Director
Apr	Tour	Romeo and Juliet	Romeo (d)
May	Tour	Romeo and Juliet	Romeo (d)
May	New	The Seagull	Trigorin
Sept	Alexandra, Toronto	Hamlet	Hamlet
Oct	Empire, New York	Hamlet	Hamlet
Oct	St James', New York	Hamlet	Hamlet

1937

Feb	Schubert, Boston	Hamlet	Hamlet
Apr	Tour	He Was Born Gay	Mason (d)
May	Queen's	He Was Born Gay	Mason (d)
May	His Majesty's	Nijinsky Matinée	Speaker
Sept	Queen's	Richard II	Richard II
Nov	Golders Green	Richard II	Richard II
Nov	Queen's	The School For Scandal	Joseph Surface
Dec	Winter Garden	King George's Pension Fund Matinée	Speaker

1938

Jan	Queen's	Three Sisters	Vershinin
Apr	Queen's	The Merchant of Venice	Shylock (d)
May	Ambassadors	Spring Meeting	Director
Jul	Piccadilly	Spring Meeting	Director
Sept	Manchester	Dear Octopus	Nicholas
Sept	Queen's	Dear Octopus	Nicholas

1939

Jan	Globe	The Importance of Being Earnest	John Worthing (d)
Apr	Old Vic	Shakespeare Birthday Festival	Hamlet
Apr	Globe	Scandal in Assyria	Director
May	Brighton	Spring Meeting	Director
May	Globe	Rhondda Roundabout	Co-producer

Jun	Lyceum	Hamlet	Hamlet (d)
Jul	Elsinore	Hamlet	Hamlet (d)
Aug	Globe	The Importance of Being Earnest	John Worthing (d)
Sept	Tour	The Importance of Being Earnest	John Worthing (d)
Oct	Tour	Shakespeare in Peace and War	Speaker

1940

Mar	Haymarket	The Beggar's Opera	Director
Apr	Haymarket	The Beggar's Opera	Macheath
Apr	Old Vic	King Lear	Lear
May	Old Vic	The Tempest	Prospero
Jul	Globe/ENSA Tour	Fumed Oak	Henry Crow (d)
		Hands Across the Sea	Peter Gilpin
		Hard Luck Story	Old Actor
Aug	Edinburgh (ENSA)	The Dark Lady of the Sonnets	Shakespeare (d)

1941

Jan	Globe	Dear Brutus	Will Dearth (d)
Jun	Tour	Dear Brutus	Will Dearth (d)
Nov	Apollo	Ducks and Drakes	Director
Dec	Royal Albert Hall	All Star Concert	Speaker

1942

Jan	Tour	Macbeth	Macbeth (d)
Oct	Phoenix	The Importance of Being Earnest	John Worthing (d)
Nov	New	Special Matinée, Way of the World	Mirabell
Dec	Gibraltar	ENSA Tour Revue	Various

1943

Jan	Haymarket	The Doctor's Dilemma	Louis Dubedat
Mar	Tour	Love For Love	Valentine (d)
Apr	Phoenix	Love For Love	Valentine (d)
Jul	Tour	Nursery Slopes	Director
Oct	Westminster	Landslide (Nursery Slopes)	Director

1944

Jan	Apollo	The Cradle Song	Director
Mar	Tour	Crisis in Heaven	Director
Jun	Lyric	The Last of Summer	Director
Jul	Tour	Hamlet	Hamlet
Aug	Tour	Love For Love	Valentine (d)
Sept	Tour	The Circle	A. Champion-Cheney
Oct	Haymarket	The Circle	A. Champion-Cheney
Oct	Haymarket	Love For Love	Valentine (d)
Oct	Haymarket	Hamlet	Hamlet

1945

Jan	Haymarket	A Midsummer Night's Dream	Oberon
Apr	Tour	The Duchess of Malfi	Ferdinand
Apr	Haymarket	The Duchess of Malfi	Ferdinand
Aug	Haymarket	Lady Windermere's Fan	Director
Oct	Far East Tour (ENSA)	Hamlet	Hamlet (d)
		Blithe Spirit	C. Condomine (d)
		Shakespeare in Peace and War	Speaker

1946

Jun	Tour	Crime and Punishment	Raskolnikoff
Jun	New	Crime and Punishment	Raskolnikoff
Jul	Smallhythe	Macbeth (Reading)	Reader
Sept	Globe	Crime and Punishment	Raskolnikoff

1947

Jan	USA/Canada Tour	The Importance of Being Earnest	John Worthing (d)
Apr	King's, Hammersmith	Lady Windermere's Fan	Director
May	USA Tour	Love For Love	Valentine (d)
Oct	Royale, New York	Medea	Jason (d)
Dec	Royale, New York	Crime and Punishment	Raskolnikoff

1948

Jul	Haymarket	The Glass Menagerie	Director
Aug	Tour	Medea	Director
Sept	Globe	Medea	Director
Dec	Globe	The Return of the Prodigal	Eustace Jackson

1949

Feb	Haymarket	The Heiress	Director
Apr	Memorial, Stratford	Much Ado About Nothing	Director
May	Globe	The Lady's Not For Burning	Thomas Mendip (d)
Jul	Smallhythe	Henry IV (Scene)	Hotspur
Sept	Apollo	Treasure Hunt	Director
Nov	Coliseum	Gala: Richard of Bordeaux (Scene)	Richard II

1950

Jan	Lyric, Hammersmith	The Boy With a Cart	Director
Jan	Lyric, Hammersmith	Shall We Join the Ladies?	Director
Mar	Memorial, Stratford	Measure For Measure	Angelo
May	Memorial, Stratford	Julius Caesar	Cassius
Jun	Memorial, Stratford	Much Ado About Nothing	Benedick (d)
Jul	Memorial, Stratford	King Lear	Lear (co-d)
Oct	Schubert, Boston	The Lady's Not For Burning	Thomas Mendip (d)
Nov	Royale, New York	The Lady's Not For Burning	Thomas Mendip (d)

1951

Jun	Phoenix	The Winter's Tale	Leontes
Jul	Smallhythe	Ellen Terry Anniversary Performance	Speaker
Aug	Tour	The Winter's Tale	Leontes
Oct	Coliseum	Salute to Ivor Novello	Speaker
Dec	Criterion	Indian Summer	Director

1952

Jan	Phoenix	Much Ado About Nothing	Benedick (d)
Mar	Memorial, Stratford	Macbeth	Director
Dec	Lyric, Hammersmith	Richard II	Richard II

1953

Feb	Lyric, Hammersmith	The Way of the World	Mirabell (d)
May	Lyric, Hammersmith	Venice Preserv'd	Jaffier
Jul	Bulawayo	Richard II	Richard II (d)
Nov	Haymarket	A Day by the Sea	Julian Anson (d)
Dec	Tour	Charley's Aunt	Director

1954

Feb	New	Charley's Aunt	Director
May	Lyric, Hammersmith	The Cherry Orchard	Director

1955

Apr	Memorial, Stratford	Twelfth Night	Director
Jun	Tour	King Lear	Lear
Jul	Palace	Much Ado About Nothing	Benedick (d)
Jul	Palace	King Lear	Lear
Jul	European Tour	Much Ado About Nothing & King Lear	Benedick (d), Lear
Nov	Memorial, Stratford	King Lear	Lear
Dec	Memorial, Stratford	Much Ado About Nothing	Benedick (d)

1956

Apr	Haymarket	The Chalk Garden	Director
Jul	Smallhythe	Much Ado About Nothing (Scene)	Benedick
Oct	Tour	Nude With Violin	Sebastian (co-d)
Nov	Globe	Nude With Violin	Sebastian (co-d)
Dec	Royal Festival Hall	The Ages of Man	Speaker

1957

Jun	Covent Garden	The Trojans	Director
Aug	Memorial, Stratford	The Tempest	Prospero
Aug	Tour	The Ages of Man	Speaker
Dec	Drury Lane	The Tempest	Prospero

1958

Feb	Globe	The Potting Shed	James Callifer
Mar	Tour	Variation on a Theme	Director
Apr	Globe	Variation on a Theme	Director

May	Old Vic then Tour	Henry VIII	Cardinal Wolsey
Jul	Comedy	Five Finger Exercise	Director
Sep	Tour (America/Europe)	The Ages of Man	Speaker

1959

Jun	Globe	The Complaisant Lover	Director
Jun	Queen's	The Ages of Man	Speaker
Sept	Boston/New York	Much Ado About Nothing	Director
Dec	Music Box, New York	Five Finger Exercise	Director

1960

| Apr | Haymarket | The Ages of Man | Speaker |
| Sept | Phoenix | The Last Joke | Prince Cavanati |

1961

Feb	Covent Garden	A Midsummer Night's Dream	Director
Mar	ANTA Theatre, New York	Big Fish, Little Fish	Director
Jun	Globe	Dazzling Prospect	Director
Sept	Memorial, Stratford	The Ages of Man	Speaker
Oct	Memorial, Stratford	Othello	Othello
Dec	Memorial, Stratford	The Cherry Orchard	Gaev
	Aldwych	The Cherry Orchard	Gaev

1962

Apr	Haymarket	The School For Scandal	Director
Apr	Tour	The Ages of Man	Speaker
Oct	Haymarket	The School For Scandal	Joseph Surface (d)
Nov	USA tour	The School For Scandal	Joseph Surface (d)

1963

Jan	Majestic, New York	The Ages of Man	Speaker
Apr	Lyceum, New York	The Ages of Man	Speaker
Jul	Tour	The Ides of March	Caesar (co-d)
Aug	Haymarket	The Ides of March	Caesar (co-d)
Dec	Australia/NZ Tour	The Ages of Man	Speaker

470

1964

Feb	O'Keefe Centre	Hamlet	Voice of Ghost (d)
Mar	New York/Princeton	Homage to Shakespeare	Speaker
Mar	Shubert, New York	Hamlet	Voice of Ghost (d)
Apr	Tour (UK/Europe)	The Ages of Man	Speaker
Jul	Lunt-Fontanne, New York	Hamlet	Voice of Ghost (d)
Dec	Billy Rose, New York	Tiny Alice	Julian

1965

Mar	The White House	The Ages of Man	Reader
Aug	Tour	Ivanov	Ivanov (d)
Sept	Phoenix	Ivanov	Ivanov (d)

1966

Mar	Shubert Theatre, New York	Ivanov	Ivanov (d)
Oct	Norway	The Ages of Man	Speaker
Nov	International Tour	Men, Women And Shakespeare	Speaker

1967

Jan	Festival Hall	Oedipus Rex	Narrator
Jun	Ankara, Turkey	The Ages of Man	Speaker
Nov	Old Vic	Tartuffe	Orgon
Nov	Queen's	Halfway Up the Tree	Director

1968

Mar	Old Vic	Oedipus	Oedipus
Aug	Coliseum	Don Giovanni	Director
Oct	Apollo	Forty Years On	Headmaster
Dec	Phoenix	A Talent to Amuse	Speaker

1970

Feb	Lyric	The Battle of Shrivings	Sir Gideon Petrie
Jun	Royal Court	Home	Harry

Jul	Apollo	Home	Harry
Nov	Morosco, New York	Home	Harry

1971

Mar	Martin Beck, New York	All Over	Director
Jul	Chichester	Caesar and Cleopatra	Caesar

1972

Mar	Royal Court	Veterans	Sir Geoffrey Kendle
Sept	Queen's	Private Lives	Director
Oct	Shubert, New York	Irene	Director

1973

Sept	Albery	The Constant Wife	Director

1974

Mar	Old Vic	The Tempest	Prospero
May	Old Vic	Tribute to the Lady	Hamlet
Aug	Royal Court	Bingo	Shakespeare
Sept	46th St Theatre, New York	Private Lives	Director
Dec	Shubert, New York	The Constant Wife	Director

1975

Apr	Old Vic	No Man's Land	Spooner
Jun	Albery	The Gay Lord Quex	Director
Jul	Wyndham's	No Man's Land	Spooner

1976

Feb	Old Vic	Tribute to the Lady	Hamlet
Apr	Lyttleton, National	No Man's Land	Spooner
Nov	Longacre, New York	No Man's Land	Spooner

1977

Mar	Olivier, National	Julius Caesar	Caesar
Apr	Olivier, National	Volpone	Sir Politick Would-Be
Nov	Cottesloe, National	Half-Life	Sir Noël Cunliffe

1978

| Mar | Duke of York's | Half-Life | Sir Noël Cunliffe |

1979

| Jan | Tour | Half-Life | Sir Noël Cunliffe |

1984

| Feb | Duke of York's | Gala Performance | Speaker |
| May | Marriott Hotel | Old Vic Tribute Dinner | Speaker |

1988

| Jan | Apollo | The Best of Friends | Sir Sydney Cockerell |
| Mar | Royalty | A Tale of Two Cities | Voice Only |

1990

| Jul | Palladium | Royal Birthday Gala | Compère |

Film and Television

Year	Production	Role	Film or television
1924	Who Is the Man?	Daniel	Film
1929	The Clue of the New Pin	Rex Trasmere	Film
1932	Insult	Henri Dubois	Film
1933	The Good Companions	Inigo Jollifant	Film
1936	The Secret Agent	Ashenden/Brodie	Film
1941	The Prime Minister	Benjamin Disraeli	Film
	Airman's Letter to his Mother	Narrator	Film
1944	Unfinished Journey	Commentator	Film
1953	Julius Caesar	Cassius	Film
1955	Richard III	Clarence	Film
1956	Around the World in 80 Days	Foster	Film

	The Barretts of Wimpole Street	Edward Moulton-Barrett	Film
1957	Saint Joan	Warwick	Film
1959	A Day by the Sea	Julian Anson	Television
	The Browning Version	Andrew Crocker-Harris	Television
1963	The Rehearsal	The Count	Television
1964	Becket	Louis VII	Film
1964	Hamlet	Voice of the Ghost	Film
1965	The Loved One	Sir Francis Hinsley	Film
1966	Chimes at Midnight	Henry IV	Film
	Alice in Wonderland	Mock Turtle	Television
	The Mayfly and the Frog	Gabriel Kantara	Television
1967	From Chekhov With Love	Chekhov	Television
	Sebastian	Secret Services Chief	Film
	Assignment to Kill	Kurt Valayan	Film
	Revolution D'Octobre	Narrator	Film
1968	The Charge of the Light Brigade	Lord Raglan	Film
	The Shoes of the Fisherman	Pope	Film
	Saint Joan	The Inquisitor	Television
	From Chekhov With Love	Cast Member	Television
1969	Oh What A Lovely War	Count Berchtold	Film
1970	Julius Caesar	Caesar	Film
	Eagle in a Cage	Lord Sissal	Film
	Hassan	The Caliph	Television
	Hamlet	The Ghost	Television
1972	Lost Horizon	Chang	Film
	Home	Harry	Television
1973	Frankenstein	Chief Constable	Television
	Menace	F.W. Densham	Television
1974	11 Harrowhouse	Meecham	Film
	Gold	Farrell	Film
	Murder on the Orient Express	Beddoes	Film
	Galileo	Cardinal	Film

1975	Shades of Greene: Special Duties	Mr Ferraro	Television
1976	Edward VII	Disraeli	Television
	The Picture of Dorian Gray	Lord Wotton	Television
	Aces High	Headmaster	Film
	Caesar and Cleopatra	Caesar	Film
	Joseph Andrews	Doctor	Film
1977	Providence	Clive Langham	Film
	Heartbreak House	Captain Shotover	Television
	A Portrait of the Artist . . .	Preacher	Film
	The Grand Inquisitor	Title Role	Television
1978	No Man's Land	Spooner	Television
	Richard II	John of Gaunt	Film
	The Cherry Orchard	Gaev	Television
	Les Misérables	Valjean's Father	Film
	Murder by Decree	Lord Salisbury	Film
	Romeo and Juliet	Chorus	Television
1979	The Conductor	Title Role	Film
	The Human Factor	Brigadier Tomlinson	Film
	Caligula	Nerva	Film
	Tales of the Unexpected	Jelks	Television
1980	The Elephant Man	Carr Gomm	Film
	Tales of the Unexpected	Cyril Boggis	Television
	Sphinx	Abdu	Film
	Seven Dials of Mystery	Marquis of Caterham	Television
	The English Garden	Presenter	Television
	Soul of a Nation	Narrator	Television
	The Lion of the Desert	Sharif El Gariani	Film
1981	Arthur	Hobson	Film
	Chariots of Fire	Master of Trinity	Film
1981	The Formula	Dr Esau	Film
	Priest of Love	Herbert G. Muskett	Film
	Brideshead Revisited	Edward Ryder	Television
1982	Marco Polo	Doge	Film
	The Critic	Lord Burleigh	Television

	The Hunchback of Notre Dame	Torturer	Television
	Inside the Third Reich	Speer's Father	Television
	Buddenbrooks	Narrator	Film
1983	Wagner	Pfistermeister	Film
	Gandhi	Lord Irwin	Film
	Scandalous	Uncle Willie	Film
	The Wicked Lady	Hogarth	Film
	The Vatican Story	Pope Pius VII	Film
	Invitation to the Wedding	Clyde Ormiston	Film
	The Master of Ballantrae	Lord Dunsdeer	Television
1984	The Far Pavilions	Cavagnari	Television
	The Shooting Party	Cornelius Cardew	Film
	Frankenstein	De Lacey	Television
	Camille	The Duke	Television
	Plenty	Sir Leonard Darwin	Film
	Romance on the Orient . . .	Charles Woodward	Film
1985	Leave Or Fare	John M. Murray	Film
	Time After Time	Jasper Swift	Television
	The Theban Plays: Oedipus	Teiresias	Television
1986	The Theban Plays: Antigone	Teiresias	Television
	The Whistle Blower	Sir Adrian Chapple	Film
	The Canterville Ghost	Sir Simon de Canterville	Film
	War and Remembrance	Dr Aaron Jastrow	Television
1987	Bluebeard	Title Role	Film
	Arthur II	Hobson	Film
	Quartermaine's Terms	Loomis	Television
1988	Getting It Right	Sir Gordon Munday	Film
	A Man For All Seasons	Cardinal Wolsey	Television
	Appointment With Death	Colonel Carbury	Film
1989	Summer's Lease	Haverford Downs	Television
1990	Prospero's Books	Prospero	Film
	Shining Through	Konrad Friedrichs	Film

	A TV Dante	Virgil	Television
	Hindemith: A Pilgrim's Progress	Narrator	Television
1991	The Best of Friends	Sir Sydney Cockerell	Television
	The Power of One	Headmaster St John	Film
1992	Swan Song	Vasily Svetlovidov	Film
1993	Inspector Morse	Lord Hincksey	Television
1994	Scarlett	Scarlett's Grandfather	Television
	Inspector Alleyn Mysteries	Percival Pyke Period	Television
	Summer Day's Dream	Stephen Dawlish	Television
1995	First Knight	Oswald	Film
	Words From Jerusalem	Narrator	Television
	Haunted	Dr Doyle	Television
1996	Shine	Cecil Parkes	Film
	A Dance to the Music of Time	St John Clarke	Television
	Looking For Richard	Interviewee	Film
	Gulliver's Travels	Professor of Sunlight	Television
	Dragonheart	Voice of King Arthur	Film
	Portrait of a Lady	Mr Touchett	Film
	Quest For Camelot	Voice of Merlin	Film
1998	Merlin	King Constant	Television
	The Tichbourne Claimant	Lord Chief Justice	Television
1999	Elizabeth	The Pope	Film
	Sergei Rachmaninov: Memories	Narrator	Film
2000	Beckett on Film	Protagonist	Film

BIBLIOGRAPHY

Allen, David, *Performing Chekhov* (Routledge, 2000)

Alpert, Hollis, *Burton* (G.P. Puttnam's Sons, 1986)

Annan, Noël, *The Dons* (HarperCollins, 1999)

Bagnold, Enid, *Enid Bagnold's Autobiography* (Heinemann, 1969)

Baxter, Keith, *My Sentiments Exactly* (Oberon, 1999)

Beaton, Cecil, *Self Portrait With Friends* (Weidenfeld & Nicolson, 1979)

Billington, Michael, *Peggy Ashcroft* (John Murray, 1988)

Black, Kitty, *Upper Circle* (Methuen, 1984)

Blakelock, Denys, *Round the Next Corner* (Victor Gollancz, 1967)

Boose, Lynda E., *Shakespeare, The Movie* (with R. Burt) (Routledge, 1997)

Brady, Frank, *Citizen Welles* (Hodder & Stoughton, 1990)

Brandreth, Gyles, *John Gielgud, A Celebration* ((Pavilion, 1994)

Brine, Adrian, *A Shakespearean Actor Prepares* (Smith & Kraus, 2000)

Brode, Douglas, *Shakespeare in the Movies* (OUP, 2000)

Brook, Donald, *The Romance of English Theatre* (Rockliff, 1945)

Brook, Peter, *The Shifting Point* (Methuen, 1987)

Brook, Peter, *Threads of Time* (Methuen, 1999)

Brown, Dennis, *Actors Talk* (Limelight Editions, 1999)

Brown, Ivor, *Theatre* (Max Reinhardt, 1955)

Brown, Ivor, *Theatre 1955–6* (Max Reinhardt, 1956)

Bull, Peter, *I Know the Face, But . . .* (Peter Davies, 1959)

Bull, Peter, *Bull's Eyes* (Robin Clark, 1985)

Burnett, Mark, *Shakespeare, Film, Fin de Siècle* (Macmillan, 2000)

Burton, Hal, *Great Acting* (BBC, 1967)

Carpenter, Humphrey, *OUDS* (OUP, 1985)

Cheshire, David F., *Portrait of Ellen Terry* (Amber Lane, 1989)

Cockin, Katharine, *Edith Craig* (Cassell, 1998)

Cottrell, John, *Richard Burton* (with Fergus Cashin) (Arthur Baker, 1971)

Coward, Noël, *The Noël Coward Diaries* (Macmillan, 1982)

Craig, Edith, *Ellen Terry's Memoirs* (with Christopher St John) (Victor Gollancz, 1933)

Craig, Edward, *Gordon Craig* (Victor Gollancz, 1968)

Craig, Edward G., *Ellen Terry and Her Secret Self* (Sampson Low, Marston)

Conrad, Peter, *Feasting With Panthers* (Thames & Hudson, 1994)

Croall, Jonathan, *Gielgud, A Theatrical Life* (Methuen, 2000)

Cronyn, Hume, *A Terrible Liar* (William Morrow, 1991)

Culver, Roland, *Not Quite a Gentleman* (William Kimber, 1979)

Darlow, Michael, *Terence Rattigan, The Man and his Work* (Quartet, 2000)

Davies, Anthony, *Shakespeare and the Moving Image* (CUP, 1997)

Dean, Basil, *The Theatre at War* (Harrap, 1956)

Denison, Michael, *Double Act* (Michael Joseph, 1985)

Drummond, John, *Tainted by Experience* (Faber & Faber, 2000)

Duff, Charles, *The Lost Summer* (Nick Hern, 1995)

Epstein, Edward, *Portrait of Jennifer* (Simon and Schuster, 1995)

Esslin, Martin, *Pinter: The Playwright* (Methuen, 2000)

Fay, Stephen, *Power Play* (Hodder & Stoughton, 1995)

Findlater, Richard, *The Player Kings* (Weidenfeld & Nicolson, 1971)

Forbes, Bryan, *Ned's Girl: The Life of Edith Evans* (Elm Tree, 1977)

Geist, Kenneth, *Pictures Will Talk* (Charles Scribner's Sons, 1978)

Gielgud, John, *Early Stages* (Falco Press, 1939)

Gielgud, John, *An Actor and his Time* (Sidgwick & Jackson, 1989)

Gielgud, John, *Shakespeare – Hit or Miss?* (Sidgwick & Jackson, 1991)

Gielgud, John, *Notes From the Gods* (Nick Hern, 1994)

Gielgud, John, *Acting Shakespeare* (Pan, 1997)

Gielgud, Kate, *Kate Terry Gielgud* (Max Reinhardt, 1953)

Gilder, Rosamond, *John Gielgud's Hamlet* (OUP, 1937)

Gish, Lillian, *The Movies, Mr Griffith, and Me* (W.H. Allen, 1969)

Gottlieb, Sidney, *Hitchcock on Hitchcock* (Faber & Faber, 1995)

Grove, Valerie, *Dear Dodie: The Life of Dodie Smith* (Chatto & Windus, 1996)

Guinness, Alec, *My Name Escapes Me* (Penguin, 1996)

Guinness, Alec, *Blessings in Disguise* (Penguin, 1997)

Guinness, Alec, *A Positively Final Appearance* (Penguin, 2000)

Gussow, Mel, *Edward Albee: A Singular Journey* (Oberon, 1999)

Guthrie, Tyrone, *A Life in the Theatre* (Columbus, 1987)

Hall, Peter, *Making an Exhibition of Myself* (Sinclair-Stevenson, 1993)

Harding, James, *Emlyn Williams: A Life* (Weidenfeld & Nicolson, 1993)

Harwood, Ronald, *Sir Donald Wolfit* (Secker & Warburg, 1971)

Harwood, Ronald, *The Ages of Gielgud* (Hodder & Stoughton, 1984)

Hawkins, Jack, *Anything For a Quiet Life* (Coronet, 1973)

Hayman, Ronald, *Gielgud* (Heinemann, 1971)

Heston, Charlton, *In the Arena* (HarperCollins, 1995)

Hoare, Philip, *Noël Coward* (Mandarin, 1996)

Hobson, Harold, *Theatre 2* (Longmans, 1950)

Hobson, Harold, *Verdict at Midnight* (Longmans, 1952)

Houseman, John, *Unfinished Business* (Columbus, 1986)

Howard, Ronald, *In Search of my Father* (St Martin's Press, 1981)

Hugget, Richard, *Binkie Beaumont* (Hodder & Stoughton, 1989)

Hurren, Kenneth, *Theatre Inside Out* (W.H. Allen, 1977)

Isherwood, Christopher, *Diaries, 1939–1960* (Methuen, 1996)

Jackson, Russell, *Shakespeare on Film* (CUP, 2000)

Jarvis, Martin, *Acting Strangely* (Methuen, 2000)

Jenkins, Graham, *Richard Burton, My Brother* (Michael Joseph, 1988)

Kavanagh, Julie, *Secret Muses* (Faber & Faber, 1986)

Keown, Eric, *Peggy Ashcroft* (Rockliff, 1955)

Laffey, Bruce, *Beatrice Lillie* (Robson, 1989)

Lambert, Gavin, *Lindsay Anderson* (Faber & Faber, 2000)

Lebrecht, Norman, *Covent Garden: The Untold Story* (Simon and Schuster, 2000)

Lewenstein, Oscar, *Kicking Against the Pricks* (Nick Hern, 1994)

Lewis, Roger, *Stage People* (Weidenfeld & Nicolson, 1989)

Lewis, Roger, *The Real Life of Laurence Olivier* (Arrow, 1996)

Little, Stuart W., *The Playmakers* (Max Reinhardt, 1970)

McBean, Angus, *Shakespeare Memorial Theatre* (Max Reinhardt, 1956)

MacCarthy, Desmond, *Theatre* (MacGibbon & Kee, 1954)

McIntyre, Ian, *The Expense of Glory* (HarperCollins, 1993)

BIBLIOGRAPHY

Manthorpe, Victoria, *Children of the Empire* (Victor Gollancz, 1996)

Manvell, Roger, *Ellen Terry* (Heinemann, 1968)

Massey, Raymond, *When I Was Young* (Little, Brown, 1976)

Masters, Brian, *Thunder in the Air* (Oberon, 2000)

Miles, Sarah, *Serves Me Right* (Macmillan, 1994)

Miller, John, *Ralph Richardson* (Sidgwick & Jackson, 1995)

Miller, John, *Judi Dench* (Orion, 2000)

Mills, John, *Still Memories* (Hutchinson, 2000)

Morley, Sheridan, *Gladys Cooper* (Book Club Associates, 1979)

Morley, Sheridan, *James Mason: Odd Man Out* (Weidenfeld & Nicolson, 1989)

Morley, Sheridan, *Our Theatre in the Eighties* (Hodder & Stoughton, 1990)

Morley, Sheridan, *Rank Outsider* (Bloomsbury, 1996)

Nesbitt, Cathleen, *A Little Love and Good Company*

Nicolson, Harold, *Diaries and Letters, 1945–1962* (Collins, 1968)

O'Connor, Garry, *Ralph Richardson: An Actor's Life* (Hodder & Stoughton, 1986)

O'Connor, Garry, *Alec Guinness, Master of Disguise* (Sceptre, 1994)

O'Connor, Garry, *The Secret Woman* (Weidenfeld & Nicolson, 1997)

Paskin, Barbra, *Dudley Moore* (Sidgwick & Jackson, 1997)

Peake, Tony, *Derek Jarman* (Little, Brown, 1999)

Perry, George, *Hitchcock* (Macmillan, 1975)

Quayle, Anthony, *A Time to Speak* (Barrie & Jenkins, 1990)

Redfield, William, *Letters From An Actor* (Viking Press, 1967)

Reynolds, Debbie, *My Life* (Sidgwick & Jackson, 1989)

Richards, David, *Played Out: The Jean Seberg Story* (Random House, 1981)

Richardson, Tony, *Long Distance Runner* (Faber & Faber, 1993)

Rossi, Alfred, *Astonish Us in the Morning* (Hutchinson, 1977)

Schneider, Alan, *Entrances* (Limelight Editions, 1987)

Shellard, Dominic, *British Theatre in the 1950s* (Sheffield Academic, 2000)

Sinden, Donald, *A Touch of the Memoirs* (Hodder & Stoughton, 1982)

Sinden, Donald, *Laughter in the Second Act* (Hodder & Stoughton, 1985)

Speaight, Robert, *The Property Basket* (Collins & Harvill, 1970)

Spoto, Donald, *Alfred Hitchcock: The Dark Side of Genius* (Collins, 1983)

Spoto, Donald, *The Kindness of Strangers* (Bodley Head, 1985)

Spoto, Donald, *Laurence Olivier* (HarperCollins, 1991)

Sprigge, Elizabeth, *Sybil Thorndike Casson* (Victor Gollancz, 1971)

Steen, Marguerite, *A Pride of Terrys* (Longmans, 1962)

Stephens, Robert, *Knight Errant* (Hodder & Stoughton, 1995)

Sterne, Richard L., *John Gielgud Directs Richard Burton in Hamlet* (Random House, 1967)

Swaffer, Hannen, *Hannen Swaffer's Who's Who* (Hutchinson,)

Taylor, John R., *The Life and Work of Alfred Hitchcock* (Faber & Faber, 1978)

Taylor, John R., *Alec Guinness: A Celebration* (Pavilion, 1985)

Terry, Ellen, *The Story of My Life* (Hutchinson, 1908)

Thomson, David, *Rosebud: The Story of Orson Welles* (Little, Brown, 1996)

Trewin, J.C., *A Play Tonight* (Elek Books, 1952)

Trewin, J.C., *Edith Evans* (Rockliff, 1954)

Trewin, J.C., *Peter Brook* (Macdonald, 1971)

Trewin, J.C., *Five & Eighty Hamlets* (Hutchinson, 1987)

Tynan, Kenneth, *He That Plays the King* (Longmans, Green, 1950)

Tynan, Kenneth, *Alec Guinness* (Rockliff, 1953)

Tynan, Kenneth, *Persona Grata* (illus. Cecil Beaton) (Wingate, 1953)

Tynan, Kenneth, *Curtains* (Longmans, 1961)

Tynan, Kenneth, *Letters* (Weidenfeld & Nicolson, 1994)

Vickers, Hugo, *Cecil Beaton* (Weidenfeld & Nicolson, 1985)

Walker, Alexander, *Vivien: The Life of Vivien Leigh* (Weidenfeld & Nicolson, 1987)

Wansell, Geoffrey, *Terence Rattigan* (Fourth Estate, 1995)

Wardle, Irving, *The Theatres of George Devine* (Jonathan Cape, 1978)

Wardle, Irving, *Theatre Criticism* (Routledge, 1992)

Warwick, Christopher, *The Universal Ustinov* (Sidgwick & Jackson, 1990)

Wells, Stanley, *The Actors' Choosing* (Long Barn, 1997)

Wells, Stanley, *Shakespeare in the Theatre* (Oxford, 2000)

Welsh, James M., *The Cinema of Tony Richardson* (State University of New York, 1999)

Williams, Dakin, *Tennessee Williams, An Intimate Biography* (Arbor House, 1983)

Williams, Emlyn, *George* (Hamish Hamilton, 1961)

Williams, Harcourt, *Old Vic Saga* (Winchester Publications, 1949)

Williams, Kenneth, *Diaries* (HarperCollins, 1993)

Williams, Tennessee, *Five O'Clock Angel, Letters to Maria St Just* (André Deutsch, 1991)

Williamson, Audrey, *Old Vic Drama* (Rockliff, 1948)

Wolfit, Donald, *First Interval* (Odhams, 1954)

York, Michael, *Travelling Player* (Headline, 1991)

Index

✿

JG = John Gielgud
Titles in italics are stage productions unless indicated otherwise.

134, 142, 274; at OUDS 83, 85–6; stage performances 92–3, 122, 189, 214, 272, 378; friendship with JG 106, 119, 152, 158, 212, 357, 411, 450–1; *Romeo and Juliet* 124–5; *The Thirty-Nine Steps* (film) 127; *Othello* (radio) 130; *The Seagull* 133–4; Broadway debut 141–2; *The Three Sisters* 155–7; *The Heiress* 201–3; made DBE 276; *The Chalk Garden* 276–7; Zeffirelli's *Othello* 311–13; *The Chalk Garden* 313–14; death 432

Ashton, Frederick 441

Assignment to Kill (film) 337

Astor, David 256

Astor, Nancy 184, 241

Atkins, Eileen 284, 439

Atkins, Robert 65, 66, 67

Atkinson, Brooks (critic) 60, 233

Attenborough, Richard 338, 345, 351, 352, 398, 417

Aubrey Smith, Sir C. 435

Auden, Lewis 383

Auden, W.H. 239, 380, 383

Audley, Maxine 214, 280

Avedon, Richard 385

Aylesbury 340

Ayliffe, Mr (Regent Theatre) 41

Aylmer, Felix 33, 287

Ayrton, Michael 178, 179

Bacall, Lauren 299, 369

Bacon, Max 191

Baddeley, Angela 102, 152, 166, 183, 248, 332

Badel, Alan 78, 212, 214, 313, 437

Bagnold, Enid 275, 303, 304

Bakst, Léon 22, 35

Balanchine, George 10, 272

Baldwin, Stanley 97

Ballets Russes 22, 23

Banbury, Frith 113

Banks, Leslie 183, 185

Bannen, Ian 311, 312, 313

Barbalu, Barbalu (film) 420–1

Barber, John (critic) 270

Barbirolli, John 146

Bardot, Brigitte 440

Barnes, Clive (critic) 350

Barrault, Jean-Louis 333

Barretts of Wimpole Street, The (Besier): 203; film 302, 279, 374

Barrie J.M. 7, 19, 32, 63, 175

Barron, Marcus 180

Barry, Gerald (critic) 316

Barrymore, Ethel 125, 227, 435

Barrymore, John 34, 53, 79, 136, 141, 143, 144, 145, 146, 225, 319

Bates, Alan 447

Battle of the Shrivings, The (Shaffer) 355, 356

Baxter, Keith 279–80, 297, 325, 327, 440; on Perry and Beaumont 160–1, 266, 306; on Martin Hensler 305–7, 447; friendship with JG 340, 448–9

Baylis, Lilian 65–7, 73–4, 76, 78, 79, 92, 142, 154, 423, 453

BBC: radio drama 183, 205, 309; television 333, 354, 362, 390

Beachcomber, The (film) 154

Beale, Simon Russell 439

Beardsley, Aubrey 73, 178

Beaton, Cecil 10, 187, 188, 201, 232

Beaumont, Hugh (Binkie) 82; homosexual circle 115, 160–1, 204, 240, 241; H.M. Tennent, 249; as impresario 159, 160, 162, 163–4, 178, 195, 237, 289, 450; and John Perry 160, 184, 265–6, 290, 306; staging Wilde's plays 166–7, 186–8; Cusack incident 182–3; exploitation of tax loophole 184–5; productions 193, 201–2, 206, 276–7, 294, 295–6, 303, 369–70; business dealings with JG 160, 219–20, 229; JG's arrest 245, 247–9; last years 304, 318, 332; death 371; *see also* Tennent, H.M., Ltd

Beaverbrook, Lord 241, 254, 277

Becket (film) 316–18

Beckett, Samuel 3, 267, 287, 345, 356, 378, 387, 452

Bedford, Brian 282, 283, 295, 297, 452

Beecham, Thomas 87

Beerbohm, Max 132

Beggar's Opera, The (Gay) 22, 34, 169

Bell, Tom 433

Bennett, Alan 3, 257, 366, 373–4, 440; *Beyond the Fringe* 334, 347; *Forty Years On* 338, 346–50, 352, 364, 407, 455–7

Index

Gay Lord Quex, The (Pinero) 385, 386
Geddes, Norman Bel 59
Genée, Adeline 21
Gerhard, Roberto 272
Getting it Right (film) 421
Ghosts (Ibsen) 21, 34, 61, 66
Gibson, Mel 129
Gielgaudskis (Lithuanian village) 8
Gielgud, (Arthur) John
 BIOGRAPHICAL SUMMARY:
  (1904–1921): childhood 5, 6, 8, 10–12;
   known as Jack 5, 28; theatrical
   ancestry 5–6, 11–12; first theatre visit
   13; Hillside preparatory school 15–16;
   brother Lewis wounded at Loos 17–18;
   avid theatregoer 14–15, 18–19, 20–1,
   24, 34–5; declining family fortunes 19;
   Westminster School 19–20, 21; love
   of art and architecture 21; and ballet
   22–3; decides on stage career 25
  (1921–1923): attends classes at Lady
   Benson's 27–30; amateur Shakespearean
   debut in *As You Like It* 28; first
   appearance in *The Importance of Being
   Earnest* 29; professional debut in *Henry
   V* 29–30; first review 30; provincial
   tour with Phyllis Neilson-Terry 30–1;
   at RADA 31–4; tutelage of Claude
   Rains 32–3; joins Nigel Playfair
   company 32
  (1923–1925): first job after RADA
   (*Charlie's Aunt*) 38; joins Oxford
   Playhouse 38–41, 44; involvement
   with OUDS 39–41; only appearance
   in music hall 42; first performance
   as Romeo 41–2; first success in *The
   Cherry Orchard* 43; offered live radio
   broadcast in *Macbeth* 43; first role
   in (silent) film *Who is the Man?* 44;
   meets Komisarjevsky 44–5; meets
   Noël Coward 46–7; understudies
   Coward in *The Vortex* 46–8; Sunday-
   night performances with Phoenix
   Society 49–50
  (1925–1929): returns to Oxford
   Playhouse 52; interest in stage
   direction 53; appears in *The Constant
   Nymph* 54–5, 58–9; poorly treated by

Basil Dean 54–5, 59; overly influenced
by Coward's performance 55; moves
out of parental home 56; discreet
homosexual life 56–8; lives with
John Perry 56; first appearance on
Broadway (*The Patriot*) 59–60; first
meeting with Mrs Patrick Campbell
61; death of Ellen Terry 62; first
acts with Edith Evans and Gwen
Ffrangcon-Davies 62–3
  (1929–1930): joins Old Vic company 66;
   unhappy attempt at Romeo 67–8; first
   Richard II 69–70; and first *Macbeth* 70;
   success of first *Hamlet* 70–2; Wolfit's
   antipathy towards 71
  (1930–1932): appears in *Importance of
   Being Earnest* with Mabel Terry-Lewis
   (aunt) 73–4; returns to Old Vic 74;
   working relationship with Ralph
   Richardson 75–7; first portrayal
   of Prospero in *The Tempest* 76;
   prickly first meeting with Edward
   Gordon Craig (cousin) 76; begins to
   understand Shakespearean verse 78;
   tackles first *King Lear* at Old Vic and
   Sadler's Wells 78–9; leaves Old Vic
   for West End 80; plays Jollifant in *The
   Good Companions* 80–7; role in (silent)
   film *The Clue of the New Pin* 81–2;
   first talking-film role in *Insult* 81–2;
   directs for the first time (*Romeo and
   Juliet* at OUDS) 82–6; meets George
   Devine 83, 86; meets Terence Rattigan
   83; meets the Motleys (designers)
   84–5, 92; works with Peggy Ashcroft
   for first time 85; importance of
   connections made at OUDS 86; works
   with Komisarjevsky 87–8; and appears
   in *Musical Chairs* 87–8; directs first
   modern play (*Strange Orchestra*) 89;
   and search for the avant-garde in
   theatre 89–90; film role in *The Good
   Companions* 90–2; standing in the
   profession 91; directs first professional
   Shakespearean play (*The Merchant of
   Venice*) 92–3
  (1933–1934): *Richard of Bordeaux*
   95, 97–100; Wolfit's enmity and

Tennessee Williams 200; failure of *The Return of the Prodigal* 201; dismissal of John Burrell 201–2; and rescue of *The Heiress* 201–2; directs and acts in *The Lady's Not for Burning* 203–8; casts Richard Burton and Claire Bloom 203–6; death of Frank Gielgud (JG's father) 205; Stratford triumph of *Much Ado About Nothing* 205–6; also directs Stratford *Love's Labour's Lost* 208; directs *Treasure Hunt* 208; has three productions in West End 208
(1950–1951): Stratford season 209, 215; Peter Brook directs *Measure for Measure* 209–12, 215–17; revives *Much Ado About Nothing* 212–13, 217; plays Cassius in *Julius Caesar* 213; co-directs and plays title role in *King Lear* 214; huge success of season 215; *The Lady's Not for Burning* in America 215–16; Brook directs *A Winter's Tale* 215–16; and influence on JG 216–17; JG directs poor production of *Macbeth* 217; strained relationship with Ralph Richardson 217–18
(1952): Beaumont takes financial advantage of JG 219; Laurie Evans becomes JG's permanent agent 219; plays Cassius in film of *Julius Caesar* 220–1; notes changes to American theatrical scene 221–2; sense of dedication 222–3; opinion of James Mason 223–4; Californian homosexual community 224–5; mentor to Marlon Brando 225, 228; death of Gertrude Lawrence 227; revives idea of resident classical company 229
(1953): Lyric Hammersmith season 231–5; first meeting with Kenneth Tynan 232; directs Paul Scofield in *Richard II* 232–3; great success of *The Way of the World* 233; Brook directs JG in *Venice Preserv'd* 234; Olivier and Richardson lobby for JG's knighthood 234–5; knighted 235; failure at Rhodes Festival 235–7; mourns death of Lewis Gielgud (JG's brother) 236–7; breaks public promise to stage *Marching*

Song 237–8; instead stages *A Day by the Sea* 237; depressed state 237–8; homophobic atmosphere 238–40, 242–3, 252–3; affair with Paul Anstee 240; arrested for soliciting 243–5; briefly considers suicide 245; court appearance 246–7; and press reports 247; Beaumont's devious approach to crisis 247–8; Sybil Thorndike's support 247, 249–50; Val Gielgud's loyalty 248–9; generous welcome in Liverpool 249; bravery at the Haymarket 250; legacy of incident 250, 257–8, 262; response of theatrical community 251; British Embassy discourages New York visit 251–2
(1954–1955): returns to *A Day by the Sea* 265; continues affair with Paul Anstee 265; has nervous breakdown 266–7; acting rapport with Richardson 267; dismisses *Waiting for Godot* (Beckett) 267; success of *The Cherry Orchard* 267–8; film role in Olivier's *Richard III* 268; directs Olivier and Vivien Leigh in *Twelfth Night* 268; and rehearsal difficulties 268–70; plans for Stratford touring company 272; disastrous Noguchi *King Lear* 272–4
(1956–1957): directs *The Chalk Garden* 275–7; directs and stars in *Nude with Violin* 277–9; and tax-exile controversy 277–8; film roles in *Around the World in Eighty Days* 279; and in *The Barretts of Wimpole Street* 279–80; failure of *The Trojans* (opera) 280–1; love of music and ballet 281–2; success as Prospero in Brook's *The Tempest* 282–5; works on *Ages of Man* with George Rylands 285, 287; acts in *The Potting Shed* 285–6; interest in avant-garde theatre 287; film role in Preminger's *Saint Joan* 287–8; friendship with Jean Seberg 288
(1958–1960): failure of *Variation on a Theme* 289–90, 291–2; portrays Wolsey in Old Vic *Henry VIII* 292–3; acting partnership with Edith Evans 293; *Ages of Man* 293–4, 301–2; and American and Canadian tour 294, 297–9; directs

332, 370; life with JG 56–8, 59, 82, 84,
103–4, 115, 150, 240; as playwright 57,
159, 161, 176, 208, 311; and business
partnership with Beaumont 161, 163–4,
189, 195, 219, 235–6, 318; war service
167, 290; leaves JG for Beaumont 160–1,
184, 265–6, 290; and Hensler 307, 340,
440–1; death of Beaumont 371
Peter (JG's staff) 447, 448, 453
Peter Pan (Barrie) 7, 9, 12
Petrified Forest, The (Sherwood) 137
Phillips, Eric 69
Phillips, Redmond 285
Phillips, Robin 362, 370
Phillips, Siân 386
Phillpotts, Ambrosine 341
Phoenix Society 49
Phoenix Theatre 87, 183, 216, 217, 332
Phoenix Too Frequent, A (Fry) 203
Piccadilly Theatre 180
Picture of Dorian Gray, The (TV) 377
Pilgrim's Progress, The (Bunyan; radio) 183
Pinero, Arthur 39, 385
Pinter, Harold 101, 399; and JG 5, 334, 452;
No Man's Land 287, 378–83, 390, 400
Piper, John 309
Pirandello, Luigi 39, 52, 276
Pitt-Rivers, Michael 238
Playbill (Rattigan) 194
Playboy (magazine) 396, 397
Playboy of the Western World, The (Synge)
182
Playfair, Giles 57
Playfair, Nigel 32, 33, 37, 43, 51, 52, 73, 74,
107, 169
Playhouse Theatre 58
Plenty (film) 397, 409, 417
Plowright, Joan 343, 428
Plummer, Christopher 398
Polanski, Roman 396
Portman, Eric 102, 194
Portrait of the Artist as a Young Man, A
(film) 390
Potting Shed, The (Greene) 285, 286, 287,
289, 300
Pound, Ezra 355
Powell, John 399
Prejudice (de Acosta) 75

Preminger, Otto 287, 288, 398
Pretenders, The (Ibsen) 342
Price, Dennis 152, 187
Price, Vincent 427
Pride, Malcolm 271
Priestley, J.B. 80
Prime Minister, The (film) 173
Prince Igor (ballet) 23
Private Lives (Coward) 122, 369, 370
Prospero's Books (film) 284, 354, 422, 430–3,
434, 447
Providence (film) 390, 391, 392, 395, 413
Puissance de L'Ange (film) 436
Puttnam, David 445
Pygmalion (Shaw) 14

QBVII (film) 362
Q Theatre (Barnes) 44
Quartermaine, Leon 151, 183
Quartermaine's Terms (TV) 420
Quayle, Anthony 190, 311; early meetings
with JG 92, 107, 159; war years 167; at
Memorial Theatre, Stratford 205, 206,
209, 212, 213, 214–15, 217, 268; death 429
Queen of Scots (Daviot) 107, 108, 122, 223
Queen's Theatre, London 71, 152, 160,
301, 451
Quo Vadis (film) 223

RADA *see* Royal Academy of Dramatic Art
Rains, Claude 31, 32, 33, 37, 184, 362
Rake's Progress, The (film) 187
Rathbone, Basil 201
Rats of Norway, The (Winter) 122
Rattigan, Terence: homosexual circle 57,
84, 115, 120, 258, 290, 370; at OUDS 83;
writes *Playbill* for JG 83, 194; *Separate
Tables* 89, 262–3; *First Episode* 104; *The
Sleeping Prince* 269; *Variation on a Theme*
287, 289–91; *The Deep Blue Sea* 289; work
out of fashion 292
Rawlings, Margaret 176
Reason Why, The (book; Cecil Woodham-
Smith) 337
Rebecca (film) 168
Recruiting Officer, The (Farquhar) 273
Red Rust (Kirchow and Ouspensky) 62
Red Sunday (Griffith) 63

INDEX